PENGUIN CLASSICS

ON GOVERNMENT

MARCUS TULLIUS CICERO (106–43 BC), Roman orator and statesman, was born at Arpinum of a wealthy local family. He was taken to Rome for his education with the idea of a public career and by the year 70 he had established himself as the leading barrister in Rome. In the meantime his political career was well under way and he was elected praetor for the year 66. His ambitious nature enabled him to obtain those honours which would normally only have been conferred upon members of the Roman aristocracy, and he was duly elected consul for 63. One of the most permanent features of his political life was his attachment to Pompeii. As a politician, his greatest failing was his consistent refusal to compromise; as a statesman his ideals were more honourable and unselfish than those of his contemporaries. Cicero was the greatest of the roman orators, possessing a wide range of technique and an exceptional command of the Latin tongue. He followed the common practice of publishing his speeches, but he also produced a large number of works on the theory and practice of rhetoric, on religion, and on moral and political philosophy. He played a leading part in the development of the Latin hexameter. Perhaps the most interesting of all his works is the collection of 900 remarkably informative letters, published posthumously. These not only contain a first-hand account of social and political life in the upper classes at Rome, but also reflect the changing personal feelings of an emotional and sensitive man.

MICHAEL GRANT has been successively Chancellor's medallist and Fellow of Trinity College, Cambridge, Professor of Humanity at Edinburgh University, first Vice-Chancellor of Khartoum University, and President and Vice-Chancellor of the Queen's University of Belfast. He was President of the Classical Association in 1977–8. He has translated Cicero's *On the Good Life*, *Selected Works*, *Selected Political Speeches* and *Murder Trials*, as well as *The Twelve Caesars* by Suetonius and *The Annals of Imperial Rome* by Tacitus, and has revised Robert Graves's edition of *The Golden Ass* by Apuleius, all for Penguin

Classics. His other books include *Roman Literature* (1958, Penguin), *The Civilization of Europe* (1965), *Gladiators* (1967), *Latin Literature* and *Greek Literature* (both anthologies in Penguin Classics), *Cleopatra* (1972), *The Jews of the Roman World* (1973), *Roman Myths* (1973), *The Army of the Caesars* (1974), *The Twelve Caesars* (1975), *The Fall of the Roman Empire* (1976), *Cities of Vesuvius* (1976, Penguin), *Saint Paul* (1976), *Jesus* (1977), *History of Rome* (1978), *The Etruscans* (1980), *Greek and Latin Authors 800 BC–AD 1000* (1980), *The Dawn of the Middle Ages* (1981), *From Alexander to Cleopatra* (1982), *The Roman Emperor* (1985), *Guide to the Ancient World* (1987), *The Rise of the Greeks* (1987), *The Classical Greeks* (1989), *The Visible Past* (1990), *A Short History of Classical Civilization* (1991; U.S. title: *The Founders of the Western World*) and *Greeks and Romans: A Social History* (1992), He has also edited *The Birth of Western Civilization* (1964; reprinted as *Greece and Rome*, 1986) and *Readings in the Classical Historians* (1992).

CICERO

ON GOVERNMENT

Translated by
MICHAEL GRANT

PENGUIN BOOKS

PENGUIN BOOKS

Published by the Penguin Group
Penguin Books Ltd, 27 Wrights Lane, London W8 5TZ, England
Penguin Books USA Inc., 375 Hudson Street, New York, New York 10014, USA
Penguin Books Australia Ltd, Ringwood, Victoria, Australia
Penguin Books Canada Ltd, 10 Alcorn Avenue, Toronto, Ontario, Canada M4V 3B2
Penguin Books (NZ) Ltd, 182–190 Wairau Road, Auckland 10, New Zealand

Penguin Books Ltd, Registered Offices: Harmondsworth, Middlesex, England

First published 1993
1 3 5 7 9 10 8 6 4 2

Typeset by Datix International Limited, Bungay, Suffolk
Printed in England by Clays Ltd, St Ives plc

CONTENTS

INTRODUCTION

Government is essential to our lives, and it is a very difficult art. One sees how difficult it is when one considers the appalling mistakes that rulers have made throughout the ages, and continue to make today. The inevitable conclusion is that they ought to know more about what they are trying to do, and about the successes and errors that have marked the careers of other governments in the past. In this respect ancient Rome is singularly relevant. It is relevant for several reasons. First, because it is, politically, culturally and socially, our direct ancestor. Secondly, because it underwent vicissitudes of the most striking and, sometimes, horrifying character. Thirdly, because it ruled a very large part of the known world, so that its experiences had enormous repercussions. And, fourthly, because it produced extremely articulate writings, which tell us what was happening.

Cicero's works, in particular, are immensely informative.[1] He played an extremely active part in the government of the Roman Republic at the most critical period of its fortunes, when despite, or because of, the immense empire that it controlled it was collapsing into convulsions and autocracy. So he had lived the issues he discussed.[2] Although his character was basically a good one, he possessed his fair share of faults and inadequacies – egotism, vanity, indiscretion, nervousness, poor judgement of men – so that his performance is very human.[3] But he also possessed one peculiarly notable advantage, consisting of his mastery of the Latin language;

1. In Penguin Classics the other volumes are *Murder Trials*, *On the Nature of the Gods*, *On the Good Life*, *Selected Letters*, *Selected Political Speeches*, *Selected Works*.

2. He has been described as the most vividly known personality of the ancient world.

3. Cicero often repeated, echoing the Stoics, that a man's true value lay not in what he actually accomplished (in regard to which he knew that he himself had frequently failed) but in what he strove for.

for he was one of the greatest prose stylists of all time. This meant that he made wonderful, lively speeches.[1]

In order to be a statesman in the Roman Republic – as in the Greek city-states that preceded it – the first essential was to be a fine orator; and Cicero was as persuasive a speaker as there has ever been. But his command of the Latin tongue went further still. For it enabled him, not only to compose superb letters illuminating the political, social and literary scenes (to Atticus[2] and his other friends), but also to produce treatises explaining his views, in the most effective and beguiling fashion. Some of these views related to abstract philosophical questions, but others concerned the practice of government in which he was so deeply involved. So here we have a man actively participating in the government of one of the greatest states of all time, to which we owe so much, and at the same time writing about its numerous aspects with incomparable literary skill. He is the only Roman statesman to have left us a comprehensive account of his political beliefs, and the first to have concerned himself systematically with the mechanics, tactics and strategies of government.

His immersion in this theme is of particular, painful interest because he lived in the last century BC, when the government of the Roman Republic was manifestly breaking down. There were various reasons for this, but the matter had been brought to a head by the stormy tribunates and violent deaths of the brothers Tiberius and Gaius Gracchus (d. 133, 121), who had sought, in vain, to introduce reforms. Then Gaius Marius pushed back invading Germans (102,101), but the result was that henceforward Roman armies began to look to individual generals rather than to the state. A dispute between Marius (and then his successors) and Lucius Cornelius Sulla led to the latter returning from the east to win a bloody civil war and establish a conservative dictatorship (83–81).

1. In addition, or in contrast, to his many less questionable qualities, Cicero excelled at all the exaggerations, reiterations, overstatements and distortions that the oratory of the time required. Indeed, they may, when he spoke, have been even more accentuated than we know, since his speeches have no doubt come down to us in a more literary form than was employed for their delivery.

2. Cicero's association with the rich, non-political knight Titus Pomponius Atticus was of immense importance to him as a source of advice and influence and funds – especially after he himself had moved into political isolation. He figures in the *Brutus*, translated in Chapter 6.

Most of his legislation, however, was swept away during the joint consulship of Cnaeus Pompeius Magnus (Pompey) and the wealthy Marcus Licinius Crassus (70). In 63 Cicero, as consul, suppressed what he described as the conspiracy of Lucius Sergius Catilina, but in 60 Pompeius, Crassus and their brilliant, ruthless junior Gaius Julius Caesar formed the unofficial First Triumvirate which reduced the Republican institutions to a shadow.

After his subsequent consulship in 59, Caesar conquered Gaul (north of the southern (Narbonese) province, which was already Roman), but the death of Crassus at the hands of an eastern people, the Parthians (53), pitted Pompeius and Caesar against one another in a confrontation which led to Civil War (49). Pompeius was defeated at Pharsalus in 48 and killed soon afterwards, and his cause suffered further and final defeats at Thapsus in north Africa and Munda in southern Spain (46, 45). The Civil War and Caesar's dictatorship (49) seemed to Cicero the negation of the Republican government for which he yearned, but he took hope when Caesar was murdered in 44, and in particular after Marcus Antonius, Caesar's would-be successor, was defeated by the Republican or governmental forces at Mutina in 43. But all hope of a restored Republic vanished when the dictatorial Second Triumvirate was formed, in the following year, by Marcus Antonius, the young Octavian (Caesar's adoptive son) and Marcus Aemilius Lepidus. They declared proscriptions, in which Cicero lost his life.[1]

Cicero had been moved by an ideal aim: national harmony, concord between the Orders, *Concordia Ordinum*, which he truly felt that the emergency coalition he had brought together, as consul, during the Catilinarian crisis, could realize.[2] Although he extended this concept to include all good men in Italy, he was thinking chiefly of unity embracing both the senators and the knights (*equites*), the men who came next to them in property and wealth.[3] When he

1. During the next decade and more, a clash developed between Marcus Antonius (Antony) in the east (with Cleopatra VII of Egypt) and Octavian in the west. The result was the battle of Actium (31), won by Octavian, who four years later assumed the name Augustus, and became the founder of the imperial régime known as the principate.

2. See below, *For Murena* (Chapter 2).

3. This name of *equites* was used from at least 88 BC. They were men of substance, not, as has sometimes been said, a homogeneous body of middle-class 'businessmen', although the *publicani* (tax collectors bidding for public contracts)

had spoken and published the *Verrines* (70; Chapter 1), he was championing a popular cause, feeling that the aristocracy, even if the ideal basis of the state, was failing to live up to its mission. But he became, thereafter, increasingly conservative, since he felt that the disturbances during his consulship, and the dangers of revolutionary violence that they disclosed, had made liberal reforms less essential than measures supporting stability.[1]

Another phrase he used to express his ideal was *otium cum dignitate*,[2] *otium* being, not 'leisure' as it literally means, but peaceful tranquillity in the state, which had been all too lacking in recent decades and was dear to Cicero's cultural inclinations and legal training, while *dignitas* represented a man of worth's capacity to express his best qualities in the hierarchical environment which such tranquillity would provide.

---

became an important pressure group. It was another issue, however, that of membership of criminal juries, which eventually developed a visible rift between senate and *equites* (on other matters, they had not regularly voted in two blocks).

1. That is why Cicero, after taking an anti-conservative line early on (e.g. in his speeches *Against Verres* (Chapter 1)), later displayed such hostility to reforming tribunes such as the Gracchi – whose activities led, he felt, to subversive demands for land distribution and debt cancellation (he was the first man to stress, articulately, the crucial role of private property, which he believed it to be the primary task of the government to safeguard). Yet he also realized that the attempts of the 'conservative' dictator Sulla (81) to restore senatorial rule had been far too bloody; and he blamed his own misfortunes (notably his exile 38–57) on the jealousy and spineless unconcern of the conservative aristocracy. Nevertheless, he sided, roughly speaking, with these same conservatives (*optimates*) against the radicals (*populares*). Neither of these groupings was consistently organized into political parties, since their members, in both cases, were competitive individuals pursuing their own power and glory. But they can approximately be described as the politicians who worked through the Senate and those who preferred to appeal direct to the Assemblies (bypassing the Senate) respectively. More will be said about the Assemblies in the treatise *On Laws* (Chapter 5).

2. The fullest statement of this concept is in the speech *For Sestius*, 96ff. *Otium* carried an implication of preserving the *status quo*, provided that the governing class lived up to a certain standard. Some men possessed *dignitas* (because of their merit, prestige, reputation and influence), others did not. Although Cicero believed in freedom, he did not believe in equality; excessive democratic liberty, he felt, meant that *dignitas* was not given its due.

Cicero did not belong to the Roman nobility, since he was the son of a country gentleman from Arpinum (Arpino) in Latium. Born in 106 BC, he received a good education in philosophy and rhetoric at Rome and later in Greece. In 90–89 he served in the army of Pompey the Great's father Quintus Pompeius Strabo, and listened to the consultations and pronouncements of two leading lawyers, the Quintus Mucius Scaevolas (Pontifex and Augur). Then, after successfully conducting his first legal case,[1] he went to Athens and Rhodes to resume his philosophical and oratorical studies (79–77). Returning to Rome, he was elected to an official post, the quaestorship (75), which took him to Sicily.

In 70, as aedile,[2] he conducted the case that truly made his reputation: against Verres, who had been governor of that island.[3] Apart from furthering his own position, he was motivated by a very strong and genuine feeling. What he felt was that Roman provincial governors ought to behave decently and properly.[4] This was his first major contribution to the art of government, and I shall include one of the speeches he delivered on the subject here.

In 63 Cicero achieved the extraordinary honour, for a 'new man' such as himself, of becoming consul;[5] and while he was consul he

1. Cicero was not, himself, a professional lawyer, although he wrote a work on the subject (*De iure civili in artem redigendo*), which has not survived. There were no specialist advocates or judges (the praetors were merely chairmen).

2. Cicero chose the aedileship rather than the more 'popular' tribunate because he did not want to offend the nobility (Dio XXXVI, 43, 5) – although these qualms vanished when he chose to attack Verres (Chapter I). The aediles were responsible for the administration of public buildings and the supervision of the archives.

3. Cicero asserted that Verres had tried to oppose his election to the aedileship by bribery.

4. Cicero, in *On Duties*, stresses that the misgovernment of subject peoples recoils on the rulers.

5. He was the only man without senatorial ancestry, in forty-four years, to become consul; and the aristocracy, from time to time, let him know it – although they backed him for the consulship, since they feared a return to dictatorship or chaos. At all times during the Roman Republic, twenty or thirty men from a dozen families almost held a monopoly of power. Cicero had no basic objection to this, provided that they were enlightened – but they were not. He went out of his way, therefore, to stress that 'new men' contributed a vital injection of *virtus*, merit. More is said on this subject in the speeches *Against Verres* and *For Murena*.

performed what he was ever afterwards to regard as the greatest achievement of his life, his suppression of what he and others believed to be the 'conspiracy' of Catiline. I have translated his orations on this subject in another volume.[1] Here I include a curious aftermath of these dramatic events. This was his defence of Murena, the man whom he and his friends wanted to succeed him as consul in the following year, so as to keep up the struggle against potential dissidents of Catiline's stamp. Murena was charged with bribery, and he was almost certainly guilty. Cicero no doubt knew this perfectly well, but felt he had to defend him all the same, in order to keep the state together. Here, then, is a morally awkward aspect of *Cicero: On Government*, but a very relevant one to how things actually were – and are. How often have we heard in this century that 'the end justifies the means'! That is what Cicero was saying.[2] And it has a strong bearing on the whole task of government, then as now. At the same time, too, he throws invaluable light on the convulsion which, he believed, was threatening to subvert all orderly government at the time.

Later, unfortunately, for all his very authentic high principles, Cicero had to compromise with these principles once again. First, it is true, he altogether declined to compromise; because when Pompey, Caesar and Crassus created the informal First Triumvirate to rule the state in an autocratic fashion (60), he rejected Caesar's overtures and refused to join them, true to his lifelong belief that Rome ought to have a true Republican government.[3] Then, however, as a direct result, he was forced into exile (58). In the following year he was allowed back. But it soon became clear – and he himself admitted[4] – that this was only on certain conditions. The conditions were that he should make speeches on behalf of the triumvirs. And that is what he did; that is why, for instance, he spoke in defence of Caesar's henchman Balbus, delivering an oration of which I have included a substantial part in this book.

1. *Cicero: Selected Political Speeches* (Penguin Classics), pp. 71–145.

2. He knows it, and elsewhere justifies unjustifiable court defences (*Letters to Friends*, VII, 1, 4, *To His Brother Quintus*, III, 5, 4). See also *For Balbus* (below, Chapter 3).

3. A number of people remained convinced that 60 BC marked the true end of the Roman Republic: R. Syme, *The Roman Revolution*, p. 8.

4. *Letters to Atticus*, IV, 5, *Letters to Friends*, I, 9.

It is highly illuminating, for two reasons. First, because Cicero tries to justify his decision to support the triumvirs after all. For one thing, he was acting under compulsion. But, apart from that, to support them seemed a lesser evil, he explained, and seemed to contribute more towards the survival or revival of a decent, stable Roman government than just to stand aside. Once again, the highest principles – this time, those that disapproved of triumviral autocracy – had to be jettisoned in favour of getting things to work.[1] I wonder if anyone, today, who has taken a practical part in the government of any country will be prepared to cast the first stone. However, *For Balbus* is also notable for another, and more optimistic, reason as well. It illustrates the skill that the Romans displayed in admitting foreigners (for that is what Balbus was) to their citizenship.

Not long afterwards Cicero began to devote himself to the two great works, *On the State* and *On Laws*, in which he put forward his main positive contributions to this art of government of which he had such great personal experience – intending these treatises not merely to be of theoretical interest but of practical application. He favours a constitution blending all the three main reputable forms, monarchy, oligarchy and democracy.[2] His own state and country, and its development, were never far from his mind, and nothing throws more light on how that extraordinary governmental organism evolved than Cicero's two analyses. And, in particular, his discussions continually have a bearing on the troubled conditions of the dying Roman Republic at the actual time when he wrote, and to see how Cicero viewed these conditions is extremely revealing. He was by far Rome's most enlightening political thinker, and perhaps its greatest.[3]

1. 'Good night to principle, sincerity and honour' (*Letters to Atticus*, op.cit.) – perhaps referring to Cicero's slightly earlier speech *On the Consular Provinces*. In *For Plancius*, 91 (delivered in 54 BC), he again explains, and seeks to justify, his recantation.

2. This 'mixed' constitution, previously admired by the historian Polybius (to whom Cicero's debts were extensive), reappeared again and again in early discussions of the constitution of the United States of America, figuring prominently, for example, in John Adams's *Defence of the Constitutions of Government of the United States* (1787).

3. M. Fuhrmann, *Gymnasium*, LXVII, 1960, p. 481. Cicero taught us how to think, said Voltaire.

Much depends on how we interpret his belief that the Republic needed a *rector*: governor, guide, protector. Was this, as many have supposed, an echo of the younger Scipio Africanus (Aemilianus), or an exhortation to Pompey, or a self-compliment to Cicero himself as a potential counsellor? But Cicero's *rector* should be seen, rather, as an unpersonalized, personified, ideal, symbolic figure, like Plato's Guardians. Yet, all the same, his delineation of the concept shows that he clearly saw that the system could not survive without some measure of personal guidance. With that single, major qualification he felt that the old, Roman Republican system (as he looked back on it with romantic nostalgia) had been the best.

So this, up to a point, was an old-fashioned traditionalistic Republicanism, which – leaving aside the vague intimations of a *rector* – had no real solution for the evils of Cicero's age. It is the attitude that has caused him to be condemned as nothing better than a muddled, desperate, dishonourable, incompetent, outmoded thinker, wedged between revolution and reaction.[1] Yet that is unjust: even *Concordia Ordinum* was better than that, and, besides, he had much more to offer as well. In particular, echoing Stoic Natural Law and the Brotherhood of Man, he believed firmly in the basic human rights which those doctrines implied. He was convinced, that is to say, that there exists a universal law, unfailingly valid, based on Reason, which (although nobody was more of a constitutionalist than Cicero) overrides all the laws of individual nations and lawgivers. This is a doctrine which has been overwhelmingly influential, and has earned a great deal of lip-service, although

1. The great Roman historian Theodor Mommsen (1817–1903) is largely responsible for this view, which R.G.C. Levens echoes – as from Cicero's consulship onwards (*Cicero: The Fifth Verrine Oration*, 1946 (1967), p. xliii). For example, in a desperately and increasingly uncontrollable situation, he failed to envisage any approach to the economic reorganization that was sorely needed. Nor did the social and constitutional framework to which he adhered keep pace with the hectic changes of his times; he was unable to see, for example, that the contemporary world could not be governed by city institutions. With hopeless, forlorn optimism, he wanted to *renew* and regenerate the state, without changing its institutions. In fact, he did not understand the roots of the troubles by which Rome was currently beset. 'Bewildered and embittered,' adds Levens, 'by the breakdown of his hopes, unable to face the future squarely, he was always struggling to link the present with a favourable interpretation of his own past, and his utterance was perpetually clouded by this obsession.'

today, as always in the past, it is far more often breached than respected in practice.

The convulsions of the Civil War between Pompey and Caesar followed (49–48).[1] Cicero was in despair, because here was the end of all the orderly, peaceful government which he had always espoused. After a period of prolonged anxiety he joined the Pompeian cause, which, for all its imperfections, seemed nearer to Republicanism than Caesar's autocracy (and had secured the allegiance of most Republicans).

After Caesar had won the war at Pharsalus (48), he pardoned Cicero, who returned to Italy. But all political life, under the dictatorship, was at an end, and although he could not help feeling a sneaking admiration for Caesar's culture and achievements he was totally out of sympathy with his autocratic domination.[2] All he could do was to return to his writing, and in addition to many vastly important philosophical works attributed to these years, popularizing abstract ideas with consummate skill,[3] he composed his *Brutus* (46) (translated here). No one can understand what Cicero meant by government without reading it.

Ostensibly the *Brutus* is a survey of Roman oratory; and it includes fascinating particulars of what Cicero did in order to become such an excellent speaker. But what has to be borne in mind is that oratory was an immensely important part of politics and government, at Rome, as earlier on the smaller stage of Athens. Indeed, Roman government depended upon, and was conducted by, oratory – as the most effective means of creating opinion and prompting action, including judicial decisions[4] – to an extent which it is by no means easy for ourselves to reconstruct and imagine, because this role is so totally alien to the practice of today, when

1. Cicero had first been proconsul of Cilicia (51–50), where he was proud of stamping out corruption.

2. Yet he three times pleaded before Caesar for the pardon of political opponents (46–45). Moreover, in December 45, he had Caesar, with a vast entourage, to dinner at his villa at Cumae.

3. It is unjust to regard him as merely a plagiarist of Greek philosophical thinking. His selection and combination of material was his own, fortified by Roman history and his own experience, and located within a universal context.

4. The solidity of a state, Cicero maintained, is very largely bound up with its judicial decisions. The *Brutus* makes it abundantly clear that the speeches in court cases often had powerful political implications.

rhetoric and its study are condemned as out-of-date stereotypes, and there is hardly a first-class speaker in any of the parliaments of the world. By way of contrast, it could be said that ancient Roman government, until the autocrats took over, *was* oratory: Cicero declares that the perfect orator (possessing a liberal culture and a sound morality) is identical with the perfect Republican statesman.[1] And what the *Brutus* does is to take its readers behind the scenes, and show them why this seemed to him to be so, and what happened. How fortunate it is for us that Cicero, shut out of politics at this time, still had the energy and the will to provide us with this invaluable study![2] It demonstrates, better than any other single work, just how the business of the Roman world was carried out.

When Julius Caesar was assassinated, in March 44, the conspirators had not taken Cicero into their confidence, because he was such a great talker. Yet he was not by any means sorry when the word went round that he had advised the murder,[3] and he greeted the news of it with delight.[4] Indeed, for a time the event had seemingly given him back his authority as a senior ex-consul. But before long it became increasingly clear that Antony intended to take Julius Caesar's place, and to become the autocrat ruling Rome. This was something that Cicero found quite intolerable. Caesar's dictatorship had already offended deeply against his Republican instincts, but he had put up with it, partly because of Caesar's personality, but mainly because he had to. He had no desire or intention to put up with Antony, whom he despised as an inferior character and who could, he believed, be prevented from fulfilling his lamentable despotic aim. So he spoke up against Antony in the Senate and Assembly, in the fourteen *Philippics*.

Cicero was not a very brave man, and he had often not been able to make up his mind what to do. But now his disgust and

1. *On the Orator*, I, 33 ff. The *Orator* attempts to portray the perfect orator. Cicero returns consciously to the humane tradition of Aristotle and Theophrastus, before philosophy and rhetoric had split apart.

2. Though Cicero himself stressed that politics were his absolute priority, and scholarship only a stopgap. He contradicts the Epicurean objections to state service and political activism (although his friend Atticus was an Epicurean). But it was his misfortune, as he saw, to live in the age when his peaceful talents were powerless against brute ambition.

3. *II Philippics*, 25.

4. e.g. *Letters to Friends*, VI, 15.

determination conferred on him both bravery and decisiveness, as he gradually induced the indifferent or reluctant Senate to realize that the constitution was in danger from Antony. Admittedly, he still made serious mistakes. The worst of them was to believe that Octavian (the future Augustus) was, and would remain, a friend of the Republic.[1] Yet his speeches against Antony were not only brilliant but truly courageous, the most courageous of all the enterprises he had ever undertaken. Cicero had at last found it possible to give public and practical voice to his profoundest conviction about government, which was that Rome must not be ruled by a single man. His declarations to this effect, in the *Philippics*, were the last that he ever uttered, for they cost him his life. Antony and Octavian came together, with Lepidus, to form the dictatorial Second Triumvirate; and upon Antony's initiative, in revenge for the *Philippics*, Cicero was put to death.[2]

But his influence remained overwhelming,[3] and what stood the test of time best of all was his famous *humanitas*, which insisted that the persons and opinions of all human beings, when the highest faculties of those beings were brought into play, had a right to be acknowledged and treated with respect – which no autocrat in the world was entitled to override.

1. See the *Philippics*, below, and *Letters to Friends*, x, 28. Ready for any expedient that would encourage the Senate to defeat Antony, Cicero – whose most congenial role was that of adviser to a natural leader – nourished, not altogether without distrust (and admitting the possibility of eventually discarding his protégé), what turned out to be the preposterous idea that he himself might become the *rector* and political mentor of the seemingly, misleadingly deferential, 'divinely inspired' Octavian (who persistently urged Cicero to come to Rome). Brutus, on the other hand – who thought an understanding with Antony might be possible – always saw that Octavian was the real danger to the Republic. But meanwhile Octavian's capacity for infighting and manoeuvring against Antony, with the help of some of the late Julius Caesar's supporters and freedmen, showed a stamina that foreshadowed his great future.

2. The dominant factor prompting these 'proscriptions' (which involved the deaths of 300 senators and 2,000 knights) was the confiscation of estates to pay troops.

3. For this see M. Grant (ed.), *Cicero: Selected Works* (Penguin Classics), pp. 25-32. It is particularly ironical that the headquarters of Al Capone's speak-easies and gambling enterprises in the 1920s, in Cook County, Illinois, was a town named Cicero.

I am grateful to David Duguid, Maria Ellis and Robin Waterfield for their very helpful contributions to this book, and to Paul Keegan, Jenny Page and Susan Piquemal for seeing it through the press.

CHAPTER I

AGAINST VERRES (II, 5): HOW NOT TO GOVERN A PROVINCE

The Verrines *were Cicero's first important contribution to the art of government. In 70* BC *Gaius Verres, governor during the previous three years of Rome's oldest, most strategic, most productive and most profitable province, Sicily, was prosecuted at Rome by Cicero, as a result of serious complaints from the Sicilian communities.*[1] *Since the restoration of large sums was demanded, his charge came before the court reserved for cases of extortion.*[2] *But it was widely understood to involve accusations of general misgovernment, and the citizen rights of Verres were at stake. So, too, in an important respect, was the position of the Roman Senate. The dictator Lucius Cornelius Sulla (81) had arranged for the extortion court to be entirely composed of members of the Senate,*[3] *whom the tribune Gaius Sempronius Gracchus, some forty years earlier, had debarred from this service – and source of patronage – in the hope of securing less lenient verdicts against Roman provincial governors (these being of senatorial rank) accused of dishonesty in their province. By the time of the trial of Verres, Sulla had abdicated and died; the Senate, as*

1. Cicero felt obliged to represent the Sicilians because he had been quaestor in Sicily (75–74). They, like other subjects of Rome, are politely described as 'allies' (*socii*). Verres would, normally, have been replaced after one year, but his governorship dragged on for three, probably because of the continuation of the Third Slave War against Spartacus in south Italy (73–71).

2. Established by the *Lex Calpurnia de repetundis* of Lucius Calpurnius Piso Frugi (tribune in 149 BC). There were also several subsequent laws on the same subject. Verres's rapacity – which he had already shown as deputy (*legatus*) to Cnaeus Cornelius Dolabella, governor of Cilicia (80–79), where he made huge profits – created fears at Rome that the Sicilians would cut their production of wheat, thus causing a loss of tithes to the Roman state; although so far Verres had sent more grain from Sicily than any of his predecessors, so that he had important friends in the city.

3. Before giving the juries to the Senate, Sulla had enlarged it by the addition of three hundred newcomers. Cicero *did* want the jurymen to continue to be senators, but wanted them to behave respectably.

strengthened by him, was still in command, but its general supremacy was beginning to weaken, since two men indisposed towards respect for its authority, Cnaeus Pompeius Magnus and Marcus Licinius Crassus, had been elected consuls for the year.

Cicero devoted all his efforts to the case (so that the Verrines *have the firmest factual basis of any of his speeches). His reasons for doing so were various. First, he genuinely hated dishonest administration. Secondly, though himself a senator since 74* BC, *he was consistently sympathetic to the knights* (equites) *among whom he had originated, the non-senatorial class whom Sulla's reforms had excluded from membership of the court and from other positions of power: Cicero honoured the memory of his own unaristocratic fellow-townsman from Arpinum and kinsman by marriage, Gaius Marius, who had been Sulla's enemy.*[1] *thirdly, this was a great opportunity for Cicero to defeat and supersede the most distinguished orator of the day, Quintus Hortensius Hortalus (we shall hear more of him in the* Brutus), *who was briefed by Verres and his noble supporters.*

Cicero's speeches against Verres are masterpieces of eloquence and liveliness, in a controlled, ironical style which he was still in the process of developing.[2] *The first of these orations (the* actio prima), *his only speech in the series that was actually delivered in court, was a complete success.*[3] *Without waiting for the second part of the trial (the* actio secunda) *– in which, according to the normal procedure, the advocates should have tried conclusions with each other again*[4] *– Verres retired to Massilia (Marseille) in Transalpine Gaul, in voluntary exile (a course open to a Roman citizen defendant up to the last moment before the verdict), and was then*

1. Cicero did not yet, as later, feel the need of senatorial solidarity: cf. above, in the Introduction.

2. 'The vigour of the picture comes from the sensational and evil . . . Of the Verrine speeches one must admit that they are splendidly and grossly Roman: vast in size and elaborate in detail, colourful, vivid and sensational, ethical and emotional, guilty and vindictive, unnecessary, but impressive' (G. Kennedy, *The Art of Rhetoric in the Roman World*, p. 165).

3. It is translated in *Cicero: Selected Works* (Penguin Classics), pp. 37–57.

4. Ibid, p. 57, note 1. It was unfortunate for Verres that he felt obliged to give way so soon, because if he had been able to hang on until 62 the elections for that year made it certain that he would be acquitted: his friend Quintus Caecilius Metellus Creticus, and Hortensius, would have been consuls, and Metellus's brother Marcus the praetor would have been presiding over the court (with the help of bribery from Verres). A third brother, Lucius, was Verres's successor in Sicily. The noble Metelli continued to be hostile to Cicero, whom they despised as a 'new man'.

condemned to outlawry and a fine of twice, or two and a half times, the amount of his extortions.[1]

Subsequently, Cicero published the actio secunda, *divided into five parts containing the additional material which he had proposed to bring forward. This sequel emphasized the significance of the case and immortalized it, impeaching the whole outrageous situation of abuses in the provinces. He may have hoped that he would never have to deliver the speech, but he could not be sure; and in the published version that has come down to us he is careful to keep up the appearance of an oration actually delivered, with the defendant actually present. The first part deals with Verres's career up to and including his praetorship (74), before he became governor of Sicily. The second deals with his administration of justice on the island, the third with his collection of tithes and purchase of grain, and the celebrated fourth with his thefts of statues and other works of art.*[2] *'But the fifth,' said R.G.C. Levens,*[3] *'with which we are here concerned, is the most varied and the most characteristic of the series. Nominally its subject-matter falls under two main heads: Verres's conduct as a military governor, and the irresponsible cruelty shown by his executions of Sicilians and of Roman citizens.*[4] *But in reality it is a carefully planned climax to the whole indictment, so constructed as to bring into play the full range of Cicero's rhetorical powers . . . His purpose is no longer mainly to furnish proofs of Verres's guilt, but rather to make him an object of contempt, indignation and hatred.'*

1. Like Cicero himself, he was executed by the Second Triumvirate (43 BC). The story was that Antony wanted one of his works of art.

2. Cicero pretends, so as to make the right impression on his Roman audience, that he himself has little acquaintance with Greek art. But the fourth part of his speech is, in fact, an important source of information on the subject. A good deal more is said about Verres's cruelty in the epilogue of the present fifth part.

3. Cicero: *Verrine V*, 1946 (1967), p. xxxix.

4. Grammarians of the fifth century AD, in view of the renown of its last portion as a model of rhetoric, gave the speech the title *De Suppliciis* (*On Punishments*).

AGAINST VERRES (II, 5)

Gentlemen, I see that you are all perfectly aware that Gaius Verres, quite openly, has robbed Sicily of everything it possesses, sacred and secular, in public and private ownership alike. It is well known to you that there is no kind of theft and plunder that he has refrained from undertaking, with unmitigated unscrupulousness, and, what is more, without the slightest concealment.

Yet, all the same, an imposing, impressive defence of his actions is being attempted. And I have to think well ahead, members of the jury, about how to oppose it. The argument I shall have to resist is this. It is the declaration of Verres's exceptional courage and watchfulness, during these times of anxiety and peril,[1] qualities which, it is said, have saved and rescued the province of Sicily from runaway slaves and the dangers of war. I have to consider, then, gentlemen, what line to take, and in which direction to frame my accusation, and which way, in fact, to turn. Verres's role as a great commander is raised like a rampart to block all my assaults. I know this type of argument very well. I see the things he will boast about. He will enlarge on the threat of fighting, on the crisis into which our country is plunged, on the shortage of generals. Then he will beg of you, or rather he will insist – as a right to which he is fully entitled – that you should not allow Rome to be deprived of such a fine general, on the strength of what Sicilian witnesses have said; and that you should not tolerate the cancellation of a general's brilliant record just because he has been accused of being grasping.

I will be frank with you, gentlemen. I am very much afraid that this account of Verres's imposing military record will mean that everything else he has done goes unpunished. I remember the trial of Manius Aquilius.[2] Marcus Antonius's speech in his defence, I recall, was considered impressive and decisive. As he brought it to a close, he showed what an intrepid, sagacious orator he was. For what he did was to go up to Manius Aquilius and grasp hold of him. Then, making Aquilius stand where everyone could see him,

1. The times not only of the Third Slave War against Spartacus in south Italy (73–71 BC), but also of the fighting against Mithridates VI of Pontus in northern Asia Minor (88–63).

2. For extortion (98 BC). Consul in 101, he had been governor of Sicily, where he had ended the Second Slave War, three years before that.

he tore open the man's tunic and bared his chest. His intention was that the people of Rome, and the jurymen, should see the scars that Aquilius had suffered – scars on the front of his body. At the same time, too, Antonius spoke at length about a wound that had been inflicted on his client's head, by the commander of his foes, no less, in person. This demonstration profoundly affected the jurymen. The man's life had been preserved from the enemy's weapons; fortune had preserved him. To save himself he had never tried. But the outlook for him was depressing indeed if, as a result of being saved, far from having the praises of the Roman people showered on him, he was going to fall a victim to the brutal blows inflicted by jurymen.

That is the line of defence which my opponents intend to employ now; and one sees the result they are aiming at. Verres may be a thief, they say, and a sacrilegious one at that, he may be the unequalled master of every crime and vice you can think of. But he is a great and fortunate commander, all the same: a man whom we should cherish, so that he can deal with the national emergency that is upon us.

Now, Verres, there are tactics that I am fully entitled to use against you; but I am not going to use them. I am not going to make an assertion which would, I suggest, be perfectly legitimate: that verdicts should be pronounced on specific, individual issues. What you would have to prove, if I insisted on this principle, would not be that you had been a good soldier, but that you had refrained from laying your hands on funds that belonged to others and not to yourself. However, that is not, as I say, how I am going to proceed. I am going to inquire, instead – and I gather that this is what you yourself would prefer – into the question whether your military achievements really were as substantial as has been said.

No doubt what you are claiming is that your courage saved Sicily from the runaway slaves. A splendid thing to have done, and a praiseworthy plea. However, what war are you speaking about? I have always understood there has been no war with runaway slaves in Sicily since the Second Slave War that Manius Aquilius brought to an end. Yet there was also a war, it will be pointed out, in Italy. Certainly, and a significant and formidable war it was.[1] Yet surely you are not suggesting that you shared the credit for that victory

1. The Third Slave War, against Spartacus (73–71).

with Marcus Licinius Crassus or Cnaeus Pompeius Magnus – although I would be perfectly prepared to believe that your impudence is monstrous enough to make even such an absurd claim as that!

No, we are invited to suppose that you stopped bands of runaway slaves from crossing over out of Italy to Sicily. But I cannot imagine where, or when, or from what direction, or what were the attempted landings, by boat or ship, that you put a stop to. I have never myself heard that anything of the kind ever took place at all. It was the enterprise and determination of the courageous Marcus Crassus, I was told, which prevented the runaways from constructing rafts[1] and crossing the straits to Messana: though that, as a matter of fact, did not actually need much preventing, if there were forces of Roman troops stationed in Sicily and ready to repel them once they had managed to land. There was war in Italy, I agree – which is certainly close to the Sicilian shore; yet in Sicily itself there was no war at all. But that is not particularly surprising. For conversely, at other times, when there *was* war in Sicily, it never crossed over to Italy, although the distance between the two regions is small.

However, I am not sure what the nearness of the two countries proves. Perhaps it is intended to show that it would have been easy for the enemy force to get to Sicily. Or that there was a danger of the rebellion spreading, by infection, to the island. But the rebels had no ships! And, without them, the passage across to the other side was not only impeded, but totally blocked. You stress that these hostile elements were close to Sicily, but they could have got to the Atlantic Ocean more easily than to Cape Pelorus. You also talk of how the contagion of the slave rebellion might have spread. But you have no more cause to speak of that, as far as I can see, than the governor of any other province might have had. Perhaps you feel you can bring the point up because of the slave wars that had previously taken place in Sicily. But that, in fact, is precisely the reason why that province of yours was, and still is, in virtually no danger at all. For ever since Manius Aquilius left, every governor has made regulations and passed edicts to make it impossible that any slave can own any weapon whatever.

In this connection, I shall tell an old story. It offers an exemplary instance of the kind of severity I have just spoken of, and may be

1. Or, 'making a bridge of boats'.

known to you for that reason. When Lucius Domitius Ahenobarbus was governor of Sicily,[1] one day a huge boar was brought to him. Domitius remarked that it was a splendid animal, and asked who had killed it. When he was told that the killer was somebody's shepherd, he summoned the man, who came readily – expecting to be praised and rewarded. Domitius asked him how he had killed such an enormous beast. The man replied that he had dispatched it with a hunting spear. Whereupon, by the governor's orders, he was crucified without delay. Perhaps that appears harsh treatment. I do not pronounce on whether it was or not. What I do see, however, is that Domitius decided to punish the man, and be regarded as cruel, rather than to ignore his offence in having used the weapon – which would have meant that Domitius must have seemed unduly lenient.

Well, when these rigorous rules were introduced for Sicily, the result was that the governor Gaius Norbanus,[2] although not a very energetic or valiant man, encountered no problems at all. That was a period when the whole of Italy was ablaze with the conflagration of the war with the allies.[3] However Sicily had, by that time, become perfectly capable of defending itself against any internal eruption that might occur. The Sicilians have extremely close links with Roman businessmen in their daily lives and material concerns; it is a sensible and harmonious relationship. Moreover, they are sufficiently content with Roman rule not to have the slightest desire for its subversion or replacement. In addition, as regards the threat of hostilities by slaves, the governors' arrangements are sufficient to look after them; and the strictness of the slave-owners themselves is a further help. For all these reasons any outbreak within the province is out of the question.

But we do have to ask whether it is, in fact, true that no insurrections by slaves and no plots were reported from Sicily while Verres was governor. Certainly nothing of the kind has come to the attention of the Senate or people of Rome, and Verres himself sent no official report on the subject back to Rome. Yet there have been suggestions, all the same, that slave risings *were* attempted, at more than one location in Sicily. True, I have no certain facts to go on,

1. In 97.
2. In 88–87?
3. The Social War (from *socii*, allies) against the Italians (91–87).

but I am making deductions from what Verres did or decreed. Please note that my motive, when I say this, is not in any way malicious. What I have it in mind to do, rather, is to transmit and record the very points which Verres himself is eager to establish;[1] and which you have not heard before.

The Triocala district is a part of the island which runaway slaves, in earlier times, had occupied. And now the slaves of a Sicilian called Leonidas fell under the suspicion of initiating a plot. Verres was told of this, and by his orders the men who had been implicated were very properly placed under arrest and taken to Lilybaeum. Their owner was summoned to appear in court, the trial took place, and they were convicted. Well, I wonder what you suppose happened next. It would certainly be reasonable for you to expect that Verres would, as usual, derive some corrupt, thieving gain from the affair. But do not expect that the same thing will happen every time: this time, I am going to tell you something different. For, once a war-scare is on, opportunities for thieving disappear. Or if there had been, in this case, any such opportunity, Verres missed it. He might, perhaps, have extracted a certain amount of cash from Leonidas when he first summoned him to appear. Or a lucrative bargain might have been struck to keep the case out of court; there would have been no novelty in that. Or, alternatively, there could have been another bargain, to get the defendants acquitted. But once the slaves have been pronounced guilty, as happened on this occasion, all possibilities of corrupt profit have vanished. All that remains is for them to be taken away and put to death.

The facts of the case, resulting in their conviction, are confirmed by the members of the court, by the official records, by the noble city of Lilybaeum, by its large and highly reputable community of Roman citizens.[2] That should have been the end of the matter; off they must go. And so, indeed, off they went, and were tied to the stake. At this point, gentlemen, I am sure you are waiting for me to indicate some improper thing that happened next; seeing that Verres, as we know, never did anything without extracting some profit or loot from it. Well, what could be done here? Expect what

1. i.e. that there *was* a danger of slave risings (which Cicero had previously minimized).

2. These provincial communities (*conventus*) were powerful, and sometimes had a say in the administration of justice in their province.

you like. Imagine the most deplorable wrongdoing you can think of. And how right you will be! For the story I am going to tell you now will surpass what any of you could possibly conjecture. For what amazingly happened was that these men, slaves who had been convicted of conspiracy and crime, slaves who had been handed over for execution and bound to the stake, were suddenly, before thousands of onlookers, liberated from their bonds and handed back to the person who owned them at Triocala!

I wonder what you, demented Verres, will say to that. And I wonder, especially, if you will have a reply to one question. It is not, I would add, a question that I am actually asking; for the very good reason that it seems shameful to raise the matter at all, when it concerns an offence of so outrageous a character. Indeed, the question should at all costs be avoided, if there were any doubt at all about what the reply would have to be; whereas in fact there is no doubt whatever. However, to get back to the question. This is what it would have been. *What did you get, Verres, for letting them go?* How much, and how did you get it? However, as I said, I will spare you the question and save you the trouble of finding an answer. Letting the men go was a criminal action which no amount of money could have induced anyone to commit – except you yourself. And no one, I am perfectly sure, can be persuaded to believe that, when you committed it, you were not paid anything whatever!

All the same, I propose to say nothing, at this juncture, about the methods you employ to thieve and loot. What I shall concern myself with instead, now, is your reputation as a general. Splendid guardian and defender of your province that you are, tell me this. First, you had learnt that these slaves intended to take up arms and create a rebellion in Sicily. And then, in consequence, you had upheld their conviction by the court. But what I very much want to know is just how, subsequently, after they had been handed over in the traditional manner for execution, you had the nerve to snatch them from the very jaws of death. You were intending, I can only suppose, that the cross you had set up for the crucifixion of slaves who had been convicted should instead disgracefully be reserved for the deaths of Roman citizens – who had not been convicted at all![1]

A country that has been ruined, and feels it must have recourse to desperate measures, often adopts the catastrophic expedient of

1. Cicero will refer later to Verres's illegal treatment of Roman citizens.

pardoning the people it has condemned, letting its prisoners go, bringing its exiles back, annulling the sentences its courts of law have pronounced. When such things take place, everyone realizes that the country in question is on the verge of collapse; and disaster looks inevitable. And wherever this kind of development occurs, one of its features, I repeat, is the cancellation of sentences of execution or banishment, to the advantage of either conservatives or radicals, as the case may be. But, even so, it has not been usual for the man who cancels the sentences to have also been the actual person who had originally pronounced them! And he does not usually do so straightaway – and does not do it at all, if the crimes of which they had been convicted had imperilled the lives and fortunes of everyone else.

On this occasion, however, we have a total novelty. The facts of the crime, taken by themselves, are hard enough to credit. It is only the character of the defendant himself, Verres, that makes it possible to believe them. The facts are these. The men released in this way were slaves. They were released by the very person who had sentenced them. They were released immediately, when their sentence had only just got under way. And they were slaves who had been convicted for a crime which imperilled the persons and the lives of every free man.

What a marvellous commander Verres turns out to be! We must no longer just compare him with Manius Aquilius, gallant though Aquilius was. It is with men of the calibre of Paullus,[1] Scipio, Marius that we have to compare him. The unrest among the slaves in Sicily that was caused by the rebellion of the runaway slaves in Italy did not, evidently, escape his notice. And having once perceived it, how effectively he terrorized them into making no move of their own! He ordered some arrests to be made. That must have intimidated them! He summoned their owners to court. What a particularly terrifying thing for a slave! He declared the accused persons guilty – and thus, by sentencing a small number of men to a disagreeable death, proclaimed that he had quenched the flames of the insurrection.

Well, what was to happen to them next? Lashes, burnings at the stake, one would suppose, and that ultimate punishment of offenders

1. Lucius Aemilius Paullus Macedonicus ended the Third Macedonian War by his victory over Perseus at Pydna (168).

and deterrent for everyone else, torture and subsequent crucifixion. No, not at all: on this occasion every single defendant was spared these penalties and set free! What a curious way to cow and terrify the slaves! Here was a governor, as they were able to see, who was so extremely amenable that he accepted bribes from the executioner himself, no less, to save the lives of those slaves, even though they had been found guilty of criminal plotting.

I suspect that you behaved in just the same way in the case of Aristodamus of Apollonia – and again in the case of Leon of Imachara. What this supposed unrest among the slaves and sudden fear of a rebellion prompted in you, I have to speculate, was not so much a tardy enthusiasm for the protection of your province as a novel method of making illicit personal profits. Eumenides of Halicyae, a man of rank, reputation and wealth, had a steward who on your initiative was accused of conspiracy. At that point, however, you accepted sixty thousand sesterces[1] from his owner Eumenides, a bribe which has recently come to light on the sworn evidence of Eumenides himself. Again, when the knight Gaius Matrinius was away at Rome, you got him to part with six hundred thousand sesterces by alleging that you had grounds for the incrimination of his stewards and shepherds. This has been reported by Lucius Flavius, who was looking after the affairs of Gaius Matrinius; and who handed over to you the sum in question. It will also be confirmed by the distinguished censor Cnaeus Cornelius Lentulus Clodianus,[2] who out of his concern for Matrinius's reputation wrote to you when the transaction was first launched, and got others to write as well.

Then there is the case of Apollonius Geminus of Panormus, Diocles's son. Here is another matter that should not be passed over without comment. It is the most notorious, scandalous and barefaced thing that has happened anywhere in Sicily. When Verres arrived at Panormus, he gave orders that Apollonius should appear before him, indeed issued a legal summons against him, in the presence of a substantial, crowded gathering of the local Roman citizens. Straightaway people began to talk: and this is the sort of thing they said. 'I was wondering how long a wealthy man like Apollonius would

1. The *sestertius* (also known as *nummus*) was one-quarter of the silver coin the *denarius*.

2. Consul in 72.

continue to evade the governor's clutches. Verres has evidently got something planned, and is getting to work on his scheme. When a rich person such as Apollonius finds himself promptly called to see him by Verres, there must be something behind it.' And so everyone was waiting to see what was going on. But then, suddenly, in hurried Apollonius himself, half dead with anxiety. His young son was with him. (His aged father had been bedridden for some time.) Verres then proceeded to name a slave, who, he said, was in charge of Apollonius's flocks. The slave, he declared, had formed a conspiracy, and had been inciting other groups of slaves in the neighbourhood.

In fact, there was no such slave whatever on Apollonius's estate. Nevertheless, Verres ordered the man to be produced. Apollonius continued to protest that he owned no slave of the name that had been indicated. So Verres had him removed forcibly from the court and thrown into prison. The wretched Apollonius, as he was being hustled away, shouted that he had done nothing, that he was innocent, that his money was all tied up and could not be made available, that he had no ready cash. Indeed, it was precisely when he was proclaiming these facts, with a great many people listening – so that anyone could understand that the reason why he was suffering this miserable fate was because he had not paid up – it was precisely, I say, when he was crying all this out about the money that he was cast into gaol.

Note the consistency which marked the governor's actions and aims. And bear in mind, too, that when these affairs come up, his defence takes the line that he is not merely the average type of governor but a general of exceptional merit. Yet when a slave revolt was feared, his reaction was to make slave-owners, who had been found guilty of no crimes, suffer the punishments from which he, at the same time, was arranging that slaves who had been found guilty should be exempted! Apollonius was a very rich man, and if a slave rebellion broke out in Sicily he would lose his substantial wealth. Yet Verres brought him into court on the improbable charge of involvement in just such an uprising, and put him in irons. As for the slaves, it was Verres himself, supported by his council, who declared that they had conspired to launch an insurrection. And yet then – this time without his council's support, and acting entirely on his own – he completely exempted the very same slaves from any penalty whatsoever!

A further point also arises. Let us imagine that Apollonius *had* done something for which he ought, according to the law, to be punished. Then, in that case, we might, it may be suggested, feel inclined to hold it against Verres, and blame him, on the grounds that he had sentenced the man to a severer penalty than he deserved. However, I am not going to be as rough with him as all that. I do not propose to follow the habit, so well known among prosecutors, of criticizing any act of clemency as unduly permissive, while at the same time whipping up hostility against the defendant by denouncing every manifestation of strictness, on his part, as cruel. That is not the line that I intend to take.

No, Verres, I shall accept the sentences you handed out. I shall support your authority so fully that you could not possibly feel any objection. But seeing that you yourself went on to annul those very same sentences that you yourself pronounced, you are hardly in a position to resent my criticism. For when a man has pronounced himself guilty from out of his own mouth, then he ought also to be pronounced guilty by the sworn verdict of this court. Apollonius is my friend and host. Yet I am not going to demonstrate my eagerness to annul your verdict by speaking in his favour. About his frugality, his fine character, his industriousness, I shall say nothing. I shall also pass over the point which I have already mentioned: the fact that his resources are invested in workers, livestock, farmhouses and loans – all of which means that, if rebellion or war broke out in Sicily, he would be the man who would suffer more than anyone else.

There is another point, too, which I shall not begin to argue. Suppose, for a moment, that Apollonius had done something seriously wrong. Then, even so, such a reputable man, belonging to such a reputable community, should never have been subjected to such a severe punishment *without trial*. Nor shall I stir up ill-will against you by telling another story that could be told. I refer to the fact that this fine man was lying in prison, in darkness, in squalor and dirt. And there, by your despotic prohibitions, his aged father, his young son, were prevented from even paying the wretched man a single visit. Moreover, there is another thing, too, that I shall pass over. On every occasion, Verres, that you visited Panormus during the whole eighteen months Apollonius spent in prison, the local senators came to see you, accompanied by the city's officials and priests, in order to plead and appeal that this miserable, innocent man should, at long last, be delivered from his calamitous fate.

About all these things, as I said, I propose to remain silent. Yet if I did choose to deal with them, I could prove, with the utmost ease, that the brutal treatment you have meted out to others has totally disqualified you from receiving any mercy from this court.

One reason why I do not intend to mobilize any of these arguments against you is that I can very well foresee the arguments with which Hortensius would reply in your defence. He would proclaim to you, gentlemen, that the age of Apollonius's father, and the youthful years of his son, and the tears of them both, count less in Verres's eyes than the advantage and safety of the province, and rightly so. He would express the view that strictness and intimidation are essential features of government. That, he would tell you, is why the rods are carried along in front of our governors, and why axes are placed among them as well, and why prisons have been constructed, and why our ancestral traditions bristle with penalties for those who do wrong.

But when he makes all these assertions, in austere and imposing language, I shall have a question to ask him. Why, with no new fact forthcoming, with no new evidence in Apollonius's favour made available, in other words for no reason whatsoever, did this same Verres then suddenly command that he should be let out of prison after all? The suspicion of criminality on Verres's part, I am prepared to insist, is overwhelmingly strong. So strong, in fact, that I shall leave it to the members of this court, without any prompting from myself, to come to their own conclusions about the sort of financial impropriety that all this involved, and about the scandalous and disgraceful nature of this kind of action in which Verres has involved himself, and about the infinite, unending possibilities of major profits with which it provided him.

First of all, estimate briefly the methods which he employed in regard to Apollonius, and note how extensive and how grave they have been. Then reckon them up in terms of cash, and see how much they amounted to. You will find that they were all committed against one single man of means, their purpose being to frighten everyone else with the prospect that similar disasters might fall upon themselves – an advance warning, that is to say, of the perils that could overtake them. The first of Verres's methods was the sudden allegation that his victim had committed a sinister, capital crime. To escape from this accusation, just calculate how much you think was paid, and how numerous were the people who had to make such payments! Then, secondly, we have a charge brought by no prosecutor, a verdict brought by no court, a conviction against which the defendant was allowed no defence. Count up, please, the sums that had to be paid for protection against such devices! And reflect, too, that while the only actual victim of these injustices was Apollonius himself, numerous other men, too, must have been faced with just the same sort of ill-treatment, and must have been forced to pay in order to avoid it. Finally, think of the darkness, the chains, the prison, the torment of being locked up, and cut off from the sight of parents and children, and prohibited, indeed, from the possibility of drawing a free breath at all – of gazing upon the light of day! These are things which I cannot assess in terms of money. Getting away from them is worth nothing less than one's life itself.

From all these horrible things Apollonius did, at long last, purchase his escape. By this time, the miseries and hardships he had suffered had left him a ruined man. Yet his experiences had at least served to teach others to come to terms with this villainous governor's criminal greed. For you cannot, surely, imagine that any motive other than personal gain for himself caused Verres to single out the extremely wealthy Apollonius as the target for such an unbelievable charge – or that one can think of any other motive whatever which could have suddenly freed him from prison. Nor, equally, can you conclude that such a form of robbery was merely tried out and put into practice against Apollonius alone, and nobody else. No: his case was designed to subject every rich man in Sicily to intimidation and terror.

Going back to the subject of his military renown, I hope, gentlemen, that Verres will not fail to remind me if I have managed to leave anything out. In my opinion, however, I have provided a complete account of his achievements, in so far, at least, as they were concerned with the alleged suspicions that a revolt of runaway slaves might be imminent. I have not deliberately, I can assure you, missed any of his exploits out. His prudence, and care, and vigilance, and his defence and protection of the province, have all been brought duly to your attention.

Military commanders are of various types. What I have tried to do is to inform you of the type to which Verres belongs. Great soldiers are in short supply today; and I should like to make sure that the remarkable qualities of Verres, in this field, obtain the recognition they deserve. True, it would be excessive to compare them, for example, with the wisdom of Quintus Fabius Maximus, or with the operational speed of the elder Publius Scipio Africanus, or with the brilliant tactics of the younger man of the same name, or with the disciplined planning of Lucius Aemilius Paullus Macedonicus, or with the force and valour of Gaius Marius. No, Verres belongs to quite a different category of commander. Yet it is a category which, clearly, we ought to cherish and maintain.

Let us speak first of all of the toilsome effort of travelling here and there, which is the most laborious of a general's duties, gentlemen, and is especially necessary in Sicily. But I have to tell you that Verres's judicious planning converted this function into quite an easy, agreeable affair. In the first place, during the winter, he discovered a very good way of dealing with the rigours of cold, and storms, and flooded rivers. For what he did was to select, as his base, the city of Syracuse, of which the situation and topography and climate are known to be such that even during the most violent, stormy weather not a single day passes without the sun having made itself visible at some time or other. Well, it was at Syracuse that this brilliant military commander spent the entire months of every winter. And he spent them in such a fashion that it was difficult for anyone to catch a single sight of him out of doors, or even out of bed. The short days were devoted to parties, and the long nights to debauchery and sex.

When spring began, it was no zephyr or constellation that announced to him, in the open air, that the year had reached this stage. No, what showed him that spring had arrived was the appearance of the first rose on his dinner table. And it was at that season that he embarked on the exacting duty of making journeys; in which task he displayed such endurance and energy that no one ever saw him on a horse. Because, instead, following the custom of the kings of Bithynia, he had himself moved about in a litter. Eight bearers carried the litter along, and inside it was a sparkling cushion from Melita, stuffed with roses. Inside it, too, was Verres, wearing two garlands, one on his head, and the other round his neck. To his nostrils he held a network bag of finest linen, delicately dappled, and once again stuffed with rose petals. That is how he made his travels; and on arrival at a town he arranged to be conveyed, in the same litter, all the way to his bedroom.

And that was the place to which Sicilian officials had to go, and Roman knights as well – as you have heard from the sworn testimony of numerous witnesses. Legal disputes were brought before him in private, and after he had heard them the documents recording his decisions were carried out of the room and presented to the public. That, then, is how Verres occupied himself: producing legal rulings from his bedroom. What was equitable did not concern him. But what was lucrative concerned him very much.

However, this sort of activity did not take up his time for too long. When it was over, he saw it as his duty to devote the rest of the day to Venus and Bacchus. In this connection, I should not refrain from recording the remarkable, exceptional perseverance displayed by our noble commander. For I have to tell you that, in all the towns in Sicily where the governors usually stay and preside over lawcourts, there is not a single community in which some woman of decent family was not selected to satisfy his sexual inclinations. Some of them were brought up, quite openly, to his table. The less brazen women arrived later on, at an appointed time, thus avoiding the daylight and the people assembled at the parties.

Now, these dinners given by Verres were not the quiet affairs that you might expect of a Roman governor and general, and did not observe the standards of decency that normally characterize the tables of Roman officials. For, on the contrary, they were accompanied by a lot of noise and abusive shouting. Sometimes the situation actually deteriorated into fist fights. This strict, diligent governor of ours had never in his life deferred to the laws of Rome. Yet as regards the laws laid down for the drinking of wine, he was extremely conscientious about fully obeying them – and imbibing a great deal. In consequence, deplorable things eventually occurred. For example, some person would be carried away from the party, in other people's arms – like a wounded man leaving the battlefield. Another would be lying like a corpse, left for dead. And most of the rest, too, would be equally recumbent, unconscious and senseless. Anyone who witnessed the scene could never have believed that what he was looking at was a governor's dinner-party. It would have seemed to him that he was watching the battle of Cannae,[1] reproduced by delinquents.

At the height of the summer, governors of Sicily are accustomed to move around. This is because they feel that the best season for inspecting their province is the time when the grain is on the

1. 216 BC, in the Second Punic War; a major defeat at the hands of Hannibal.

threshing-floor. For that is when the workers are all gathered together, so that the size of the slave households can be reliably estimated, and the sort of work they are doing can be most easily seen. Yet at this time of year, when all other governors travel about, this novel type of commander, Verres, instead remained stationary, and had a camp set up for him at the city of Syracuse, and indeed in its most agreeable section. Precisely at the entrance of the harbour, where the gulf turns in from the sea-coast towards the city, he pitched a series of pavilions; they were constructed of fine linen, stretched on poles. Moving out of the governor's residence – the former palace of King Hiero[1] – he established himself on this new site so completely that, throughout all this time, it was impossible for anyone to catch a glimpse of him in the outside world.

Moreover, the only people allowed into this new dwelling of his were people whose job it was to share, or minister to, his sensualities. Here flocked all the women with whom he had had relations (and the number of them, at Syracuse, is past belief). Here assembled, also, the people whom Verres deemed worthy to be his friends – worthy, that is to say, to share the life of revelry in which he indulged. And Verres's son, too, by now a grown man, spent his time with men and women of the same type. His own character might incline him to be different from his father. But habit and upbringing made him his father's true son, all the same.

To get the woman Tertia away from Rhodius the flute-player, Verres employed a cunning trick.[2] Yet the abduction is said, all the same, to have created something like an upheaval in the camp. For the upper-class wife of Cleomenes of Syracuse, and Aeschrio's wife,[3] who was also well born, resented the entry of the daughter of a ballet-dancer, Isidorus, into the group to which they belonged. Yet this Hannibal of ours maintained that precedence should go, within his camp, to merit rather than social position.[4] Besides, he became so fond of this Tertia that, when he finally left the province, he took her with him.

1. Hiero II, king of Syracuse (270–215 BC).

2. The 'cunning trick', as described by Cicero elsewhere, was her transfer to Docimus, so as to make her available to Verres.

3. Later she is identified as Pipa.

4. According to Ennius, Hannibal, during the Second Punic War, declared that anyone who struck a Roman enemy down should be deemed a Carthaginian.

Dressed in a purple Greek cloak and a tunic down to the ankles, Verres spent all this period having a good time with his women. However, while he was thus engaged, the absence of the chief magistrate from the Forum, the lack of any legal decisions and hearings, caused no one to feel in any way offended or displeased. Where Verres was staying, on the coast, there resounded a constant din of female voices and vocalists. In the Forum, on the other hand, laws and lawsuits had ceased to exist. But nobody minded. Men did not worry at all because, with Verres away, the law and the courts were suspended. On the contrary, his absence, they felt, was sparing them violence and brutality, and the savage, unprovoked plundering of their possessions.

Surely, Hortensius, you cannot argue, in his defence, that a man of such a kind was an impressive general! Try, as you may, to eulogize his alleged noble achievements and his reputation as a commander, his thefts, his robberies, his graspingness, cruelty, arrogance, criminality, impudence, evil behaviour, are things that you cannot conceal. I hope we do not have to fear, as the climax to your speech for the defence, that you will resuscitate that old imposing oratorical device employed by Marcus Antonius: making Verres stand up, and bare his chest, and display his scars to the Roman people – scars which were, in fact, in his case, made by women's teeth, and which testify to immorality and lechery and nothing else.

All the same, if you do find the gall to enlarge any further on military affairs and operations of war, you will be doing me a favour! For then, indeed, the true facts of all those old campaigns will be fully apparent. You will learn, gentlemen, not only how Verres behaved as a commander, but how he had earlier comported himself in subordinate capacities as well. For the story of his early 'service' will come out all over again; the story of the time when he was escorted from the Forum not, as he says, to his own home, but into the arms of a male lover. You will also hear of that camp at Placentia which was a gambling den, and was attended regularly by Verres, although all he got from it was to be deprived of his pay as a punishment. Reference can also be made to his other, numerous, financial losses while he was serving: and to how he paid them off, with additional compensation, by offering his debtors the enjoyment of his youthful body. He submitted, passively, to these disgusting practices. And it was not he who put a stop to them, either, but the others who had had enough of him.

Next came his behaviour when he had become a grown man. No fortress of modesty and chastity was strong enough to resist his violent attacks. But it is not for me to talk of all these, and tell of his evil doings, involving, as they do, other people's shame. No, gentlemen, I prefer not to, and I shall pass those early scandals over, and only refer, without damaging anyone else's reputation, to two recent matters, which will enable you to form your own idea about the rest of what was happening.

One was an entirely notorious fact, known to all the world: so well known that, during the consulships of Lucius Licinius Lucullus and Marcus Aurelius Cotta,[1] every plainest rustic, from any country town, who came to Rome on legal business was aware of it. This fact that everyone learnt was that every single decision which Verres pronounced as city praetor[2] had been made on the prompting of the prostitute Chelidon, and according to her wishes. A second matter that everyone knew about was this. Verres had, by this time, left the city, in his military commander's cloak. He had already offered his vows relating to his period of office and the welfare of the state. And yet time after time he got himself carried back to the city in a litter after darkness had fallen, in order to commit adultery with a woman who had a husband; though she was also available to everyone else. It was a proceeding entirely opposed to morality, to the auspices,[3] to every principle of religion and human behaviour.

Heavens above, what different attitudes men have from one another, and what different intentions! Take my own case. If it is not true that I, when assuming the offices with which the Roman people has up to now honoured me, have felt the most solemn obligation to carry out my duties with the utmost conscientiousness, then, gentlemen, I will feel obliged, voluntarily, to sacrifice all the goodwill that you and our country have been kind enough to lavish upon my plans and hopes for the future! When I was elected quaestor,[4] I felt that the post had not only been conferred on me,

1. In 74.

2. Verres was city praetor (*praetor urbanus*) in 74 and thus responsible for the administration of justice in Rome.

3. Divination undertaken on all solemn occasions.

4. In 75. A comparatively junior rung on the official ladder. The dictator Sulla (81) had fixed the total number of quaestors at twenty, fixed thirty as their minimum age, and automatically made them members of the Senate.

but was a solemn trust committed into my hands. When I was carrying out the duties of my quaestorship in Sicily, I was convinced that all men's eyes were turned upon myself, and myself alone. It seemed to me that my own person, and my office, were set upon a stage, acting before an audience which was nothing less than the whole of the world. And so I denied myself all the amenities which are permitted to the incumbents of such offices, not only for the gratification of out-of-the-way tastes but even to satisfy the most orthodox and indispensable requirements.

Now I am aedile elect.[1] Once again, I am well aware of the responsibility that the Roman people has entrusted to me. In my celebration, therefore, of the holy festival of Ceres, Liber and Libera, I shall be meticulous and ceremonious in the extreme. By holding Games, which many will attend, in honour of the lady Flora, I shall intercede with her for the people and community of Rome. With the utmost solemn devotion I shall perform the most antique festival of all, the earliest to be given the name of 'Roman', in honour of Jupiter and Juno and Minerva.[2] The maintenance of our sacred buildings has been entrusted to my care. And so, indeed, has the protection of the whole of our city.

In return for the labour and worry which these functions will involve, I shall be the recipient of certain privileges. I shall have the right to speak early in the Senate. I shall be entitled to wear a purple-bordered toga, and sit in a curule chair.[3] I shall be permitted a portrait bust, as my memorial for later generations. And yet, over and above all these things, gentlemen – as I hope for the favour of all the gods in heaven – I must assure you of something else. Certainly, I am very happy that the Roman people has honoured me with this post. And yet my happiness is overtaken by a feeling of consuming anxiety. What I am anxious about is that men should

1. For the aedileship, see the Introduction.

2. Ceres and Liber Pater were the Greek Demeter and Dionysus respectively (Bacchus also corresponded with Dionysus). Libera was the partner of Liber. Flora was an Italian goddess of flowering plants, whose Games, the Ludi Florales, were celebrated annually. Jupiter (Zeus), Juno (Hera) and Minerva (Athena) were the Capitoline Triad. The Roman Games were also known as the Ludi Magni.

3. An ivory folding seat, reserved for senior, 'curule' officials (Cicero was to be a 'curule' aedile; there was also a grade of 'plebeian' aediles).

not just think that I was given this office because it had to go to one or another of the candidates. What I want is that they should believe that the people came to a correct decision, and that the appointment went to the right man.

But, in contrast, Verres, consider yourself. I do not propose to talk about the circumstances of your election as praetor.[1] But think of the moment when your election was announced, when the crier declared that you had been invested with this high office, by the votes of the entire Assembly, its senior and junior sections alike. I cannot see how, on that occasion, the very sound of the crier's voice could have failed to inspire you with a feeling that a share in the government of your country had been entrusted into your hands – so that for this one, forthcoming, year at least you would have to keep away from the houses of prostitutes!

When the drawing of the lots regarding the praetorships assigned to yourself the function of administering the law, I should have supposed that you must have reflected what an extremely heavy and burdensome responsibility this involved. And you might also have concluded – if you could have come to your senses sufficiently to do so – that duties which are, indeed, difficult enough even for the wisest and most honest of men to perform had, in this case, been allotted to a person of exceptional stupidity and vileness. But no. And far from excluding Chelidon from your house while you held the office of praetor, you instead transferred the entire praetorship, lock, stock and barrel, to her own home. Next followed your provincial administration. The power of your position, the rods and axes its symbols, was enormous; and its dignity was majestic and splendid. Yet it never, apparently, crossed your mind that these assets had *not* been placed in your hands so as to allow you to utilize their force and authority to breach every barrier of decent and dutiful behaviour. It was *not* their purpose, you could have realized, just to make it possible for you to treat any and every man's possessions as your own personal loot: with the result that nobody's property could be safe, nobody's house secure, nobody's life protected, nobody's chastity intact, against your rapacious aggressions.

That is how you behaved all the time. The evidence against you is overwhelming. That is why you have to take refuge in this story about a rebellion of Sicilian runaway slaves. But you should appreci-

1. In 74.

ate that this story is very far from supplying you with a defence. On the contrary, it provides numerous additional charges against you. As for that aftermath of the slave war on the mainland, or that setback at Tempsa,[1] I do not suppose that you will want to say anything much about them. The latter was an incident in which fortune very conveniently gave you an excellent chance – if only you had possessed the slightest courage or energy. But all you did, instead, was to demonstrate that you were still just the same as you had always been.

A delegation from Vibo Valentia called on you, and its spokesman, the eloquent, high-ranking Marcus Marius, requested you to deal with the situation there. You possessed the authority and position of governor, he pointed out. So would you not accept the leadership and command, and wipe out the small band of rebels that was threatening them? However, you preferred to shirk the obligation. Indeed, at that very same time, you were to be seen on the seashore with that woman of yours, Tertia, whom you had taken off to keep you company. And although it was a town as reputable and distinguished as Vibo Valentia to which, regarding this important matter, you had given such a negative and unhelpful reply, you just continued to walk around in a workman's tunic and a Greek cloak, and were quite happy to do so.

Just think of the contrast: first imagine the way in which Verres conducted himself when he was setting out for his province and when he was there; and then look at him on his way home – destined not for a triumph but for a trial! Yet even then, when the question of achieving sexual pleasure no longer arose, he still could not help behaving abominably. Earlier on, at that crowded meeting of the Senate in the temple of Bellona,[2] there had been murmurs of disapproval when the question of Verres's intervention at Tempsa came up. You will recall the moment, gentlemen, early in the evening, when the bad news from the place was reported. We could not think of anyone of sufficient military rank to dispatch there. Then someone remarked that Verres was not far from Tempsa. But there was a groan of protest from every side; and the leading speakers opposed the proposal openly. I fail to see, therefore,

1. This incident is unknown; but Verres was evidently held to have responded uncourageously to some appeal from Vibo Valentia relating to Tempsa.

2. The goddess of war.

how this very same man they were complaining about, who has been convicted of so many crimes on such manifold evidence, can now entertain the slightest hope that any of the jurymen's votes will operate in his favour, seeing that, by word of mouth, they have condemned him before the trial even began!

Let us accept, then, that he scored no credit whatever from any rebellion, or suspicion of rebellion, among runaway slaves: because in Sicily no such rebellion or threatened rebellion occurred, and he took no steps to prevent one, because there was nothing to prevent. Yet we shall be told, all the same, that he kept his fleet in good shape to repel pirates, and that he performed this task most meticulously, thus protecting his province in an exemplary fashion. But listen, gentlemen, to what I shall tell you about this Sicilian fleet, and its fighting against the pirates. The nature of my explanation will enable me, at the outset, to emphasize that this matter brought out the very worst features of his character: his avarice, treachery, folly, lust and brutality. You have so far paid careful attention to what I have told you. Please continue to do so, when I briefly recount what happened on the occasion to which I am referring.

The first thing that I have to point out is that the purpose of Verres's conduct of his naval affairs was not to defend the province at all. No, it was to extract personal financial profit out of what was meant to be expended on the fleet. Previous governors had regularly required the Sicilian towns to provide ships and a fixed quota of sailors and soldiers. But you, Verres, chose to exempt Messana, an extremely important and wealthy city, from supplying any of these requirements at all.[1] How much money the people of Messana secretly paid you for this exemption we shall later, if need be, find out from their own documents and witnesses.

What I next have to report, however, is that a very large, fine and handsomely fitted-out cargo-ship, the size of a trireme, was openly constructed at the expense of Messana *for your own use*. And the vessel, as the whole of Sicily knew, was presented to you as a gift by the chief official and Senate of the city. Now, this was the ship which Verres, when he left Sicily, loaded up with the plunder of the island, of which, indeed, it formed a part. On the way home,

1. Messana, unlike other 'federated' cities, was under an obligation to contribute a warship to Rome – which liked this arrangement, since it did not trust all Sicilians to serve in the armed forces.

the vessel put in at Velia with its substantial cargo, including objects which he did not want to dispatch, along with the rest of his loot, to Rome, because of their exceptional value and the fondness that he felt for them. Not long ago, I myself saw this ship at Velia; and many others have seen it as well. It is very splendid, gentlemen, and magnificently equipped. And everyone who saw it, I may add, understood that it gave advance notice, as it were, of its owner's future exile, looking ahead to the time when he would be obliged to sail away into banishment.

I wonder how you propose to reply to me about this. Whatever you say will be entirely implausible, but presumably your answer will be on the lines which any man accused of extortion is obliged to follow: you will answer that the ship's construction was paid for by yourself. Well, that is what you will have to say, so the least that you can do is to say it. Do not be afraid, Hortensius, that I might be going to ask whether a senator has a legal right to build a ship. The laws prohibiting it are antique – what you yourself often describe as dead letters.[1] They belong to an epoch when our nation was of such a high-principled character, and when, in particular, our lawcourts observed such austere standards, that prosecutors ranked any charge relating to this matter as one of the gravest they could put forward. That, however, was long ago.

Yet we may well inquire why you yourself needed a ship anyway. Whenever you make a journey on official business, ships are provided at the public expense to convey you and ensure your safety. Unofficially, you are not entitled to travel at all. Nor was it justifiable that you should have had your personal possessions dispatched, by sea, from places where you are not permitted to own them. And, indeed, this raises the question how it was that, in Sicily, you illegally acquired such possessions. In the old days, when strict moral standards prevailed in the country, that would have been a serious offence. But today, on the other hand, I do not even bother to bring it forward as a charge to be launched against you.

Nor will I even – though I should have a lot of people on my side if I did – offer this specific criticism of your behaviour: that you failed, evidently, to realize that your possession of such a

1. The *Lex Claudia* of the tribune Quintus Claudius (218) forbade senators and their sons to own sea-going vessels capable of carrying more than 300 *amphorae* (225 bushels).

merchant vessel, constructed as your own personal property, at a populous centre in the province of which you were governor, was scandalous, improper and offensive. I am surprised you did not appreciate what those who saw it would say, or those who heard it would think. Would they imagine, do you suppose, that you were proposing to take the ship over to Italy without first loading it with any cargo at all? Or that when you arrived at Rome you were going to enter the shipping business? People could hardly be expected, surely, to recall your ownership of an estate on the coast of the mainland, and believe that the reason why you had acquired a sea-going vessel was merely to market your produce from that estate! Indeed, you were perfectly willing to let everyone discuss your actual intentions quite openly. You explained, that is to say, that your motive in purchasing the ship was to export your loot out of Sicily, and then to send the vessel back to the island again to fetch whatever of your thefts you had left behind.

However, I am prepared to withdraw all these allegations, to let them all go in your favour, if you are only able to do one thing: to persuade me that it was you yourself who paid for the construction of the ship. But you have been stupid about this. Because you must surely realize that your chances of making any convincing explanation that you had paid were abolished during the first part of this trial. They were abolished by the people of Messana – the very men who speak so highly of you. For Heius himself, the leader of the delegation they sent to sing your praises, stated that the ship had been built for you *by men who worked for the city*, and that a senator of Messana had been officially made responsible for its construction. Then came the question of the timber. Messana does not have any; so you yourself, officially, ordered the people of Rhegium to supply what was needed. They say so themselves. And you are in no position to deny it.

So both the materials required to build the ship, and the workmen who built it, were procured by your orders – though not from your own funds. Where, then, I want to know, are we to find a record of the money which you yourself, you assure us, spent on the project? We are told, in support of that suggestion, that the accounts of the city of Messana show no signs of any expenditure on their part. But first of all, I must point out, it may well be that the city treasury was not called upon to make any financial contribution on its own account. Even when our ancestors built Rome's

Capitoline temple long ago, it proved possible, by compulsorily enlisting masons and conscripting labourers, to construct and complete the building without paying anything at all. But I have a second point as well: I have no doubt about it at all, and I shall prove it when I call the appropriate witnesses. It is to this effect, as their own documents confirm. Extensive sums of money paid out to Verres were fictitiously entered in the records as applying to contracts that were, in fact, entirely imaginary.

It is not really surprising that the people of Messana made sure that their public accounts did not list items that might ruin the man who had been so very useful to them, and who was indeed, as they knew, more of a friend to themselves than to Rome. But let us concede for a moment, Verres, that the omission from Messana's accounts of any allusion to money paid to yourself might, alternatively, be satisfactory evidence that no such payments were, in fact, made. Even if that had been so, your own failure to provide any document relating to purchases or contracts effected by yourself in connection with the building of the ship is ample proof, without a doubt, that its construction cost you, personally, nothing at all!

The reason, you go on to say, why you did not order the Messanians to furnish a ship was that their treaty with Rome guaranteed them certain privileges. How lucky we are, indeed, to find a man so expertly trained in international law,[1] so exceptionally scrupulous and vigilant about fulfilling our solemn treaty obligations! All previous governors that have ever existed, then, ought to have been, we now see, handed over to the people of Messana for punishment, because they broke the treaty by ordering them to provide a ship!

All the same, if you were as conscientious and scrupulous as all that, I cannot help wondering why you *did* request a ship from the people of Tauromenium. The terms of its treaty with Rome are exactly the same as Messana's. Here were two cities which, in this respect, possessed exactly comparable treaty rights. Yet you chose to treat them, instead, as if their rights and positions were quite different. What can be the explanation of this, except that you were bribed to do so?

But I can issue a proviso at this juncture, gentlemen of the jury,

1. Trained, Cicero says, by the 'college' of *fetiales*, which was responsible for the appropriate formulas of peace treaties and declarations of war.

and show that, in fact, the treaty rights of the two cities were *not* comparable after all. For the treaty with Tauromenium specifically exempts it from providing the Romans with a ship – while the treaty with Messana, with equal explicitness, prescribes that it is under a formal obligation to supply one. So Verres, by demanding a ship from Tauromenium and excusing Messana from furnishing one, was guilty of infractions both of the one treaty and of the other. The obvious deduction is that, while he was governor of Sicily, the provision of the ship brought more advantage to Messana, which did not have to provide one, than Tauromenium's treaty brought to Tauromenium, which did. [*Let the text of the treaties be read aloud.*]

You may call this an act of generosity by Verres towards Messana. But the facts show that it was the outcome of bribery and corruption. By acting as you did, Verres, you have lowered the stature of your country. You have weakened the strength of the Roman state. You have diminished the resources that the valour and wisdom of our ancestors handed down to us. Our imperial authority, the status of our allies, the reputation of the treaties that we made with them – you have demolished them all.

By the terms of their treaty, it was incumbent upon the people of Messana to arm and equip that vessel, and also to send it, if ordered to do so, even as far as the Atlantic Ocean, at their own expense and risk. And from those obligations, to which the treaty and their duty to ourselves as the imperial power made them subject, they bribed you to exempt them. So effectively did they do so, that they were not even left with the duty of patrolling their own strait, in front of their own dwellings and homes, or of protecting their own walls and harbours.

When this treaty with the Messanians, gentlemen, was originally drafted, just think how much toil and trouble and cash they would very willingly have expended in order to keep this clause about the vessel out of the text – if there had been the slightest possibility of inducing our ancestors to make a concession of such a kind. For the imposition of so onerous a responsibility upon their community meant that the treaty of alliance implied a suggestion of servitude. From those ancestors of ours, however, they failed to extract any such concession at all, although they had recently provided us with assistance, and there was no special hampering precedent, either, and Rome was not, at the time, faced by any sort of critical situation.

And yet now, after all these years, they obtained precisely this exemption from Gaius Verres by bribery, although they have done nothing new to help us, and our imperial rights have been asserted, without a break and continuously, year after year. And now is the time, moreover, when we stand seriously in need of ships! Besides, it was not only exemption from providing a ship that the Messanians secured from you, Verres. During the three years of your governorship, you cannot point to a single sailor, either, whom they provided for our fleet, or a single soldier for our army.

Furthermore, it was decreed by the Roman Senate, and enacted by the Terentian–Cassian law,[1] that grain should be purchased from all the Sicilian towns, according to an equitable division of the responsibility between them. This was a light enough duty, and applied, without exception, to all of them. Yet, once again, you exempted the Messanians. You argue that the Messanians were not under any obligation to 'supply' grain. But it depends on how you would define the term 'supply'. It surely should not mean that they were under no obligation to *sell* us any; for, on the contrary, this was not grain extracted as a tax, but grain to be bought. If you take the opposite view, and interpret the situation as meaning that the people of Messana were equally exempt from having to offer us any grain for sale, then you could go further, and say that they had no obligation whatever to help the Romans by doing any trade or business with us at all!

In that case one would have to ask why this interpretation did not apply to other communities as well. Yet it evidently, in your view, did not, since not only were the occupants of state-owned lands, by way of contrast, compelled to provide the quantity of grain fixed by the censors' law, but you also ordered them to supply a further amount, in accordance with different regulations. Again, according to Hiero's law,[2] each of the farmers on a tithe basis is only required to provide the tenth of his produce. But you, for some reason (which we should like to know), named an additional quantity of grain which they had to make available for purchase. Then, too, there was the question of certain towns that

1. This law of the consuls Marcus Terentius Varro Lucullus and Gaius Cassius Longinus (73) provided for a supply of cheap grain to the city of Rome.

2. The *Lex Hieronica* of Hiero II of Syracuse (269–215 BC) formed a basis for a system of taxation founded on tithes, which the Romans later took over.

were explicitly exempted from such a requirement. So, obviously, they were not obliged to supply anything at all. Yet you ordered them to do so all the same. And you also demanded from them the 60,000 measures that you had allowed Messana, on the other hand, to keep for itself; which meant that these other communities were forced to provide more than they could possibly manage to. I would not go so far as to argue that it was wrong to requisition these quantities from all the other towns. But what I do say is that the Messanians were in exactly the same category as the rest. All earlier Roman governors, I would point out, had demanded grain from them on exactly the same basis as the others, in return for the payments laid down by the appropriate senatorial decree and law. So I conclude that, by letting the Messanians off, Verres acted wrongly.

And now let me nail down this benefaction of his (if that is what you want to call it) to the Messanians once and for all. Verres brought their case before his council, and then announced that he would not be requiring them to supply grain, 'in accordance with the council's decision'. Listen to the decree issued by this money-grubbing governor, excerpted from his own records. Read it, please. [*It is read.*] He gladly acts, he says, on his council's resolution. And then he continues in similar terms. If you had left out the word 'gladly', I suppose we should have had to assume that you found making money for yourself by such improper methods distasteful! And consider that phrase 'the council's resolution'. You have heard, gentlemen, who the members of this eminent council were. But, when you listened to their names being read out, I wonder if you really took them for a governor's council at all, rather than just as the partners and cronies of a robber and a crook.

Have a look at these men entrusted with the negotiation and interpretation of our treaties, and the duty of reminding us where our solemn obligations lie! Grain had never before been officially purchased in Sicily without the Messanians being ordered to provide their appropriate share: until Verres put this select and distinguished council on the job. Its task was to get money out of them for his own personal benefit, in accordance with his general practice. And this decree I am speaking of remained in force longer than it ought to have. This was because Verres had accepted a bribe in exchange for it – had sold it, that is to say, to the very people from whom he should have been *buying* instead: buying grain. As soon, however, as

Lucius Caecilius Metellus became governor in Verres's place,[1] he returned to the recorded procedure of the earlier governors Gaius Licinius Sacerdos and Sextus Peducaeus, and ordered the Messanians to supply grain as before. And they, in turn, then realized that they could no longer hold on to what they had bought from a man who was entirely out of order in making the transaction.

Well, Verres, you like to be regarded as a scrupulous interpreter of treaties. So tell us this. Why was it that you required Tauromenium and Netum to provide grain, when both towns enjoy treaty rights that entitle them to avoid doing anything of the kind? Indeed, the people of Netum duly pointed out their privileged status. As soon as you had announced that you were, gladly, exempting Messana, they came to you and reminded you that their treaty, too, conferred on them precisely the same exemption. That being so, their position being identical with the position you had accorded to Messana, you could not decide to treat them differently. So you announced that Netum, too, was under no obligation to deliver grain. And yet, all the same, you then proceeded to compel them to provide it! Let us hear the governor's ruling, and then the contradictory requisitioning order that followed. [*Documents read out.*] In the light of this brazen, scandalous inconsistency, gentlemen, there are only two, alternative, deductions that we can draw. The first is that he asked Netum for a sum of money, which Netum, however, refused to pay. The second is that he wanted to demonstrate to the Messanians how wise it had been of them to hand him over all those rewards and bribes, when they could see that others, who had a perfect right to receive the privileges that they had received, were unable to get them from him at all.

I wonder if, in this connection, he will have the nerve to cite the eulogy the Messanians delivered in his favour. You must all of you realize, gentlemen, the numerous reasons why that encomium is valueless. First of all, when a defendant cannot produce ten witnesses to praise him, he will be well advised to produce none whatever, rather than try to make up the traditional, regular number of ten – and fail to do so. In your case, however, Verres, after you have governed Sicily for three years, almost all its communities are testifying against you. A few small places, alone, remain silent,

1. Lucius Metellus had at first been hostile to Verres, but then friendly: he rebuked Cicero for making a speech to the council of Syracuse in Greek.

because they are frightened. Only one, Messana, speaks up in your support.[1] What this means is clear enough. The advantage of an authentic, sincere eulogy is unmistakable. But it is an advantage of which your conduct as governor has deprived you. As to my second point – and here I have to repeat something I have already said elsewhere – that single Messanian eulogy takes on a curious appearance when we learn from the very people dispatched to deliver it, and from their leader Heius himself, about the ship which was constructed for you at their expense; not to speak of the ways in which they themselves, personally, had suffered plunder and robbery at your hands!

So these were the men who now felt obliged to sing your praises – the only Sicilians who sang them. For they had got back what they lost, and what they were doing, in effect, was to record, before us all, what you had given them – something you had achieved by robbing Rome instead! Throughout the whole of Italy, during these years, no colonial city rights, no municipal tax immunities, have begun to equal, in terms of lucrativeness, the exemptions of every kind from which Messana has benefited at your hands. For in the course of those three years Messana was the one and only Sicilian community which did not provide what the treaty required it to. Its people alone, so long as Verres remained governor, remained exempt from every obligation. For them alone, under his governorship, the condition that ruled their lives was this. They need never give Rome anything at all – provided that, to Verres, they never gave the answer 'no'.

But I must go back to what I was talking about before that digression. I was speaking of the fleet. First, by accepting that one ship from the Messanians, you broke the law. Secondly, by exempting them from providing further supplies, you violated the treaty. In your relations, that is to say, with this single community, you have been guilty not of a single offence, but of two. You have granted them an improper exemption. And you accepted from them an improper gift. It was your duty to get them to provide a ship to keep looters in check; instead, it was you who got the loot on board for your own personal benefit, and then you sailed away

1. But Syracuse, too, had organized a festival, the Verria, in his honour (*II Verres*, 2. 114, 154; 4. 151). Sicily included sixty-eight communities of various statuses.

with it. The ship should have protected the province from plunder, not carried the plunder that had been extorted from it. The Messanians furnished you with a port, at which you could gather together all your thefts from every region of the island. And they also furnished you with the ship in which you could take them all away. This was the town in which everything you had embezzled could be stored. Its inhabitants were the witnesses of your thieveries, and their custodians as well. It was they who found you a place to deposit what you had stolen, and who found you the ship in which you could take it all away.

As a result of all this, even after your criminal avarice had caused the loss of the fleet, you still did not summon up the courage to order the Messanians to provide a ship to help replace the losses. And yet this was a time when our serious shortage of ships, and the disaster that had overtaken the province, could very well have induced them to supply you with a vessel, merely as a favour. But the fact was that you were in no position at all to issue imperative commands or urgent requests. They were ruled out because of the existence of that notorious ship of your own. It could not possibly be described as a warship contributed to the Roman state. On the contrary, it was a merchant vessel presented to the governor as a personal gift. Its presentation bought exemption from Roman orders, from rendering aid to Rome, from responding to the Roman people's right to receive such a ship; exemption from customary procedures, from obligations under the treaty.

You now have the story of how the valuable assistance that one Sicilian state might have rendered to the Romans was sold away, and lost, in return for a bribe. Let me now tell you, also, of Verres's novel scheme for extracting loot – which he was the first man ever to devise. The normal practice had been that all communities should make provision for their own fleet's costs, comprising food and pay and all other such expenditure. This was done by supplying their commander with the necessary sum. Let us bear in mind that he, for his part, was never likely to venture to incur the danger that he would be charged with misappropriation by people in Rome. For it was his obligation to submit accounts to his fellow-citizens. Thus his conduct of his duties at all times involved not only work but personal risk. This, I repeat, was the invariable practice, not only in Sicily but in every other of our provinces as well. Indeed, it even applied to the pay and expenses of our Italian allies, and of the

Latins too, during the period when we used to employ them as auxiliary troops.[1]

Verres, however, was the first man, ever since our imperial rule began, to have ordered that all these funds should be counted out by the provincial communities, to himself in person, and looked after by individuals who were his own nominees. Now, why you chose to introduce this innovation, changing a custom that was so longstanding and universal, must be perfectly clear to all. It must be clear enough, too, why, although it would have been so manifestly convenient to leave the handling of the money in other hands, you nevertheless preferred to do nothing of the kind; and why you were willing to take over, personally, a function which was not only tiresome and troublesome but made you the object of suspicions of the most disagreeable nature.

Other schemes for making money, too, were set on foot by Verres. In this connection you should note, gentlemen, how many opportunities of the kind the naval situation alone supplied, quite apart from anything else. For cities were only too ready to pay Verres to exempt them from the requirement of providing sailors. Enlisted men could secure discharge for a fee. Then the pay they would have been due to receive would be diverted by Verres to himself, while at the same time he would fail to hand over to all the rest the pay to which they were entitled. You will find all these facts in the evidence provided by the cities. Read it aloud to us. [*It is read out.*]

Have a look at this man, gentlemen! Note his disgustingly impudent behaviour. He drew up a list, you know, of the sums of money that corresponded to the numbers of men that the various communities were under an obligation to provide. The fee he fixed for discharging sailors was six hundred sesterces. Any man who paid it up got his discharge, for the entire summer. And the money that Verres had received for that man's pay and subsistence he kept for himself. By these means, one single discharge enabled him to profit twice over. This was a time when pirates were extremely threatening, and the province in grave danger. And yet this outrageous character conducted all his deplorable activity so openly that the pirates were perfectly well aware of what he was doing, and the entire province saw it happen before its eyes.

1. i.e. until the *Lex Julia* (90 BC), by conferring Roman citizenship on the Italians, replaced this obligation by voluntary enlistment in the legions.

Because of all Verres's embezzlements, the Roman fleet in Sicily was a fleet in name alone. Indeed it consisted of vessels that had become virtually crewless, and were better suited to furnishing the governor with loot than frightening the pirates. All the same, while Publius Caesetius and Publius Tadius were at sea with their ten undermanned craft, they did encounter one of the pirates' ships, crammed with plunder. They did not exactly capture it, because it was already incapacitated, you could say, and indeed virtually captured, by the sheer weight of its cargo and nothing else. But at least they managed to tow it away. The ship proved to be full of handsome young men, as well as of silver plate, silver coin and a quantity of textiles.

The discovery – since I can hardly say capture – of this one single ship took place in the region of Megara Hyblaea, which is not very far away from Syracuse. When the news was brought to Verres, he was lying on the beach, drunk, in the company of certain females. However, he got up, and immediately dispatched a number of his bodyguards to his quaestor and deputy, ordering that everything should be brought, intact, for him to look at as soon as possible. So the ship was taken into Syracuse. Everyone expected penal sentences against the pirates. But Verres's behaviour, instead, was that of a man whose loot has just been brought to him. As for the prisoners, if they were old or unattractive, he classified them as enemies, and had them put down. When, however, there happened to be some who were at all good-looking or young, or possessed any skills, he took them all away. Then he distributed a number of them among his secretaries or staff, or presented them to his son; and six of the captives, who were musicians, he dispatched as a gift to a friend in Rome. The whole night was spent unloading the ship.

The chief of the pirates ought to have been put to death. But he was nowhere to be seen. Everyone is convinced, today, that Verres was secretly bribed by the pirates to spare the man's life. You must use your own judgement to guess whether that is correct. All right, you can call it guess-work, if you like. But no one can be a sound judge if he does not give due weight to convincing suspicions. You know, Verres, whom we are speaking of. And you know of the invariable custom which requires every commander who has captured a pirate or enemy leader to allow him to be displayed before the eyes of the public. And yet, gentlemen, amid all that extensive population of Syracuse I did not find one single man who said he had set eyes on the pirate chief. One must ask why this person was so completely hidden away that no one was even able to get a casual look at him. The people of Syracuse, who are seafarers and had often heard, and feared, the pirate's name, were very keen to feast their satisfied gaze upon the spectacle of his torture and execution. But none of them was permitted even to have a glimpse of him.

Contrast the behaviour of Publius Servilius Vatia Isauricus.[1] He took more pirate chieftains prisoner than all his predecessors put together. Was the enjoyable experience of getting a view of the captives denied to anyone? On the contrary. Wherever Servilius travelled to, he regaled the public with the welcome sight of its captured foes in chains. In consequence, crowds collected to come and look at the show, flocking in not only from the actual towns through which the pirates were being taken, but from neighbouring communities as well. Moreover, Servilius's subsequent triumph in this city was the most popular and welcome Roman triumph that there has ever been. And one can see why. It was not only because victory was welcome, as it always is, but also because its most impressive evidence is the spectacle of those who have often caused us to tremble being taken in chains to be executed.

So one cannot help wondering, Verres, why you did not do the same; and why that pirate was hidden from everyone's eyes, as if it would have been a crime to display him; and why, for what reason, you did not put him to death. Do you know of a single pirate leader who has ever before been captured in Sicily and not had his head cut off? Quote me just one single precedent, or model, for how you behaved. You preferred to keep this pirate chief alive. Why did you do so? Presumably, you intended to have him led before your chariot when you celebrated your triumph. Triumph, I say. For indeed, after you had lost that whole fine fleet of Roman ships, after you had shattered that Roman province to pieces, all that remained for us to do was to reward you with a naval triumph!

Well then, instead of following the normal practice of having this pirate chieftain beheaded, Verres chose to introduce an innovation, and keep him prisoner. So one must next ask what sort of imprison-

1. Consul in 79. As governor of Cilicia in 78–76 he took vigorous measures against the pirates of southern Asia Minor. He was also one of the jurymen at this trial.

ment the man was required to undergo, and among what kind of fellow-prisoners, and in what fashion. Now, you have all heard of the Stone Quarries at Syracuse, and most of you have seen them.[1] They are a huge and grandiose piece of work, created by the city's past kings and tyrants. The whole affair has been dug into the rock to an extraordinary depth by the excavations of a great host of labourers. It would be impossible to construct or imagine any prison that was more completely barred, more securely guarded, more impossible to get out of. People officially sentenced in the courts are relegated to these quarries not only from Syracuse but from all the other towns of Sicily as well.

Verres's plan was to send a substitute pirate chief to this place instead of the real one. But since he had already imprisoned a number of Roman citizens in the quarries, and had had the remaining pirates put away there as well, he saw that, if he sent the bogus pirate chief to join them, a number of the other detainees would realize that he was not the real one. So, although this was the best and securest of prisons, Verres did not dare send the man to be confined in it. Indeed, he was afraid that nowhere in Syracuse would do. Perhaps Lilybaeum might be better. Ah, but that would be on the assumption that he is not afraid of people who live on the coast. So Lilybaeum would not do either. That objection aside, Panormus would have been another possibility. But since the pirate had been captured in Syracusan waters, Syracuse was the right place for his execution or, failing that, his custody. Not Panormus then.

Well, I wonder if you can guess where Verres sent the man instead. He sent him to Centuripa. It was a place where the population had not the slightest reason to feel fear or anxiety about pirates, and indeed had nothing whatever to do with maritime matters or sailing on the sea. On the contrary, it was situated firmly in the interior of the island;[2] its inhabitants were capable farmers. No sea-going pirate had ever caused them alarm. While you, Verres, were governor, the only person who alarmed them was that dry-land buccaneer Apronius.[3] The reason why the governor chose Centuripa as his fake pirate's prison was to enable the prisoner to

1. These *lautumiae*, dating from the early years of the Greek colony, were stone quarries which were also employed as prisons.

2. It is cut off from the east coast by Mount Aetna.

3. A friend of Verres, who appointed him to collect tithes.

pass himself off, without difficulty or embarrassment, as the man he was not. And Verres let this purpose be quite easily known, since he ordered the Centuripans to supply the substitute with food and other amenities on a liberal and lavish scale.

The people of Syracuse, however, being men of experience and education, could do better than just perceive what was obvious. It was not beyond them, that is to say, to make their own further deductions, as well, about what had been kept secret and why. So they kept count, one and all, every day, of the number of pirates who were beheaded – calculating what the total ought to be from the dimensions of the captured ship and the number of its oars. Verres, as we heard, had removed anyone who possessed any skill or looks, and taken them elsewhere. So now, when this much larger number had been removed than were left behind, he concluded that the general realization that this was what had happened might cause a public outcry if he followed the customary practice of having those that remained just herded together and tied to the stake. So what he did instead was to have them brought out to be put to death in small groups, on different days. And yet, even so, there was not one single person amid all that large population of Syracuse who failed to keep an account of the numbers, and notice how many were missing, and demand clamorously that the missing men, too, should be included among those who were executed.

Nevertheless, a lot *were* still missing. So the lamentable Verres took steps to replace these missing pirates – whom he had, in fact, removed to his own house – by certain of the Roman citizens whom he had on earlier occasions flung into prison. Some of them, he claimed, were deserters from the army of Quintus Sertorius,[1] who on their journey back from Spain had been obliged to land in Sicily. Others were people who had been travelling for commercial or other purposes, and had been captured by pirates; but Verres accused them of having joined the pirates of their own free will. And so these Roman citizens were dragged out of their prison to die at the stake – their heads covered up, so that no one could see who they were. A number of others *were* recognized by their fellow-citizens, who unanimously protested that they were innocent. Yet they, too, were executed, all the same. They were subjected to cruel tortures as well; and their deaths were horrible. Of this I shall

1. Leader of the rebellion in Spain (82–72).

have more to say when the time comes to speak on that subject. Indeed, when I speak of Verres's savagery, in massacring those innocent Roman citizens, no language will be too strong for me. If my strength fails me when describing these horrors, if my very life itself is extinguished, I should reckon it as a glorious, welcome outcome, provided only that the story is not left unrecorded!

This, then, is the deed that was done, this the magnificent victory. A light pirate vessel is captured. Its captain is set free. Some musicians are sent to Rome. The attractive men, and the youths, and those who have some talents, are packed off to the governor's house – and an equal number of Roman citizens is put in their place. These are tortured and put to death, as if they were enemies of Rome. As for the textiles and gold and silver, the whole lot are taken away and appropriated.

You will recall how during the first hearing of this case Verres convicted himself out of his own mouth. For days he kept silent. But then, after the distinguished Marcus Annius had testified that a Roman citizen had been beheaded, but the pirate chief had not, Verres suddenly leapt up. Consciousness of his criminal acts, and the mental disturbance brought about by all these wicked deeds, had put him into a frenzy. In this state, he offered his admission. He realized, he confessed, that he would be charged with accepting a bribe and with having failed to put the real pirate chief to death; and actually, he said, he had *two* pirate chiefs in his house!

It seems to me that the mercifulness, or should I rather say patience, that the Roman people displayed on your behalf, at that juncture, was quite remarkable and exceptional. Marcus Annius, a Roman knight, had stated that a Roman citizen was beheaded. And you remained silent. He had stated that the pirate chief was spared. And you admitted it! Groans and shouts were heard from all sides. The people of Rome might well have struck you down on the spot. But they did not do so; they held themselves back, they left it to the strictness of the court to ensure that they themselves, as Roman citizens, were protected.[1] You were perfectly well aware, it appears, that you were going to be charged in this connection. One wonders how you knew about this. But we do know that you felt you had good reason to suspect it would happen. You had no enemies, you

1. i.e. their own lives were endangered by the way Verres had treated other Roman citizens.

tell us. If you had, surely, however bad your behaviour had been, you did not need to fear that you would be prosecuted! But perhaps it was your bad conscience – which plagues other people too – that made you afraid of what was going to happen.

Well, if when you were still governor you were frightened by the prospect of prosecution and trial, there must surely be no possibility of your getting off now, when all these witnesses are testifying against you. Anyway, let us accept that you did fear you would be accused of replacing the pirate chief, due for execution, by a substitute. Then one has to consider, next, the two possible lines of defence you might develop at your trial, and consider which of them, in the end, you decided would be the more effective. One of the possibilities was to produce in court, in response to my insistence – before men who had never seen him – the man who, you claimed, was the pirate chief. The other possibility was straightaway, at Syracuse itself, to have that same man put to death, in front of people who knew him, with virtually the whole of Sicily watching. You can see which of the two alternatives was the more convincing. The former, in fact, was not a plausible defence. The latter would have avoided leaving you open to attack. That is why all other governors have adopted the latter method. But you preferred to follow the former course, and I have yet to find anyone else who has ever done so, except yourself.

You kept that pirate alive. We have to ask how long. The answer is, as long as your governorship lasted. One must then ask why, and following what precedent, you kept him alive throughout that time. One has to try to find out, too, the reason why, while beheading, without delay, the Roman citizens whom the pirates had captured, you nevertheless allowed one of the pirates themselves to continue to enjoy the light of day for all that lengthy period. All right, then; let us go on to the next stage. We may concede that you enjoyed freedom of action as long as you remained governor. But one cannot help wondering why, even after you had ceased to hold that post, even after you had been committed for trial, even after you had virtually been found guilty, you still continued to keep these men in your own home – these leaders of our country's foes. For a month, two months, in the end almost a year after the time when those pirates of yours were captured, they remained in your house. They remained, indeed, as long as I allowed them to. As long, that is, as they were allowed to by Manius Acilius

Glabrio,[1] who ordered, at my request, that they should be brought out and taken to prison.

No right, no custom, no precedent justifies the way you behaved. This pirate was a ferocious, deadly enemy of the people of Rome. Indeed, I would go so far as to call him the common enemy of all countries and nations. Surely, then, no private person, in all the world, could be permitted to harbour him within the walls of his own home. Let us imagine, now, that on the day before you admitted, under compulsion from myself, that, after beheading Roman citizens, you had this pirate chieftain alive and living in your house; and then let us suppose that, on that very same day, he escaped from your house, and directed an armed rebellion against the Roman state. Well, if that had happened, what would you say? This, I suppose: 'Yes, he lived in my house, we were together. The reason why I kept him alive and unharmed was with an eye on my forthcoming trial, so as to help me to contradict the accusations my opponents were proposing to bring against me.'

That would be it, then! Your plan is to save yourself by imperilling the safety of everyone else. The capital penalty is the fate our defeated enemies ought to suffer. But you only propose to inflict it when it suits yourself, and not when it suits Rome. Meanwhile, Rome's enemy is to be kept in custody in a private residence! Certainly, generals celebrating triumphs, too, keep enemy leaders alive, for a while. They do so in order to parade them in the triumphal procession, so that the people of Rome can enjoy the fine spectacle, victory's due reward. Yet even those generals, as their chariots turn out of the Forum up to the Capitol, order their captives to be taken off to prison, and the day that ends the conqueror's tenure of his command ends those enemies' lives as well.

As you yourself confessed, you had decided your prosecution was inevitable. In view of this, you would scarcely be likely, one would think, to run the risk of sparing the pirate chief's life – since, alive, he was a manifest danger to yourself. You told us, I repeat, that you feared a prosecution was on the way. So you might well, indeed, have preferred to declare that he was dead. But the problem was this. If you had said so, who would have believed you? True, nobody at Syracuse, as was very well known, had actually set eyes

1. The president of the extortion court (*quaestio repetundarum*).

on the pirate, and everyone had looked for him without success. But it was universally known that you had been bribed to set him free. People were saying freely that another man had been substituted for him – whom you were maintaining was the pirate chief himself. You had also, as you yourself conceded, been afraid, for a long time, that you were going to be prosecuted on this very charge. Who, then, would believe you for a moment if you declared that the man had died?

Even as it is, when you produce this person of yours, whoever he is, alive, you can see how people laugh at you. But just imagine if that substitute of yours had escaped, had broken his chains like the famous pirate Nico, whom Publius Servilius Vatia Isauricus, however, recaptured as successfully as he had captured him in the first place. I wonder what you would have said then. However, the fact of the matter was this. If the authentic pirate had been beheaded, you would have lost your money. So you would not have been likely, in any case, would you, to reintroduce him, to take the place of the lost substitute; and, besides, if that substitute died or escaped, it would have been easy to replace him by someone else altogether.

I have spoken about this pirate chief at greater length than I intended to. Nevertheless, even so, I have still not yet quoted the most damning proofs of the charges against Verres in regard to this matter. That is because I propose to set it aside for the present, as something that will have to be dealt with on its own account. That is to say I want to reserve it for the particular location, law and court to which it belongs.[1]

So Verres had enriched himself by acquiring a great amount of plunder, slaves, silver and fabrics. Yet this did not by any means make him pay more attention to the equipment of his fleet or the recall, or sustenance, of his absent soldiers – although to have done so, in addition to benefiting his province, could have provided him with additional booty. Midsummer is the season when it has been the custom of all previous governors to travel actively round the province. And sometimes, too, when the threat of attacks from pirates was as dangerous as it was at that time, they put out to sea as well. But Verres, on the other hand, possessed dissolute, extravagant tastes which his official residence, formerly the palace of King Hiero II, was unable to satisfy. Desiring, therefore, to spend the summer

1. The court that tried cases of treason (*quaestio maiestatis*).

according to his usual life-style, he gave orders, as I indicated earlier, that tents of linen canvas should be erected. They were set up on the shore of the island of Syracuse,[1] beyond the spring of Arethusa, close to the mouth of the harbour. It was a pleasant position, out of sight of any possible observers.

It was here, then, that Rome's governor, the guardian and protector of the province, spent the summer giving parties for female companions every day, with no men at table except himself and his youthful son; and since they were the only men present, I might equally have said that there were no men present at all! At times, however, the freedman Timarchides was also brought in to join them. The women were married and of good class, with the single exception of the actor Isidorus's daughter Tertia, of whom Verres was so fond that he took her away from Rhodius the flute-player. Another of the women was Pipa, the wife of Aeschrio of Syracuse, a lady who had formed the theme of a number of comic poems, referring to Verres's lascivious feelings towards her, which enjoy a wide circulation throughout Sicily. There was also the wife of another Syracusan, Cleomenes. Her name was Nice, and she was said to be extremely pretty. Her husband was devoted to her, but had neither the ability nor the courage to oppose the sensual intentions of Verres, and was inhibited from doing so, moreover, by the numerous gifts and favours which the governor had bestowed on him.

Verres, of course, as you know, is entirely shameless. And yet even he did not feel quite relaxed and comfortable about spending all those days on the beach with Cleomenes's wife while her husband was actually in Syracuse. However, he thought of a singular method for dealing with this problem. The fleet had hitherto been under the command of Verres's deputy. But Verres now made Cleomenes its commander instead. Here was a Roman fleet, under the orders and command of a Syracusan – Cleomenes. Verres's motive was not only to keep Cleomenes at sea, away from home, but actually to make him feel *glad* that he was away, because of the important position and advantage this absence brought him. As for Verres himself, with the husband removed to a good distance, he would be able to enjoy the wife's company, I will not say more unrestrictedly than before, since nobody ever restricted

1. Ortygia.

Verres's gratifications, but at any rate in a more tranquil frame of mind than before, once the man who was both her husband and his rival had been transported elsewhere.

Well, there were the ships of our allies and friends, given into the hands of Cleomenes the Syracusan. It is hard to decide what aspect of this bad situation I ought to protest against and censure first. Let us note, to begin with, that this powerful, important command, which ought to have been held by the deputy governor, or quaestor, or even the governor himself, had been given to a Sicilian. As for yourself, Verres, I expect your time was fully taken up with parties and women. But one may still inquire what had happened to your quaestors and deputies, what had happened to the grain valued at three *denarii* a measure and intended for the defence of the island, what had happened to the mules, the tents and the extensive and diversified equipment authorized by the Senate and people of Rome for allocation to their officials and their deputies. And what had happened, for that matter, to your own junior officers? – who would have been more appropriate, as commanders of the fleet, than Cleomenes.

Or if, in fact, there was no Roman citizen who could have been suitably entrusted with the command, there were surely the cities which have remained, for all time, the loyal friends of Rome. There were, for example, Segesta and Centuripa, which are so intimately associated with ourselves, not only by their service and loyalty over very many years, but by blood relationships as well, that they virtually deserve to be called Roman. It was these very communities which had furnished the men and ships and captains that had now been subordinated to this Syracusan, Cleomenes. And indeed Verres, in taking that action, had pushed aside every decent conception of what is honourable and just and merited. I cannot think of a single war in Sicily in which Centuripa was not our ally, and Syracuse our foe. In saying this, I have not the slightest desire to cause offence to the Syracusans. I am merely calling attention to historical facts.

It was because of those facts that the great and glorious general Marcus Claudius Marcellus[1] took the action that he did. By his gallantry he had captured Syracuse,[2] and by his mercifulness he

1. Consul in 222 etc.

2. In 211.

spared the city destruction. But then he ordered that, henceforth, no Syracusan should be allowed to live in that portion of the town which is situated on the Island. Indeed, still, to this very day, I would remind you, no Syracusan is permitted to live there. For it is a site which even a very small garrison could defend against attack. Because this was so, Marcellus did not want it to be in the hands of men who could not wholly be trusted. Besides, this is the point at which the city can be reached by sea; and the Syracusans had frequently kept Roman forces out. So Marcellus refused to allow the keys of the place to be at their disposal.

Note the contrast, Verres, between your own lecherous pleasures and the decisive authority of our ancestors, between your obsession with sexual indulgence and their prudent farsightedness concerning affairs of state. What they did was to debar the Syracusans from access to the coast. What you did was to allow them complete control of the sea. They, our ancestors, refused to permit any Syracusan to live at a location at which ships could arrive. You, on the other hand, decided to give a Syracusan the command of our fleet and our ships. They took a part of the Syracusans' own city away from them. You, on the other hand, gave them a share in Rome's imperial power. The Syracusans do what we tell them to do because of the help we receive from our allies. As for you, you have ordered our allies to obey a Syracusan.

Cleomenes sailed out of Syracuse harbour in a quadrireme[1] from Centuripa. After him came ships from Segesta, Tyndaris, Herbita, Heraclea, Apollonia and Haluntium. They were an impressive fleet to look at, but weak and ineffective, because so many soldiers and oarsmen had been discharged. The fleet was under the authority of this meticulous governor of ours, but the only glimpse he got of it was when the ships passed beside the place where he was holding one of his disgusting parties. Verres himself had not been on view for many days past, but on this occasion he did display himself briefly to the sailors. So there was the Roman governor, leaning upon one of his female companions, as he stood beside the shore, in his purple Greek cloak and a tunic down to his ankles; this was a costume in which numerous Sicilians and Roman citizens had often seen him before.

The fleet continued its journey for a little, and after four days at

1. Ship with four banks of oars.

sea put in at Pachynus. By that time food had run short. But there were a lot of wild palms in the region, as in most parts of Sicily. So the sailors went out to collect their roots, and it was on these that the unfortunate wretches kept themselves alive. While this was happening, Cleomenes, who saw himself as Verres's equal in power and licentious self-indulgence alike, followed his lead by spending entire days drinking in a tent upon the shore.

But now, while he himself was the worse for liquor whereas his men were starving, it was suddenly announced that pirate ships had arrived in the port of Odyssea (our fleet was in Pachynus harbour). There was a garrison of our troops at Odyssea. Or rather, there was not, but there was supposed to be. Anyway, Cleomenes hoped to be able to detach troops from this hypothetical garrison in order to bring his total number of sailors and oarsmen up to their regular complement. It now became clear, however, that Verres's personal acquisitiveness had affected the size of the land forces as well as of the fleet. For most of the garrison had been let go, and very few men were left.

However, Cleomenes led the way towards Odyssea. On his quadrireme from Centuripa he had the mast erected, the sails spread and the anchor cables severed; and he signalled to the others to follow him. Now, while Verres remained governor, no one could be sure how fast any ship's oars would prove able to take her. But the vessel from Centuripa moved with remarkable rapidity. For Cleomenes, who was on board, had been conceded – as a sign of favour, and in recognition of his rank – the least stringent rate of numerical shortage in respect of his oarsmen and soldiers. The quadrireme's high speed almost took her out of sight of the other ships, which were still struggling to get going at their point of departure. Yet their crews were not lacking in determination. Few in numbers though they were, and difficult as their situation was, they nevertheless shouted out that they were eager to give battle. Such life and strength, they declared, as had survived their starvation diet they were willing enough to dedicate freely to whatever armed combat lay in store for them.

Indeed, if Cleomenes had not speeded away so far ahead of them, there would, in spite of everything, have been some possibility of making a fight of it. His quadrireme had a deck – it was the only one of the ships to possess one – and it was large enough to offer protection to the rest of the fleet: in any fight with the pirates, it would have towered like a city above their light, marauding galleys and defended the other vessels in its squadron. As it was, however, left unprotected by their absent fleet commander, all the other ships could do was to follow behind him. So, proceeding in his wake, they made for Helorus. This was not so much to escape an attack from the pirates. What they were doing was to follow their commander, taking the same course as he did. The hindermost ships in this fleeing flotilla were the first to run into danger, as the pirates fell in turn on the vessels in the rear. The first to be captured was the ship from Haluntium. Its captain, an upper-class Haluntine named Phylarchus, was later ransomed from the pirates by the people of Locri, at the expense of the community. In the earlier hearing, he told you, under oath, what had happened and why. Next the ship from Apollonia was captured, and its captain Anthropinus killed.

Meanwhile Cleomenes himself had reached the shore at Helorus, where he hastened to disembark, leaving his quadrireme where it lay. The captains of the other ships saw that their commander had landed, and realized that they themselves had no chance either of fighting off the enemy or of escaping by sea. So they, too, put in at Helorus, and went ashore like Cleomenes. That is to say, the pirate chief Heracleo had suddenly become victorious – which he had never expected at all. Nor did he owe it to any valour of his own. He owed it to the criminally avaricious conduct of Verres towards his own weakened fleet. Whereupon Heracleo, seeing this Roman naval force relegated to the shore and abandoned, waited until the evening, and then set the ships on fire and burnt them.

What a bitter and lamentable incident in the history of the province of Sicily this was! For a host of innocent people, it meant ruin and disaster. It was an exceptionally repulsive and deplorable piece of bad behaviour by Verres. On one and the same day we were able to see the governor blazing with disgusting sexuality, whereas the blaze which the Roman fleet were experiencing was that of the real fires in which the pirates had demolished them.

The news of the calamity reached Syracuse late at night, and everyone rushed to the governor's palace. He himself had returned there slightly earlier, brought back by his women from a grand party, to the accompaniment of singing and music. Although it was night, Cleomenes did not have the courage to display himself in public, but shut himself into his house. His wife could have comforted him in his distress. But of her there was no sign.

As for our own glorious general, discipline in his household was so austere that even in so serious an emergency, when such grave news had arrived, no one was allowed into his presence, or dared to awaken him while he was asleep, or interrupt him when he was awake. Very soon, however, everyone discovered what had happened, and a huge crowd collected from every part of the city. This time, it was not the flames of some beacon on a watch-tower or a mound that gave warning of the pirates' approach. It was the conflagration of the ships themselves that proclaimed the catastrophe that had occurred, and the peril that was imminent for everyone on land.

However, no one, it became clear, had told the news to the governor, and people tried to find out where he was. An excited multitude rushed to his house. He was woken up, and heard the whole story from Timarchides. Then he put on his military cloak, and as dawn was breaking came out, still replete with wine and drink and sex. The people yelled when they saw him, and he felt that he was in the same hazardous position as he had been at Lampsacus.[1] But this time the peril seemed even worse, because the mob was not only equally hostile but very large indeed. It called out allusions to the times he had spent on the seashore, and to his dissolute orgies there. The crowd also shouted out references to his women by name. Then they asked, openly, where he had been throughout all those successive days, when no one had even caught sight of him. They demanded that Cleomenes, whom he had put in command, should be given up to them. It looked very much as though what had happened to Gaius Fabius Hadrianus at Utica[2] was nearly happening again at Syracuse, so that two bad governors would go down to their graves in two provinces.

However, the crowd restrained itself. It remembered that the situation was tense, and that hostilities were under way. And it also bore in mind the high position and reputation of Syracuse, where the community of Roman citizens does credit, according to the

1. As Cicero had described in his first Verrine speech, Verres, on his way to Cilicia to serve as staff-officer of Gnaeus Cornelius Dolabella (80), had been mobbed by an angry crowd at Lampsacus because he had behaved so badly there.

2. Hadrianus, governor of Africa in 83, had been burnt alive in his house at Utica by the Roman residents there, because of his oppressive conduct.

general belief, not only to the province but to the Roman state itself. Verres just stood half awake and stupefied. But the crowd shouted at one another urging action, and seized weapons, and occupied the whole of the Forum and the Island of Ortyqia, which forms a substantial part of the city.

After stopping for only that single night at Helorus, the pirates left our ships still smoking and made off towards Syracuse. They had frequently been told, no doubt, that the walls and harbours of that city were the finest sight in the world, and they must have concluded that their only chance of seeing them was during the governorship of Verres! The first place they came to was that summer dwelling-place of the governor, on that very location upon the sea-shore where he had earlier pitched the tents of his orgiastic camp. They found the place abandoned. Evidently, they realized, Verres had moved his camp elsewhere. So they pushed on straightaway, without a care, right inside the city harbour. And I must now explain the local topography in some detail, gentlemen, for the benefit of those who are unacquainted with it. Well, when I report that the pirates moved right into the city harbour, that is the same as saying that they entered the city itself, and penetrated as far as its inmost part. For the harbour of Syracuse does not encompass the circumference of the city, since, on the contrary, it is the city which surrounds and encircles the harbour. Instead, that is to say, of the waters of the harbour lapping against the outermost section of the city walls, they extend directly into the very heart of the city itself.

So at the time when you, Verres, were governor, the pirate Heracleo and his four diminutive light galleys sailed into Syracuse without meeting the slightest impediment! Heaven help us! The city belongs to the Roman empire and is the Roman governor's capital. Yet a light pirate vessel had sailed right up into its Forum, and to every one of the quays that the city possessed. It got as far as a point which even the famous fleets of Carthage, when its naval power was at its height, had never managed to reach, despite repeated attempts in war after war. It was a location which even the splendid fleet of Rome itself – a stranger to defeat until you were in charge – never succeeded in reaching, in any of our Carthaginian and Sicilian wars. None of Heracleo's enemy ships, either, had ever made its appearance in the harbour before. Yet now, right at that most central spot, his triumphant armed vessels were to be seen, inside the very walls of Syracuse, within its city, in the Forum itself. While you were governor, that is to say, these diminutive pirate ships were able to roam to and fro freely in waters into which only once before, in the memory of humankind, a fleet had managed to force its way. This was the massive, formidable fleet of the Athenians, with its three hundred craft;[1] and the topography of the harbour showed how their fleet was defeated and overwhelmed in that very same place. It was there, then, that the power of that Athenian state suffered its downfall and collapse. It was in that harbour that the imperial splendour and glory of Athens was shipwrecked.

So a pirate was able to penetrate to a point where the city of Syracuse no longer lay in front of him, but a large part of the town was actually now behind him. He sailed on right beyond the Island. This, at Syracuse, is a city in itself, by name and in virtue of its fortifications. It is the region in which, as I mentioned before, our ancestors would not allow any Syracusans to live, because they realized that people who dwelt there would be capable of dominating the harbour. Yet look, by way of contrast, at the free and easy way in which Heracleo was now able to sail around in those waters!

His men had come upon the wild palm roots that were on board our ships, and waved them about. Verres's appalling behaviour, and its terrible effects upon Sicily, were now visible to all. The Sicilian soldiers were the sons of farmers whose labours produced enough grain to feed the people of Rome and the whole of Italy. And yet these men, it was now learnt, the offspring of Ceres's own island, where grain, it was said, had been originally discovered,[2] had been obliged to eat the very food from which their ancestors rescued themselves, and all the rest of the world too, by their discovery of grain!

While you, then, were governor of Sicily, Sicilian soldiers had to eat palm roots, while Sicilian pirates fed on grain. What a depressing, miserable spectacle! Think of the glory of Rome, the dignity of the Roman people, the extensive Roman community dwelling at Syracuse, all made a mockery by that little pirate galley! Think of that pirate inside the harbour of the city, triumphantly celebrating his

1. The Athenian expedition during the Peloponnesian War (415–413).

2. Henna in Sicily was believed to have been the scene of the rape of Proserpina (Persephone), the daughter of Ceres (Demeter), by Dis (Pluto); Ceres's subsequent search for her daughter was symbolic of the growing of grain by burying seed in the ground.

victory over the Roman fleet, while his oars spattered the face of that idle scoundrel of a governor with spray!

Eventually the pirates sailed out of the harbour again. Nobody had frightened them away. But they had got enough. And now people began to ask what had caused this calamity. One thing was asserted and argued, quite openly. With all those oarsmen and soldiers discharged, it was declared, and with those that remained undermined by destitution and hunger, and with the governor spending all the time boozing in female company, such a humiliating disaster was only to be expected. This censorious abuse directed against Verres was backed up by reports from the captains whom the various communities had appointed to command their ships. Each of these captains who had got away to Syracuse, following the loss of the fleet, indicated the number of men on his own ship whom he knew to have been demobilized and were therefore missing. The whole matter was perfectly clear. Verres's lamentable conduct was demonstrated by the explicit testimony of witnesses, as well as by other evidence of numerous kinds.

As he knew, because he was told, the undivided attention of the Forum and the Roman community at Syracuse was devoted, throughout the day, to inquiring from the captains about how the fleet had been lost. The captains, for their part, replied by insisting to everyone that its loss was caused by the release of so many oarsmen, the starvation of those who were left, and the flight of the terrified Cleomenes. When Verres learnt that this was being said, he began to reflect. As you heard him say himself, during the earlier hearing, he had already concluded, before these developments, that he was certain to be prosecuted. And if the captains' evidence was heard, he would be wholly unable, he realized, to answer this serious charge that would be laid against him.

The plan that he first devised to counteract this danger was not exactly harsh, but it was stupid. He ordered the captains to be brought to him, and when they arrived rebuked them for talking about him in such terms. Then he requested each one of them to confirm that he did, in fact, still have the full complement of sailors on his ship, and that not a single one of them had been discharged. They, in response, agreed to fall in with his demand. Then at once, without delay, he summoned his friends, and in their presence interrogated each of the captains, one by one, about how many sailors he had had on his ship. Without exception, they gave the answers they had been told to give; whereupon Verres had these statements written down and stamped with his friends' seals, his far-sighted aim, no doubt, being to use this testimony in his defence against accusations on the subject, should the necessity arise.

I imagine, however, that the silly man's advisers laughed at him, and warned him that these documents would not help his case, and, indeed, that such exaggerated precautions on the part of a governor would arouse still further suspicions that the accusation was justified. Verres had already employed the same foolish tactics on a number of earlier occasions, ordering that, to suit his requirements, passages should be officially erased from municipal records, or, alternatively, inserted in their texts. But none of this, as he now appreciates, is doing him any good at all. For there is definite, authoritative, written and oral evidence which unmistakably demonstrates his guilt.

He did realize, finally, that the captains' testimonies, and his own statements, and the written records, would none of them be of any use to him. At that juncture, therefore, he developed a new plan. It was not just the sort of plan a crooked governor would devise; that would have had to be endured. It was a plan that no one but a ferocious, unhinged tyrant could have thought of. For what he now decided was that if he wanted to minimize the charge (he saw no chance of getting rid of it altogether), every single one of those ships' captains, the men who could testify to his criminality, must be killed. And another thought, too, kept coming into his mind. This was the problem of what could be done with Cleomenes. To take action against mere subordinates, Verres reasoned, while acquitting the man whom he had put in command and authority over them, was something that he could not get away with. It was just not practicable to put the men who followed Cleomenes's lead to death, and yet to let off Cleomenes himself, who had ordered them to follow him and to run away just as he himself had done. Severity towards men whose ships were short of crews and lacked any decks, combined with leniency to the one and only person who had a decked ship and something like a full complement of crew, was surely out of the question. So let Cleomenes die with the rest!

Ah, but what about all those promises, those solemn vows of friendship, those handshakes and embraces, how about that tent-companionship in the sex war waged upon that voluptuous shore? No! Cleomenes simply had to be spared after all. So Verres sent for him, and announced that he had decided to punish all the captains of the ships. It was necessary and imperative, in the interests of self-protection. 'But you, and you only,' continued Verres, 'I shall spare. I would rather take upon myself the blame for what has been done wrong, and suffer abuse for inconsistency, than act cruelly to yourself – or leave so many dangerous witnesses alive and unharmed.' Cleomenes thanked him, expressed satisfaction with his proposals, and agreed that that was what had to be done. But at the same time he reminded Verres of a point that had not occurred to him. Phalacrus, the captain of the quadrireme from Centuripa, could not be proceeded against, because Cleomenes himself had been with Phalacrus on his ship. Did this mean, then, that Phalacrus, a young man of high rank from a city of good repute, would be left free to offer whatever testimony he wished? 'Yes, for the moment,' replied Cleomenes, 'since it is evidently unavoidable. Later on, we can take steps to make sure that he does not get in our way.'

Once all this had been planned and decided, Verres hastened away from the governor's palace, fired with his criminal, lunatic, brutal design. He came into the Forum, and ordered the captains of the ships to be sent for. Unsuspicious, unafraid, they turned up without hesitation. Whereupon he commanded that the wretched, innocent men should be arrested and chained up. They appealed to Verres's sense of justice, and begged to know why he had done this. His answer was that they had betrayed the fleet to the pirates. The result was an outcry from the amazed population. It seemed quite extraordinary that the man could be so impudent and outrageous as to blame others for something that was entirely due to his own acquisitiveness, and to accuse others of treachery when he himself, so people believed, was a friend of the pirates. Furthermore, it was not until two whole weeks after the loss of the fleet that Verres had launched his accusation.

Meanwhile, people kept on asking where Cleomenes had got to. Not that anybody believed that Cleomenes himself, whatever sort of man he was, deserved to be penalized for the defeat. For what could he have done? To make unjustified accusations against anyone is something I want to avoid; and I repeat, therefore, that there was nothing effective that Cleomenes could have achieved with those ships which Verres's money-grubbing had denuded of their crews. However, here was Cleomenes, as people could see, sitting by the governor's side, and whispering in his ear in his usual intimate manner. At this juncture, then, there was an outbreak of universal indignation at the fact that while highly reputable men, nominees of their various cities, had been shackled and chained, Cleomenes himself remained the governor's close friend – because he was his partner in the deplorable dissipations in which Verres spent his time.

So, a man was designated by Verres to prosecute the captains. He was a certain Naevius Turpio, who had been convicted of assault while Gaius Licinius Sacerdos was governor. Turpio was singularly well adapted to the unscrupulous purposes of Verres, who had, indeed, employed him regularly as an intelligence agent and a spy in questions relating to tithes, capital charges and fabricated accusations of every kind.

The parents and relations of these unfortunate young captains, devastated by the sudden announcement of the catastrophe which had overtaken them, appeared in Syracuse. There they saw their sons loaded with chains, their necks and shoulders weighed down by the fate which the governor's avarice had brought upon them. They flocked into court and pleaded for the young men, and appealed, Verres, to your sense of what is right – something that did not exist, and never had! Among the fathers in this group was Dexo of Tyndaris, a man of the highest rank whom you had accepted as your host when you stayed in his house. Now, on the other hand, you saw this deeply respected man laid low by unhappiness. His tears, you would have thought, and his advanced years, and the rights and significance of hospitality, should have diverted you from your evil intentions and caused you to show some small element of humanity.

But there is little point in speaking of the rights of hospitality in connection with such a bestial horror. Another of his hosts had been Sthenius of Thermae Himeraeae, and Verres, as his guest, had stripped and gutted Sthenius's home of all its contents, had arranged for him to be prosecuted in his absence, and had sentenced him to death without his case even having been heard. That, surely, is not the man from whom we should expect deference to the ties binding host and guest. What we have here is not just a cruel human being, but a savage and monstrous beast.

The father Dexo's tears, wrung out of him by his son's peril, failed to touch your heart in the slightest. Yet you yourself had a father, whom you had left at home. You also had a son, who was with you. But the presence of your son did not manage to remind you how much parents love their children; nor did your absent father prompt you to remember the love that fathers feel for their sons. Dexo's son Aristeus, who had entertained you, was there in chains. And why? Because, you say, he had betrayed the fleet. For what reward? Well, he himself had been allowed to get away. Or take Cleomenes, for that matter – what had he done? He had shown himself a coward. But how was this, when you had decorated him for bravery? He had discharged a lot of sailors. But it was you who had got hold of the exemption fee for every one of them, without exception.

On the other side stood another father, Eubulida of Herbita, an eminent man in his town. Eubulida, attempting to defend his own son, had ventured to criticize Cleomenes. So he had been reduced to destitution and nakedness. It was hard to see what plea, what defence, could be put forward at all. No allusion, they were told, must be made to Cleomenes. Yet there was no other way to offer a defence. Mention his name, and you were as good as dead – and Verres's threats could never be taken lightly. Then there was the shortage of oarsmen. Ah, you are going to blame the governor, are you? Break the man's neck. Well, it is hard to see what could be done at all, if we may not refer to the governor, or, for that matter, to his rival for the lady Tertia's affections, although the whole of our defence depends precisely upon those two men.

Another of the accused captains was Heracleus of Segesta, whose family ranked very high in his town. Listen to his story, gentlemen, with the sympathy that your humane instincts demand. For it is a tale of great troubles and injuries inflicted upon our Sicilian allies. You should appreciate what Heracleus's situation was. Because of a serious eye infection he did not, on that occasion, go to sea at all, but by doctor's orders stayed behind at Syracuse on sick leave. So he, very definitely, did not betray the fleet, or run away in terror, or desert his post. For if his sick leave had been regarded as culpable the proper time for bringing him to book was when the fleet was sailing out of Syracuse. Here was a man against whom no charge of misconduct, however lacking in justification, could possibly have been alleged. Yet he was treated as if he had been caught in the very act of committing some crime.

Another of the captains was a certain Furius of Heraclea (for some of these people have Latin names of that kind). Furius was a man of distinction and reputation beyond his home town even while he still lived; and, after his death, he became famous throughout the whole of Sicily. For he had had the courage to denounce Verres in the severest terms; conscious that he would have to die, he knew he risked nothing by doing so. And so with determined resolution, on the point of death, while his mother sat weeping by his side in the prison all day and all night, he wrote down a speech in his own defence. There is no one in Sicily today who does not own a copy of that speech, and has not read it, and learnt from it all about the crimes and cruelties that you committed. In this document Furius described how many sailors his town allotted to him, how many he let go and in exchange for what sums, and how many he kept; and he also gave similar information about the other ships as well.

Yet when he made these statements before you in court, what happened was that he was beaten about the face with sticks. Faced by the prospect of death, Furius patiently endured the pain. But he persisted, loudly, in asserting the facts, just as he left them in writing. That the kisses of a totally immoral woman, he declared, should influence you more in the direction of acquitting Cleomenes than the tears of a mother were influencing you to spare his own, Furius's, life was disgusting and shameful. Moreover, I understand that he said another thing as well. It was a dying man's message to yourselves, gentlemen, and if the Roman people is right in its opinion of what sort of people you are, then what he said will strike home. Verres, he affirmed, may put the witnesses to death. But justice is something that he cannot kill. He himself, from beyond the grave, Furius proclaimed, would offer more convincing testimony, for the ears of understanding judges, even than if he had been brought into court in his lifetime. Alive, he would say, I could only describe Verres's greed. Slaughtered, I shall be able to explain how utterly criminal he was, how outrageous and how cruel.

And Furius made another splendid statement as well. When your trial, Verres, takes place, he declared, it is not only a multitude of human witnesses that will come forward. For the avenging demons from the tombs of innocent men will be there as well – and the spirits of vengeance who haunt guilty men. His own personal fate, Furius asserted, will seem of relatively minor importance – after all, he had already seen your lethal axes with his own eyes, and had gazed upon the face and hands of Sextius your executioner – when here, in the community of Roman citizens that exists in this town, some of those citizens, at your command, were actually beheaded by those very axes. Gentlemen, I need not continue. You have given our allies freedom. And Furius made the fullest use of that freedom, while suffering the sort of excruciating death which might have been the lot of some wretched slave.

Verres found them all guilty – through the verdict of his own court. Although the charge was so serious, he had not called in his quaestor, Titus Vettius, to offer advice. Nor had he called in his own deputy governor Titus Cervius – whom subsequently he challenged as one of the judges in his own case, precisely because Cervius had been his deputy in Sicily.[1] No, Verres convicted the defendants, every one of them, on the basis of a decision made by his own friends, that is to say a collection of robbers.

It was a verdict that greatly upset the Sicilians, our loyal allies from ancient times. For they felt that their own lives and fortunes were now precarious. They were horrified by the degeneration of our own imperial rule from its earlier lenient mildness into a regime of such inhuman brutality. The mass condemnation of those innocent men appalled them, and so did the attempt of our disgraceful governor to evade condemnation for the thefts which he himself had committed by the undeserved massacre of people who were guilty of nothing at all.

You will think, gentlemen, that this story of criminal brutality must by now be complete. And that you should think so is reasonable enough. In competition with other evil men Verres would easily be the winner, by a large margin. But he competes with himself: with each new horrifying action he ensures he will outdo what he has done before.

I mentioned that the name of Phalacrus of Centuripa was erased from the death-list on the proposal of Cleomenes, because it was on Phalacrus's quadrireme that Cleomenes had sailed. All the same, however, the young man felt nervous, because he realized that his position was the same as that of the perfectly innocent people who had been condemned to death. But Timarchides went to see him, and told him he was not in any danger of execution. Nevertheless, he would do well to take steps, Timarchides added, to make sure that he was not flogged. To cut the story short, you have heard from the young Phalacrus himself that this prospect frightened him

1. i.e. Cervius, as *legatus*, had been too honest to suit Verres.

so much that he passed Timarchides a bribe. But these are trivial matters to bring against a defendant who has to face such serious charges as Verres. All right, it was he, in fact, who took, through Timarchides, the bribe which saved Phalacrus from being scourged. People do behave like that. He did accept money to refrain from convicting a defendant. Well, that is not entirely unusual. The Roman people are hardly interested in having such conventional accusations brought against Verres. What they feel they need, what they demand, are charges that are quite unusual and unprecedented. Because this case, they are convinced, is not just the trial of a Roman governor. It is the trial of a dreadful tyrant.

The convicted men were cast into prison. The punishments to which they were sentenced, however, were passed on to their unfortunate parents, who were denied access to their sons – prohibited from bringing food and clothing to their own children. You can see the fathers here in court. Imagine them lying there, in the entrance of the prison. And the unhappy mothers, too, spent their nights at the same prison doorway, shut out from a final glimpse of their children, praying only for permission to receive their sons' last breath on their lips.

The prison warder, Sextius the lictor, stood by. He was the governor's executioner, a terrifying dealer of death to the allies and citizens of Rome. Every groan, every moan of pain meant more money for him, at a rate that had already been fixed. 'To be allowed to see him, the sum you will pay will be this. To take food and clothes inside, the fee will be such and such.' No one refused. 'Well, what will you let me have if I agree to kill your son with a single blow of the axe? That will mean that, as he dies, he does not have to suffer prolonged torture, one blow after another, a ferocious pain.' Yes, the lictor was paid for that too. Think of the ghastly, unbearable sadness, the bitter and tragic destiny, of those parents who were compelled to pay bribes, not to have their children freed, but actually to allow them a quick death. Moreover, the young men themselves spoke with their good friend Sextius about the execution that was coming to them, about their preference for that single stroke of the axe. And the last appeal these children made to their parents was that money should, indeed, be paid to the lictor, in order that they should not have to suffer so greatly.

So many, many horrible agonies were inflicted upon those parents and relatives. One would suppose, however, that their sons' death would put an end to those agonies. But that will not be the case. It is hard, certainly, to imagine how cruelty could go any farther. Yet a way will, nevertheless, be found. When the young men have been beheaded, by the axe, their bodies will be thrown to wild animals. If, however, that distresses the parents, then they can pay for permission to bury them instead. Onasus, a leading gentleman of Segesta, bears witness, as you have heard, that he paid over a sum of money to Timarchides for leave to bury the captain Heracleus. There is no question, here, of having to discount the fathers' versions, on the grounds that they obviously lament their bereavement. For here is supporting evidence from a man of rank and position who is not one of the fathers at all. Furthermore there is not one single person in the whole of Syracuse who has not heard, and is unaware, that bargains of this sort about burial were arranged with Timarchides by the doomed men themselves before they died. They spoke with him about the matter quite openly. They all brought in their kinsmen to back them up. They arranged for their own funeral rites while they were still alive. And once these arrangements had been fixed and concluded, they were taken out of prison, and bound to the stake, and put to death.

No one in the world could be unfeeling and inhuman enough not to feel deeply sorry for the miserable fate of those very decent young men – except you. Nobody could help weeping, could help believing that the calamity which had overtaken them was a personal attack upon himself, a menace to everyone. The axe fell. There were screams of grief. But you rejoiced and gloated. It gave you pleasure that these witnesses to your graspingness had been removed. Yet you were mistaken, Verres, very mistaken indeed, in supposing that the stains of your robberies and other disgraceful deeds would be washed clean by the blood of those innocent allies of Rome. To imagine that the harm your graspingness had inflicted could be cured by recourse to such cruel behaviour showed that you had lost all contact with reality and sanity.

It is true that those witnesses to your dreadful behaviour are dead. All the same, their relations have not forgotten them. And they have not forgotten you either. Besides, a number of the captains are still alive; and here they are. Destiny, I would suggest, has preserved them, to avenge their innocent colleagues, and appear in this trial. Phylarchus of Haluntium is here. He did not run away when Cleomenes did. So he was caught by the pirates and taken prisoner.

And that misfortune proved his salvation, for if the pirates had not captured him he would have fallen into the hands of this other pirate Verres, who plunders our own allies. Phylarchus tells us, in his evidence, about the demobilization of sailors, about the starvation of those who remained, about how Cleomenes ran off. Another man who is here is Phalacrus of Centuripa, an eminent member of an eminent city. His evidence agrees, totally, with what Phylarchus has said.

Now I must ask you, gentlemen, what you are feeling and thinking as you sit there and listen to what I say. You cannot, surely, believe that I am judging the matter wrongly, or that the catastrophes which have overtaken our unfortunate allies have caused me greater distress than is reasonable. Would it not, instead, be right to say that the agonies and miseries inflicted on these innocent persons have distressed yourselves just as much as they have distressed me?

As I speak of men of Herbita and Heraclea perishing by the executioner's axe, I feel a vivid sense of the shameful injustice of their fates. They were citizens of communities, and grew up in the fields of those communities, which, year after year, by their laborious work, contributed huge quantities of grain to feed the populace of Rome. Their parents brought them up and educated them to have the highest hopes of our rule and our justice. And the outcome was this: that they were struck down by Verres's outrageous inhumanity – struck down by his death-dealing axe. When I think of the ships' captains from Tyndaris and Segesta, the rights that those cities have legitimately enjoyed cannot fail to come to mind, and the services they have rendered to Rome. Publius Cornelius Scipio Africanus the younger decided that the spoils of war should fittingly be employed for the beautification of those cities. As for Verres, on the other hand, not only did he rob them of the things of beauty that were theirs,[1] but he criminally deprived them of their most distinguished citizens as well.

The inhabitants of Tyndaris could well be proud to speak of themselves in the following sort of terms. 'We are counted among the seventeen loyal peoples of Sicily.[2] Throughout Rome's Punic and Sicilian wars we invariably maintained our ties of faithful

1. This was dealt with at length in *II Verres*, 4.

2. i.e. the seventeen that had remained loyal to Rome during the Second Punic War (218–201).

friendship with the Roman nation. We have always provided the Roman people with every assistance in war and every contribution in time of peace.' But what a lot of use this loyalty has been to them while Verres has been in charge and in power! Once upon a time, men of Tyndaris, it was Scipio Africanus the elder who led your sailors against Carthage. Today it is Cleomenes who leads your ship against the pirates; and it is almost devoid of crew. Scipio Africanus the younger passed you a share of the spoils of war and rewards of victory.[1] But now, by way of contrast, despoilment is your fate: despoilment by Verres! Your ship is snatched away by the pirates. You yourselves are classified as enemies.

There is also that blood relationship between Rome and Segesta.[2] The Segestan archives show it in their records, and evidence to the same effect has been handed down by word of mouth. Besides, the relationship is reaffirmed and demonstrated by the numerous services the city has rendered to us. But what benefit, one may ask, did Segesta derive from that link while Verres was governor? In such great regard, gentlemen, did he hold it that one of the most prominent young men of the city was wrenched from the bosom of his native place and handed over to Verres's executioner Sextius. Our ancestors granted Segesta substantial, fertile lands, and immunity from taxes. It remained for you, Verres, to show such total disregard for the Segestans' claims of kinship, fidelity and ancient tradition, and for the dignity of their town, that when they appealed to you to spare the life of that single, honoured, guiltless son of theirs, they appealed in vain.

Where our allies can take refuge, to whom they can plead for help, what hope, indeed, they can cherish of living any worthwhile lives at all, I am at a loss to say, if you, gentlemen, abandon them. To approach the Senate, and ask it to have Verres punished, would serve no purpose. Such an approach is not customary; that is not what the Senate is for. An appeal to the Roman Assembly would be equally ineffective. It had passed a law, it would answer, for the benefit of its allies,[3] and it was you yourselves whom it had

1. After the sack of Carthage following the Third Punic War (146) he restored to the Sicilian cities numerous works of art which the Carthaginians had taken from them.

2. The Segestans, like the Romans, claimed Trojan descent.

3. The Cornelian Law about extortion (*Lex Cornelia de pecuniis repetundis*) of the dictator Lucius Cornelius Sulla (81).

appointed to keep an eye on that law, and see that it was adhered to. Your court here, then, is the only place in which they can seek compensation. But the refuge that they now look for is not as effective as the refuge they were accustomed to look to in earlier days, when they applied to get stolen property back. Indeed they suspect, wrongly no doubt, that the Roman people has come to condone such robberies, and has no objection to their continuance. And it is true that we have permitted these outrages to continue, year after year, and we have said nothing. We have seen the entire wealth of the world pass into the hands of a very small number of men. Our willingness to tolerate and allow this state of affairs is all the more clearly perceptible because none of these persons troubles to pretend that he is not indulging in acquisitiveness, or makes the slightest effort to conceal that he is doing so.

The beautiful, elegant objects that adorn this city of Rome and are the property of our state have, in every case, been brought here after they have been captured from a defeated enemy of our nation. The men to whom I am now referring, on the other hand, have adorned and crammed their own personal country residences with a very large number of beautiful things taken, as spoils, from our own loyal allies. You can easily see what has happened to the riches of the foreign states that have now become so poor, when you find the entire wealth of Athens, Pergamum, Cyzicus, Miletus, Chios, Samos, indeed the whole of Asia and Achaea and Greece and Sicily, concentrated in this small number of Italian country mansions!

And today, gentlemen, as I have said before, your allies have had to let all those treasures go, without attempting to recover them. At one time, by their record of loyal service, they safeguarded themselves against official Roman depredations. In due course, however, there came a few Romans whose greed they proved unable to resist. Somehow or other, nevertheless they managed to satisfy it. But today they have lost the capacity not only to resist, but even to supply all that has been demanded. And so they let their property go. They give up the funds which this court – as its name shows – was created to recover; they do not claim it back. Instead, they just take refuge here, dressed as you see them. Look, look, gentlemen, at the filthy, dishevelled appearance of these people – people who are your faithful allies![1]

1. i.e. they were dressed as bereaved mourners.

One of them, standing here, is Sthenius of Thermae Himeraeae. Note his unkempt hair, his mourning clothes. You have pillaged that man's home, Verres, from top to bottom. Yet he remains entirely silent about your robberies. It is only his own restitution of his own person that he asks for – nothing more than that. For it is you, Verres, whose villainous unscrupulousness has expelled him from his own home country, where his many fine qualities and generous actions had made him a leader. And here, gentlemen, you see Dexo of Tyndaris. What he, for his part, demands from you, Verres, is not the wealth that you have stolen from his city – and not even what you have stolen from him personally. What he asks for, instead, this unhappy man, is the corpse of his only son, his excellent and entirely innocent son. He is not, I repeat, trying to recover any of the money he has been made to pay. But he does have one additional demand, and that is to offer to the bones and ashes of his dead son the small degree of consolation that your own downfall will bring. Here, too, is the elderly Eubulida. In spite of his age, he undertook the wearisome enterprise of travelling to Rome. To recover some portion of his property was, once again, not the motive he had in mind. His one aim was that his eyes, which had witnessed the blood welling from the neck of his son, might now look upon yourself, after you have been condemned by the court.

The mothers and sisters of the unfortunate young victims, gentlemen, had also wanted to come, if Lucius Caecilius Metellus[1] had allowed them to. One of them came to see me, as I was arriving one evening at Heraclea. She was accompanied by all the married women of the city; many of them were carrying torches. She hailed me as her saviour, and denounced you, Verres, as an assassin. Crying out the name of her son, the poor woman hurled herself down at my feet, as if I had the power to raise her son from the dead. In the other towns, too, the aged mothers and even the small children of those wretched victims had behaved in just the same way: old and young alike, they begged me to make the effort to help them, and appealed to your trust and compassion.

And that, gentlemen, is how Sicily has entrusted me with the present protest, in addition to all the rest. It is pity, not ambition,

1. The successor of Verres as governor of Sicily.

that has prompted me to respond. It is my aim that the conviction of innocent men, prison chains, floggings and the wielding of axes, the torment of our allies and the bloodshed of innocent men, and, worst of all, the blood-drained bodies of the dead and the sorrow of their parents and relatives, should not be allowed to enrich Roman officials. If, gentlemen, thanks to your honesty and integrity, I manage to get this man condemned and thus relieve Sicily of its terror, I shall feel that my own sense of duty, and the wishes of those who asked me to do what I am doing, have received full and complete satisfaction.

But if you, Verres, can find someone willing to try to defend you on this charge concerning the fleet, he must do so without bringing forward the well-worn type of irrelevant arguments. He must not, for example, suggest that what I call culpable action was really just plain bad luck, or that what I describe as a crime was merely a regrettable setback. Nor must he assert that when I blame you for losing the fleet I am unfair, since many valorous commanders in the past, liable like everyone else to the uncertain hazards of war, have frequently suffered reverses on land and sea alike. No, it is not just bad luck that I hold against you. To mention other men's ill-successes, and to list the shipwrecks that have, fortuitously, caused the downfall of earlier commanders, will not do you any good at all. For my charges are different. Your ships were unmanned. Oarsmen and sailors had been discharged. Those who were left had to feed on palm roots. A Roman fleet was placed under a Sicilian. A Syracusan was put in charge of men who had always been our allies and friends. And as for you yourself, Verres, at that very time, and for many immediately preceding days, I must repeat that you had just been drinking on the sea-shore in the company of females. Those are my accusations. I have witnesses to support every one of them.

You cannot, I think, complain that I am trampling you when you are down, unfairly brushing aside your defence of ill-luck, assailing and abusing you for what were merely the chances of war. As a matter of fact, the imputation of ill-fortune, even if you yourself choose to invoke it, is not, generally, palatable to men who have had to allow fortune to guide them, and who have had experience of its hazards and shifts. But, in any case, fortune has played no part in these calamities of yours. It is upon the battlefield, not at the dinner table, that men test the chances of war. It is not

Mars the god of war, but Venus the goddess of love, whose indiscriminate favours may be said to have swayed the issue.[1] Furthermore, if it is misguided to blame you when you were merely unfortunate, one may ask why you yourself showed no consideration or pardon to those innocent young men whose sufferings were certainly due to misfortune.

Furthermore, it would be equally illegitimate for you to cut me short, and claim that I am seeking to work up feeling against you, because you had recourse to the axe to inflict capital punishment – which was, you maintain, in accordance with our ancestral custom. Your penal methods do not form part of my charge. I do not claim that no man ever ought to have his head cut off. Nor do I suggest that fear should play no part in military discipline, or severity in our system of rule, or punishment when a crime has been committed. I willingly admit that our allies, and indeed our own Roman citizens and soldiers, have often, legitimately, been punished with sternness and vigour. So you had better leave that line of argument alone.

What I am seeking to demonstrate, however, is that you were to blame, and the ships' captains were not. I accuse you of discharging oarsmen and sailors, and receiving payment for doing so. All the surviving captains confirm that this was the case. So does our ally, the city of Netum. So do the people of Amestratus and Herbita, of Henna and Agyrium and Tyndaris. And so, finally, does your own witness, your own admiral, your sexual rival, your guest Cleomenes. He went ashore, he says, to obtain soldiers from the garrison at Pachynus, in order to replenish his crews. This is something that he would obviously never have done if his crews had been at full strength, since a completely manned and equipped vessel has no room, not only for a substantial number of additional persons, but not even for one.

I also maintain that the sailors who had remained, undischarged, on Cleomenes's ships were all weakened and undermined by starvation and the lack of necessities in general. I maintain, too, that this was not their fault. Alternatively, if any of them has to be censured, it should be Cleomenes himself, who had the best ship and the most sailors and was in command of the fleet as a whole. Or if, on the other hand, every one of the captains *was* to blame, then certainly Cleomenes should not have been just permitted to remain a looker-on

1. Cicero is referring to Cleomenes's alleged sharing of his wife with Verres.

while all the rest were tortured and executed. And I further maintain that, when their executions took place, it was a very wicked thing to extract fees from their weeping relations, fees for the fatal wounds that were inflicted on them, fees for their deaths and their burials.

If, therefore, you propose to answer the accusations I am bringing against you, this is what you will have to say to contradict me. The fleet, you will have to argue, was completely manned and completely equipped. None of the fighting men had gone. None of the oars was towed along for lack of rowers. There was ample grain on board. The captains, the representatives of all those responsible cities – of the whole island of Sicily – were all just telling lies. Cleomenes, too, when he stated that he had gone ashore at Pachynus to embark soldiers, was also lying – in order to let you down. What the captains were short of was not a larger quantity of men, but a greater degree of courage. They deserted and abandoned Cleomenes when he himself was fighting bravely. Nobody was paid anything at all for the burial of the executed men. If all this is what you are going to declare, it will be proved, in every respect, to be a fabrication. Whereas if you say anything else, it will mean that you find my charges against you impossible to refute.

I cannot feel that you will now have the effrontery to assert, 'One of the jurymen is my personal friend, another is a friend of my father's.' On the contrary, the closer a juryman's relationship with you, the more ashamed you should be to proclaim it, when you are faced with such grave charges. A friend of your father's? But if your father himself were a member of the jury, the only thing he could do, God knows, would be to address you in terms such as these. 'You are the man,' he would say, 'who, as governor of a Roman province, in charge of warfare at sea, for three years allowed the men of Messana exemption from providing the ship which the treaty required them to provide. It was for your private use that these same Messanians constructed a large merchant ship, at the expense of their own city. It was you who compelled the Sicilian communities to pay *you* money, ostensibly for the fleet. It was you, once again, who accepted money from the oarsmen, in exchange for their release. It was you, when your quaestor and deputy governor captured a pirate ship, who concealed its captain where no one could trace where he was. You were shameless enough to behead men who were stated, and widely known, to be

Roman citizens. You had the audacity, also, to take pirates away to your own house, and it was actually from there that you brought out their leader to appear at your trial.

'Here in this splendid province,' your father would go on to say, 'among our loyal allies and a respected Roman community, in the midst of the perils which threatened the island, what did you do? You reclined day after day beside the shore, plunged in debauchery. Throughout all that period, it was impossible for anyone to meet you in your home, or even catch a sight of you in the Forum. Your companions in these dissipations were married women, the wives of our allies and friends. Those were the sort of females whom you brought your young son, my grandson, to meet. This meant that at the most critical, hazardous period of his life his father's behaviour set him the worst possible example.

'You, a Roman governor in his province, allowed yourself to be seen wearing a Greek tunic and purple cloak. For the better gratification of your erotic lusts, you took the command of the fleet away from the Roman deputy governor and gave it to a Syracusan instead. Sicily is a province fertile in grain; yet your soldiers had to go without that grain. Because of your extravagance, your mean graspingness, a Roman fleet was captured and burnt by pirates. No enemy had ever penetrated into the harbour of Syracuse since the city had been founded. Yet under your governorship pirates sailed about freely inside that same port.

'Nor did you make the slightest attempt to cover up all these disreputable happenings by pretending you had no knowledge of them, or allowing them to be forgotten or passed over in silence. On the contrary, you took your ships' captains, who were guiltless, tore them away from the embrace of their parents, whose guest you had been, and hastened them off to torture and death. Appeals to my name, as your father, cried out by those weeping, grieving parents, did nothing to soften you. For the blood of those innocent men brought you not only satisfaction but financial gain.'

I have now done everything I can for the Sicilians. I have carried out my duty towards them, I have satisfied the claims of friendship, I have fulfilled the promise I made them.[1] What still remains of my case, gentlemen, is not something I have just taken on, but something

1. Cicero is referring to the friendly ties he formed when he was quaestor in Sicily (75).

I feel a powerful, inborn impulse to persevere with. It is not something that has been placed in my hands from outside, but is inextricably rooted in my inmost instincts and feelings. It is no longer a question of the safety of our allies. For what is at stake is the life and life-blood of Roman citizens, that is to say of ourselves, of every one of us. Do not expect me to launch out on arguments, gentlemen, which sound as if I am feeling that some part of what I tell you could be doubted. On the contrary, everything I shall say will be so crystal clear that I could make the whole of Sicily a witness to its truth.

The folly of Verres, a quality which goes together with brazen wrongdoing, has driven his savage mind and ungovernable feelings into insanity. That is the only way one can describe how he never held back, although the whole of the Roman community was looking on, from openly arranging that punishments designed for condemned slaves should be inflicted upon citizens of Rome. I need not remind you of the number of citizens he ordered to be slashed with rods. The plain fact, gentlemen, is this. During Verres's governorship of Sicily, he did not ever draw the slightest distinction, for such purposes, between Roman citizens and everyone else. Eventually, indeed, the lictors actually formed the habit of seizing hold of our citizens without even waiting for his order to do so.

In Lilybaeum there is a substantial Roman community. And you, Verres, are unable to deny that in its Forum Gaius Servilius, a Roman citizen of advanced years belonging to our community at Panormus, was struck with staves and knocked down before your own tribunal. Summon up the courage to say that this was not so, if you can. There was not one person at Lilybaeum who did not see what happened, not one person in Sicily who did not hear of it. So I charge you with having a Roman citizen beaten by your lictors until he fell to the ground before your eyes. And one must ask what the pretext for this action was – although, heaven knows, it is damaging enough to our common interests and the rights of Roman citizens that any such question even has to be asked. When I do so, therefore, in connection with Servilius, it is with the added proviso that such a thing ought never to happen to a Roman citizen at all. In respect of this one man, then, gentlemen, I shall venture to ask the question; and forgive me when I do. In the remaining cases I shall not spend much time inquiring about pretexts.

Well, what Servilius had done was to talk with some freedom

about Verres's criminal and sinful behaviour. This was passed on to Verres, who promptly ordered him to give surety for his court appearance at Lilybaeum[1] to answer a charge brought by an attendant at the temple of Venus.[2] Servilius obeyed, and duly appeared. But no one came forward to bring the charge. Verres therefore set about bringing pressure upon him to accept a challenge from one of his lictors, involving the sum of one thousand sesterces to prove that he, Verres, was not a swindler;[3] and the governor added that he would supply members of his own staff to conduct the case. Servilius protested strongly against being tried for a capital offence,[4] before a biased court, when no one had even come forward to bring the charge. While in the process of making this appeal, however, he found himself surrounded by six lictors, tough characters who knew all about assaulting people and beating them up, and who now proceeded to strike him savagely with their batons. Next, the head lictor Sextius, whom I have frequently mentioned before, began to hit the unfortunate man violently across the eyes with the butt end of his stick. His face and eyes streaming with blood, Servilius fell to the ground. While he lay there, his assailants continued to aim blows at his body – until finally he agreed to accept the legal challenge. That was how he was treated. He was carried off, taken for dead, and soon afterwards did in fact die. Whereupon Verres, that devoted follower of Venus, so full of every sort of gallantry and charm, spent the proceeds of the dead man's property on the dedication of a silver image of Cupid in Venus's

1. This was the procedure applicable to civil suits heard at Rome or in courts of local jurisdiction, whereby the defendant was required to give surety to the plaintiff for his appearance on the day fixed for the hearing.

2. The famous temple of Venus Erycina on Mount Eryx. Verres had, apparently, suborned one of the 'servants' of the goddess to make a charge against Servilius which would involve his attendance at nearby Lilybaeum, so that he would not have to appear at his home town Panormus, which might have favoured him.

3. This *sponsio* was a procedure whereby a point of fact was submitted to a judge or a board of arbitrators (*recuperatores*). The party against whom the decision went forfeited a named sum. In this case Verres was perhaps getting his lictor to challenge his supposed swindling of the managers of the temple of Venus.

4. i.e if the case went against him he was likely to be convicted on a charge of *maiestas* (treason) for having slandered the governor.

temple. This, then, was how he misused the possessions of others, to fulfil the nocturnal vows of his own libidinous desires.

Concerning the torments inflicted on other Roman citizens I prefer just to offer a general, comprehensive description, rather than considering them one by one. While Verres was governor, the prison built at Syracuse by the cruel despot Dionysius I,[1] and known as the Stone Quarries, was the place where Roman citizens had to live. If the thought or sight of any of them caused Verres displeasure, the man was immediately thrown into the Quarries. I can see, gentlemen, that this makes you all very angry. Indeed, I already noticed that this was the case at the first hearing, when witnesses told the same story. It is your conviction, I know, that we Roman citizens ought to be able to enjoy our rightful freedom not only in Rome, but elsewhere as well. In Rome, of course, we have the tribunes of the people, the other officers of state, the lawcourts with which our Forum is filled, the authority of the Senate, the people's judgement in the Assembly, to protect us. But you believe, as I am well aware, that the freedom and position that we Romans share with one another are at stake if our citizen rights are infringed among any people whatsoever, anywhere in the world.

So one wonders, Verres, how you could have had the nerve to use that place of confinement for foreign malefactors and criminals and pirates and enemies of Rome to incarcerate Roman citizens, in substantial numbers. It is remarkable that the prospect of your future trial never occurred to you, nor the thought of a gathering such as this, at which such a mass of listeners are staring at you with censorious, hostile gaze. How strange that the greatness of the Roman people never entered your mind or presented itself to your imagination, not to speak, as I said, of this great concourse that you might have to face. That you would never again have to appear before their eyes, never re-enter the Forum of the Roman nation, never again be obliged to submit to the authority of our laws and our courts, was surely more than you could have hoped for.

It is necessary to demand what lay behind this passion for cruelty, this massive involvement in crime. What mainly made it possible, gentlemen, was a novel, exceptional device for performing swindles. The poets have told us stories of men who lurked in inlets of the sea or occupied promontories or jagged cliffs so that anyone who was

1. 406–367.

shipwrecked there should suffer death at their hands.[1] And it was with a precisely similar aim that Verres menaced the entire stretch of sea surrounding every part of Sicily. Whenever a ship arrived from Asia or Syria or Tyre or Alexandria, the spies and guards he had appointed for the purpose promptly seized hold of it. The people travelling on it were cast into the Quarries, one and all, and the cargoes and goods they had been proposing to sell were taken off to the governor's palace. After so very many years Sicily had once again become the prey, I will not say of a Dionysius or a Phalaris[2] or one of the many other savage despots that the island has produced in its time, but rather of a different kind of monster, as fierce as any of those that reputedly haunted the region in remote antiquity. Indeed, it is my opinion that neither Charybdis nor Scylla presented as grave a menace as Verres to the men who were sailing in that strait.[3] For he was more dangerous than they were, since he had flanked himself with much more numerous and ferocious hounds than Scylla's. He was a second Cyclops.[4] But he was more horrible than the Cyclopes, who had only held sway over Aetna and that part of Sicily, whereas Verres beset the whole island.

If you want to know, gentlemen, what explanation for this appalling cruelty Verres offered at the time, it was the same explanation as his defence will be putting forward now. Whenever anyone disembarked in Sicily with an appreciable quantity of goods, Verres denounced them as soldiers of Quintus Sertorius, who were in flight from Dianium.[5] In order to avert this peril, they used to display the wares they were bringing: Tyrian purple robes, incense, scents, linen fabrics, gems and pearls, Greek wines, Asian slaves for sale. What they hoped was to prove by the nature of this merchandise where they had come from. They had hoped, that is to say, that this demonstration on their part would save them. But

1. e.g. the Laestrygones in Homer's *Odyssey* (x, 80ff.).

2. Phalaris of Acragas (Agrigentum) ruled from *c.* 570/565 to 554/549.

3. Charybdis was a whirlpool in a narrow channel of the sea, later identified with the Sicilian Strait (Strait of Messina), opposite the six-headed sea-monster Scylla, which was believed to have a girdle of dogs' heads round her loins.

4. The Cyclopes were giant one-eyed beings, one of whom, Polyphemus (the son of Poseidon), was tricked by Odysseus in Homer's *Odyssey*, and was believed to have lived in Sicily.

5. Otherwise known as Artemisium; formerly the naval arsenal of the rebel Sertorius (82–72).

what it did instead was to bring about their ruin. For Verres declared that it was from the pirates that these goods had come into their possession. Then he ordered the merchants to be consigned to the Stone Quarries, and took their ships and their cargoes into detention.

By these methods, the prison was soon crammed full of men who had been engaged in trade. Next followed the events of which you have learnt from Lucius Suettius, a Roman knight of excellent character, and you shall hear of them from the other witnesses as well. What happened was that innocent Roman citizens, consigned to that prison, had their necks broken. 'I am a Roman citizen' is a declaration and an appeal which has, many times, brought men rescue and safety among uncivilized peoples at the ends of the earth. Yet all it achieved, for these men, was a quicker penalty and a nastier death.

Well, Verres, I simply fail to see how you propose to ward off these accusations. That I am lying, or inventing, or exaggerating, you are really unable to claim. I cannot believe that you will dare to advise your defence counsels in any such sense. Let us have, please, out of the fold of his toga those Syracusan records which he feels were put together in such a way as to favour his case. Let us have, also, the prison roll, which is meticulously kept so as to indicate the dates on which prisoners are first detained, and the dates on which they die, or are put to death. [*The roll is read out.*] You see how Roman citizens were herded into the Stone Quarries, how all your fellow-citizens were massed together in that place of degradation. Search, if you like, for some trace indicating their subsequent departure from the prison. There is none. Did they all die natural deaths? Even if that plea were open,[1] it would still not be plausible. But in that very same record we find a phrase which this careless and uneducated man was incapable of noticing or understanding: 'Justice was done to them', which was the Sicilian way of saying 'they were executed'.

If it had been some monarch, or foreign people or nation, that had treated Roman citizens in this way, we should surely be taking official measures to punish those responsible, and dispatch our armies against them. For we could not possibly have endured such a disgraceful slur upon the honour of Rome without exacting venge-

1. As it is not, since it is ruled out by documents that contradict it.

ance and punishment. Remember all those important wars upon which our ancestors embarked, because Roman citizens were said to have been insulted, Roman ship-masters placed under arrest, Roman traders subjected to robbery. Yet I, on this occasion, am not complaining because these merchants were arrested, I am not declaring it unendurable that they were robbed. My accusation is that, after their ships and slaves and trading goods had been taken away from them, they were hurled into prison, and in that prison, although Roman citizens, they were killed.

My theme, then, is the brutal execution of that multitude of Roman citizens. And I am speaking about it in Rome itself, before this vast gathering of Romans. I am speaking to a jury composed of senators, members of the most eminent body in the state. I am speaking in the Forum of our Roman people. Yet, if my audience were Scythians instead, what I am saying would move even their barbarian hearts. For so magnificent is our empire, so greatly is the name of Rome respected among all the nations of the world, that it is not felt permissible for any man whatsoever to treat our citizens with such savagery.

I cannot imagine where you can escape to, Verres, or where you can find refuge. For it is clear to me that the strict justice of the jurymen who are trying your case has thoroughly trapped you, and that the crowded Assembly of the Roman people has caught you in its meshes. And just suppose – though I know it is out of the question – that you *did* manage to wriggle yourself out of the net that entangles you, and find some means and method of getting clear, it would only be to fall into a snare that was even deadlier still. For it will still be my own particular duty to make an end of you and cut you to pieces, and I shall be doing so, then, from a more commanding position.[1]

Suppose I went so far as to accept Verres's line of defence. Yet, even so, that ill-founded plea on which he relies would, in fact, turn out to be no less damaging to his case than my own well-founded accusation. For this is his defence: that he intercepted fugitives from Spain, and put them to death. But one has to ask, Verres, who authorized you to adopt these measures, what right you had to adopt them, who had ever done the same before, what entitled you to take such unprecedented action. True, we see our Forum and our

1. i.e. as aedile (69).

public halls filled with men who have acted with the same sort of violence; and we do not find the sight disquieting. For we can at least not regret that this civil strife of ours, this madness, this stroke of fate, ill-fortune – call it what you will – has reached a conclusion which enables us to preserve, unharmed, those of our fellow-citizens who have managed to survive the disturbances. But Verres has done worse. Long ago, you will remember, he betrayed the consul under whom he was serving as quaestor,[1] and transferred his allegiance to those who were against him, misappropriating public funds as he went. Then Verres set himself up as a national leader. As a mark of this, he seized men who were perfectly entitled, as far as the Senate and Roman people and every state official were concerned, to appear in the Forum, vote, live in Rome and take part in political life; and it was his intention to put all such citizens to a painful and brutal death, if any of them happened to land at any point on the coast of Sicily.

A considerable number of soldiers who had been in Quintus Sertorius's army took refuge with the eminent and valiant Cnaeus Pompeius Magnus, after Marcus Perperna Veiento had been put to death.[2] As for Pompeius, he took every possible step to ensure that they remained unharmed. To every one of his fellow-citizens who appealed for help, Pompeius's invincible arm extended its protection, and gave them reason to hope that they would be saved. It seems unbelievable that these men could have found a haven of refuge with the man against whom they had been fighting, while you yourself, by way of contrast, who had never counted for anything at all in public life, had nothing to give them except torture and death.

See, now, what little use this line of defence – arguing that the men were Sertorians – has been to your cause! I honestly feel I would be happier if the court and the Roman people accepted your defence than I am when I have to ask it to believe the terrible things that I have to say against you. I would feel happier, as a prosecutor, I mean, if disbanded rebels should have been victims of your

1. Cnaeus Cornelius Dolabella, governor of Cilicia 80–79 (he had been consul in 81). Verres plundered Cilicia and Asia in association with him, but after their return helped to convict him for extortion.

2. Perperna, who had joined Sertorius and then murdered him, was defeated and executed by Pompeius (Pompey) in 72.

enmity, rather than the harmless merchants and ship-owners that they actually were. For what my arguments demonstrate is just that you are unpleasantly grasping. But your own chosen line of defence convicts you of a monstrous mental derangement, of cruelty of unheard-of dimensions, of what is virtually a new proscription.[1]

However, this remarkable advantage that Verres himself places at my disposal[2] is not available for me to employ after all. The reason why, instead, I have to pursue my own, different, course of argument is this. The entire people of Puteoli is here. Its rich and respected merchants have flocked to join us at this court. And what these men tell us is that their partners, their freedmen, or their fellow-freedmen, were robbed and thrown into prison, and some of them were slaughtered within the prison itself, while others were taken out and had their heads cut off. And now note, Verres, how fairly I propose to treat you. I am going to call upon Publius Granius of Puteoli to testify. He is to tell us how many of his freedmen you beheaded. He is also going to ask you to give his ship and cargo back. If you can prove him a liar, do so. And if you succeed in doing so, I will willingly leave my own witnesses in the lurch, and agree with you, and support your demonstration in any possible way. You shall show that those men had been serving with Sertorius, and had disembarked in Sicily while in flight from Dianium. That would, from my point of view, be the best thing that you could prove. For it would be impossible to find or cite a crime that deserved severer punishment.[3]

At the first hearing, you chose not to cross-examine anyone at all. Your counsel declared this a sensible innovation. But, as everyone knows, it was really because you knew that you were guilty, and that my witnesses carried conviction. Anyway, because you refrained from any cross-examinations before, I am prepared, if you wish, to call Lucius Flavius to give evidence again.[4] Let Flavius, if you like, be cross-examined; and let him be asked who Titus

1. The *proscriptio* of the dictator Sulla (82–81) listed Roman citizens who were declared outlaws and hunted down and executed.

2. i.e. the advantage that he would gain if Verres could prove that his victims were Sertorians.

3. i.e. Cicero propounds, for argument's sake, the fantasy that to execute disbanded rebels is a worse crime than the execution of harmless merchants.

4. The agent of Gaius Matrinius, whom Verres (as Cicero earlier recorded) had imprisoned.

Herennius was.[1] Flavius said earlier that Herennius was a banker at Lepcis Magna. Now, Herennius was able to mobilize more than a hundred Roman citizens from the community at Syracuse who not only knew him personally, but launched an appeal to you on his behalf with tears in their eyes. Nevertheless, with all Syracuse looking on, he was beheaded. Once again, if you could show that my witness was telling lies, and demonstrate and prove that Herennius had been, as you said, in Sertorius's army, it would give me nothing but pleasure.

We must say something more about the numerous Roman citizens who, on your orders, were taken out, among the captured pirates, to be executed. Their heads were covered up; and one must inquire about the significance of this novel step you took to prevent their identification, and consider why you had planned it. It may be that the distressed protests of Lucius Flavius and the others against your treatment of Titus Herennius had had some effect on you. Or perhaps the very authoritative objections put forward by the eminent and respected Marcus Annius had frightened you and made you more circumspect. For Annius testified, just recently, that one man whose execution you ordered was not just some foreigner or other who had arrived from elsewhere, but a Roman citizen who had been born in Syracuse and was known to the entire Roman community of the city.

After those men's loud complaints, after Verres's outrageous behaviour had become universally known and condemned, he continued his killings not with greater mercifulness, indeed, but with greater caution. He still had Roman citizens executed in public. However, when they were taken out to die he arranged, as I said before, that their heads should be covered. This was because, as I also mentioned, the members of the Roman community were making inconveniently exact calculations about the number of victims who had truly been pirates – and the number who had not.

Surely, this was not the proper treatment that you, as governor, ought to have meted out to Romans: surely this was not the fate to which their trading ought to have led them, or the protection to which their rights and lives were entitled. Traders have enough hazards and accidents to face without having to encounter terrors such as these, in Roman provinces and at the hands of Roman

1. Another of the captives.

governors. This, surely, was not the appropriate destiny of our loyal near neighbour Sicily, or a due reward for the generous welcome it has always extended to every Roman citizen who wanted to make the island his home. Men used to come sailing back to Sicily from remotest Syria and Egypt. They were people whose Roman togas had earned them respect even among barbarian nations. They had escaped the ambushes of pirates, and the perils of tempests. And now, when they already believed that they had safely reached home, they fell victims to the executioner's axe in Sicily!

Next, gentlemen, I want to speak of Publius Gavius of the municipality of Compsa.[1] And I shall speak on this subject in the most convincing tones and with the weightiest oratory that I can muster, and with truly heartfelt sorrow! For there is, indeed, abundant sorrow in my heart. And what I must strive to do is to attain an eloquence that lives up to that sorrow, and to the theme to which I have addressed myself. For the accusation that I now have to bring against Verres is so extraordinary that when the facts were first made known to me I really could not see how I would be able to make use of them. Certainly, I had no doubt that they were true. But how anyone could be expected to believe them I could not think. At the first hearing of this trial I only called sufficient witnesses to convince everybody what had happened. That much action I felt obliged to take, in response to the tearful appeals of all the Roman citizens who do business in Sicily. The evidence of the excellent people of Vibo Valentia was a further inducement. And so was the information provided by a number of Roman knights who happened to be at Messana at the time.

But what am I to do now? For hours I have been speaking about one single theme, the dreadful cruelty of Verres. While putting examples of that cruelty before you, I have practically exhausted the entire vocabulary which matches the evil things that he has done. Nor have I taken any particular trouble to vary the character of my charges, as I might have done so as not to lose your attention. The question, therefore, of how best to deal with the peculiarly terrible affair which I now have to bring before you needs serious consideration. Only one course, I think, only one method, is open to me. And that is to put the plain facts before you. They are of such a compelling nature that no eloquence on my part is required and in

1. A *municipium*, i.e. a Roman citizen community.

any case I could not hope to provide it – or on anyone else's part either – in order to arouse your fury.

The person I am speaking about, Publius Gavius of Compsa, was one of the Roman citizens whom Verres imprisoned. Somehow or other he managed to escape from the Stone Quarries, and got away to Messana. From there he could see Italy nearby, and the walls of Rhegium, of which the inhabitants are Roman citizens. From the grim shadow of death he had come back to life, revived by the bright light of freedom and the fragrant air of justice. And so now, in Messana, he started to complain about how he, a Roman citizen, had been thrown into prison. And he added that he was going straight to Rome, and would raise the question of Verres when he got there. The unfortunate man, however, did not realize that saying such things in Messana was the same as saying them to Verres himself, in his own house. For Verres, as I indicated earlier, had selected this city to help him in his crimes, and receive his stolen goods, and share the secrets of all his abominable actions. So the result was that Gavius was immediately rearrested and hauled before the principal member of the city government of Messana. Verres himself happened to arrive there on the very same day; and he was told that there was a Roman citizen complaining that he had been imprisoned in the Stone Quarries at Syracuse.

At this juncture Gavius was just going on board a ship, uttering violent threats against Verres. But now he was dragged ashore again and detained, for the governor to deal with him as he thought fit. Verres thanked the men who had arrested him, expressing appreciation of their thoughtful attention to his interests. Then he proceeded to the Forum, ablaze with evil malice. His eyes flashed fire, cruelty stood out from every feature of his face. Everyone was wondering to what lengths he would go and what he intended to do. Then, suddenly, he ordered Gavius to be dragged out, stripped of all his clothes and tied up in the middle of the Forum. And he commanded that the rods should be made ready.

The wretched man shouted out that he was a Roman citizen, of the municipality of Compsa. He had served in the Roman army, he declared, with the respected Roman knight Lucius Raecius, who was a businessman at Panormus from whom Verres could obtain confirmation that his story was true. To this, Verres responded that Gavius, he had learnt, had been dispatched to Sicily as a spy by the leaders of the fugitives from Sertorius's army – although this was an accusation which had not been lodged by any informer, and was not supported by a single scrap of evidence, or even by the smallest grain of suspicion. He then commanded that the man should be severely beaten on all parts of his body.

So there, gentlemen, in the middle of the Forum of Messana, a Roman citizen was chastised with rods. While it was happening, as the strokes cracked down, not one sound came from the wretched victim himself except the single cry, 'I am a Roman citizen.' By that declaration he had hoped to ward off the blows, and protect himself from these onslaughts. Yet not only did he fail to secure remission from their violence, but when he continued to appeal and insist on his citizen's rights, a cross was made ready to crucify him: a cross was prepared for that unhappy, miserable man, who had never seen such an abomination before.

That precious thing called freedom, the privileged rights that our citizenship confers, the Porcian and Sempronian laws,[1] the powers of the tribunes of the people – powers whose elimination was felt so profoundly, until they were at long last restored[2] – we must conclude, alas, that all these things, in the end, have come to mean nothing at all. For there in a Roman province, in the Forum of a town bound to us by treaty rights, it was possible for a Roman citizen to be tied up and lashed with rods – by a man who owed the rods and axes of his governorship to the office conferred on him by the people of Rome! Fire, and hot metal plates, and other instruments of torture were brought up to add to Gavius's torment. But even if, Verres, his passionate appeals and agonized cries failed to touch you, it is hard to see how the tears and resounding groans of the Roman citizens standing by left you unmoved.

How could you have had the audacity, Verres, to crucify any man who declared himself to be a Roman citizen? At the first hearing of this trial, gentlemen, I refrained from pressing this point with the vehemence that I am displaying today. I refrained because,

1. In 199 BC the tribune Publius Porcius Laeca extended the right of appeal (*provocatio*) in capital cases to Roman citizens in Italy and the provinces, and in the following year the praetor Marcus Porcius Cato (consul 195) forbade the flogging of citizens without appeal. Laws of Tiberius and/or Gaius Sempronius Gracchus (133, 123–1) evidently safeguarded their immunities further.

2. The dictator Lucius Cornelius Sulla (81) had abolished or curtailed most of the tribunes' powers, but in 75 they were readmitted to the higher offices, and in 70 their powers were fully restored.

as you were able to see, the audience was already, without any additional stimulus from myself, stirred up strongly against Verres by feelings of indignation, and hatred, and alarm for the safety of us all. On that occasion I exercised a self-imposed restraint, both upon my own assertions and upon the evidence of Gaius Numitorius, the leading Roman knight whom I called as a witness. And I was glad when Manius Acilius Glabrio took the prudent step of adjourning the hearing before that witness had finished his speech. For Glabrio, in fact, feared that the people of Rome might take it into their own hands to inflict on Verres the retribution from which they were afraid your judicial verdict would enable him to escape.

But as the situation is now, Verres, no one has the slightest doubt which way your case is going, and how you will fare as a result of losing it. So I feel free, in these circumstances, to pursue the matter further. You allege that Gavius suddenly turned spy.[1] Well, I will prove that he did not, since, in fact, he was in the Stone Quarries at Syracuse, imprisoned there by your orders. And I will not merely prove this by reciting the prison records. For you might, in that case, object that, because *a* Gavius is mentioned in those records, I am seizing on this name with the mendacious aim of declaring that he is *the* Gavius. No, I shall produce witnesses, as many as you wish, who can testify that this Publius Gavius of Compsa, and not someone else of the same name, was the man you consigned to the Stone Quarries at Syracuse. I shall also call some of his fellow-townsmen and close friends from Compsa itself, who will demonstrate to you, Verres, and to the jurymen who are trying your case – will offer a demonstration that is too late to save yourself, but not yet too late for them to hear – that the Publius Gavius whom you put to death on the cross was a Roman citizen from that municipality of Compsa, and not a spy from the fugitive army.

First, then, it is incumbent upon me to prove that everything I am saying is true, to the ample satisfaction of even your closest supporters; and this I undertake to do. Next, I will take up the point with which you yourself present me; and I will declare myself content with that. Well, first let us remember what you said quite clearly the other day, when you jumped to your feet terrified by the hostile shouts of your fellow-countrymen. What you said was

1. i.e. for the army of Sertorius, which had been defeated in Spain.

that the reason why Gavius went on crying out 'I am a Roman citizen' was merely in order to put off his execution, but that he was, in fact, a spy. This is, actually, an admission, on your part, that he claimed Roman citizenship, and proves that my witnesses were telling the truth. For that is exactly what we were told by Gaius Numitorius, by the very reputable Marcus and Publius Cottius from the Tauromenium district, by Quintus Lucceius, a substantial banker at Rhegium, and by all the rest. For the witnesses I have so far produced have not just been people who said that they knew Gavius personally, but men who actually claimed that they saw him, with their own eyes, being dragged off to be crucified – and heard him protesting that he was a Roman citizen.

And that is precisely what you yourself say and admit, Verres, that he repeatedly cried out that he was a Roman citizen. Quite evidently, this assertion of his citizenship did not make you feel in the slightest degree hesitant, or cause you to postpone, even for a short while, the infliction of that brutal and horrible penalty. Gentlemen of the jury, I stress this admission by Verres. I insist on it. I am content with it. I let everything else pass. This actual admission that Verres himself has made cannot fail to become his trap – and to bring the knife to his throat. You did not know Gavius's identity, you thought he might be a spy? I refrain from asking you why. Instead, I indict you out of your own mouth. Gavius claimed to be a Roman citizen. If you, Verres, had been imprisoned in Persia or the farthest regions of India, and were being dragged away to be put to death, your one cry would be this: *I am a Roman citizen.* If you were a stranger among strangers, among barbarians, among people inhabiting the remotest and most outlandish territories of the earth, the glorious and universally renowned title of your Roman citizenship would still have stood you in good stead. Let us revert, then, to this man Gavius, whom you were hustling off to be executed. Whoever he was, he was unknown to you; but he pronounced himself a Roman citizen. To that statement, that claim of citizenship, you from your governor's seat ought manifestly to have responded, if not with the total annulment of his sentence of death, at least with its postponement.[1]

Men of no particular importance sail across the seas and arrive at

1. Or he could have sent him to Rome – as St Paul was sent to Rome, after declaring that he was a Roman citizen.

places they have never seen before. There they come among strangers, and cannot always muster acquaintances who can vouch for their identity. Yet they trust so completely in the single fact of their Roman citizenship that they remain confident of their safety. And those are not places where they can find our own state officials, who are kept straight by their fear of the law and of what the public may think. Nor will they find their own fellow-countrymen, with whom they are united by the bonds of a common language, and by shared legal rights and many other things as well. None of these advantages will be available, and yet, all the same, they feel wholly assured that this one, single fact of their Roman citizenship will ensure their protection.

Deprive them of this confidence. Deprive Roman citizens of this protection. Rule that the cry 'I am a Roman citizen' will be of no assistance at all. Allow any provincial governor, or anyone else, to inflict upon someone who calls himself a Roman citizen any penal fate that he chooses, on the grounds that he does not know who the man is. Then what you have done, by defending such actions, is to make all our provinces, all foreign countries, all free states, out of bounds to Roman citizens, who have always, to an exceptional degree, had free access to them up to now. Another point, too. When Gavius cited the name of the Roman knight Lucius Raecius, who was in Sicily at the time, it surely would not have been too difficult to write to him at Panormus. Your Messanian friends could have seen that Gavius was safely detained, or you yourself could have kept him chained and locked up, until Raecius arrived from Panormus. If, on arrival, he had identified your prisoner, it was open to you to modify the rigour of Gavius's sentence. Should Raecius, on the other hand, have failed to do so, you would be free to make it a general rule that persons who were unknown to yourself, and could not provide a substantial witness to their identity, might be put to death by crucifixion, even if they were, allegedly, Roman citizens.[1]

About Gavius, however, I need say no more. For it was not, at that time, against Gavius, personally, that your animosity, Verres, was directed. No, what you were declaring war against was the entire title and concept of Roman citizenship, and the rights that it

1. Here Cicero touches lightly on the possibility that Gavius's claim to be a Roman citizen may not have been justified.

conferred. You were not, I repeat, just the enemy of that single man. You were the enemy of everyone's freedom. For that was what you had in mind when you issued that order to the Messanians. They, in accordance with their custom, had set up the cross for Gavius's crucifixion upon the Pompeian Road behind their city. But you, instead, commanded them to erect it in the section of the town that overlooks the Strait, so that it was visible to all. And, indeed, you yourself added a comment, which you are not in a position to deny, since you made it openly, in the presence of everyone. What you said was that, since this man claimed to be a Roman citizen, you chose this spot deliberately, so that he could get a sight of Italy, his home country, from the cross on which he was to be crucified!

That is the only cross, gentlemen, that has ever been set up at that particular spot, throughout the entire history of Messana. Its location, with the view of Italy, was chosen by Verres with a deliberate purpose. It was chosen so that his victim, as he perished in torment and suffering, should realize that the narrow strait in front of him marked the boundary between lands of freedom and slavery. And it was chosen so that Italy should see its crucified son suffering the most dreadful and fatal of penalties that was normally reserved for slaves. To shackle a Roman citizen in chains is a criminal act. To have him beaten is an outrage. To execute him is little short of murder. And as for death on the cross, there are no words sufficiently horrible to match the perpetration of such a deed. But as for yourself, Verres, not even this degree of cruelty contented you. 'Let him gaze upon his native land,' he joked. 'Let him die where justice and freedom can be seen before his eyes.'

It was not just Gavius, one single ordinary man, whom you consigned to that agonizing death by crucifixion. It was the principle of freedom and citizenship, shared by us all. Just note how scandalously Verres behaved. One must suppose it caused him disappointment that he could not set up this cross, for the death of Roman citizens, within the Roman Forum itself, in the place of Assembly, upon the speakers' platform. Yet he did choose the section of his province which resembled Rome most closely in respect of its large population, and was nearest to Rome, too, in its geographical position. He chose that this memorial of his shameless wrongdoing should stand in sight of Italy, at the gate of the island of Sicily, at a point where all who travelled in one direction or the other by sea must pass nearby.

Suppose that these words of mine were not addressed to Romans, to a number of our country's friends, to people familiar with the name of Rome. Suppose that my hearers were not even human beings at all, but wild animals – or, to go one step further, that it was only to the stones and rocks of some uninhabited region that I was telling this tale. Then, even so, even in that silent, lifeless waste, an account of such appallingly inhumane behaviour could not fail to arouse pity! Yet the jurymen to whom I am, in fact, addressing this speech are Roman senators, guardians of the laws and the lawcourts and justice. So I can feel confident, surely, that whereas no other Roman citizen ought ever to be treated in such a way at all, the one and only citizen who utterly deserves that penalty of crucifixion is Verres himself.

A short while ago, gentlemen, the miserable, undeserved fate of those sea-captains was bringing tears to our eyes. That the tragedy of our innocent allies should move us to such an extent was entirely right and proper. And now, when we hear of the sufferings of our own flesh and blood, how much more deeply still we ought to be moved! I call them our own flesh and blood, because the link between one Roman citizen and another is nothing less than a blood relationship. This has to be said, not only because it is true, but because our common safety requires it. And now, in this place, the entire citizen body of Rome, those who are present in person and those who are not, are united in demanding that you, gentlemen of the jury, should pronounce a strict verdict. All these people appeal to your honesty. They beg for your help. Upon your decision, they know very well, depend every one of their rights and interests and means of protection – in fact everything that makes them free men.

From myself, these people have nothing more to ask. Yet if, by any chance, things should turn out against my expectations,[1] it may well be that I should still have further services to perform: even over and above what they are requiring now. That some violent upheaval should rescue the man from your just retribution is not something that I am afraid of, gentlemen, since I do not see it as within the bounds of possibility. Yet let us imagine, for a moment, that my calculations prove mistaken, and the alternative, unfortunate outcome that I have mentioned is, in fact, what occurs. Then in that

1. i.e. if Cicero loses the case.

case the Sicilians will be deeply upset that their case has been defeated – and I will share their distress. However, the Roman people has entrusted me with the power to initiate jurisdiction, and so – before the first of February of next year[1] – it will once again be able to execute its rights unimpeded: that is to say, I shall lay the case before the Assembly, with which the decision will then rest.

In so far as my own credit and reputation are concerned, it would suit my interests perfectly well if Verres contrived to escape my attack here and now, but then, on that later occasion, came up for trial before the Assembly. That type of prosecution has an impressiveness of its own.[2] For myself, it would be a proper form of procedure, and a convenient one. And to the people of Rome it would be acceptable and satisfying. Suppose that I had been hoping to further my own career at Verres's expense; though in fact that has not been my aim at all. But following that line of thought let us reflect that Verres, in this present trial, can only be acquitted if a great many men accept criminal bribes. His acquittal, then, would give me excellent chances of self-advancement – by bringing accusations against the men who took such bribes.

All the same, gentlemen, for your own sakes and for the sake of our country, I would be very reluctant to see such a serious offence – I refer to the acquittal of Verres – committed by a body whose members have been selected as you have. Indeed it was I myself, exercising my rights of challenge, who chose you after scrutiny.[3] So I should not like to see you going about the city so polluted with the disgrace that Verres's acquittal would bring upon you that you would look as if you had been smeared not just with the wax of the voting tablets but with dirt.[4]

In this connection I should like to offer you, too, Hortensius, some advice, in so far as my position as accuser permits me to do so. I would advise you to think deeply, and reflect upon what you are doing and in what direction you are moving. Just consider the sort

1. i.e. before Cicero has been a month in office as aedile.

2. i.e. an official bringing an indictment before the Assembly is more impressive than a prosecutor appealing to a jury.

3. This was true in so far as they had remained after he had exercised his right of rejection.

4. The voting tablets (*tabellae*) employed by jurymen were smeared with wax, on which they scratched C(*ondemno*) or A(*bsolvo*).

of man you have to defend, and the methods you have to adopt in order to do so. Far be it from me to curtail your freedom to match your abilities and oratorical resources against mine. Yet, leaving that aside, I must ask if you truly believe that by what you do outside this court you can achieve anything inside its walls; if you imagine, I mean to say, that any sort of intrigue or stratagem or influence or friendly relations or Verres's money will enable you to fix matters up in his favour. If such is indeed your opinion, I strongly advise you to abandon the idea. Moreover, as regards the attempts in that same direction that have already been set on foot by Verres himself, take note that I have already detected and investigated them; and my advice is that you should suppress all such endeavours, and prevent them from going any further forward. Any misconduct on your part in this trial will involve you in great danger, greater than you have any idea of. Because you are consul elect and have held a whole series of offices of state, you may think that you no longer have anything to fear. But, believe me, those honours conferred by the Roman people's favour require as much of an effort to keep as they required to gain.

The country has endured you, Verres, and your friends' autocratic domination of the courts and the government as long as it could, as long as it had to.[1] But on the day when the tribunes were given back to the Roman people,[2] all your power in the courts and government, although you may not yet realize it, was, in effect, removed from the hands of you all and lost to you. What, at this particular juncture, the eyes of all the world are turned upon is the entire body of us senators assembled here, to see how scrupulously I prosecute, how honestly you jurymen return your verdict, what tactics you employ in defending your case. If any one of us deviates ever so slightly from the highest possible standards, the result will no longer be that unspoken disapproval which you have all, up to now, been accustomed to ignore, but open, vigorous condemnation by the entire people of Rome.

The defendant is no relation of yours, Hortensius, he is not your

1. The dictator Lucius Cornelius Sulla (81) had made all the jurymen senators again, and Cicero takes the line that he approves of this, provided that they do not behave corruptly.

2. i.e. in 75, when the tribunes were readmitted to the magistracies; as has been said, in 70 their powers were fully restored.

personal friend. In the past, in this or that trial, you have excused excessive partisanship on grounds of that kind. But no such excuses are available to you in this trial of Verres. When he was in charge of his province he used to declare and repeat, openly, that he was acting in the way he did because he had full confidence that you jurymen would not let him down. And you will have to ensure, carefully, that people do not come to the conclusion that he had an excellent reason for saying so.

As far as my own obligations are concerned, I believe that I have now discharged them to the full, to the satisfaction of my severest critics. The first hearing of this trial did not last for more than a few hours. But during those few hours I made everyone on earth agree that Verres was guilty.[1] What remains to be tried is not my personal honesty, since that has been confirmed, and not Verres's behaviour, since that has been condemned. It is only the members of the court, that is to say, to be quite frank, yourselves, gentlemen of the jury, who remain on trial.

And now let us just think of the circumstances in which your verdict will be pronounced. This is a matter which deserves to be seriously thought about. For in political life, as in everything else, the mood and bias of the times is of pre-eminent importance. The verdict will be pronounced, as you know very well, at a juncture when our nation is demanding a different type of jurymen, drawn from a different order in the state. The text of a proposed law revising the membership of the courts on those lines has already been published.[2] Now the man behind this proposed law was not really the praetor Lucius Aurelius Cotta, whose name is attached to it. The man who prompted it was rather, involuntarily, Verres himself, the man who stands accused in this case. For it is his hope of your dishonest support, his unworthy conviction that you were bribable, which caused people to feel that, in order to resist such things, such a bill had to be drafted and passed. At the moment when this case began, it had not been published at all. For at that time Verres was dismayed by your evident integrity, and for that reason had given various indications that he did not propose to offer

1. *Cicero: Selected Works* (Penguin Classics), pp. 35–7.

2. This *Lex Aurelia*, subsequently passed, provided that criminal juries were no longer to consist wholly of senators, but were to be divided equally between senators, knights and a third category (*tribuni aerarii*). Cotta was consul in 65.

any defence. It was only after he had begun to change his mind about you, thus recovering his spirits and confidence, that the publication of the bill took place, to block his plans. For he is mistaken, and you are honest men; and that is a strong argument against the bill becoming law, and depriving senators of their membership of the court. Yet Verres's illusory, impudent certainty that he was able to bribe you encourages those who want to see it passed. Suppose that any member of the court, as it is now constituted, behaves improperly, and accepts a bribe. Then either the Assembly will place him on trial, a thing that was not considered suitable before, or else he will be tried by the non-senatorial jurymen, set up by the new law to censure their predecessors for the unsatisfactory way in which they had administered the courts.

As for myself, everyone can see why it is essential for me to persevere with this case; I do not need to provide an explanation. It is quite impossible for me to hold my tongue, Hortensius, or to pretend not to care, when such things have been done. Our country has sustained a damaging wound. Our provinces have been devastated. Our allies have been pillaged. The immortal gods have been stripped of their treasures. Roman citizens have been tortured and put to death. Meanwhile, the criminal whom I am accusing of all this still goes unpunished! It is out of the question for me to walk out of this court and leave such a responsibility behind. And if, that being so, I continue to shoulder the burden, then I cannot remain silent. The matter has to be pursued to the end, dragged out into the light. The honour of the people of Rome is unavoidably invoked. It is essential that the men who corrupted our jurymen, and the jurymen who allowed their integrity to be corrupted, should be summoned to trial for the crimes they have committed.

'Do you really propose', someone is likely to ask me, 'to embark on such an onerous task, which will mean that you acquire so many thoroughly hostile enemies?' Not with any eagerness, I assure you, or at all willingly. But I do not have the same opportunities as men of aristocratic origins, upon whom our country's honours are showered without their even having to interrupt their slumbers. My own career, in this state of ours, has to proceed in a very different fashion. I am reminded of that wise and vigilant man Marcus Porcius Cato the elder.[1] Cato was convinced that, lacking noble

1. Consul in 195.

birth as he did, he could endear himself to the Roman people solely by merit; and it was his ambition to found and propagate a renowned family of his own. By these efforts, however, he attracted the enmity of extremely powerful persons. Yet all the same, after enormous exertions, he lived on to become a very old man, enjoying ample renown. Subsequently Quintus Pompeius Rufus too,[1] whose origins were entirely humble and obscure, likewise made numerous enemies, and likewise underwent heavy labours and grave perils, but reached the top position in the government in the end. More recently, we have seen Gaius Flavius Fimbria and Gaius Coelius Caldus[2] once again grappling with formidable oppositions and burdens in order to win the elevated offices of state which you yourselves, gentlemen, have instead attained with carefree ease. Theirs, on the other hand, is the course along which men in my non-aristocratic situation must proceed. Theirs is the school, theirs the methods, that have to be followed by people like myself.

For it is clear enough that the qualities and energies of 'new men' are regarded by certain nobles with jealousy and distaste.[3] If we 'new men' shut our eyes for a moment, we know we shall fall into some trap. If we lay ourselves open to any suspicion or charge, an attack will immediately be launched against us. All the time we have to be watchful, and work hard. We have foes. Let us face up to them. We have tasks to perform. Let us get on with them. An enemy who is open and declared is less dangerous than one who keeps quiet, and acts secretly. There is hardly one member of the great noble houses who looks upon my efforts with favour. Whatever services we 'new men' render them, we cannot attract their goodwill. They remain as coldly distant, and unsympathetic, as if we and they did not belong to the same human race. But for this very reason their hostility need not inspire any fear – since they have started regarding us with ill-will and envy long before we have done anything to antagonize them.

What I very much hope, gentlemen of the jury, is that having done what Rome expected of me, and having fully performed my

1. Consul in 141.

2. Consuls in 104 and 94.

3. 'New men' (*novi homines*) meant, at this time, men whose families had never attained the consulship before: see the Introduction (p. 14 n. 4) and the speech *For Murena* (Chapter 2).

duty towards the Sicilians, this case will mean that I can stop being a prosecutor. All the same, as I said, I have fully decided, should the result of this trial fall short of the high opinion I have formed about you, to bring to trial both those who will be most to blame for bribing members of the court, and those who, as accomplices, will be infected with the same guilt. To all, therefore, who intend to employ their influence and their drive and their cunning on behalf of the defendant in this case, I offer this message. Let their readiness to behave in such a way be tempered by the knowledge that they will have myself to reckon with before the judgement-seat of the Roman people itself. I trust they have not found me lacking in vigour, determination or vigilance in prosecuting this man whom the Sicilians presented to me as an opponent. If, as I hope, that supposition is correct, they will be able to note, in the future, that my vigour and pertinacity as a prosecutor will not have diminished, but increased. Indeed, I shall quite deliberately be inciting them against me. Because I shall be speaking in defence of the people of Rome.

Hear me, Greatest and Best Jupiter: whose offering of royal magnificence, worthy of your noble temple, worthy of the Capitol that is the citadel of all the world, worthy of the royal donors of that gift which they dedicated and vowed to you, Verres sacrilegiously stole out of their hands.[1] And it was he, too, who despoiled Syracuse of your sacred, beautiful image.[2]

Hear me, Queen Juno: whose two holy, ancient sanctuaries, built by our allies on the islands of Melita and Samos, Verres, by an equally criminal act, denuded of all their offerings and adornment.[3]

Hear me, Minerva: whom he has likewise despoiled by stripping your two renowned, revered temples, your shrine at Athens of its massive weight of gold, and your shrine at Syracuse of all but its

1. A jewelled candelabrum which the two sons of the Seleucid monarch Antiochus XII Dionysus Epiphanes had got ready for the inauguration of the new temple of the Capitoline temple of Jupiter, Juno and Minerva, which was to be rededicated in 69 (the old temple had been burnt down in 83). Cicero claimed that Verres persuaded one of the princes to let him have it to look at, and omitted to return it.

2. A statue of Zeus Ourios (giver of fair winds).

3. The thefts at Samos and other cities in Asia and Greece were attributed to Verres's journey eastwards to serve as *legatus* of Cnaeus Cornelius Dolabella, governor of Cilicia (80–79).

roof and walls.[1]

Hear me, Latona and Apollo and Diana: whose temple – and indeed ancient home, as devout persons believe – he broke open and burgled by a thievish attack under cover of night.[2] And hear me, Apollo, again, whose image he carried off from Chios. And Diana again and yet again, whom he robbed at Perga, and whose most sacred statue at Segesta, twice dedicated there, first by the piety of the Segestans themselves and then by Scipio Africanus the younger after his victory,[3] Verres caused to be taken down and carried off.

Here me, Mercury: whose statue had stood, as Scipio had planned, in the recreation-ground of our allies the people of Tyndaris, to be the guardian and patron of its young men, until Verres transferred it to the gymnasium of a private house.[4]

Hear me, Hercules: whose sculptured figure at Agrigentum, at dead of night, with a gang of slaves he had recruited and equipped, Verres endeavoured to wrench from its place and remove.[5]

Hear me, holy Mother of Ida:[6] whose sacred, venerated temple at Engyium he left so thoroughly plundered that nothing remains there now but the memory of the name of Scipio Africanus the younger and the traces of the sacrilege that was perpetrated, since the trophies of Scipio's victory, the splendid objects that adorned the shrine, are there no longer.

Hear me, Castor and Pollux: you who have your abode in the crowded centre of Rome, who witness and supervise all that takes place in our Forum, all our gravest deliberations, our laws and our

1. Verres was accused by Cicero of removing the panels, decorated with two-hundred-year-old battle-scenes, from the temple of Minerva at Syracuse, and transferring them to a brothel.

2. At Delos, described as the 'home' of the three deities because Latona (Leto) was believed to have given birth there to her twin children Apollo and Diana (Artemis).

3. Over the Carthaginians in the Third Punic War (146).

4. Verres had induced the people of Tyndaris to part with it, according to Cicero, after having their chief citizen bound to an equestrian statue on a winter day. Mercury (Hermes) was 'the young men's patron', because he was the patron of all Greek sports.

5. But Verres failed, because the slaves he sent for the purpose made such a noise trying to prise up the statue that the local population woke up and objected.

6. i.e. Cybele (Magna Mater), though the temple was in fact dedicated to the nymphs who were said to have nursed the infant Jupiter (Zeus) in Crete.

lawcourts: you from whom Verres so disgracefully extracted acquisitions and loot.[1]

Hear me, all those gods who are carried in sacred waggons to watch over our solemnly appointed festivals. Verres had to have the road on which you went your way constructed and kept in repair. He did so, however, not to uphold the sanctity of that ceremonial, but for his own personal profit.[2]

Hear me, Ceres and Libera, whose rites, according to the assertions of religious believers, rank above all others in grandeur and mystery.[3] You by whose agency, it is said, the means of sustaining life, morality and law, humanity and civilization, were first bestowed upon humankind and its various peoples; whose worship the Roman people has adopted and taken over from the Greeks, and now conducts with such corporate and personal devotion that it seems difficult to believe that it is an import from Greece – one feels rather that it must have gone forth to all other nations from here. Yet this worship was polluted and desecrated by one single man, Verres, who had the statue of Ceres at Catana – which it was sinful for any but women to touch or even see – uprooted from where it stood in the shrine and borne away.[4] And the other sculptured image of Ceres too, which belonged to the city of Henna, an image so beautiful that those who gazed upon it felt that it must be the goddess herself, or, if not, was her likeness fashioned by no human hand but fallen down to the earth from heaven – that, too, Verres caused to be taken from its home, where it belonged.[5]

And so I beg and implore you, most worshipful gods and goddesses, who dwell in the lakes and woods of Henna, and who

1. Verres made a large profit out of the resetting of the columns of the temple of Castor in the Forum during his praetorship (74).

2. This was acquired, according to Cicero, because Verres, as praetor, had deliberately neglected the procession route, which in consequence had to have expensive repairs, from which he derived a financial advantage.

3. This is a reference to the Eleusinian Mysteries in honour of Ceres (Demeter), of which Cicero was himself an initiate. As mentioned earlier, Libera was the partner of Liber (Bacchus, Dionysus).

4. Cicero asserted that Verres had the statue removed by his slaves during the night.

5. Henna was the place where Proserpina (Persephone), the daughter of Ceres (Demeter), was supposed to have been seized by Dis (Pluto), and taken to his kingdom of the underworld.

preside over this entire land of Sicily, whose defence has been entrusted to myself: you whose discovery of grain, and its distribution throughout the world, has filled all countries and peoples with adoration of your divinity. And I implore all the other gods and goddesses as well, against whose shrines and rituals this brazen, deranged ruffian has unceasingly waged impious and blasphemous war: hear me! Hear my appeal!

And agree with me, please, about this: that in my prosecution of this man, in my conduct of this case, I have unwaveringly directed all my attention to the welfare of our allies, the honour of our country, the demands of my conscience. Agree that my endeavours and cares and thoughts have at all times been devoted to the honest performance of my duty. If so, then I have a right to demand, too, that my purpose in undertaking this case, and the integrity with which I have pursued it, may be rewarded by the verdict that you will be pronouncing. The actions of Gaius Verres, it appears to me, display a blend of criminality, brazenness, treachery, lust, greed and brutality that has never been witnessed or heard of before. If you are of the same opinion, then I pray that your verdict may bring upon him the doom that his life and misdeeds deserve. I beg also that my country should find it enough that I have served as prosecutor in this one case alone – and I beg that my conscience shall not have to demand that I offer further services. Henceforward, may I be free to act for the defence of decent men, instead of being compelled to undertake the prosecution of rascals.

CHAPTER 2

FOR MURENA:
When to Sacrifice a Principle

Cicero always believed that the greatest of his contributions to government, and indeed the greatest achievement of his life, if not the greatest thing that had ever happened in Roman history, was his suppression, during his consulship (63), of the 'conspiracy' of Lucius Sergius Catilina (Catiline) – an action, on his part, about which he never ceased to reassure himself. While presenting the four speeches that he directed against Catilina,[1] *I commented that Cicero had undoubtedly exaggerated, but that there is little doubt that Catilina, even if he did not get very far towards revolution, did* intend *to bring down the Republic by force. Indeed, faced with Cicero's onslaught, he fled from Rome, and died confronting the Republican forces in battle (January 62). Despite his charm and energy, and if we discount Cicero's picture of him as a devil incarnate, he was not a particularly able or significant figure. He resented having twice been defeated for the consulship. And these disappointments, enhanced by poverty, inspired him with rather a vague anger against the injustice of things in general, which earned him numerous equally discontented supporters (Cicero, as we shall see, rebukes him for defending the poor).*[2]

Between his Third and Fourth Catilinarian speeches Cicero delivered another oration, in defence of Lucius Licinius Murena, which is translated here. Murena was one of the four candidates for the consulship for 62, the year following Cicero's own tenure of the office. The other candidates were Decimus Junius Silanus, Servius Sulpicius Rufus and Catilina himself. Because of Catilina's activities, the election was postponed, by order of the Senate. But when it subsequently took place, Lucius Murena and Decimus Silanus were elected. Marcus Porcius Cato the younger, a stern Stoic moralist, had already announced that he would prosecute the successful candidates, whoever they turned out to be, because bribery had been liberally employed by one and all. Silanus, however, was his brother-in-law, and Cato shelved his otherwise unbending principles sufficiently to

1. *Cicero: Selected Political Speeches* (Penguin Classics), pp. 74–145.
2. *For Murena*, 50.

refrain from prosecuting him. He did, however, join forces with one of the defeated candidates, Servius Sulpicius Rufus, to prosecute Murena.

Murena's defenders were Cicero, Quintus Hortensius Hortalus, who had been Rome's most distinguished pleader before him – and had, as we have seen, been Cicero's opponent in the Verres case (Chapter 1) – and Marcus Licinius Crassus, who had been consul in 70 and was to become, ten years later, a member of the dictatorial First Triumvirate. Something has been said about Cicero's motives in the Introduction. It was a question of the end justifying the means. The desired end was that there should be the full complement of two *consuls in the critical post-Catilinarian year 62 – during which Cicero feared that the revolutionary peril would outlive his own tenure – and that one of them should be Murena, who was suitably dedicated to the respectable, anti-Catilinarian cause. To achieve this, Cicero had to forget that Murena, whom he was defending, was in fact guilty; that is to say, like so very many others in these years, he had unmistakably paid bribes.*[1] *This was surely not unknown to the orator. Yet he, no less than Cato, felt he had to forgo his principles; because it seemed to him that the cause, and the interests of the state, demanded him to do so. This is a concession that people engaged in government often have to make, and Cicero made it.*[2]

His speech shows that he achieved this acrobatic feat very ingeniously, in superb style.[3] *Of the actual charge against Murena he steers pretty clear, as he must. Instead, he stresses the peril to the state if his client should have to be disqualified. And then he makes jokes. His irony has become lighter and more refined than it had been when he was prosecuting Verres. Here, for a change, there is good humour – which no doubt was a relief, at a tough and vicious time. Cicero makes fun of the legal*

1. It was an ironical fact that Cicero himself, early in his consulship, had passed a law against bribery, the *Lex Tullia de ambitu*, a more stringent amendment of the *Lex Calpurnia de ambitu* of Gaius Calpurnius Piso (consul 67), restricting the amount of money a candidate for office might spend on public entertainments, and increasing the penalty to expulsion from the Senate and ten years' exile. From the traditional institution of *clientela*, binding patrons in a mutual relationship with their clients (for which *For Murena* is a classical source; as it also is for elections in general), it was only a short step to bribery, which was rampant, despite repeated attempts to check it.

2. He had also to explain how and why he had, originally, supported Servius Sulpicius Rufus's candidature against Murena.

3. The speech was referred to by Quintilian, the oratorical expert of the first century AD, no less than sixteen times.

profession, of which Servius Sulpicius Rufus was a prominent luminary. And he makes fun, too, of the rigours of Stoicism, of which Cato the younger was an adherent. So the high moral standards of both prosecutors are made to sound silly, and – though they neither of them bore a permanent grudge[1] *– Murena was duly acquitted, and became one of the consuls in 62. In the interests of governmental stability, Cicero had supported the election of a not very honest client, and had won.*

FOR MURENA

On that day when, having taken the auspices, I notified the Assembly of the election of Lucius Licinius Murena to the consulship,[2] I followed the custom and precedent of our ancestors and prayed to the immortal gods that this might be an event which would prove happy and beneficial not only to myself, my reputation and my high office,[3] but also to the Roman community and people as a whole. And now again today, by the same token, I pray to the same immortal gods that this Murena shall be permitted to retain his consulship and secure his acquittal. Moreover, I offer another prayer as well: that your own inclinations and decisions, members of the jury, may correspond with the will and vote of the Roman people, and that, as a result, peace and quiet and calm and harmony may be yours and theirs.

That is a prayer which customarily accompanies elections, and is

1. 'What a witty consul we have,' Cato rather sourly remarked; but he became the close adviser of Murena, who intervened on his behalf (Plutarch, *Cato Minor*, 28. 2, cf. 21. 5f). As for Servius Sulpicius Rufus, he remained the lifelong friend of Cicero, to whom he wrote two famous letters; and the orator praised him in the Ninth Philippic.

2. The Assembly of the Roman people (*comitia*) was summoned in three groups, *curiae*, tribes and centuries (originally military groups of one hundred), so that it was variously described as the *comitia curiata, tributa* and *centuriata*. The Assembly indicated here was the *comitia centuriata*, which, among other responsibilities, elected senior officials. The auspices (*auspicia*), of which more will be said in the treatise *On Laws*, were a form of divination, mainly based on the movement of birds, which was taken by senior officials (possessing the *ius auspiciorum*) and conducted by the official diviners, the priestly college of the augurs at elections, inaugurations into office, etc.

3. i.e. the consulship, held by Cicero in 63.

endowed with religious force by the consular asupices, so that it carries with it all the power and sanctity that the dignity of our nation demands. Supported by this conviction, I also prayed that this same event, the election, might have a favourable, happy and successful result for the actual men upon whom, according to my presiding initiative, the office of consul has been conferred. That is to say, gentlemen, since the immortal gods have transmitted the totality of their power to yourselves, or at least share it with you, I, who formerly commended Lucius Licinius Murena to the gods, now commend him to your own goodwill. By which means, declared consul and now defended by myself who announces his election, he will be in a position to justify the honour the Roman people has conferred on him, protecting the well-being of you senators and of every other citizen.

Yet critics have censured my devotion to his defence – and even the fact that I accepted the case at all. So before I begin to speak on behalf of Lucius Murena I propose to say a few things on my own personal behalf. I am not suggesting, by doing so, that this self-justification is more important than Murena's acquittal. But my point is that, if you approve of what I am doing, this will add greatly to the force of my efforts to ensure that his enemies' attacks on his honour, reputation and entire welfare will be routed.

The first man to whom I have to justify the duty I have undertaken is Marcus Porcius Cato. He is a man who guides his life according to fixed rules, and weighs the requirements of every duty most meticulously. Cato asserts that I ought not to have agreed to defend Lucius Murena, seeing that I not only occupy the consulship – an office which I have administered with all the scrupulousness in my power – but am also the initiator of a law against bribery.[1] His criticism moves me very deeply, and I feel impelled to justify my defence of Murena, not only to yourselves, gentlemen, to whom I have the strongest obligation in such a matter, but also to the upright and high-minded Cato himself.

Tell me this, Cato: who could be a more appropriate man to undertake a consul's defence than a consul? For no member of our community can or should be closer to myself than the man to whom I am transmitting the care of our entire nation. For the preservation of that nation, I have undertaken mighty labours, and

1. The *Lex Tullia de ambitu* (63): on which see the Introduction to this speech.

undergone huge perils. And now it is for him to preserve our country in his turn.

When a property is sold, it is the seller who assumes the contractual obligation to guarantee its title, with the consequent risk.[1] By analogy, it is even more appropriate, when a consul elect is put on trial, that the consul who formally announced his election should be the man who takes the responsibility for the honour the Roman people has conferred on his successor, and who defends him when he is in peril. In some states it is customary to appoint a special advocate for such cases.[2] Well, surely they would, when such a situation arises, when they are defending a man elected to the highest office, be right to appoint a man who already held the same office to defend his successor. For he would be in a position to contribute authority and ability alike to the defence he was undertaking.

Sailors who have just come into harbour out of the open sea are very willing to offer those who are about to start out all the information that they can muster about winds and pirates and waters, because it is natural for us to want to assist the men who are about to incur the same dangers as we ourselves have been through. You can see, therefore, how warmly I myself, who after a formidable tempest[3] am now in sight of land, must feel towards the man who, I am convinced, will likewise have to undergo severe political storms. A consul who is doing his job has to see not only what is being done but also what is going to be done in the future. And so I feel it is my duty to emphasize how important it is for our national safety that the government should have *both* its consuls on the first of January.[4] This being such a necessity – and I shall return to the point later – we need not think of the present case as one in which duty is just summoning me to defend the fate of a friend. It is more a question of our country summoning the consul to defend the safety of the nation.

Let us go back to the fact that I passed a law against bribery. Yes,

1. Murena's consulship is thought of as the property of which Cicero is the seller and Murena the purchaser.

2. e.g. Athens.

3. The Catilinarian 'conspiracy'.

4. If Murena were convicted, and therefore disqualified from candidature, there would only be a single consul in 62 (Decimus Junius Silanus).

I did so, but without cancelling another rule which I had also, long ago, laid down for myself: my obligation to protect Roman citizens from danger. Certainly, if I admitted that bribery had taken place, and argued that this could be justified, I should be acting disreputably, even if it had not been I myself who proposed the bribery law. When, on the other hand, I argue, as I do, that no illegal act has been committed by Murena at all, I cannot see why the fact that I proposed the law against bribery could be said to have any negative bearing at all upon my decision to defend Murena.

Cato maintains that I have deviated from my own strict standards. That is to say, I expelled Catilina from the city by menaces and virtually by military force when he was plotting the destruction of our nation within the walls of this city. And yet, he says, here I am defending Lucius Murena. But it is natural for me to be lenient and compassionate, and that, indeed, is a form of conduct that I have always been happy to adopt. To adopt the opposite attitude of sternness and severity has never appealed to me. Nevertheless, when those were the qualities the country needed, I provided them; since that, during an extreme national crisis, was what the great responsibility of this consular office made imperative. That is to say, when force and severity were what Rome demanded, I overcame my natural character and was as stern as I was compelled to be – regardless of how I myself liked to behave. But now, on the other hand, when I am prompted by every sort of reason to display kindness and humanity, I very much want to behave accordingly, following what is, after all, my natural inclination and custom. However, with regard to this subject of obligation to conduct this present defence, and the censure you have directed against me for doing so, I shall have more to say in another part of my speech.

But it is the criticism of Servius Sulpicius Rufus, gentlemen, who is an extremely wise and eminent man, which has moved me just as deeply as Cato's strictures. Sulpicius declares that he is profoundly and grievously hurt because I am defending Lucius Murena against himself. This, he says, shows I have forgotten our close ties of friendship. Jurymen, I am very anxious to justify myself in his eyes. So I want you to decide between us. If a charge such as he is making, calling our friendship into question, proves to be warranted, I shall regard it as a very serious matter; whereas, conversely, if such an accusation is made, and turns out *not* to be warranted, we must pay due attention to the fact.

Now, when you were canvassing your own candidature for the consulship, Servius Sulpicius, I agree that since you and I were friends I owed you all my most enthusiastic support. And I believe that that is precisely what I provided, and that while you were canvassing I fell in no way short of what might be required from a friend or a sympathizer or a consul. But that time is now past. The situation has changed. I will tell you what I think, and I am convinced it is right. In opposition to Murena's promotion to high office I certainly owed you whatever you felt impelled to ask of me. In defence of his present acquittal, on the other hand, I owe you nothing at all. For even though I supported you when you were a candidate for the consulship, I have no obligation whatever to offer you the same support now, when you are prosecuting Murena. And the suggestion that whenever the prosecutor is a personal friend he ought never to speak for the defendant whom he is prosecuting is, surely, improper and inadmissible – even if the defendant is someone we do not know at all.

Far from a stranger, however, Murena is my close friend, and has been for a long time. There can be no question, then, of this friendship just being cancelled out by Servius Sulpicius – in a lawsuit upon which Murena's entire civil status depends – merely because, earlier, when the two men stood as rivals for the office of consul, it was my friendship with Servius to which I assigned priority. And indeed, even if such considerations are not to be applied, Murena's own worth, and the great office to which he has been elected, would both have convicted me of outstanding selfishness, not to say cruelty, if I had refused to defend a man whose career has been marked by such personal distinction and national honours alike.

If someone is in danger, it would be out of the question, and entirely wrong, for me to fail to devote my energies to giving him assistance. And indeed such efforts, on my part, have hitherto been granted rewards which have never previously been bestowed upon anyone else. That being so, I feel that to abandon, once one has become consul, the activities one has been engaged in up to that time would be to display both unscrupulousness and ingratitude. I would only desist – and would do so gladly – on one condition: that you yourself, Servius, assume the full responsibility for clearing me of any imputation whatever of culpable slackness or lack of compassion or hard-heartedness. But if on the other hand it is true, as it is, that to shirk hard work demonstrates laziness, that to reject suppliants is a sign of inhumanity, that the abandonment of one's friends is disgraceful – then, surely, the present case is one which no one with any claims to industry or a heart or a sense of duty could refuse.

Indeed, Servius, your own legal profession can very easily offer you a relevant comparison. If someone consults you on a point of law, you would feel it necessary to supply him with a ruling, even if he happened to be at odds with some of your friends. Likewise, too, if a man whom you once opposed in court subsequently had another lawsuit stopped by the judge because he had failed to make out his case, it would be perfectly legitimate for you yourself, if you were now defending him, to regard that judge's decision as improper. By the same token, then, do not be so unfair as to believe that, whereas *you* open all the dam-gates of your support to your enemies, *mine* have to be closed even to my friends.

Let us suppose, however, that considerations of friendship, and now I refer to my friendship with yourself, had caused me to decline this case. Let us suppose, too, that the same had applied to the eminent Quintus Hortensius Hortalus and Marcus Licinius Crassus, and all the other men, also, who attach so much importance, as I know, to your goodwill. Then, in that event, we should have a consul-elect who could find no one to speak in his defence! And this would be happening in a country in which our ancestors intended that no one, however humble, should lack someone to stand up for him. Gentlemen of the jury, if I failed a friend, I should regard myself as infamous. If I failed someone who was in trouble, I should consider myself cruel. If I failed a consul, I would brand myself as arrogant. Certainly, Servius, I shall make every concession to my friendship with yourself that I can. Indeed, I shall treat you as if you were my own brother, whom I dearly love. But I must also think of the demands that duty, loyalty and conscience must make of me. And in bearing these demands in mind I shall have to remember that, although I am speaking against the wishes of one of my friends, I am doing so, in order to help another, who is in critical peril.

The accusations against my client, gentlemen, as I understand them, come under three different headings. The first consists of attacks upon his life-style. The second concerns the comparative merits of the rival candidates. The third deals with the imputation of bribery. Now, the first of these three charges, gentlemen, ought to have carried the most weight. But, instead, it seemed insubstantial and trivial. In fact, what made it obligatory for the accusers to say something about the life of Lucius Murena was merely a sort of prosecutor's routine rather than any authentic possibility of saying something unpleasant about him. The name of Asia is brought up to censure him. But he did not seek out the Asian job in order to have a good time and enjoy himself. On the contrary, he moved from place to place all over the area, as a soldier. If he had failed to serve in Asia, if, young as he was, he had refused to serve under his father, who was in command,[1] it would have appeared that he was frightened either of the enemy or of his father's authority – or that his father had disowned him.

Young sons often ride the horses when their fathers are celebrating a triumph, and that is what Lucius Murena did.[2] He contributed military trophies to the adornment of the celebration; having shared in his father's campaigns, he shared also in his triumph. And I cannot see why he should have done anything else. Certainly he was in Asia, gentlemen, and his gallant father received his valuable assistance in hazardous times, his relieving efforts amid laborious endeavour, his congratulations in victory. Does the word 'Asia' carry some suspicion of luxurious behaviour?[3] If so, to have avoided visiting Asia altogether would not have deserved any particular praise, but it is praiseworthy, rather, to have been there and lived a decent life. So Asia should not be made into an accusation against Murena. On the contrary, it brought renown to his family, glory to his clan, a fine reputation to his name. If he had done something wrong in Asia, or brought back a disgraceful record from the country, it would have been a different matter. But what he did, instead, was to play a part in the greatest, indeed the only, war that Rome was fighting at the time.[4] And to have done so was a proof of his courage. Likewise, to have served, very willingly, under his

1. Lucius Licinius Murena the elder broke the terms agreed by Sulla and Mithridates VI at the Treaty of Dardanus (85) and ravaged the king's territory, but was heavily defeated.

2. When a general celebrated a triumph, his sons, if old enough, rode beside him, or (if younger) rode horses attached to his chariot. (The triumph of Murena's father was singularly undeserved – see last note.)

3. Asia was notorious for the ease with which it corrupted Roman officials.

4. The Third War against Mithridates VI of Pontus.

father's command was a proof of his dutifulness as a son. And, finally, the fact that his service should have culminated in his father's victory and triumph was a proof of his successful good fortune. This whole series of events, therefore, offers no grounds whatever for abusive charges. Instead, it gives occasion for nothing but praise.

Cato calls Murena a professional dancer. If that accusation is true, the prosecutor who produced it is a conscientious researcher. If it is false, however, he is a foul-tongued slanderer. For a man in your position, Marcus Cato, to pick up slanders off the street, or from some altercation among buffoons, and then go on to pronounce that a Roman consul is a dancer, is not at all desirable. For this is what you ought to realize: a man who can rightly be described as a dancer must have something seriously wrong with him. In the first place, hardly anyone dances when he is sober; unless he is out of his mind. Nor does anyone dance when he is on his own, or at a respectable, decorous party (at best, a reputable party of such a kind, in some agreeable location, might terminate in a dance, among other entertainments). But what you are doing, Cato, is to drag in what is, of necessity, the last and least significant of the vices, without pausing to consider the others, without the prior existence of which it cannot exist. These include scandalous debauchery, for example, and sexual indulgence, and over-lavish expenditure: pleasures, if you like, but they are really vices. In Murena, there is no trace of them at all. In him, no such luxurious conduct can be found; you cannot find even the shadow of it.

Nothing, then, can be said against Lucius Murena's way of life, nothing at all, I insist, gentlemen of the jury. That is a key-point in my defence of the consul-elect. No deceitfulness, no avarice, no treachery, no cruelty, no ill-natured utterances can be charged against him throughout his entire life. Good, then. The foundations of my defence have been laid. Later I shall pass on to positive praises. But even before we come to these, his enemies must virtually admit that my client is a man of decent, honourable life-style. Now that this has been established, the way is clearer for me to pass on to an estimate of his positive merits, which was the second point in the charges against him.

It does not escape me, Servius Sulpicius, that you yourself are abundantly endowed with the qualifications of family, character, industriousness and all the other distinctions which a man has to be able to cite when he becomes a candidate for the consulship. Yet Murena, I insist, possesses these qualifications too, in equal measure. Indeed, so equally does he possess them that, in respect of such merits, even if he could not outrank you, he would not be outranked by you either. You have expressed contempt for Murena's family, and have glorified your own. But if what you mean by this is that no one is of distinguished birth unless he is a patrician, you are suggesting that the plebeians will have to secede to the Aventine once again![1] Admit, then, that eminent and honourable plebeian families *do* exist. Thus the great-grandfather of Lucius Murena was a praetor, and so was his grandfather as well.[2] His father, too, held a praetorship, and when it came to an end celebrated a magnificent and amply merited triumph. And this made it easier for his son to aspire to the consulship. For what he was aiming at had its foundation laid by his father.

Your noble birth, on the other hand, Servius Sulpicius, although very lofty indeed, is, one must admit, better known in literary and historical circles; the people and the voters are less well acquainted with your pedigree. Your father was a knight, your grandfather was not renowned for any notable achievement. So awareness of your aristocratic origins is not exactly common talk today. On the contrary; it has to be dug up from antique records. For this reason I am inclined to place you in the same category as myself. That is to say, although your father was a knight, you yourself have come to be thought eligible for the highest office in the state.[3] By the same token, I have never rated the valorous Quintus Pompeius Rufus[4] lower than Marcus Aemilius Scaurus,[5] although the former was a new man and the latter of highly aristocratic lineage. True, Scaurus, by his own merits, resuscitated the memory of his family when it was almost defunct.[6] But to transmit to posterity, as Quintus Pompeius Rufus did, a glorious reputation which he had not inherited, demands just as high standards of mind and of character.

1. According to tradition, there were five 'secessions' of the plebeians – protesting against the patricians – mostly to the Aventine Hill (494–287 BC).

2. Not later than 147 and not later than 101 BC respectively.

3. Having been defeated, however, in the election for 62, Servius did not become consul until 51.

4. Consul in 141.

5. Consul in 115 and 107.

6. It had not held office for three generations. But Scaurus became the chairman of the Senate (*princeps senatus*).

I used to believe, gentlemen, that my endeavours had prevented many excellent persons from being reviled for their humble origins. For I have gone out of my way to eulogize new men. And I do not only mean antique heroes like Manius Curius Dentatus, Marcus Porcius Cato the elder and Quintus Pompeius Rufus.[1] For I am also referring to recent figures, men such as Gaius Marius, Titus Didius, Gaius Coelius Caldus.[2] And I myself, too, after the passage of a good many years, likewise broke through the barriers set up by the nobility.[3]

This meant that, just as in the time of our ancestors, the consulship had become as accessible to merit as to birth. That being so, I never imagined that when a consul-elect, himself a member of an ancient and eminent family, was being defended in court by a consul who was the son of a Roman knight, the prosecutors would be talking about new men. As for myself, when I was a candidate for the consulship, my rivals were two patricians. One, Lucius Sergius Catilina, was evil and outrageous. The other, Publius Sulpicius Galba, possessed a fine character and great integrity. But I had a better character than Catilina, and my popularity was greater than Galba's. If those are facts for which a new man deserves to be criticized, then certainly I should have been a target for hostility and envy. However, let us stop talking about birth, for in this respect both Servius Sulpicius and Lucius Murena enjoy an impeccable standing. Let us look at other matters instead.

'Murena', Servius points out, 'was a candidate for the quaestorship when I was, and I received more votes and was placed above him.'[4] Well, we cannot deal with every objection. You can all see that, while a number of candidates may possess equal qualifications, only one can obtain the first place. Merit, that is to say, and the placing in the election do not necessarily correspond, because those who are

1. Consuls in 290 etc., 195, 141.

2. Consuls in 107 etc., 98, 94.

3. A *nobilis* in the strict sense was a man who had held senior (curule) office, or had an ancestor who had done so; but in the last years of the Republic the consulship was the only office that counted for this purpose. Cicero therefore, even if 'noble' in his home town Arpinum, was a 'new man' (*novus homo*) at Rome. On his awareness of this, see the Introduction and note to the speech *Against Verres* (Chapter 1).

4. Servius is here made to argue that this prior election for the quaestorship in 75 indicated his greater popularity.

elected are often indistinguishable from the point of view of merit, yet they have to be placed and announced in order, one after another. In any case, the assignments you and Murena received as quaestors were not so very different. Murena, under the Titian Law, was allocated a quiet and tranquil province.[1] You were assigned a post that always produces groans when the quaestors draw lots – Ostia, which is not particularly agreeable or distinguished, and carried a troublesome work-load. Both men's reputations went into a state of suspension while they were quaestors. For they had each drawn a lot which gave them no scope for displaying their ability, or getting it recognized.

The controversy now turns upon what happened later. The two men came to be occupied in quite different ways. Servius here worked in the city with myself. His job consisted of giving legal opinions, drafting documents, protecting people's interests. It was an anxious and worrying activity. In the course of it, he learnt civil law, he stayed up late at night, he laboured long and hard, he helped a lot of persons, he put up with the stupidity of a lot more, he endured their pretensions, he swallowed their captiousness, his life was dictated by other men's whims, he had no life of his own. That one single man should work so industriously in a field of knowledge which will bring benefits to numerous people is extremely praiseworthy, and greatly appreciated by the public.

What about Murena meanwhile? He was an officer serving with that valiant, wise and eminent general, Lucius Licinius Lucullus.[2] While occupying that post he commanded an army, pitched his standards here and there, fought battles, defeated large enemy forces, and captured cities by storm and by siege. As for that Asia you were referring to, crammed with riches and refinement, he passed through the country without absorbing the smallest trace of extravagance or greed. It was a war of considerable importance, and

1. Two quaestors were assigned to duties in the city of Rome, four to places outside. The Titian Law may have been proposed by Sextus Titius (tribune in 99).

2. Lucullus conducted the Third Mithridatic War against Mithridates VI of Pontus for eight years (74–66), but in spite of successes failed to win the war because his troops began to mutiny, and the knights (*equites*) at Rome objected to his financial settlement, which had cleared the province of Asia of debt, to their disadvantage. Murena was one of Lucullus's staff officers (*legati*).

you could describe his conduct in these terms: he did many great things without his general, and his general did none without him. I know that I am speaking in the presence of Lucullus. But even if he would authorize me to exaggerate somewhat, in the emergency of this trial, I do not want to avail myself of the privilege. For, in fact, all the facts that I quote are confirmed by official documents. In these, Lucullus gives Murena a share of his glory in very complimentary terms, such as no selfish or jealous commander would ever permit himself to employ.

Both Servius and Murena possess enormous merits, and reputations to match. If Servius would give me permission, I should like to honour them equally. But that he does not let me do. He goes on about the military situation, he criticizes Murena's entire role as an officer, he sees the consulship as nothing but a series of day-by-day matters requiring the consul's personal attention. 'As far as I can see, Murena,' he objects, 'you have been with the army all these years. You have not been near the Forum. So how can you expect to compete, for high posts, with men who have been living in the Forum, when you have just come back after being away for so long?' First, Servius, a word about the desirability of always being available on the spot. You do not, I think, realize that people can have enough of seeing one, and in the end it may disgust them. True, the fact that my popularity was visible, for everyone to see, did do me a great deal of good at the time. All the same, they got tired of me, and it caused me a great deal of trouble to set this in reverse – and I think the same applied to you. It would have done neither of us any harm to have been away – and to have been missed!

But let us drop this subject and return to the contentious issue of which occupations and qualifications are best. Surely you must agree that a distinguished war record is more valuable to a candidate for the consulship than distinction in civil law. You stay up late to give legal opinions to people who consult you. He stays up so that his army can arrive rapidly at the place it is making for. You are awakened by the crowing of the cock, he is awakened by the sound of the trumpet. You arrange how you are going to plead, he arranges how he is going to fight. You take precautions to save your clients from suffering loss; his are to ensure that cities and camps shall not be overwhelmed by the enemy. He knows, and understands, how to keep enemy forces away. All you know about keeping away is rainwater.[1] He spends his time enlarging the boundaries of the Roman empire. You spend yours looking after the boundaries of your clients' properties.

I must say what I believe, and what I believe is this: military ability takes precedence over ability in every other field. That is what has won the Roman people its fame, and has won this city of Rome eternal glory. It has compelled the entire world to obey our Roman state. Everything that goes on in this city, every worthwhile activity that we undertake, every labour that occupies us in the Forum together, and the applause it commands, why are all these things safe and secure? Because the army, with all its valour, is looking after them and protecting them. The very moment that there is any whisper of violence, our civilian occupations straightaway fall dumb!

As for you, Servius, it seems to me that you cherish your knowledge of the law with loving caresses, as if it were your own little daughter. Certainly, you have taken trouble over acquiring this knowledge, but I am not going to allow you to make the mistake, any longer, of regarding it as something of peculiar value. I have always believed that you deserved the consulship, and every other office as well, because of your other great qualities: self-restraint, natural dignity, just conduct, honesty and all the rest. But as regards your knowledge of the civil law, I will not suggest that you have wasted your energy, but I will say this: it is a pursuit which offers no sure road to the consulship.

For every activity that gains us the votes of the Roman people should possess not only outstanding worth, but also an inviting practical usefulness. Now, the worthiest men are those who have won the greatest military eminence. For it is the general conviction that they are the protectors and upholders of our entire government and state. It is they who provide the counsel, they who run the risks, which enable us to enjoy our national life, and our private affairs as well. And that makes them our benefactors to a unique degree.

Now, one matter that has often influenced the election of a consul is the ability to speak, which is indeed a weighty and dignified qualification. I mean, the ability, by a combination of good sense and eloquence, to direct the decisions of Senate and

1. Bad drainage of surface water frequently resulted in lawsuits.

Assembly and jurymen. We need a consul whose speech-making will, on occasion, be capable of quelling the violent passions of tribunes, of swaying excited multitudes, of standing up against bribery. It is hardly surprising that men who are not of aristocratic birth have often attained the consulship because they are able public speakers. Nothing wins deeper gratitude, closer friendship, more devoted support.

But your own profession on the other hand, Sulpicius, enjoys nothing of the kind. First, it is based on a lightweight sort of knowledge, lacking in solidity. For its subject-matter is trivial, devoted to matters such as spelling and the stops between words. Secondly, even if the profession was regarded with some respect in the time of our ancestors, it lost all of its prestige and came to be seen as contemptible once its mysteries were published. Before that, very few people had even known whether a lawsuit could be undertaken at all, since the calendar itself was not available to the public. The men who pronounced on legal points, therefore, enjoyed enormous power. They were invited to name the day on which a case could be brought into court, as if they were Chaldaean astrologers.[1] There came a time, however, when a clerk named Cnaeus Flavius 'put out the eyes of the crows', that is to say displayed exceptional enterprise, by publishing a calendar which made it possible for the people to learn the days on which a lawsuit could be heard. So, in this way, Flavius plundered the expertise which the clever legal advisers had previously monopolized.[2] This infuriated the advisers in question, who were afraid that these cases could be conducted without their intervention, now that the list of appropriate days was published and generally known. So they then proceeded to invent a series of legal formulas which would mean that they would be indispensable in every case after all.

A lawsuit could have been neatly framed in the following terms. The Sabine estate belongs to me. No, it belongs to me. Then the

1. The Chaldaeans (from south-eastern Mesopotamia) were famous as astrologers.

2. In 304 BC Cnaeus Flavius, the secretary of Appius Claudius Caecus, published a calendar of court days, thus providing the people with a knowledge of civil law precedure. The crow supposedly attacked other animals in the eyes, so that the saying quoted by Cicero was a proverbial description of how even the watchful could be blinded.

hearing would follow. The expert, however, prefers to say: 'the estate which is located within the territory which is described as Sabine'. Well, that is verbose enough. But there is more to come. 'I affirm that this property is mine by Quiritary title.'[1] And then: 'From this place I summon you to that place to join hands with me and contest the issue in accordance with the law.'[2] The defendant has no clue about how to provide an answer to this prolix, litigious person. So then the same legal adviser changes over to the opposite side, like the man who plays the flute in a Latin play and accompanies the two actors one after another.[3] 'From the place', he says, 'from which you have summoned me to contest the issue in accordance with the law, I in my turn summon you to that other place.'

Meanwhile, too, steps are taken to ensure that the presiding praetor should not be so pleased with himself that he proposes to make some statement on his own account. That is to say, he too has a legal formula set out for him. It is a lot of nonsense, and contains the following particularly stupid item: 'The witnesses for both parties being present, I indicate that yonder road should be followed. Proceed along that road.' And the learned man remained in attendance, to show them what road he meant. 'Return by the road.' They do so, with the same expert to guide them. I imagine that this seemed ridiculous even to our bearded ancestors: that is to say, the fact that men who had duly reported to a place should be instructed to leave it and return forthwith to the place from which they had originally departed.

All procedures were tinged by the same sort of absurdities. Such as: 'Since I recognize your presence here as a legal fact,' and 'Would you indicate the grounds on which you base your claim to the property?' As long as these procedures remained secret, it was necessary to learn them from those who were in the know. Subsequently, however, when they had been published and circulated and

1. The *ius Quiritium* was the most ancient part of the civil law, and applied only to Roman citizens (Quirites) and others who had been admitted to their privileges.

2. Originally the formal joining of hands and laying claim to the disputed property took place on the site in the presence of the praetor.

3. A flautist accompanied the actors as they recited the song or intoned portions of the play in alternation. He was traditionally a Latin, not a Roman citizen.

pored over, it was discovered that they were senseless, and indeed crammed with deception and stupidity. It was true that our laws had defined numerous matters, and had done so perfectly clearly. But, when cases came to court, these definitions came to be perverted and twisted by astute legal brains.

Again, it was our ancestors' decision that all women should be subject to the authority of guardians. But the lawyers thought up a category of guardians who are subject to the women instead.[1] Our ancestors decided that sacrifices for the dead should continue perpetually. But these cunning lawyers discovered how to utilize old men to bring the sacrifices to an end, by a fraudulent sale.[2] In general terms, they deprived the civil law of its principle of equality, while retaining its strict verbal literalism. To take one example, they found, in a book someone had written, the female name 'Gaia' employed as a general term for women, and in consequence ruled that all women who perform a civil marriage ceremony should be described as 'Gaia'.[3] And I do regard it as strange that such a large number of clever men, after so very many years have gone by, should still not have been able to decide whether one ought to say 'two days from now' or 'the day after tomorrow', or whether 'judge' or 'arbitrator',[4] 'lawsuit' or 'case', is correct.

Such are the reasons why I have concluded that this legal profession of yours was never impressive enough to aspire to the consulship. For it was a profession which was made up of fictions and fabrications, and was conspicuously lacking in any power to acquire popularity. For something which is at everyone's disposal, and is equally at the disposal, that is to say, of myself and my opponent in this court, cannot possibly gain popular support. You have lost all hopes of doing people a personal favour, and your ancient right of

1. That is to say, women found it possible to choose their own guardians, who would do what they told them.

2. Women with an obligation to perform religious duties could avoid them by undertaking a secular form of marriage with a childless old man without resources, who freed them from the obligation (for a fee).

3. Cicero is again describing a fraudulent application of *coemptio*, the civil marriage ceremony in which a woman made a formal sale of herself to her husband. In the formula of *coemptio* the woman's name was 'Gaia'.

4. The technical difference is that an appeal to a judge (*iudex*) is for a fixed sum, whereas an appeal to an arbitrator (*arbiter*) is for an amount to be determined according to the circumstances.

saying 'consultation permitted' is no longer attractive.[1] For no one can be regarded as a wise man when his knowledge is valueless anywhere outside Rome, or even inside the city once the courts have been adjourned. Besides, nobody can rank as an expert when the subject is one with which everybody is familar, so that any authentic differences of opinion are out of the question. And, in addition, when a subject is concentrated within a very diminutive series of documents – and not very abstruse documents at that – it cannot be defined as a field of study involving any particular difficulty.

So if you should arouse my anger I can guarantee, busy man that I am, that I will make myself a lawyer in no more than three days. For once a topic has been entrusted to writing, everything relating to it can be found written down somewhere or other; although nothing is written down very exactly, and you may need to cover yourself against risk by some such phrase as 'the matter with which we are concerned'. And when it is a question of oral advice, this, too, can be given irresponsibly, with a minimum of risk. If you offer the right answer, you can make it seem that you are giving the same correct reply as Servius. But even if you do not, you can make it appear that you are discussing a knotty legal point, with which you are fully acquainted.

I declared earlier that the glory of the military life is greatly preferable to the lawsuits and technical terms with which you concern yourself. But what I want to say now is something different, and it is this: another career which is far superior, once again, to your legal profession, as far as promotion to high office is concerned, is that of the orator. It is my impression that a great many men, in the past, began by wanting to be orators, but when they failed to achieve this, lowered their ambitions and came down into your profession instead. It is said about Greek musicians that those who do not succeed in playing and singing to the lyre play and sing to the flute. And in precisely the same way we can observe that those who do not succeed in becoming orators descend to becoming lawyers instead.

1. In the period before the secrets of their procedure were known, lawyers were approached with these words: *licet consulere?* Their affirmative reply was *consule* – consultation permitted. Now that the law is available to all, argues Cicero, lawyers have lost their chance of conferring a favour, and are not even asked for one.

Public speaking means hard work, important affairs, lofty responsibility and great popular favour. The matters about which a client consults you, on the other hand, affect his own personal welfare and, sometimes, his life, but that is all. And another point: your legal opinions, your legal rulings, are often completely overturned by a speech – pronounced by an orator – and even when they are not, they cannot get themselves accepted unless they have an orator to defend them. If I myself had become a good enough speaker, I should not be praising oratory in such unmeasured terms. But I am not talking of myself. I am talking of great orators, at the present time and in the past.

Let us conclude, then, that there are two professions which can elevate a man to the highest office in the state: that of the military commander, and that of the able orator. For the former wards off the perils of war, and the latter maintains the amenities of peace. Certainly, merits in other fields as well carry a great deal of authority – justice, good faith, modesty, self-control. And these are virtues in which everyone knows that you, Servius, are pre-eminent. But the pursuits that I am considering now are those that lead to high office; it is not merely a person's inborn qualities I am referring to. All those other occupations, in which you spend your time, are knocked out of your hands as soon as any new disturbance sounds its trumpet-blast of war.

For as that brilliant poet and marvellous writer Ennius observed,[1] 'when battles are at hand, from our midst are cast' not only your worldly pretence to good judgement but even that mistress of the world, wisdom. 'Force directs action: the diplomat is cast aside', and not only if he speaks boringly and verbosely, but even if he is 'good – it is the rough soldier who is loved'. In that situation your job becomes wholly ineffective. 'They enforce their claims not by a legal contest, but by the sword.' If that is true, Servius, as it is, the Forum must, of necessity, give place to the camp, peace to war, the pen to the sword, the shades of a quiet life to the glare of the sun. In other words, be willing to grant the highest importance, in our national affairs, to what enables our nation to take the first place in the world.

But Cato is objecting that I have made too much of all this in my speech. I have forgotten, he protests, that in the war with Mithridates

1. *Annals*, VIII, 2ff.

our enemies were little more than feeble women. I entirely disagree, gentlemen, though I am not going to go into the matter at any length, since that is not the point upon which the case turns. However, if we are going to despise all the wars we have fought against the Greeks, then we shall have to pour scorn on the victories of Manius Curius Dentatus against King Pyrrhus of Epirus, Titus Quinctius Flamininus against Philip V of Macedonia, Marcus Fulvius Nobilior against the Aetolians, Lucius Aemilius Paullus Macedonicus against King Perseus of Macedonia, Quintus Caecilius Metellus Macedonicus against Pseudo-Philip, Lucius Mummius against Corinth.[1] These were, in fact, extremely troublesome wars, and our victories at the end of them were very welcome.

So I cannot see why you see fit to despise the Asiatic nations, and that enemy of ours, Mithridates. For, as regards Asia, I see from our early records that the war the Roman people fought against Antiochus III was a very important one.[2] It was won by Lucius Cornelius Scipio, who thus earned renown equal to that of his brother Publius. For just as the name Africanus which was given to Publius bore witness to the glory he had won by the conquest of Africa, so Lucius, too, was awarded a similar distinction when he assumed the surname Asiaticus after conquering Asia. That was a war, Cato, in which your great-grandfather displayed conspicuous courage.[3] And if he was the man I suppose him to have been he would never have gone out with Lucius Scipio to fight that war if the enemies had only been feeble women! On the contrary, the Roman Senate evidently regarded it as a war of the most serious, significant, character. For otherwise they would never have arranged for Publius Scipio Africanus to serve on his brother's staff, just after Publius had rescued our country from the gravest of perils by driving Hannibal out of Italy and Africa, and crushing Carthage.[4]

1. The victories of Dentatus and Flamininus were at Beneventum (275) and Cynoscephalae (197) respectively. Nobilior subjugated the Aetolians in 187, and Paullus defeated Perseus at Pydna in 168. 'Pseudo-Philip' was Andriscus, who claimed to be an illegitimate son of Philip V, and was captured by the praetor Q. Metellus in 148. Mummius sacked Corinth in 146.

2. The Seleucid Antiochus III the Great invaded Greece but was defeated at Thermopylae and Magnesia ad Sipylum, and at sea, and forced to sign the Treaty of Apamea in 188.

3. Marcus Porcius Cato the elder served under Manius Acilius Glabrio at Thermopylae (191).

4. At the end of the Second Punic War (218–201).

As for Mithridates, think carefully about what he was capable of accomplishing, and what he accomplished, and what sort of a person he was. And if you do this you must surely conclude that he comes first and foremost among all the kings against whom the Roman people has fought wars. Lucius Cornelius Sulla, an aggressive, alert and experienced general (to say the least), commanding a large and formidable army, let him go in peace only after he had invaded the whole of Asia.[1] Then Lucius Murena, the father of my client, fought against him with great determination and energy, and left him very substantially worn down, though not altogether subdued.[2] Subsequently the king spent some years building up his resources and strategies for war. His hopes and prospects ran so high that he actually expected to form a link between the Black Sea and the Atlantic Ocean, by allying the forces of Quintus Sertorius with his own.[3] Two consuls were dispatched to direct the warfare that ensued.[4] One was to attack Mithridates, while the other defended Bithynia. This second consul's activities, on land and sea alike, were catastrophic, with the result that the king's strength became much greater, and so did his reputation.

However, the campaigns that Lucius Licinius Lucullus launched against him were so successful that it would be difficult to think of any other war that achieved such a massive scale, or was more wisely and courageously conducted. The central point of the warfare, at this stage, was Mithridates's assault on the walls of Cyzicus, which he designated as his gateway into Asia. If he could shatter and obliterate Cyzicus, he reasoned, the entire province of Asia would be at his mercy. However, Lucullus fought back so effectively that this city, of which the inhabitants were our loyal allies, was able to keep the enemy at bay, and the prolonged siege severely diminished the resources of the king.

1. In the First Mithridatic War against Mithridates VI of Pontus, Sulla won the battles of Chaeronea and Orchomenus and made the Peace of Dardanus in 85.

2. As stated earlier, however, the elder Lucius Murena did not fare so well. He was heavily defeated crossing the River Halys (84), although he was subsequently awarded a triumph, to which Cicero has already referred. His son served under him.

3. Sertorius's revolt against the Roman government in Spain lasted from 82 until his death in 72.

4. Lucius Licinius Lucullus and Marcus Aurelius Cotta (74).

Nor, surely, can you dismiss the naval battle at Tenedos as just a small-scale, insignificant engagement; when the enemy's fleet, under very competent leadership, was proceeding at full speed, and with the highest and keenest hopes, towards Italy itself. About all the other battles and sieges I shall say nothing. But I must add that Mithridates, even after he had finally been expelled from his kingdom, still possessed enough astuteness and influence to reconstitute his resources and his army by forming an alliance with the king of the Armenians.

To recall Lucullus's many important battles, testifying to the mighty achievements of his army and its commander, is, as I have already mentioned, not my purpose today. But one point I do want to make. If this war, this enemy, that monarch, had been so contemptibly insignificant as Cato said, then the Senate and Roman people would not have seen the whole matter as such an anxious business as they did. Nor, indeed, would Lucius Lucullus have conducted his operations for so many years and with such distinction.

Nor, after that, would the Roman people have so enthusiastically bestowed the task of finishing off the war to Cnaeus Pompeius Magnus. Pompeius was a man who fought innumerable battles. But the fiercest and most grimly contested of the lot seems to me the engagement that he fought against Mithridates himself.[1] When the defeated ruler had got away, and had fled to the Cimmerian Bosphorus where the Roman army could not go after him, even in the desperate crisis of his flight he still kept the title of king. Pompeius had occupied his kingdom. He had expelled his foes from all their coasts and all their notable strong-points. Everything that Mithridates had possessed, had come near to possessing, had hoped to possess, had fallen into Pompeius's triumphant hands. And yet the victor still regarded that one single person, Mithridates, as so vitally important that he would not consider the war was over until he had put an end to his life.

So that, Cato, is surely not an enemy whom you can despise. Think of all the many battles so many Roman generals fought against him for so many years. This was the man, fugitive and exile though he was, whose life was still considered so enormously significant that nothing short of the announcement of his death was deemed enough to prove that the war was finally over.

1. The battle of Nicopolis in Pontus (66).

This, therefore, is what I claim, in my defence of Lucius Murena. He was well known to have been an officer of superlative courage and wisdom and industry. This military career of his, I insist, played as dominant a part in winning him his consulship as my own hard work in the Forum played in gaining a consulship for myself.

You also point out that when, earlier, the elections for the praetorship had taken place Servius Sulpicius came first on the list, before Murena. Yes, but surely you do not intend to suggest to the Assembly that the place granted to a candidate for one office should, contractually, be guaranteed to him over and over again in all his candidatures for subsequent posts! Elections are changeable, disturbed affairs. No strait, no Euripus,[1] has such powerful eddies, such varying turbulences and veering currents. The passing of a day or the coming of a night often sets matters on a totally different course, and the slightest breath of rumour transforms everyone's opinions. Frequently, and without any evident cause, things happen that are totally unexpected, so that sometimes even the general public are surprised by the course of events, even though they themselves, in fact, have been responsible for what has occurred.

Let me give some examples. Nobody, nobody at all, imagined that the brilliant, experienced, popular, aristocratic Lucius Marcius Philippus could be defeated by Marcus Herennius.[2] Or that the cultured, wise and upright Quintus Lutatius Catulus could lose an election to Cnaeus Mallius.[3] Or that Marcus Aemilius Scaurus, such an excellent character and citizen and senator, could be beaten by Quintus Fabius Maximus Eburnus.[4] No, no one believed that any of these things could happen, and even after they had happened no one could understand why things had turned out as they had. Although the appearance of certain constellations in the sky frequently means that there is going to be a storm, it is equally true that storms often appear unexpectedly, for some obscure reason for which no explanation can be provided. And the same is true of these tempestuous elections. You may sometimes, it is true, be able to detect the influence which made the storm overtake them, but

1. The narrow strait between the mainland of Greece and the island of Euboea.

2. Consul in 93.

3. Consul in 105.

4. Consul in 116.

on many occasions, also, the cause is so undetectable that it looks as if mere chance has been at work.

Still, if we have to offer explanations, two things are required of a praetor, and both of these proved of great assistance to Murena in his candidature for the consulship. One was the expectation of Games, and this was enhanced by rumours that spread around, and by the interest and critical comment of his rivals.[1] His other asset was the continued presence in the city of those who had served with him in Asia, bearing witness to his generosity and courage. Those were two advantages that fortune bestowed upon him in his candidature for the consulship. For the army of Lucius Lucullus which had come to Rome for his triumph was still on hand for Murena's election. Magnificent Games, too, which he had not been able to supply when he was campaigning to become praetor, were instead provided, at his expense, after his election, during his tenure of the praetorship; and they were remembered.

You will not, I think, argue that these two points only amounted to insignificant aids and supports, when he was aiming to become consul. Take the army first. Friendly feelings among the soldiers, and their votes, are powerful factors, because the soldiers are so numerous, and, besides, they can influence their friends. Indeed, their sentiments, in a consular election, exercise an influence upon the entire Roman people. For the men who are elected on these occasions are military commanders – not specialists in legal terminology! This is the sort of testimony that carries weight: 'He looked after me when I was wounded. He gave me a share of the loot. He was our leader when we captured the camp, when we fought the battle. He never gave the soldiers tougher tasks than he was prepared to undertake himself. He was a brave man: and a lucky one as well.' You can see very clearly how talk such as this makes a man popular, and wins him support. Nor is it surprising that, in such a case, the talk and reputation of *luck* has been a decisive factor, when so much religious feeling is involved in these elections, so that up to now the omen established by the initial returns has invariably proved accurate.[2]

1. Probably what Cicero means is that his rivals' propaganda, intended to criticize the proposed Games, actually increased people's expectation of them.

2. The 'centuries' of the Assembly (*comitia centuriata*) voted in an order determined by lot. The vote of the century which voted first was regarded as an

These are points that carry weight. But even if you disagree with this, and prefer to rate such considerations as somewhat trivial, ranking the civilian vote above that of the soldiers, you would be ill-advised to extend your contempt to the magnificence of Murena's Games and the splendour of the spectacles they provided. For, in fact, they helped him a great deal. There is no need for me to emphasize the remarkable pleasure that the public and the uneducated masses derive from Games. There is nothing surprising about this. It is enough, for my argument, to point out that they are an occasion when the people get together in huge numbers. So if the splendour of Games causes pleasure to the people, it was only to be expected that they should win Murena popular support.

We ourselves are kept away from these public performances by pressure of business, and instead derive our satisfaction – of quite a different kind – from our work. Yet even we, too, find the Games enjoyable and fascinating. So why should you be astonished that the ignorant crowd feels the same? My excellent friend Lucius Roscius Otho[1] has given back to the order of the knights not only its dignity but its entertainments: and the most popular of all his laws is the regulation relating to Games, which not only restores the distinction of that highly respected order, but also allows it to enjoy its amusements again.[2] For, believe me, people do have a good time at the Games. And I am referring not only to those who admit that this is so, but also to the others who pretend the contrary. I learnt that in my own electoral campaign. For spectacles of this kind were employed as a means of competing with me. I myself had given three sets of Games when I was aedile.[3] Yet, all the same, I was shaken by the large scale of the Games my fellow-aedile Gaius Antonius Hybrida[4] offered. Since that was so, then, you cannot suppose that the silver-tinted stage shows of your opponent Murena, which you make fun of, failed to do your rival candidature any harm. Especially since you yourself, as it happened, had given no Games at all!

---

important clue to the final result. 'Luck', *felicitas*, was considered a valuable quality – and was associated with religion (Tyche (Fortuna) being a goddess).

1. Tribune in 67.

2. His law restored to the knights (*equites*) the front fourteen rows of seats in the theatre, immediately behind the *orchestra* where the senators sat. Sulla had deprived the knights of this privilege.

3. They were dedicated to Ceres, to Liber and Libera, and to Flora.

4. Consul in 63.

But, all right, let us assume for a moment that, despite what I am saying, these things even out in the end, that civilian activity counts the same as military service, that the votes of soldiers count the same as the votes of civilians, that to have given superb Games amounts to precisely the same as giving no Games at all. But consider, in addition, your and Murena's praetorships. You cannot, surely, suppose that there was no difference between the ways in which you and he fared on that occasion. His assignment gave him what all your friends hoped that you would get: the duty of conducting lawsuits.[1] This is an activity in which the importance of the business transacted enhances the chairman's credit, and the handing out of justice confers influence. In performing this task a wise praetor, which is what Murena was, provides impartial rulings that avoid causing offence; and he makes himself popular by the sympathetical manner in which he conducts his cases. It is a distinguished occupation, and one which fits a person for the consulship. It offers the chance of enhancing one's reputation for fairness, honesty and affability. And these benefits receive their crowning glory when attractive public Games are subsequently held.

Your assignment on the other hand, Servius, was very different indeed. It offered you the dreary, disagreeable, criminal court that brings embezzlers to trial.[2] One side offers nothing but squalor and weeping:[3] on the other side are chains and informers. Jurymen attend under compulsion, and are kept on against their will. The secretary, we learn, is convicted for a criminal offence,[4] and his whole group become hostile. Sulla's allotments are inveighed against.[5] Many admirable men, indeed practically an entire section of society, become totally alienated. Heavy damages are imposed. People who win forget to remain grateful; the loser remembers.

And finally, when your praetorship was over, you refused to

1. i.e. Murena was lucky in drawing the lot for the *praetura urbana*, one of the two praetorships allotted to the civil courts (the other was the *praetura peregrina*). The six remaining praetors presided over the criminal courts.

2. The *quaestio de peculatu*.

3. The defendants sought to excite pity by wearing the shabbiest possible clothes.

4. Nothing more is known about this case.

5. Those who had received state property from the dictator Sulla (81) were now afraid of becoming the targets of actions for embezzlement. His veterans, 'many admirable men', were a force to be reckoned with.

accept the administration of a province. I cannot criticize you for that, since I did the same after I had served both as praetor and as consul. All the same, there is no denying that the province Murena accepted brought him a lot of popularity and goodwill. After he had left Rome, he raised troops in Umbria. The national situation made it possible for him to be generous, and by being so he placed many of the tribes, to which Umbrian towns were attached, under an obligation towards himself.[1] In Transalpine (Narbonese) Gaul,[2] too, by his fair and energetic conduct, he made it possible for our countrymen to gather in debts of which they had despaired. Meanwhile you remained in Rome, performing services to your friends. Certainly, I admit that. But you should nevertheless bear in mind that the support of quite a number of friends is inclined to dwindle if they realize you have rejected a province.

What I have demonstrated, gentlemen of the jury, is that Murena and Servius Sulpicius were equally well qualified to stand for the consulship, but did not enjoy equal fortune as regards the administrative duties that had been assigned to them. I shall now pass on to indicate, quite frankly, certain respects in which my friend Servius ranks *below* the other man. For now that the election is past I propose to state to you, openly, gentlemen, what I often said to him in private before it took place. What I pointed out to you, Servius, more than once, was that you had no idea how to promote your candidature for the consulship. The things that I saw you doing and saying, and you were doing and saying them with courage and determination, appeared to me, as I frequently told you, the actions and assertions of a courageous prosecutor rather than a sensible candidate. Every day, you issued menaces, and threats of legal action.[3] Such gestures display an intrepid spirit, but they dampen people's hopes that they are going to gain any benefit, and diminish the keenness of one's friends. So the same thing always follows, in one way or another; it has been observed to happen not just in one or two cases, but in many. That is to say, once a candidate is seen to be thinking in terms of prosecutions, it begins to be suspected that he has despaired of winning the election.

1. The Umbrian towns which received Roman citizenship under the *Lex Julia* of Lucius Julius Caesar in 90 were attached to specific Roman 'tribes'.

2. This was the province of which Murena was governor (*propraetor*) in 64.

3. i.e. in case he was defeated in the election he was already preparing to prosecute his successful rivals.

Am I suggesting, then, that it is undesirable to take legal action against a wrong that has been done? No, on the contrary, it is highly desirable. But there is a time for such prosecutions – and that is not when one is seeking election to an official post. A candidate for office, and particularly for the consulship, should in my view be escorted to the Forum and Campus Martius amid lofty hopes, keen enthusiasm and large supporting crowds. If a candidate starts to think of launching prosecutions, it is a sign of forthcoming defeat, and I do not like it. Nor do I like him collecting witnesses when he should be collecting voters, or uttering menaces when he ought to be distributing compliments, or bawling out personal attacks when friendly greetings would be more appropriate. And this sort of behaviour is particularly unsuitable now that we have this new fashion according to which almost everyone rushes into the candidates' homes in order to judge from their expressions how much drive and resourcefulness each of them possesses. 'Did you see how glum and depressed he's looking? He's lost hope, he's finished, he's thrown his weapons away.' The rumour creeps round. 'Do you know he's planning to launch a prosecution? He's investigating the rival candidates, and trying to find witnesses against them. As far as he himself is concerned, he's evidently given up; and I'm going to vote for someone else.' Even the candidates' closest friends are shaken when this sort of rumour goes about. Their enthusiasm vanishes. They abandon the whole thing, because his failure seems an accomplished fact. Or they save up their efforts and influence for the trial and prosecution that lie ahead.

In such a situation the candidate is simply not in a position to inject the necessary determination and attention and energy and perseverance into his electoral campaign. For he cannot stop thinking about the prosecution he has in mind, which is, after all, important for him, and indeed uniquely so. To collect all the evidence that will enable you to expel a man from the country is no small matter: especially if your victim is neither impoverished nor weak, and can rally to his defence not only his own endeavours but those of his friends, too, and even of strangers. For we hurry to his defence, every one of us, and, except for those who may be the defendant's open enemies, undertake the duties and responsibilities that would be appropriate to an extremely close friend, even if the man being tried is, in fact, a total stranger.

I am not unacquainted with the hard problems of seeking office and of conducting legal defences and prosecutions. And these personal experiences have brought it home to me that, in standing for office, the most important qualification is keenness, in conducting a legal defence it is the performance of one's duty, in undertaking a prosecution it is hard work. And, in consequence, I am entirely convinced that it is impossible for one single person to combine, effectively, the two activities of preparing a prosecution and standing for the consulship at one and the same time. Few men could do either, without the other. No one can do both. When you turned aside from your candidature, and devoted your attention to a prosecution instead, you believed you would be capable of responding to the demands that both those tasks would make. But you made a bad mistake.

For once you had started announcing that you were going to prosecute, not a single day passed which you did not dedicate wholly to that project. You demanded a law against bribery. Actually, there was one available. It was the Calpurnian Law,[1] and it was very severely phrased. It fell in thoroughly with your wishes, and what your position required. That law, taken as a whole, would have added a powerful sanction to your charge that bribes had been received – if, that is to say, you had a guilty defendant. But it spelt ruin for your electoral campaign. For what you were saying meant that the masses would be subject to more stringent punishments; and the result was that the feelings of the poorer classes were inflamed against you.[2] For men of our status, your attitude spelt out exile. However, the Senate gave way to your demand for harsher legislation. But it was not happy that, by meeting your request, it established harsher conditions for the population as a whole. (A penalty was set up, too, against pleas of ill-health. That alienated a lot of people, who either had to struggle against the discomforts of illness, or, in addition to these discomforts, now found themselves deprived of life's other amenities as well.)[3]

1. The *Lex Calpurnia de ambitu* of the consul Gaius Calpurnius Piso (67), which supplemented the existing penalties of a fine and civil disability by imposing expulsion from the Senate as well. Cicero's *Lex Tullia* (63) added exile.

2. Because they were deprived of the hope of making money by receiving electoral bribes.

3. i.e. if defendants could maintain a plea of illness until they entered office (when they would be immune), they could evade prosecution. But Cicero's *Lex*

Well, who put those measures through? I did, in obedience to the Senate, and to your own wishes, although I had least of all to gain from their enforcement.[1] As for your further proposals, which a crowded meeting of the Senate turned down – once again, with my fullest agreement – you must admit they did your candidature considerable harm. You wanted an individual vote, not by centuries and tribes.[2] You advocated the passage of the Manilian Law, establishing a popular veto.[3] You wanted thoroughgoing equality, with no distinctions of privilege or rank or voting power. Respectable men with influence in their neighbourhoods and towns were not pleased that a man with a background like yours should level down their rank and privileges in this way. You also wanted jurymen to be selected by the prosecutors.[4] But this would have meant that any man's secret animosities, which are now restricted to disagreements that do not get voiced, would in future be able to burst out openly against thoroughly reputable people. All these things prepared the way for the prosecution you intended to launch. But they prevented you from getting elected to the consulship.

Moreover, your candidature also encountered an even greater obstacle. I warned you about it in advance. It is a matter on which the brilliant, eloquent Quintus Hortensius Hortalus has enlarged convincingly and at length. Indeed, the order of our speech-making that has been allotted to us here presents me with problems. For Hortensius spoke before I did. And so did that eminent, thorough, excellent orator Marcus Licinius Crassus. So I am speaking last. That means that I do not just have to deal with part of the case, but that I have to recapitulate the whole of it, as best I can. Inevitably,

---

Tullia de ambitu either ruled out such pleas or accepted them only under strict conditions.

1. Because Cicero, having held the consulship, could not, according to the law, immediately be a candidate for further office.

2. To prevent any particular group of voters from having undue influence, and to prevent bribery.

3. Gaius Manilius (tribune in 67) proposed the distribution of freedmen throughout all the tribes (which was annulled). But it is doubtful if that is the regulation to which Cicero refers here.

4. As it was, the panels of jurymen selected by the prosecutors could be modified by challenges from the defendants.

therefore, I am going over the same points as they did. However, to the best of my ability, gentlemen, I shall try not to bore you by this repetitiveness.

Well, Servius, surely you must see that you put paid to your candidature altogether when, although prompting the Roman people to fear that Catilina might be elected to the consulship,[1] you were, at the same time, by concentrating on the prosecution, effectively giving up and abandoning your own electoral campaign! For people were able to notice how you were grimly setting up investigations; and your friends were despondent. They could observe how you were noting everything down, concerning yourself with evidence, trying to attract witnesses, moving around to get men to join you as accusers. A candidate busying himself with that sort of matter cannot fail to look pretty glum.

While Catilina, at the same time, surrounded by a gang of young men, protected by informers and assassins, could well offer the appearance of being quite alert and happy. He had high hopes of his soldiers; and additional sources of encouragement, as he himself said, were promises made by my fellow-consul Gaius Antonius Hybrida. Moreover, an army of settlers from Arretium and Faesulae had flocked around him. On the whole, it is true, they were just a mob. But among them were men of superior calibre – sufferers from the catastrophes of the epoch of Sulla. The look on Catilina's face was demented. His eyes seemed like those of a criminal. His speeches were full of insolence. He gave the impression that the consulship was already in his grasp, and that he had got it and taken it home. Murena he viewed with contempt. Sulpicius he saw as his prosecutor, and no sort of rival at all, and threatened him with violence. Indeed he issued threats against the entire Roman state.

You do not need me to remind you of the terror which this situation inspired in all honest men, and how desperate everyone felt at the prospect of Catilina becoming consul. For you can remember it all yourselves. You can recall how word had got round of something which that deplorable gladiatorial character was supposed to have said at a meeting in his home. What he had said, it was reported, was that no reliable champion of the unhappy

1. Lucius Sergius Catilina was one of the candidates for the consulship of 62, and Servius pointed out that his own defeat might have won Catilina the election in his place.

masses could be seen anywhere except himself, who was one of them. Those who were distressed and unhappy, he was thought to have added, had better not believe the promises of those who were prosperous, and doing all right. So anyone, he said, who wanted to replenish his resources, and get back what he had lost, would be well advised to look at Catilina himself, and note the size of his debts, and his lack of possessions, and the ferocity he was prepared to display. He was the right man to be the leader and standard-bearer of those who were in trouble, because he was in trouble himself.

When this pronouncement by Catilina became known, you will remember that, on my proposal, the Senate passed a decree putting off the consular election that had been due to be held on the following day, so that senators could have a chance to discuss the whole matter. On that next day, therefore, at a packed meeting of the Senate, I called upon Catilina, and told him to speak about the matters that had been reported to me, if there was anything he wanted to add. Being, at all times, a man who spoke freely, he did not attempt to offer excuses, but assumed full, self-incriminating responsibility for what he had said. Then he went on to assert that the state possesses two bodies: one weak and with a feeble head, and the other strong but lacking a head altogether. This second body, he added, if it proved to deserve his help, would never be without a head again, as long as he lived. The crowded Senate groaned deeply, but nevertheless did not pass a decree which was stern enough to match up to the affront it had received. For some of the senators avoided a severe measure because they saw nothing to fear, and others because their fears were too great.

Catilina rushed out of the Senate-house, triumphant and content. He never ought to have been allowed to get out alive. For this was the man who, at a similar meeting a few days earlier, had declared to the eminent Marcus Porcius Cato the younger, who was denouncing him and threatening to bring him to trial, that if a conflagration did away with Catilina's prospects,[1] one must expect him to put it out, not just by the use of water, such as one employs to extinguish a fire, but by inflicting ruin upon one and all.

This moved me very deeply. And I had also been told that Catilina was bringing armed men, with swords in their hands, into

1. i.e. of becoming consul.

the Field of Mars:[1] a conspiracy was already under way. So I myself, too, went into the Campus, accompanied by a powerful guard of intrepid men. I was wearing that massive, conspicuous cuirass. It would not, I knew, protect me, for I was aware that Catilina was accustomed to strike, not at the side or stomach, but at the head and neck. But what I intended was that all reputable citizens would note what was happening, and that, when they saw their consul alarmed and imperilled, they would rush to help and defend him: which is precisely what happened.

While people could detect that you, Servius, were only pressing your candidature rather languidly, they were able to note that Catilina, on the other hand, was burning with optimistic ambition. So everyone who wanted to rid our nation of that pestilential figure at once transferred their votes to Murena. In consular elections, major shifts of attitude occur very suddenly. And this especially happens when opinion veers towards a man who is not only worthy in himself, but is also favoured, in his campaign, by other advantages as well. Murena conscientiously pushed his candidature forward. The records of his impeccable father and ancestors helped him. So did the respectable way in which he had spent his youth, and his eminent service as a military officer. Another help, too, was his praetorship, in which he had administered the law with such distinction, and earned popularity because of his Games; and his provincial service had further enhanced his reputation. As a candidate, too, he neither gave way before threats, nor threatened anyone himself. And we can scarcely be surprised that Catilina's sudden hope of becoming consul gave a further boost to Murena's cause.

Now remains the third section of my speech. It relates to the charge of bribery. This has, in fact, been refuted by those who spoke before me. Yet I must discuss it again, all the same, because that is what Murena wishes. In dealing with this matter I shall answer my very talented friend Gaius Postumus[2] about the alleged evidence of bribe distributors and the funds that were seized. I shall also answer the able, excellent young Servius Sulpicius Rufus the younger (son of the lawyer) about how the centuries of the knights may have been involved. And I shall answer Marcus Cato, that man

1. A northern area of the city full of important public buildings.
2. Nothing is known of him, except what is mentioned below.

of such outstanding integrity, about the charge that he has personally brought, and about the relevant senatorial decree, and about our national affairs in general.

But first I must mention, with distress, a few things about Murena's current ordeal that have recently struck me. Even before this present time, gentlemen, reflecting upon other people's troubles and my own cares and labours every day, I repeatedly came to the conclusion that those who live quiet and tranquil lives far removed from ambitious political struggles are indeed fortunate men. And now, too, these great and sudden troubles that have overtaken Murena move me so profoundly that I feel unmeasurable sadness about his plight and ill-fortune – and about the way, I must add, in which the lives of us all turn out. The first point is this. What Murena was trying to do was to secure an office just one single grade beyond those that his family and his ancestors have so frequently held. Yet, in attempting this, he has now risked losing every single thing that had come to him as their inheritance, in addition to what he himself had won. In his desire to gain new distinctions, then, he is gravely hazarding those which he already possessed.

That is hard for him, gentlemen. But what is most painful of all is this. The accusers are not induced to prosecute him by personal feelings of hatred. The opposite is the case: it is their eagerness to bring the prosecution which has caused them to hate him. I will say nothing more, at this point, about the lawyer Servius Sulpicius Rufus, who is motivated, I know, not by any belief that Murena has done him wrong, but by their rival claims to the consulship. But Murena's accusers also include Gaius Postumus, a longstanding neighbour, as he himself records, and a friend, who had also been a friend of his father. Postumus, then, had more than one reason for friendship; and he could name no reason for becoming Murena's enemy. Murena is also accused by the younger Servius Sulpicius Rufus – son of the other who was so close to Murena – and the young man ought to have employed his talents to ensure that all his father's friends were better looked after. The other accuser is Marcus Porcius Cato. He was never Murena's enemy in any respect whatever. Moreover, his family position, in this state of ours, should have made him devote his resources and gifts to protecting a large number of people – including, perhaps, even strangers – and not to aiming at the ruin of any man at all, even if he was a personal opponent.

I shall begin by answering Postumus. He himself has not got beyond the stage of having been a candidate for the praetorship. Yet he is interfering with the consular election, it seems to me, rather like a circus rider's horse which collides with a four-horse chariot.[1] If his own fellow-candidates for the praetorship had done nothing illegal, he acknowledged that they were his superiors when he withdrew his candidature for that office. If, on the other hand, they had been guilty of bribery, he did them a good turn by prosecuting someone else instead, involved in another election altogether – a prosecution, incidentally, which helps another man, a consular candidate, but does no good to himself.[2]

I now come to Marcus Porcius Cato the younger. It is he who provides the prosecution with its entire foundation and force. He is such a formidable man, and such a vigorous accuser, that I am more afraid of his influential personality than of his prosecution itself. Speaking of Cato's role as accuser, my first prayer, gentlemen, is this: that his position, and his expectation of the office of tribune,[3] and his entire glorious, powerful record, may not become factors that operate against Murena. And my second prayer is this. Marcus Cato acquired his resources with the purpose of providing aid to a whole host of people. I beg, therefore, that they should not be employed to injure just this one man alone, namely Murena.

Publius Cornelius Scipio Africanus the younger provides an analogy.[4] At the time when he brought an action against Lucius Aurelius Cotta,[5] he had twice served as consul, and had consigned

1. i.e. if he was going to prosecute, he should have prosecuted one of his own competitors, not Murena, who was a competitor of Servius Sulpicius Rufus (a higher rank).

2. If, that is to say, his own competitors had offered bribes, they had found a friend in Postumus who had prosecuted Murena – a candidate in quite another, consular election – instead of themselves; but Postumus's action gets him no nearer the praetorship – he had better have left the consular candidates to their own affairs.

3. Cato had just been elected to a tribuneship, which he would take up on 10 December.

4. Cicero is now citing precedents of eminent men in the past who have failed in their prosecutions because the Roman people did not like them mobilizing their prestige against an individual in court.

5. In 138.

the two cities that menaced our country, Carthage and Numantia, to destruction. He was a man of extraordinary eloquence, honour and integrity. His influence was as potent as that of the entire Roman government, which, indeed, was kept going by his labours. But I have often heard older men remark that when Scipio prosecuted Cotta his outstanding power and dignity were actually of considerable help to the defendant. For the wise men who were serving as jurymen in that court did not believe it right that anyone should seem to have lost his case just because the superior personal authority of his opponent had been too much for him. And it was the Roman people itself, as tradition informs us, which rescued Servius Sulpicius Galba from the clutches of your own staunch and successful great-grandfather Marcus Porcius Cato the elder, despite all Cato's efforts to bring about his destruction.[1]

For in this country, at all times, the entire people, and its wisest and most forward-looking jurymen, have invariably resisted prosecutors whose power was excessive. For it is wrong that a prosecutor should employ his great personal power, or his overwhelming capacity to apply force, or his outstanding influence, or his excessive popularity, as a means of affecting a court's decisions. Let these assets, by all means, be utilized to protect innocent men, to help the helpless, to rescue those who are in trouble. Yet in a trial which is aimed at inflicting ruin upon Roman citizens they ought to be rejected. Besides, someone might assert that the younger Cato would never have stooped to bring the case at all unless he had prejudged that its outcome would be in his favour. But if that was really so, gentlemen, he would be creating a very unfair precedent. And if it should be assumed that this prejudgement by the prosecutor should carry weight against the defendant, that would indeed mean that everyone up for trial is in a lamentably unfavourable situation.

It is not for me to find fault with your intentions, Cato. I admire your character too much. But perhaps I might offer a few detailed criticisms, and suggest minor rectifications. 'You do not make many mistakes,' said that old guardian Phoenix to his valorous ward Achilles, 'but you do make some. I can put you right.'[2] Putting it

1. In 149 BC Lucius Scribonius Libo and the elder Cato accused Servius Sulpicius Galba of massacring the Lusitanians in the previous year.

2. Said to have been a quotation from Accius's tragedy the *Myrmidones*.

right, however, I am afraid, is something that I cannot hope to do. Indeed, I would not be far wrong if I said that you never make a mistake at all, and that correcting you is out of the question; although small amendments would still seem to be in order. Nature has made you a man of pre-eminent honesty, seriousness and self-control, a man whose conduct is generous and just. In fact, she has made you a man who possesses every noble endowment to an exceptional degree. But to these qualities you have added a creed of your own. It is neither gentle nor mild. On the contrary, it is, in my opinion, somewhat more grim and harsh than the conditions of actual life and natural existence make it possible to tolerate.

I am not speaking, I know, before a crowd of uneducated people or a collection of rustics. So that encourages me, at this stage, to make a few additional remarks about the cultural studies in which both you and I, Cato, engage with so much pleasure. Here, we must make a distinction. The truly admirable, superhuman qualities which we see in Marcus Cato were inborn. Those of his qualities, on the other hand, which we may feel inclined to criticize are derived not from his nature at all, but from his teacher. I mean Zeno.[1] Certainly, Zeno was a man of outstanding gifts. The people who try to follow his teachings are the Stoics. And the sort of maxim and precept that he offered them went as follows. A wise person never allows himself to be influenced – and never forgives anyone else who has done anything wrong. Only fools and triflers show mercy. A real man is not affected by prayers or attempts to placate him. Philosophers are people who, however ugly, remain handsome; even if they are very poor, they are rich; even if they are slaves, they are kings. All sins are equal, so that every misdemeanour is a serious crime. The man who unnecessarily strangles a cock is as guilty as the man who has strangled his father. The philosopher has no need to offer conjectures, never regrets what he has done, is never mistaken, never changes his mind.

Marcus Cato, being a highly intelligent man, took over this doctrine, under the direction of learned professors. And he adopted it not merely, like most men, as a theme for theoretical debate, but as the guide to his life. This is the sort of thing it involves. The tax-collectors put forward a demand. They must make sure that favouritism does not in any way influence them in what they are demanding.

1. Zeno of Citium (335–263 BC), founder of the Stoic school.

Wretched suppliants come in, men who have suffered disaster. Yet if your response were dictated by compassion, you would be acting immorally and criminally. A man admits he has acted wrongly, and asks to be excused for what he has done. But to forgive wrongdoing is sinful. The offence, perhaps, was only a trivial one. Yet all misdeeds are equal. Or, you have made some assertion. Once you have said it, it is fixed, and you cannot take it back. But what you had said was not based on fact at all, but only on conjecture. However, the philosopher does not conjecture. Or, if you *did* make a mistake, it must not be taken literally, for you made it, he would maintain, on purpose, in order to be deliberately misleading.

Once this sort of philosophy becomes involved, here is the kind of thing that happens to us. 'I declared in the Senate that I was going to prosecute one of the candidates for the consulship?' Yes, you said that; but when you said it, you were angry. But the philosopher, he objects, is incapable of being angry. All right, then, you were just playing for time. 'To tell a lie', he replies, 'is a wicked act. To change one's opinion is deplorable. To pardon anyone is a crime. To show compassion is deplorable.'

Now I will admit, Cato, that I too, when I was young, feeling diffident about my own intellectual resources, sought the assistance of philosophy. And what my teachers told us – Plato's and Aristotle's followers, moderate and reasonable men – is that it *is* sometimes possible to make philosophers change their minds. It *is* a virtue, they comment, to show compassion. Offences are not all equally serious: they differ in gravity, and deserve different punishments. However steadfast a man may be, he can sometimes pardon. As for the philosopher, he *does* sometimes guess about things he does not know for certain, he *is* sometimes angry, he *is* sometimes influenced by prayers and attempts to placate him, he *does* sometimes alter what he has said if he finds a reason to improve, he *does*, on occasion, change his opinion. That is to say, all virtues, I learnt, are subject to modification by the Mean.

If you, Cato, able as you are, had had the good fortune to learn from those teachers, you would not, certainly, be a better man or stronger or more self-controlled or more just. For that would be impossible. But you would have been a little more inclined to show kindness. You would not, unprompted by any background of enmity, unprovoked by any injurious act, have prosecuted a thoroughly decent, worthy and honourable man. Since, moreover, you and Murena had happened to hold official posts in the same year,[1] you would have felt bound to him by some sense of comradely responsibility after your joint involvement in national affairs. And then you would not have launched those savage charges in the Senate. Or, at least, you would have put them forward more mildly.

As far as I can surmise, Cato, you are suffering from some state of mental turmoil, which has, at the moment, caused you to become overwrought. The intellectual gifts with which nature endowed you have transported you into a state of excitement, to which your recent philosophical studies provided an additional stimulus. But experience, I am sure, will supply the necessary check, time will soften you, and you will become mellowed with age.

Indeed, those very professors of yours, who instructed you in ethical matters, have, in my opinion, enlarged the demands of duty a bit farther than nature actually intended. For surely, although our intellects had directed that we should aim at perfection, we were nevertheless meant to stop at the appropriate point on the way. 'Forgive nothing.' No, do not forgive everything, but forgive *something*. 'Do not ever do anything under influence.' Yes, resist influence – as far as duty and honour demand. 'Do not be moved by mercy.' No, certainly, when you have to fight against cruelty. But, all the same, it is not always a bad thing to be kind. 'Stick to your opinion.' Certainly – unless some other opinion should take precedence, because it is better!

Our Scipio Africanus the younger was not ashamed to go in for philosophy as you do, when he made the learned Panaetius his guest at his home.[2] Panaetius taught the things that give you such satisfaction. Yet, all the same, his talks and his precepts did not make Scipio a sterner person. On the contrary, from what old men have told me, they made him milder. Moreover, the same sort of studies made Gaius Laelius, too, quite exceptionally affable and agreeable, though no one could have been wiser and more impressive than he was. The same can be said of Lucius Furius Philus and Gaius Sulpicius Galus.[3] But now let me take you into your own

1. Murena as consul, Cato as tribune.

2. Panaetius of Rhodes (*c.* 185–109 BC) was head of the Stoic school for the last twenty years of his life.

3. Philus was a member of the Scipionic circle, and Galus famous for his knowledge of astronomy. They were consuls in 136 and 166 respectively.

family home. Do you imagine that anyone was more obliging and unpretentious and accessible to every kindly inclination than your own great-grandfather Marcus Porcius Cato the elder?[1]

You spoke very accurately and convincingly about his exceptional qualities. They meant, you said, that your own family provided you with the model whom you ought to imitate. Yes, indeed, he is a model, set before you in your own home. In consequence, you yourself, who are one of his descendants, can imitate him more easily than the rest of us can (though he is a model whom I feel I should imitate quite as much as you do). But if you would only temper your own gravity and strictness with the affability and friendliness that he displayed, I am not saying that the great qualities which you yourself possess would be improved, since that would not be possible – but I do say that they would be more agreeably seasoned.

But let me return to the point where I began. I ask you to imagine that Cato's prestige be ignored in this case. Forget his influence. That is a thing, in a trial, which ought not to have any weight at all, or which, if it has, should work in favour not of condemnation but of acquittal. Concentrate on the specific accusations themselves as the matters on which we are joining issue.

Well then, what exactly is the accusation that you are making, Cato? What is the true nature of your charge – and what is the argument you are employing in order to press it? What you are attacking, of course, is bribery. That is something that I do not defend. You criticize me because I am defending a man accused of the very offence that I myself penalized. But what I penalized was bribery – not innocence. I am only too glad to join you in your attack on bribery, if you would want me to. You pointed out, I repeat, that it was I myself who proposed a relevant decree of the Senate. According to this decree, the Calpurnian Law was contravened if men were paid to meet the candidates, if people were hired, for a fee, to act as escorts, if at gladiatorial combats places were allotted to the crowd according to tribes,[2] if free dinners were given to the public. So the Senate decided that these actions

1. Is this a joke? Cicero can hardly have meant it seriously about this blunt and ill-mannered man.

2. It was illegal to provide seats for a whole tribe, which might then be induced to vote for the provider.

would be illegal *if* they were committed. The decree satisfied the candidates. Yet it does not solve the question we are considering today.[1]

For the pressing question is: was bribery committed, or not? If it was, it was clearly illegal. It is ridiculous to leave ambiguity unresolved, while adjudicating on something unequivocal. Every one of the candidates was in favour of the resolution, so that there was no knowing who benefited from it and who did not. If you could only prove that one of them, Lucius Murena, was guilty of bribery, then I myself am perfectly prepared to admit to you that he was behaving illegally.

'Many people', it is insinuated in support of the charge, 'went out to meet him when he came back from his province.' That is surely not unusual, especially when the man is a candidate for the consulship. And, besides, people do go out to meet anyone who is returning home. 'But why was that enormous multitude there?' Well, perhaps I cannot offer a detailed explanation, but it is in no way exceptional, as I said, for a large number of men to go out to meet a returning official, especially if he is standing for the consulship. Indeed, if that had *not* happened, there would be more reason to feel surprised. And if I was prepared to add that many members of the crowd had been *asked* to go, even that would be nothing unusual, and no occasion for criminal charges, or for amazement. It is a common Roman practice for people, in response to a request, to escort even the sons of very humble citizens into the Forum, almost before daylight, and from the remotest parts of the city.[2] So I do not see why people should be reluctant to come to the Field of Mars well after day has dawned, and particularly if they are invited in the name of so distinguished a personage.

So people belonging to the trade associations joined the crowd. Well, what if they did? Such persons include many of the jurymen who are sitting here today. What if many members of our own honourable senatorial order were there too? What if that entire collection of assiduous seekers after office were also there, the men

1. Because it could not, obviously, pronounce on whether anything illegal, in any specific case, had been done – which Cicero now goes on to discuss.

2. e.g. when a young man entered the Forum for the first time at his coming of age and assumption of the *toga virilis*, he was escorted by all the friends of his family.

who permit no one to enter the city without ceremony? If, finally, our prosecutor Postumus himself chose to go and meet him, with his own substantial group of supporters, I see nothing extraordinary about the mass of people who evidently assembled. One need not speak, surely, of Murena's clients, neighbours, fellow-tribesmen,[1] who no doubt swelled the size of the crowd, not to mention the entire army of Lucullus which had come to Rome, during those days, to celebrate their commander's triumph. But I assure you of this. Crowds have always been available to perform this duty entirely of their own free will, when the position of the man entering the city warranted such a gathering – and the men to whom they flocked, no doubt, were glad that they came. 'Yet such an enormous mass of people gathered around him.' Prove that they were paid to do so. If you can, I will accept that it was illegal. But if you cannot, what offence is involved?

'What does a man want', the prosecutor then goes on to ask, 'with all that accompanying multitude?' Why choose me to answer that question? For, after all, it is a practice that every one of us has followed. Men without resources of their own have only one way of earning and repaying favours from us senators: they can support us by coming to be in our company while we are campaigning for office. Certainly, they cannot attend their friends who are candidates for whole days at a time. Nor could we, or the knights, demand such a thing. But if they arrive at our houses, if on occasion they escort us to the Forum, if they honour us with their presence just for a single turn within a public hall, we are grateful for the trouble they have taken to show us respect and attention. That is the way in which persons without important occupations, persons of slender means, can display their solidarity. And they are always ready to back good, generous candidates in this fashion.

Cato, do not deprive these lesser men of that way of demonstrating their support. All their hopes are centred on what we can give them: so let them be permitted to give us something in exchange. Their votes, if they vote at all, are not enough to let them have any influence on their own account. As they themselves often apologetically declare, they cannot speak up for us, or guarantee us, or invite us to their homes. They ask favours from us, on a considerable

1. The territorial tribes were divisions of the Roman state, the units for census, taxation and the military levy.

scale, but the only thing they believe they can offer us in return is their personal attendance. That is why they opposed the Fabian Law limiting the dimensions of escorts, and the senatorial decree passed in the consulship of Lucius Julius Caesar.[1] Sanctions do not exist which can prevent the humbler classes from observing this ancient method of fulfilling their obligations.

'But free shows were laid on for entire tribes, and hosts of people were invited to banquets.' Actually Murena himself, gentlemen, did no such thing. Certainly, it was done by his friends, but on no unusual scale, and in moderation. Still, the fact that this happened reminds me, Servius, what a large number of votes we ourselves lost[2] because of complaints on the subject made in the Senate. For neither in the years that we can remember nor in those that our fathers could recall was there ever a time when people did not aspire, motivated either by a desire to better themselves or merely by generous feelings, to present seats in the Circus Maximus or at the Forum Games[3] to their friends and fellow-tribesmen. The bestowal of such gifts upon members of one's own tribe, as rewards and favours, is an ancient tradition. On one occasion, the chairman of the craftsmen's corporation was criticized by a decree of the Senate for giving seats to his fellow-tribesmen. So I wonder what they are going to decree against men of the highest rank who erected whole shops in the Circus for people who belonged to their tribe!

However, the general view is that all these charges about escorts, shows, banquets, are merely products of excessive conscientiousness on your part, Servius. Besides, in any case, Murena is protected against this sort of accusation by the authority of the Senate. If you ask how this can be, the point is that the Senate does not regard it as a criminal act to go out and meet a candidate for office who is returning home. For it does not, does it? 'No, not unless people are paid to go.' Which you have got, in this case, to prove. Or is it criminal to have a large escort flocking around one? No, not unless they are hired. Prove that they were. Or to give away seats for a

1. Nothing is known about these two measures. Lucius Caesar was consul in 64.

2. i.e. you, as candidate, and I, as your supporter.

3. Gladiatorial Games took place in the Forum Romanum before the amphitheatres were constructed.

show, or issue invitations for a dinner? No, not unless it is done promiscuously, and the beneficiaries are an enormous crowd. What do you call an 'enormous crowd'? Well, the entire city. Take the case of Lucius Pinarius Natta, a young man of eminent position. We see what he already is, and his character, and what sort of a man he is going to be.[1] If Natta decided, as he did, to show generosity to the knights, bearing in mind both the claims of friendship and his own ambitions for the future, surely that was no reason to brand his stepfather Murena as a delinquent or a criminal. And if a Vestal Virgin, his relation and his friend, chose to give Murena her seat at a gladiatorial show, she was acting perfectly properly and he, too, was not doing anything wrong.[2] All these are things that friends have to do. They are what poor men like to have done for them. They are expected by candidates for office.

But Cato disagrees with me, in austere Stoic fashion. Men should not, he says, be enticed to show goodwill by food, and decisions in elections should not be corrupted by the offering of enjoyments. Does he mean, then, that anyone who offers an invitation to dinner in order to promote his election campaign should be condemned? 'Yes, certainly,' he replies, 'it would be entirely wrong to seek election to the highest post and authority of the state, the office that guides our nation, by indulging people's senses, and appealing to their feelings, and pandering to their pleasures. Are you applying', he might go on to say, 'to a crowd of dissipated youths for a job as a pimp? – or are you asking the Roman people for an office that controls the entire world?'

That is a frightening way to talk. And experience, life, custom, our country itself, declare it to be misguided. For neither the Spartans, who invented your life-style and way of talking,[3] and who recline daily at their meals upon couches made of wood, nor even the Cretans, who never even reclined at meal-times at all, maintained their states more successfully than the Romans – who find time to enjoy themselves, as well as to work. It needed only a

1. Actually, he turned against Cicero, and helped to destroy his house in 58.

2. The Vestal Virgins (priestesses of Vesta) had fixed seats assigned to them at public entertainments. Presumably, in this case, the suggestion was that she had given him her seat so that he could give it to someone else in return for political support.

3. i.e. 'Laconic' – named after Laconia, of which Sparta was the capital.

single campaign for our army to overthrow Crete.[1] And as for Sparta, it was only under the protection of our imperial rule that it was able to preserve its way of life and its laws at all. So you should avoid, Cato, delivering such harsh attacks upon the customs of our ancestors, which have, in fact, been vindicated by the historical facts, and by the length of time for which our nation has remained in existence.

In the epoch of our fathers there was a learned man who belonged to the same philosophical school as yourself, the noble and honourable Quintus Aelius Tubero.[2] When Publius Cornelius Scipio Africanus the younger died,[3] his nephew Quintus Fabius Maximus Allobrogicus[4] gave a funeral banquet to the Roman people in Scipio's honour. Tubero, since he was the son of Scipio's sister, was asked by Maximus to provide the coverings for the couches. And that erudite Stoic covered Fabius's simple Carthaginian benches[5] with shabby goatskins, and laid out cheap Samian crockery. You might have thought that the dead man was Diogenes the austere Cynic,[6] and not that it was the death of the immortal Scipio Africanus which was being honoured: the man who in the course of his funeral inspired Maximus, when he delivered the funeral oration, to thank the gods because such a man had been born in our country rather than in another; since where Scipio Africanus was, there, inevitably, must reside the direction of the entire world.

Now, the Roman people, honouring Scipio Africanus's death, were far from impressed by Tubero's misapplied meanness. So Tubero, although he was the grandson of Lucius Aemilius Paullus Macedonicus,[7] and although, as I said before, he was the son of Scipio Africanus's sister, was defeated for the praetorship – and it was those goatskins that did it. For although the people have no taste for private extravagance, they enjoy public grandeur. I am not saying that they love elaborate banquets; they do not. But they like

1. Under Quintus Caecilius Metellus, subsequently known as Creticus, in 68–67 BC.

2. Tribune in 130(?).

3. In 129.

4. Consul in 121.

5. 'Punic' couches were long, low, benches made of wood.

6. Diogenes of Sinope (*c.* 400–*c.* 325 BC) founded the Cynic school of philosophy.

7. Consul in 182 and 168.

boorish squalor a good deal less. That is to say, they distinguish between what is appropriate for different observances and occasions, and they know that there are times for work and times for pleasure.

You assert that decisions about electing men to office should be determined entirely by their work. But I have to add that you yourself do not maintain the highest standards in this respect. For ought you, Cato, in that case, to ask people to back you and to help you?[1] What you are asking me, in effect, is to allow you to be my boss, to allow you to take over my interests. But note where this leads. In matters affecting my personal fortunes, when I have to undergo both toil and danger, should it not rather be myself appealing to you for your protection, rather than the other way round?

And then there is the fact that you employed a prompter, to remind you of people's names.[2] By doing so, you are playing rather a shameful game. For if it is decent behaviour, as it is, for you to address your fellow-citizens by name, it is, on the other hand, degrading that they should be better known to your slave than to yourself. But if you were, genuinely, already acquainted with them, I cannot see why, when you are standing for election, you have to use a prompter before you address them – which implies that you had no knowledge of who they were! Then, after you have been prompted, you greet them as if you knew them. When your election was over, however, your greetings became much more casual. Well, if you judge all such behaviour according to the common practice at Rome, there is nothing wrong with it; it is only when you assess it according to your own philosophical principles that it seems rather shabby. And if you are going to behave like that, I cannot see why the Roman masses should not be allowed to enjoy Games, or gladiatorial combats or banquets – all of which our ancestors established. And I cannot see why candidates for official posts should be prevented from performing acts of kindness: which are products of generosity, not of bribery.

1. Ought you not, that is to say, to rely upon your own merits and nothing else? Cato had evidently asked Cicero to help him become a tribune: you ask me, Cicero replies, to support you, so that you, when you become an official, may protect me in turn – which you are not doing now.

2. A *nomenclator*, a slave whose duty it was to accompany a candidate and whisper to him the names of those whom he was canvassing.

What you emphasize, Cato, is that the national interest is what has prompted you to conduct this prosecution. And no doubt it was, indeed, with this conviction and impression that you launched it. But you have gone badly wrong. What I myself am doing, certainly, I am doing because of my friendship with Murena, and to protect his position. But I am doing it also, I sincerely declare, for the sake of national peace, tranquillity, concord and freedom, and for the lives and safety of us all. Listen to what I am telling you, gentlemen, listen to a consul's words – I will avoid saying anything more presumptuous, but I must say this: you are listening to a consul who spends all his days and all his nights thinking of the interests of our country.

Catilina's contempt and disdain for this country of ours are not so utterly overwhelming, surely, that he can bring himself to believe that he is able to overthrow the government merely by using the armed men he has taken out with him. No, the infection of his evil actions is more widespread than anyone imagined – and reaches a larger number of people. I declare that the Trojan Horse is within this city itself.[1] But it will never overwhelm you in your sleep as long as I remain consul. You ask if I am afraid of Catilina. No, I am not: and I have taken steps to ensure that no one else need be afraid of him either. But I do feel that his men whom I see with us here in Rome are something to be afraid of. And what we need to fear even more than Catilina's army are the people who are said to have deserted from it. For, in fact, they have not deserted at all. He has left them behind in watch-towers and hiding-places, from which they threaten to emerge, and slice off our heads, and cut our throats. And what they desire, with this in mind, is that you should decide to deprive an honest consul and a good general, dedicated by character and responsibility to the safety of our country, of his task of guarding our city. They want to strike the protection of our country out of his hands.

These were the men whose criminal violence I thwarted in the Field of Mars, foiled in the Forum, and on more than one occasion suppressed in my own house.[2] If you give up one of the two

1. The Wooden Horse, loaded with soldiers, was the stratagem by which the Greeks were believed to have captured Troy.

2. Gaius Cornelius and Lucius Vargunteius tried to enter his house and assassinate him.

consuls into their hands, they will have gained more by that decision than their swords could ever be able to give them. In the face of redoubtable opposition, I have made it my task to ensure that on the first of January there shall be two consuls in the state. That, gentlemen, is vitally necessary. Do not imagine that our enemies are employing designs of any ordinary kind, or methods we are accustomed to. It is not just a matter of an immoral law, of damaging bribery, of rumours about a national peril that lies some time in the future. No, gentlemen, plans have been laid, here and now, in this land of ours, for nothing less than the obliteration of our city, and the massacre of our citizens, and the blotting out of the very name of Rome.

And these actions have been plotted, and are being plotted today, by Roman citizens – if one can call them that – against their own nation. I fight against their schemes every day. I try to wear their ferocity down. I resist their crimes. Yet I warn you, gentlemen of the jury: my consulship is coming to an end. But there exists one man who helps me in all these labours. Do not, I beg you, cast him aside! It is to him that I want to hand over our country, unharmed, so that he can continue to protect it from these massive dangers. Do not force him out!

I must also direct your attention, gentlemen, to a particular threatened calamity, a special aspect of the general menacing situation. It is really you I am speaking to, Cato. Can you not foresee how tempestuously your year of office as tribune is going to turn out? Already, when the Assembly met yesterday, the lethal tones of another tribune-elect, your future colleague, thundered out.[1] True, your own comprehension of the situation has effectively frustrated him, and so have all the excellent men who urged you to stand for the tribunate. Three years ago, as you know, Catilina and Cnaeus Calpurnius Piso conceived the idea of massacring the Senate.[2] And all the plots which have been boiling up ever since then are now ripening suddenly, in these very months and days. There is not a place or time or day or night when I do not have to be rescued and preserved from the ambushes and assassination attempts of that gang

1. Quintus Caecilius Metellus Nepos attacked Cicero for his execution of the conspirators and vetoed his final speech at the end of the year.

2. Piso had been subsequently sent to Spain, but was murdered by adherents of Pompey (64).

– rescued by my own endeavours, certainly, but much more by the intervention of the gods. It is not just the individual, Cicero, whom they want to kill: they want to kill me in order to deprive the state of a vigilant consul's care.

Moreover, they would be equally glad to eliminate you yourself, Cato, in some way or other, if they could. Indeed, believe me, that is what they are actually planning and plotting to do. They note your determination, and resourcefulness, and authority, and ability to protect our country. But when they see you in the office of tribune, deprived of the additional authority and assistance that a consul could give you, they conclude that, thus disarmed and weakened, they will find you easier to destroy. The substitution of another consul, in Murena's place, does not frighten them. They see that the question whether there is to be such a substitute at all will lie in the power of your fellow-tribunes;[1] and what they are hoping is that Murena's excellent fellow-consul, Decimus Junius Silanus, will be at their mercy when he holds office without any colleague whatever. You too, then, will have no second consul to support you. And the state will have no one to protect it.

You, Marcus Cato, were in my opinion born to serve not yourself but your country. And in circumstances of this highly critical nature it will be incumbent upon you to realize what is going on, and to retain this consul-elect, Murena, as your helper, your protector, your ally in the nation's service. He will not be a consul who is after his own advantage. He will be the consul whom this present time most greatly needs: just the man, as his record confirms, who is suited by his position to cherish peace, the man whose expert knowledge qualifies him to fight, the man whose determination and experience will enable him to conduct any affairs that you can think of.

It is with you, gentlemen, that the entire decision rests. It is you, with this issue before you, upon whom the whole control and guidance of our country depends. If the decision rested with Catilina instead, accompanied by the gang of criminals whom he has taken out of Rome to support him, he would condemn Lucius Murena. Indeed, if he could, he would kill him. What Catilina is after is that our state should be deprived of its defences, that its commanders

1. One of them, by his veto, could prevent new consular elections from being held.

opposed to his lunatic career should be fewer, that greater power should be bestowed upon the tribunes of the people,[1] by getting the man who could put a stop to the sedition and discord out of the way. I urge then that the decision of you senators, men who are both honourable and wise, selected from the highest ranks of our citizen body, should totally reject the schemes of that most disreputable gladiator, Catilina, the enemy of our country.

Believe me, gentlemen, what you will be voting about in this case is not only Lucius Murena's life, but your own lives as well. We have come to the end of the road. We have no resources left from which we could recover our strength or, having fallen, could rise up once again. We must be sure not to weaken the assets that we have, and in addition new assets, if possible, must be procured. The grimmest moment in the Second Punic War was on the River Anio.[2] But now the enemy is not on the Anio but in the very city and Forum of Rome. My god, it is difficult to talk like this without weeping! For there are enemies even in that national shrine of ours, the Senate-house itself.

May heaven grant that my courageous colleague shall be able, with his army, to suppress this filthy gang of Catilina's brigands![3] I too, as a citizen, with the help of yourselves and all decent men, will shatter and crush this monstrosity which our country has conceived and is bringing to birth. Let us consider, however, what will happen if these plots elude our grip and come flooding back again next year. There will be only one consul, and he will be preoccupied, not in organizing the war but in trying to find a substitute colleague. There are people who will be impeding what he does. And then that appalling, pestilential horror of Catilina's sedition will burst out once more. It will spread speedily over the lands adjoining the city. Frenzy will rage on the speakers' platform, terror in the Senate-house, plotting in the Forum, military occupation of the Field of Mars, devastation throughout the countryside. In every home and

1. Cicero again has the hostile Quintus Caecilius Metellus Nepos (tribune in 62) in mind.

2. In 211 Hannibal had advanced as far as the Anio, only three miles from Rome.

3. In fact Cicero's fellow-consul, Gaius Antonius Hybrida, cautiously absented himself from the final battle against Catilina's army, which was defeated, and Catilina killed, by Marcus Petreius near Pistoria in January 62.

every place we shall have violence and incendiarism to fear. All these catastrophes have long been brewing. But if our state is duly equipped with the guardians it needs, the wisdom of our officials and the vigilance of private citizens will have no difficulty in averting even the greatest disasters.

What should carry the greatest weight with everyone is the safety of our nation. And in supporting that cause, gentlemen, since things are as I have described them, I cite my devotion to our country, of which you are very well aware, as my motive for presenting you with a warning. I cite my authority as consul to exhort you. I cite the formidable danger that threatens us as the cause of my entreaty. And what I warn and exhort and entreat you is this. Lucius Murena is enduring serious physical and mental distress. He is an unhappy person now, but has recently had cause to rejoice.[1] Do not bury his newly found joy beneath a new load of grief! It was only just now that he seemed a fortunate man, honoured by the highest reward that the Roman people could give him; because he was the first man to have honoured his long-established family, and his ancient home town,[2] with a consulship. And yet at this present time instead, gentlemen, he is suffering and mourning. He is ill. Tears and sorrow have torn him apart. He is your suppliant, gentlemen, he calls on your loyalty, he begs for your compassion, he looks to your power and your resources. Jurymen, I beg you by the immortal gods! He believed that this office would glorify his name. Do not, instead, wrest it out of his hands! If you did so, you would also be depriving him of all the distinctions he had already won in the past. You would be destroying every particle of his rank and position.

Murena has never unjustly injured anyone. He has never caused offence, or acted against anyone's wishes. He has never provided a motive for anyone at home or abroad to hate him – and that is putting it mildly. Gentlemen of the jury, Lucius Murena pleads and appeals to you, if you can find it in your hearts to respond, begging you to grant him your sympathy, to offer a place of refuge for a man who is in trouble, to support the claims of decency! One ought to feel very sorry, gentlemen, for a man who has been robbed of his consulship. For with the consulship lost, everything else is lost too. As for *envying* a man who has become consul, on the other hand, no

1. i.e. because he has been elected consul.

2. Lanuvium in Latium.

one could possibly do so at a time like this – when that office stands isolated and exposed to seditious crowds, and the plots of conspirators, and the weapons of Catilina, and every possible danger and injurious assault. So how, gentlemen, anyone could be jealous of Murena, or any other consul for that matter, because of election to this noble office, I fail altogether to see. But what I do see, because they are before my very eyes, are the reasons why compassion should be felt. And you can see and appreciate them too.

May Jupiter avert the omen from what I am going to say next. But let us just suppose, for a moment, that you are going to vote to condemn Murena. Then, in that case, I am completely at a loss to say in what direction the poor man will turn. Not, surely, to his home, where he would behold the mask of his eminent father,[1] which only a few days ago he saw crowned with a laurel wreath in thanksgiving for his election as consul: whereas now, in sharp contrast, his father would have been utterly cast down into mourning and humiliation, if he knew that his son had suffered such a dishonour! Nor could Murena go, it is abundantly clear, to his poor mother, who has just kissed her son when she learnt he had been elected consul but would now be tormented by the anxious fear that this very same son was in imminent danger of being robbed of his entire position.

But I am wasting time by speaking of his mother and his home, since the new legal penalty[2] would deprive him of both, not to speak of the company and sight of all his friends as well. Would the unfortunate man, then, have to go into banishment? One wonders, however, where he could go. To the east, perhaps, where for so many years he was a staff officer, and commanded armies, and performed great deeds? Yet to go back, in disgrace, to a place which you had earlier left, loaded with honours, is utterly degrading. Or should one think of him hiding himself at the opposite end of the world? There, Transalpine Gaul could see the man whom it so recently and happily beheld, no longer crowned with the grandest authority as he had been then, but a grieving and mourning exile. One can imagine, too, how he would feel in that province when he

1. In the more distinguished houses, the masks of leading forebears were preserved, and decorated with wreaths, when a member of the family had been awarded a triumph or elected to a high office.

2. Under Cicero's own *Lex Tullia de ambitu*, of this year 63.

saw his brother Gaius Murena.[1] How sad Gaius would feel! How gloomy would the feelings of Lucius be! Their fortunes and their talk would indeed have suffered a mighty change. For that would be the place where, only a few days before, messengers and letters had made it known that Lucius Murena had been elected consul, and guests and friends had sped off to Rome to congratulate him. Yet now he would be appearing, in that very same place, to bring the news that he had become the victim of total disaster.

Such a situation would be cruel, miserable and grievous. It would also, gentlemen, be wholly out of keeping with your own record of kindness and compassion. If I am right in saying that, confirm the honour that the Roman people has conferred upon Lucius Murena! Give our country back its consul! Reward him for his decency! Grant this gift to his dead father, to his clan and to his family, and to the noble town of Lanuvium, whose many, sorrowing, representatives you have seen throughout this trial!

At the ancestral shrine of Juno the Deliverer at Lanuvium every Roman consul is obliged to offer sacrifice.[2] This consul Murena is her fellow-townsman and her very own. Do not drag him away from that holy place. If my testimonial carries any weight at all, if my endorsement has any authority whatever, I, as consul, commend him as consul to yourselves. And I do so with this promise and guarantee. He will make every effort for peace. He will strongly favour honest men. He will oppose rebellion most actively. He will be courageous in war. And he will be a formidable opponent of this conspiracy which is now undermining our country.

1. Whom he had left in charge of the province when he returned for the consular election.

2. The famous temple of Juno Sospita.

CHAPTER 3

FOR BALBUS: The Admission of Foreigners to Citizenship

Cicero's speech for Balbus is important for two reasons. First, because it shows him, in the interests of statesmanship, deserting his principles once again. And secondly, and more important, because it illustrates, and demonstrates, one of the greatest and most telling strengths of the Roman government, which was its comparative readiness to accept foreigners as citizens, something that the Greek city states had never been willing to do on anything like such a scale.[1]

For Lucius Cornelius Balbus was a foreigner, a man of Gades (Cadiz) in Spain who was, therefore, a Phoenician, a Semite who no doubt did not look like a Roman at all. But he was a very powerful person at Gades, and had made himself indispensable to the leaders of Roman political life. During the war against the rebel Quintus Sertorius in Spain (79–72/71) he had served the Romans with distinction, receiving their citizenship as a result, through the agency of Pompey (72).[2] *Subsequently, he formed a close connection with Julius Caesar, who, as governor of Further Spain, employed him as a senior staff officer (61). Then, towards the end of 60, Balbus played a prominent part in the negotiations which brought Pompey, Caesar and Crassus together in the informal but dictatorial First Triumvirate.*

During the Gallic War, Caesar took Balbus on to his staff once again. But when, in 56, the Triumvirate seemed to be breaking up, its enemies launched an attack on Balbus's right to citizenship, and brought their case

1. Though J.S. Reid, *Ciceronis Pro Balbo Oratio* (1879), p. 12, thought that Rome was far too grudging.

2. His citizenship was ratified by the *Lex Gellia Cornelia* (of the consuls Lucius Gellius Poplicola and Cnaeus Cornelius Lentulus Clodianus) of that year, in common with other enfranchisements conferred by Pompey. Balbus probably took his name Cornelius from Lucius Cornelius Lentulus Crus (consul in 49), who must have recommended him for citizenship.

before one of the standing courts.[1] *They mobilized a man from Gades as prosecutor, and the defence was entrusted to Pompey, Crassus and Cicero. Cicero's acquiescence in this role was questionable on moral grounds. First, there was a shadow over his relations with Balbus himself. For Balbus had tried to induce him to join the Triumvirate when it was formed, but Cicero had refused, since, as a convinced Republican, he had a rooted objection to the autocratic Triumvirate and all that it stood for. But the Triumvirate, apparently breaking at the seams, had just been revived at the Conference of Luca (Lucca) in 56, and Cicero, as we saw in the Introduction, had lost his independence of action. He had lost it so thoroughly that he was persuaded to make a number of speeches in the Senate on behalf of the triumvirs.*[2] *The second was his defence of Balbus.*

Numerous technicalities were involved, and these I have omitted in the translation that follows.[3] *I have instead concentrated on the two points I mentioned at the beginning of this note. The more important of them was Rome's relative willingness to give citizenship to foreigners, which was to prove extremely valuable. And the other was Cicero's own* volte-face, *and his explanation of it. He had been against the triumvirs, but now he was speaking on behalf of a cause they favoured. He was doing so because they were in power, and because the demands of orderly government (as well as his own interests) required that he should support them. He explains this with care, and reminds us of the dilemmas which afflict politicians at all periods, and is not therefore entirely unconvincing.*

FOR BALBUS

If neither our generals, nor the Senate, nor the Assembly of the Roman people, are going to be allowed, by offering rewards, to induce the bravest and best of men from allied, friendly states to incur perils for our own benefit, then in tough and dangerous times

1. Probably the *quaestio de maiestate*, set up by the tribune Lucius Appuleius Saturninus in 103. Subsequently the court, concerned with 'injury' to the Roman people, played a large part in the savage infighting of the late Republic. Balbus's enemies cited the *Lex Papia* of Gaius Papius (65) which, although its exact provisions are unknown, was evidently designed to stop the illegal exercise of citizen rights, by the expulsion of foreigners.
2. The first was *On the Consular Provinces* (56); cf. Introduction.
3. I have indicated some of these matters in Appendix 1.

we shall be depriving ourselves of a tremendous advantage and, on many occasions, of the most vital assistance.

Heavens above, I cannot hope to imagine what sorts of alliance and friendship and treaty we can possibly have in mind for ourselves if we are going to interpret them to mean that our country, when it is in danger, has to be deprived of the support of citizens of Massilia or Gades or Saguntum![1] If these are states that have produced men who by their own endeavours have rendered aid to our leaders, who at their own risk have safeguarded our supplies, who have many times engaged in hand-to-hand battles against people who are our enemies, who have repeatedly exposed themselves to the weapons of our foes, imperilling their own lives and confronting the prospects of death, are they never, on any conditions whatever, to be rewarded by the citizenship which it is in our power to offer them?

For the Roman people, it would indeed be a serious matter not to be able to make use of allies of exceptional merit, the sort of men who are willing to share whatever perils we ourselves become involved in. And as for our allies, and the communities we are now talking about who are bound to us by treaties, it is an injury and an insult that these most loyal of allies with whom we have been so closely associated should be dismissed as ineligible for honours of the kind – which are available even to communities that pay us tribute,[2] and even, indeed, to our enemies, and often, actually, to slaves.

For we know very well that Roman citizenship has been conferred even on numerous members of tribute-paying communities in Africa, Sicily, Sardinia and our other provinces. We are aware, also, that enemies, once they have defected to our commanders and performed important services to our country, have likewise been rewarded with citizenship.[3] And even slaves, too, whose legal position and situation are as low as can be, are very frequently

1. Friendship between Rome and Massilia, a Greek (Phocaean) colony founded in *c.* 600 BC, dated from at least *c.* 400. Gades, originally Phoenician as we have seen, was a *civitas foederata* (city bound to Rome by a treaty) from 206. Saguntum's protection by the Romans, dating from *c.* 231, was one of the principal causes of the Second Punic War.

2. The *civitates stipendiariae*, the least privileged category of community.

3. The prototype, according to tradition, was Lucius Mamilius, dictator of Tusculum, in 458 BC.

granted their freedom – that is to say, citizenship – because of the valuable contributions they have made to our national interests.[1]

I find it strange, therefore, that you, as patron of treaties and of states bound by treaty-rights to Rome, should wish to demote the people of Gades, your own fellow-citizens, to such a debased condition that they do not enjoy this privilege.[2] What you are saying is that, although those whom, with important assistance from your own forefathers,[3] we have reduced by force of arms and brought under our rule are entitled to be presented with our citizenship by the Senate and our generals, with the authorization of the Roman people, the same right is to be denied to your own people of Gades! . . .

Imagine, for a moment, that rewards for valour were abolished. That would practically be the same as saying that these people have been totally forbidden to take any part whatever in the wars that we fight. In the whole of human history you can find extremely few men who, even on behalf of their own country, have gone to the lengths of actually hazarding their lives in face of an enemy's weapons when no reward was offered them for doing so. Well, that being the case, do you really suppose that anyone whatever would be willing, in aid of a foreign state, to expose himself to the same sort of mortal peril, when not merely no reward is offered him for doing so, but, worse, any such action on his part is explicitly prohibited! . . .

I want to lay down the general proposition that no community exists in any part of the world, whether estranged from the Roman people by hostile feelings and animosities of some kind or bound to it by ties of affectionate loyalty, which forbids us to transfer one of its citizens to ourselves, and present him with Roman citizenship. Conversely, our own ancestors, right from the very beginnings of Rome, were enabled, by divine guidance, to establish our own truly admirable legal arrangements. They laid it down that none of

1. Slaves had been rewarded in this way on several occasions in the Second Punic War.

2. The prosecutor, an unknown man from Gades, is described sarcastically as its 'patron' (Gades had also appointed Balbus to that role). This prosecutor, we are told (*For Balbus*, 32), had lost his civil rights owing to a criminal conviction. But he would get them back if he launched a successful prosecution.

3. This reading is uncertain. It has been alternatively suggested that there was a reference to Cnaeus Pompeius Magnus (Pompey) here.

us can be a citizen of more than one state (since a different state inevitably means a different legal system). And those same men also provided that it was impossible for anyone to be removed from the register of citizens against his will,[1] or compelled to remain on it against his will either. For the immovable basis of our freedom rests on the unrestricted power of every one of us to keep or renounce his citizenship as he wishes.

Yet what has unquestionably done more than anything else to create our empire and increase the glory of the Roman people is the fact that Romulus, the founder of our city, instructed us by the treaty he concluded with the Sabines[2] that it is desirable for this nation of ours to be enlarged by the enrolment even of enemies as citizens. Relying on Romulus's authority and precedent, our forefathers never paused in their conferments and bestowals of citizenship. That is why numerous inhabitants of Latium – the men of Tusculum and Lanuvium for example – and whole communities of peoples such as the Sabines and Volscians and Hernicans, were admitted as citizens.[3] And none of those peoples would have been compelled to change their status in this way, unless they had actually wanted to. Nor, when they acquired this citizenship of ours by the gift of the Roman people, was this ever regarded as an infringement of any treaty that we had concluded with them . . .

The men of Gades call to our generals to support their case: men who are now dead, although their immortal memory and glory still

1. Cicero also recalls this principle in two other speeches, *For Caecina*, 95ff., and *About his Home*, 77.

2. Sabines coalesced with the Latins in Rome at a very early date; their homes were on the Quirinal and Esquiline Hills, whereas the Latins dwelt on the Palatine.

3. The Latin League had made a treaty with Rome (the *foedus Cassianum*, named after Spurius Cassius Vecellinus), supposedly in 493 BC. It was abolished in 338. Tusculum was absorbed into the Roman state in 381 and again, after rebellion, in 338, when Lanuvium and other towns also obtained Roman citizenship. The Sabines in their own country, after conquest, received second-class citizenship (*civitas sine suffragio*) in 290, and full citizenship in 268. Latin colonies were established in Volscian territory in the early fourth century. Some Hernican towns received second-class citizenship after a war against Rome (306).

remain alive: the Scipios, the Brutuses, the Crassuses, the Metelluses.[1] They also call upon Cnaeus Pompeius Magnus, who is here with us today, to offer his testimony. When he was fighting a fierce and mighty war a long distance from their own walls,[2] they assisted him with supplies and with money. And now, at this present time, they call also upon the Roman people – whom they helped by providing grain, when grain was expensive, as indeed they have often done before. They call upon the Romans to confirm that they, the people of Gades, can justifiably demand that if any Gaditan has shown exceptional bravery on our behalf he shall have a right, for the sakes of himself and his children, to be admitted to our camps, to the headquarters of our generals, to the places where our standards are pitched and the ranks of our soldiers in battle. And by these onward steps he shall finally be promoted to citizenship.

But what you are claiming, on the contrary, is that whereas Africans, Sardinians and Spaniards, men whose lands and whose money, in taxes, we have taken away from them, should be allowed, nevertheless, to gain our citizenship when they have performed courageous actions, the people of Gades on the other hand, whose services, time-honoured traditions, loyalties, shared perils and treaty relations bind them to ourselves so closely, should be forbidden to enjoy the same privilege! Then, surely, the conclusion of the Gaditans will be that their treaty with us means nothing at all, since, instead, they have received nothing at our hands except a set of supremely unjust restrictions . . .

I suggest we can offer you a precedent for the alternative course of action that I am proposing: under the name of Gaius Marius.[3]

1. e.g. Publius Cornelius Scipio Africanus the elder and younger (Aemilianus), and Decimus Junius Brutus Callaicus (consul in 138) who triumphed over the Gallaeci while governor of Further Spain. After 'the Brutuses' a name seems to be missing, and the 'Crassuses' is not certain: the reference could be to Publius Licinius Crassus Dives (consul in 97), who commanded in Spain and triumphed in 93. The next reference is to Quintus Caecilius Metellus Pius (consul in 80), who commanded during the war against Quintus Sertorius as proconsul of Further Spain (79–71).

2. i.e. the war against the rebel Quintus Sertorius (see last note). Pompey assumed the command in 76.

3. Gaius Marius (consul 107, etc.) was Cicero's fellow-townsman from Arpinum, and hero.

You cannot, I am sure, think of anyone more distinguished for his impressive and steadfast conduct, more pre-eminent as a man of courage, wisdom and conscientious principle. Now, Marius made Marcus Annius Appius, a fine and admirable man from Iguvium, a Roman citizen. He also conferred citizenship upon two entire cohorts from Camerinum,[1] although he was fully aware that our existing treaty with that town was already impeccably impressive and equitable.[2] It is impossible, then, to condemn Balbus without condemning Marius as well.

So let your imagination, for a while, rest upon that great man: because he can no longer be with you in person. Look at him with your mind's eye, since you cannot actually gaze on him yourselves. Let him remind you that he knew about the treaties with Iguvium and Camerinum, that he was conscious of the precedents, that he was not unversed in warfare. And here, too, are other matters that he can call to your attention. He was a learner under the younger Publius Cornelius Scipio Africanus (Aemilianus), and served under him in the army.[3] He had got his training while engaged in military duties, and as an officer in time of war. Even if he had merely read in books about all the important wars which, instead, he actually fought and won, even if he had only served under as many consuls as the consulships which he had held himself,[4] he could still, even so, have learnt all about the laws of war, and got to know them thoroughly. And what emerged was his total certainty that no treaty in the world could prevent him from acting in the interests of the Roman state. What he did was to select the most valorous citizens from communities which had shown us exceptional friendliness and devotion. And neither the treaty with Iguvium nor the treaty with Camerinum contained any clause whatever which suggested that rewards for bravery should not be conferred upon their citizens by the people of Rome . . .

If, then, the countenance of Gaius Marius, his voice, his piercing

1. The cohort was a military unit divided into six centuries. There were ten cohorts in a legion. In 101 Marius enfranchised two cohorts from the town for their gallant fighting against German invaders, the Cimbri.

2. Rome's treaties with Camerinum and Iguvium dated from 310 and *c.* 308 respectively. The former at least was the better, 'equal' type of treaty (*foedus aequum*).

3. In the Numantine War in Spain (139–133).

4. Seven in number.

general's eyes, the military triumphs he had lately won,[1] his physical presence, were so potent while he was alive, then let our memory of him, let the eternal renown of that most noble and intrepid of men be no less potent now! Let us distinguish between citizens who just make an impression on their contemporaries and those who are truly valiant. The former, as long as they live, may enjoy the fruits of their popular appeal. But the latter, such as Marius, even after they are dead – if any man who has defended our empire can ever be said to die – shall retain their immortal prestige for evermore . . .

And then take this man who is present with us today, Marcus Licinius Crassus, by whom all this material that I have just been briefly surveying has already been set before you with great thoroughness. For he too bestowed citizenship upon an inhabitant of the federated town of Avennio.[2] And Crassus is a wise, imposing personage, whose record in granting citizenship can certainly not be described as over-generous. Nor would you, in this record, wish to invalidate the same sort of favours, or rather decisions taken and deeds performed, by Cnaeus Pompeius Magnus, too, whose actions were on similar lines.

For the fact is that if the men who fight for our country at the cost of their own exertions and their own perils deserve other rewards, as they do, then they surely also deserve the status of Roman citizens – since it is for the citizens of Rome, after all, that they have been facing dangers and confronting the weapons of war. If, in any place whatever, they have been fighting to defend this empire of ours, then I profoundly desire that they should become our fellow-citizens. (And I hope, conversely, that everyone who has launched an attack on our nation should be deprived of our citizenship, if he possessed it.) Our eminent poet Ennius made Hannibal exhort his soldiers in these terms: 'Any man who smites our enemy shall be, as far as I am concerned, a Carthaginian, whoever he is, and whatever his country.'[3] Nor did Ennius merely mean these

1. In 104 he celebrated a triumph for victory over Jugurtha, king of Numidia. In 101, he triumphed, with Quintus Lutatius Catulus, over the Germans (Cimbri and Teutones).

2. In Gallia Narbonensis (the Roman province in southern Transalpine Gaul). Originally a dependency of Massilia, Avennio became a Latin colony (Pliny the elder, *Natural History*, III, 4, 36).

3. Ennius, *Annals*, VIII, referring to Hannibal's invasion of Italy during the Second Punic War (218–201).

words to be an exhortation by Hannibal on that particular occasion: he meant them to be an assertion which any and every commander might make, at any time. The country from which a soldier actually comes is regarded by a general as irrelevant; that has always been so, and it still is. And so they have admitted courageous men, of whatever origin, to their citizenship – and have very often preferred the merit of people of no exalted birth to gutless noblemen . . .

Now, take Balbus. To calm the feelings of those who feel envious of Balbus is a relatively simple task. They display their envy as men usually do. They speak nastily about him at parties. They are malicious about him in social conversation. They attack him with the venom of envy, but also with the venom of slander. The people, however, whom Balbus has greater reason to be afraid of are those who are the enemies not of himself, but of his friends – or who envy those friends. For as regards Balbus himself, no one has ever been his enemy, or could justifiably have become one. He has always been a man who supported sound people,[1] who showed respect for men of position and status. While on the closest terms with an extremely powerful Roman[2] at a time of our gravest troubles and disagreements, he none the less avoided ever causing offence to people who belonged to the other side, and the other way of thinking, by word or by deed, or even by the expression on his face.

It was my destiny, or the destiny of my country, that the burden of those times, which involved us all, should have fallen upon myself and myself alone. But Balbus never exulted in my downfall,[3] or on the miseries which, it must be added, all you fellow-Romans also underwent. On the contrary, while I was away, his assistance of every kind, his compassionate tears, his industrious endeavours, his keen sympathy, were a blessing to the whole of my family. It is on the basis of what they told me, and in response to their entreaties,

1. *Boni*, which often means 'conservatives' in Cicero, though that was hardly the cause dearest to Balbus, who supported Caesar: see next note. Yet Balbus, as Cicero adds here, tried not to offend the conservatives.

2. Julius Caesar. The 'troubles and disagreements' relate to the accusations of illegality launched against Caesar during his consulship (59), and the Senate's opposition to his alliance with Pompey and Crassus in the First Triumvirate.

3. Cicero's exile (58–57) – which, at the time, he had been inclined to blame, not unjustly, on Caesar.

that I am now offering him my own services in return, with a view, as I stated at the outset, to repaying him the debt of gratitude that I owe him.

Jurymen, I know very well that you feel affection and love for those who took the lead in championing my welfare and securing my rehabilitation. That being so, I earnestly hope that all that Balbus did, which was everything a man could possibly have done, and everything his situation[1] allowed, will meet with your approval and concurrence. Now that he is attacked, it is not his own enemies who are attacking him. For, as I said, he does not have any. No, his attackers are the enemies of his friends,[2] and those attackers are both numerous and powerful. It was against himself, not anyone else, that Cnaeus Pompeius Magnus, in the eloquent and powerful speech he delivered yesterday, told those assailants to direct their attack, if they wanted to, seeking, by that proposal, to divert them from their unequal, unjust contest and conflict with Balbus.

May I suggest, gentlemen, a rule of behaviour that will be not only objectively fair in itself but also extremely advantageous both to ourselves and to every one of our intimate friends. The rule I propose is that we should limit our enmities to actual enemies of our own, but that we show restraint when it comes to dealing with those enemies' friends. What I would like these attackers to do therefore, if my advice carries any weight in the matter – and they will be able to see that altered circumstances and personal experience have taught me a lot – what I would like them to do is to profit from my example and distance themselves from that vicarious type of feud I have mentioned, which carries more serious consequences. Certainly, in defence of what one believes to be a rightful cause, I have always maintained that political disputation is an activity fully worthy of notable and courageous men. Nor, I hope, in the performance of that labour, duty, obligation, have I myself ever been found wanting. But it is a type of behaviour that only makes sense so long as it is beneficial to our country, or if not beneficial at least not injurious.

While others just felt sad, however, about what was happening, I

1. i.e. his friendship with Caesar.

2. Caesar and Cnaeus Pompeius Magnus (Pompey), who with Crassus had formed the dictatorial First Triumvirate in 70.

personally, at the time, grieved and mourned aloud.[1] But as to how things have turned out, what is the point of trying to overthrow what we cannot alter, instead of just accepting what has, in fact, happened? The Senate has honoured Gaius Julius Caesar with the most complimentary form of public thanksgiving, to last for a number of days exceeding all precedent.[2] It has also agreed to pay his victorious army (although the treasury is so short of funds). It has approved the allocation of ten officers to its commander's staff. It has ruled that he should not be superseded under the Sempronian Law.[3] It was I myself who initiated and moved these proposals.[4] For I believed it less desirable to be influenced by my old difference of opinion with Caesar than to adjust myself to the present needs of our country, and work for national harmony.

Others do not take the same view. They are people, perhaps, who are harder to budge from an attitude, once they have decided to adopt it. I am not apportioning blame to anyone. But I do not agree with everybody either, and I do not regard it as inconsistent to change my views and my course, like a ship's course at sea, according to the weather in which our country finds itself. But some people, I see, having once disliked a man, are determined to go on disliking him for ever. If I am right in saying that such people exist, what I ask them to do is to direct their attacks against the leaders of the state themselves, and not against those leaders' subordinates and adherents. Some, it is true, will regard attacking the leaders as merely perverse. But others will consider it a virtue. In any case, attacks on mere subordinates will be generally seen as unfair, not to say cruel. Some people's feelings, perhaps, cannot be soothed by any means whatever. But as for your own feelings, gentlemen, I am sure that they have been soothed, not by anything that I myself have said, but by your own humane instincts.

What I would also suggest is that Balbus's friendship with Caesar should in no way be considered a reason for blaming Caesar, but

1. Cicero refers again to the First Triumvirate (60), which overrode all the institutions of the Republic.

2. For his victories against the Gauls.

3. The *Lex Sempronia de provinciis consularibus* of Gaius Sempronius Gracchus (122 or 123), which instructed the Senate, before the consular elections, to allot the provinces to be governed by the new consuls after their year of office at Rome.

4. In his speech *On the Consular Provinces* (56).

ought, on the contrary, to be regarded as a major compliment to him. They became acquainted when Balbus was still very young. Caesar is an extremely discriminating man, but Balbus made an impression on him. Caesar had numerous friends, but Balbus ranked as one of the closest of them. When Caesar became praetor and then consul,[1] he appointed Balbus as his Chief Engineer.[2] He valued Balbus's judgement, he applauded his loyalty, he warmly appreciated his services and devotion. Time after time, Balbus has shared many of his labours. Today, perhaps, he shares some of his advantages.[3] But if these are facts that damage him in your eyes, it seems to me that what you are saying is that reliable behaviour ought not to be recompensed by rewards.

Gaius Julius Caesar, now, is far away. He is in regions which, geographically speaking, are at the ends of the world, and which, in terms of his own achievement, are the boundaries of the Roman empire. Gentlemen, do not, in heaven's name, permit that this bitter news be conveyed to him: that his Chief Engineer, a man whom he loves and with whom he is very close, has been destroyed by your votes – not because of anything that he himself has done wrong, but because he is Caesar's friend.

1. Consul in 59.

2. *Praefectus fabrum*; but the title bore little relation to his duties, which were those of a general assistant to the commander.

3. e.g. some of the gold which Caesar had acquired in Gaul.

CHAPTER 4

ON THE STATE
(III): THE IDEAL FORM OF GOVERNMENT; (V, VI): THE GOOD STATESMAN

It is important to see what sort of state a man who was as experienced in government as Cicero was, and who wrote as brilliantly as he did, thought that Rome ought to have.

He gave us the benefit of his views on this subject, which no other Roman had ever handled before in anything like so systematic a form, at a time when he was no longer in the forefront of affairs, because the Republic had been, in fact – as we have just seen – superseded by the autocratic First Triumvirate of Pompey, Caesar and Crassus. Cicero started work on his study On the State *(otherwise known as* On Justice*) in 54, and, after various changes of plan, completed it in 51, if not earlier. It takes the form of a discussion which had supposedly occurred in 129, in the garden of Publius Cornelius Scipio Africanus the younger (Aemilianus).*[1] *Besides Scipio himself, eight others took part in the discussion.*[2]

In Book I of the six-book work, Scipio defines the nature of the state, and discusses the three principal forms of reputable government (kingship,

1. Scipio (consul in 147 and 134), the conqueror of Carthage in the Third Punic War, was not a professional philosopher, like Plato's principal speaker Socrates, but a practical man. The idealistic picture Cicero paints of him (identifying him, sometimes, with himself) is modified by accounts from others, which refer to Scipio's harder side. Cicero indicates, elsewhere, that his reason for placing the discussion in a past epoch was so as not to cause offence. Moreover, that past time had been a Golden Age, it seemed, when Republican institutions were still sound and not threatened by autocracy.

2. Gaius Laelius 'Sapiens' (consul in 140), Lucius Furius Philus (136), Manius Manilius (149), Quintus Aelius Tubero, Scipio's nephew (118), Publius Rutilius Rufus (105), Spurius Mummius, Stoic, orator and poet, Gaius Fannius (122), and Quintus Mucius Scaevola Augur, the son-in-law of Laelius (117). The 'dialogue' form, which seems rather artificial and ineffective but does allow new points to be made, goes back to Aristotle rather than Plato (*Letters to Atticus*, XIII, 19, 4); long speeches predominate.

aristocracy and democracy). In Book II he briefly traces the history of the Roman state. Book III, of which the surviving portions (which form its greater part) are translated in the pages that follow, turns on the defence of justice, and contains a vital discussion of the eternal, immutable law, based on reason, which draws an absolute distinction between right and wrong.[1] *Books IV and V, like so much of the work, have survived only in a very fragmentary condition, but what remains of V will be reproduced here: it speaks of the ideal statesman and 'leader'* (rector reipublicae) *and the qualities he needs. Book VI emphasizes the value and reward of the statesman's endeavours, and concludes with* Scipio's Dream.[2] *Cicero's own political position, as well as the identity of the* rector, *has been discussed in the Introduction.* On the State *seeks to present the ancestral constitution as it was – or should have been – a century earlier, accepting the Stoic view that individual rights could be reconciled with those of society.*

ON THE STATE (III)

When Reason found people uttering formless, confused sounds with uncouth voices, it took these sounds and divided them out into separate classes, and fastened names upon things just as one must fasten labels. By this means, human beings, who had been isolated from each other before, were joined together, one with another, by the convenient means of communication provided by speech.[3] Reason also noted and represented all the sounds of the voice, innumerable though they seemed, by a few characters which it invented for the purpose, so that conversations could be conducted with persons who were not present, and our aspirations, and records of what had happened in the past, could be written down. The addition that came next was the system of numbers, which is both indispensable for human life and unique by virtue of its

1. This doctrine of Natural Law, based on Stoic ideas, dominated the thought of many eighteenth-century scholars.

2. Translated in *Cicero: On the Good Life* (Penguin Classics), pp. 337–55.

3. Aristotle, in his *Politics*, I, 1253a, had written of how language distinguishes human beings from animals and enables human society and political life to come into being.

unchangeability and permanence.[1] This, too, was the art which first prompted us to look up into the sky and gaze, with understanding, upon the motion of the heavenly bodies, and to list nights and days in numerical order.

Finally, people's minds rose to even greater heights, and the actions and thoughts they were able to achieve proved worthy of the gift which, as I have said, they received from the gods.[2] Certain thinkers discuss the principles according to which we should direct our lives, and they are certainly great men. We must recognize their learning, and their ability to instruct us about mental and moral excellence.

Yet we must not forget that there is another science, too, which is by no means contemptible: whether it was discovered by men who had personal experience of various sorts of state, or was evolved by secluded study of the abstract thinkers of whom I have just spoken. I refer to the art of government and of maintaining good order among nations. This is an art which, in men of good qualities, brings into being, as it often has in the past, merits of an extraordinary and almost superhuman calibre. Some of the men who were engaged in the discussion that I am recording here maintained the view that the faculties with which the human mind is naturally endowed, and which are broadened by public experience, can be improved still further by study and by the wider knowledge of life that it confers. If that is so, then, clearly, anyone who has supplemented his natural and practical qualifications by learning of this kind is superior to everybody else. For, unmistakably, the union of experience in the conduct of great affairs with study and erudition of that wider sort must be something of unique value. Publius Cornelius Scipio Africanus the younger, Gaius Laelius and Lucius Furius Philus came extremely close to that ideal. For they were eager to miss nothing whatever that might help a leading man to achieve the highest degree of excellence. And, in consequence, they enriched their own local, ancestral customs by adding the foreign erudition that went back to Socrates.

And, certainly, anyone who is desirous and capable of achieving both those objectives – that is to say, who has broadened his

1. Cicero enlarged on the consequences of the discovery of numbers in his treatise *On the Nature of the Gods*, II, 153.

2. i.e. intelligence.

inherited traditions by the infusion of additional scholarship – merits, in my opinion, the highest possible praise. But let us suppose that only one of these two paths towards wisdom is feasible. Then, in that case, even if, to some people, a studious life devoted to the higher learning may appear to have superior attractions, surely a statesman's life is, in fact, more distinguished and more admirable. For that is the life by which a truly great man achieves his greatness. Consider, for example, Manius Curius Dentatus, 'whom none could overcome by sword or by gold'.[1]

True, both classes of men, the theoretical thinker and the practical statesman, can rightly be described as wise. But the difference between them is that the one class nourishes the gifts of nature by study and instruction, whereas the other does so by the guidance of institutions and laws. Our own country, itself, has produced a great many men – perhaps one should not after all call them actually 'wise', since that is a term of which the employment has been so heavily restricted; but anyway they have deserved the highest degree of commendation, since it is they who have given effect to what the 'wise' first invented and taught.

Think how many excellent states exist at this present time, and have existed in the past. And remember that to establish a state that is going to be durable demands the greatest intelligence that nature can provide. That being so, we must conclude that even if each of those states possessed only *one* such man, they must have added up to a remarkable number![2]

LAELIUS: For the purposes of argument, see if you can offer a defence of injustice!

PHILUS: What a fine cause you have handed over to me – to speak in favour of evil!

LAELIUS: Yes, I can see what you have reason to fear. You are afraid that, if you repeat the customary arguments against justice, you might be supposed also to approve of them. Yet you yourself, I must point out, stand for old-fashioned integrity and honour to an

1. Ennius, *Annals*, XII. Dentatus had been consul in 290 etc.

2. The fragmentary passage that (perhaps) followed here referred to the Latins, Sabines, Volscians, Samnites, Etruscans, Magna Graecia (the Greek cities of southern Italy and Sicily), the Assyrians, Persians and Carthaginians. Thereafter, Philus is evidently asked to defend the cause of injustice.

almost unparalleled degree! And your habit of arguing on the other side – on the grounds that you find it the easiest way to arrive at the truth – is something with which we are quite familiar.

PHILUS: All right, then. In order to humour you, I will smear myself with dirt, quite deliberately. For that is what people who are looking for gold always feel that they have to do. So we who are looking for justice, which is far more valuable than all the gold in the world,[1] surely ought to do the same, without shrinking from any hardship whatever.

But I only wish that since I am now going to make use of what someone else has said, I could also use his own language! The man I am referring to is Carneades.[2] For he, with his gift for sophistical disputation, was quite accustomed to making the best causes sound ridiculous! And so, after reviewing the arguments of Plato and Aristotle in favour of justice – a subject on which the latter filled four large books[3] – what Carneades then proceeded to do was to refute them![4] From Chrysippus I did not expect anything substantial or impressive.[5] He uses his own peculiar method of argument, analysing everything from a purely verbal rather than a factual point of view.

These heroes acted correctly in exalting the virtue of justice, in disrepair as it was. For justice, when it exists, is the most generous and liberal of all virtues, loving itself less than it loves all the people in the world, and living for the benefit of others rather than of itself. In seating it, therefore, upon that heavenly throne, not far from wisdom itself, those philosophers were perfectly right. But one more thing has to be pointed out. They did not, evidently, lack the desire to exalt justice. For, if they had, what would have been their reason and purpose for writing at all? Nor did they lack the ability to do so, in which, indeed, they surpassed everyone else. Yet their enthusiasm and eloquence alike were undermined by a certain weakness. For the justice into which we are inquiring is not just

1. Cf. Plato, *Republic*, I, 336e.

2. Carneades (214/213–129/128 BC) was the founder of the New or Third Platonic Academy.

3. Aristotle's four-book study of justice is lost.

4. This assertion, quoted by Lactantius, precedes a considerable lacuna.

5. Chrysippus (*c.* 280–207 BC) succeeded Cleanthes as head of the Stoic school.

something that naturally exists, but a quality that is created by those who are occupied in government. It cannot be merely natural, because if it was, justice and injustice would be the same thing to all human beings, like heat and cold, or bitter and sweet.

But that is not the case; on the contrary, beliefs on the subject vary enormously. If, for example, one could climb into Pacuvius's 'chariot of winged snakes'[1] and drop in on many diverse nations and have a good look at them, one would find, first of all, that in Egypt, that most unchanging country of all in which the written records of the events of a vast series of centuries are preserved, a bull is considered a god – which the Egyptians call Apis.[2] And numerous other monsters and animals of every kind are ranked among divinities and regarded as holy. That, to us, appears thoroughly alien. Here in Rome, on the other hand, as in Greece, splendid shrines can be seen, adorned with statues of deities in human form.

Yet the Persians have always considered that to be a blasphemous custom. Indeed, Xerxes I is said to have commanded that the temples of Athens should be burnt down, for this sole reason, that he considered it blasphemous to keep the gods shut up within walls, when they belong to the entire world. Indeed subsequently Philip II of Macedonia, who planned to attack the Persians, and Alexander III the Great, who actually did so,[3] quoted as their pretext their determination to avenge the Greek temples – which the Greeks had decided that they must never rebuild, so that later generations would always have before their eyes this visible memorial of Persian sacrilege.[4]

Furthermore, a considerable number of peoples, unlike ourselves, have believed that the practice of human sacrifice is pious and thoroughly pleasing to the immortal gods. They include the Taurians on the coast of the Euxine Sea, King Busiris of Egypt,[5] and the Gauls and the Carthaginians. Indeed, people's life-styles are sometimes

1. The play of Pacuvius (220–*c.* 130 BC) from which this quotation may have been taken was the *Medus*.

2. The sacred bull worshipped at Memphis.

3. Philip II and Alexander III the Great ruled from 359 to 336 and from 336 to 323 respectively. Xerxes I had reigned in Persia from 486 to 465.

4. Doubtful, because Pericles had undertaken the restoration of these temples.

5. Busiris, in mythology, was the son of the god Neptune (Poseidon), and was killed by Hercules (Heracles).

so divergent that the Cretans[1] and Aetolians consider banditry respectable. As for the Spartans, they declared, habitually, that any territory whatever that they could touch with their spears belonged to themselves![2] And the Athenians, too, swore oaths, in public, pronouncing that every piece of ground that produced olives or grain was their own property. The Gauls, however, consider it degrading to grow grain by manual labour. For that reason they take up arms so that they can go and reap other people's fields. But consider the customs that we – who are, of course, the most just of men! – habitually follow. What we do is to tell the Gauls across the Alps that they must not plant olives and vines, because we want to increase the value of our own. That, you might say, is prudent; 'just' is not the word you could apply to it. One can see, from this example, that what is sensible is not always truly wise. Consider Lycurgus.[3] He invented a series of admirably wise and sensible laws. Yet he felt able to insist, all the same, that the lands of the rich should be cultivated by the poor as if they were slaves.[4]

Moreover, if I wanted to describe the differing ideas of justice, and the divergent institutions and customs and ways of life, that have prevailed, not only in various nations of the world, but even in this single city of our own, I could show you, also, that they have not remained the same, but have been changed in a thousand different ways. Take for example Manius Manilius here, our interpreter of the law. The advice that he generally gave you about women's legacies and inheritance when he was a young man, before the Voconian Law was passed, was not at all the same advice as he would give you now.[5] (Yet that law, I might add, was passed for the benefit of males, and is very unfair to women. For why should a woman not have money of her own? And why should a Vestal Virgin be permitted to have an heir, when her mother cannot? Nor

1. The Cretans had joined the Cilician pirates against the Romans, who annexed the island in 67. The Aetolians had become subject allies of the Romans in 189.

2. This was believed to have been asserted by the fourth-century Spartan general Antalcidas.

3. The legendary founder of the Spartan social, military and constitutional system (*agoge*).

4. Or rather, Helots (the subordinate population).

5. The *Lex Voconia de mulierum hereditatibus* of Quintus Voconius Saxa (169) limited the right of inheritance by women.

can I see why, if a limit had to be set to the amount of property a woman could possess, the daughter of Publius Licinius Crassus Dives Mucianus,[1] provided that she were her father's only child, should be authorized by law to own a hundred million *sesterces*, while three million is more than my own daughter is entitled to own.)[2] . . .

So laws, then, can vary considerably, and can be changed. If they had all come from God, that would not be so. For, in that case, the same laws would be applicable to all, and, besides, a man would not be bound by one law at one time of his life and by another later on. But what I ask, therefore, is this. Let us accept that it is the duty of a just and good man to obey the laws. But *which* laws is he to obey? All the different laws that exist?

There are difficulties here. Inconsistency, between laws, ought to be impermissible, since it is contrary to what nature demands. But the point is that laws are *not* imposed on us by nature – or by our innate sense of justice. They are imposed by the fear of being penalized. In other words, human beings are not just, by nature, at all.[3]

Let us reject, moreover, the argument that, although laws vary, good men naturally follow the true, authentic path of justice, and not merely what is thought to be just. That argument maintains that what a good and just man does is to give everyone his due.[4] (One problem which arises in this connection is what, if anything, we are to grant *dumb animals* as their due. Men of far from mediocre calibre, indeed men of powerful learning such as Pythagoras and Empedocles, insist that identical standards of justice apply to all living creatures, and declare that inexorable penalties await those who ill-treat animals.[5] To do them harm, in other words, seems to them to be criminal.)[6]

★

1. Consul in 131.

2. About fifteen lines are lost here.

3. This is an allusion to the famous Greek controversy about the relative rights of nature (*physis*) and law (*nomos*). Cicero does, however, believe in 'natural law', which overrides specific, local laws.

4. Cf. Plato, *Republic*, I, 331ff.

5. Pythagoras, founder of the Pythagorean philosophy, emigrated from Samos to Croton in *c.* 531. Empedocles of Acragas lived from *c.* 493 to *c.* 433.

6. A passage is lost here.

PHILUS. Anyone who has the power of life and death over a people is a despot – though they prefer to be known as kings, following the example of Jupiter the Best.

When however, instead, a group of men seize the state by exploiting their wealth or noble birth or some other resource, that is a political upheaval, though they call themselves conservatives.[1] If, on the other hand, the people gain the supremacy, and the whole government is conducted according to their wishes, a state of affairs has arisen which is hailed as liberty, but is, in fact, chaos. But when there is a situation of mutual fear, with one person or one class fearing another, then because nobody has sufficient confidence in his own strength a kind of bargain is struck between the ordinary people and the men who are powerful. The result, in that case, is the mixed form of constitution which Scipio recommends.[2] Which means that weakness, not nature or good intention, is the mother of justice.

For we have to choose one of three things. We can perform injustice and not suffer it. Or we can both perform and suffer it. Or we can neither perform it nor suffer it. The most fortunate choice is the first, to perform injustice, if you can get away with it. The second best is neither to perform it nor suffer it. And the worst is to engage in an everlasting turmoil consisting of both performing it and suffering it.[3]

Wisdom, as commonly understood, prompts us to increase our resources, to multiply our riches, to enlarge our frontiers. For the essential significance, surely, of those eulogistic words inscribed upon the monuments of our greatest generals, 'he extended the boundaries of the empire', is that he had extended them by taking territory from someone else. That, then, is the teaching of 'wisdom', that we should rule over as many subjects as possible,

1. *Optimates*, 'the best men' (cf. *boni*). These were the conservatives, who put their measures through the Senate in traditional fashion, in contrast to the *populares*, 'radicals' who bypassed the Senate and applied direct to the Assembly. The term will be analysed further at a later point.

2. A blend of monarchy, oligarchy and democracy.

3. It is perhaps in a hiatus which occurs here that the story of Alexander the Great and the pirate should be placed. When the king asked the pirate what wickedness drove him to harass the sea with his single ship, the answer was: 'The same wickedness that impels you to harass the entire world.'

indulge in pleasures, hold on to power, be rulers and masters. But justice, on the other hand, demands that we should be merciful to all men, act in the interests of the entire human race, give everyone what they are entitled to, and never tamper with religious property or what belongs to the community or to private persons.

If you follow the dictates of what we call wisdom, then, you acquire wealth, power, resources, lofty status, military commands and positions of supreme authority, whether you are a state or a private person. What we, however, are at present considering is the former of these two categories, the state, and so what is done by states assumes priority for our present purpose. True, the same standards of justice apply to states and individuals alike, but the former are what we now have to consider. In particular, not to mention other nations, it is clear enough that our own Roman people, whose history Scipio traced from its beginnings in yesterday's discussion, and whose empire is now world-wide, grew from the smallest to the greatest dimensions by wisdom, and not by justice.[1]

When, however, one sets justice against wisdom in the way I have attempted to do here, the contrast is sometimes blurred by arguments that complicate the issue. The men who put these arguments forward understand very well how to argue;[2] and their reasoning on the subject carries all the more impressive weight because, in the course of their investigation into how to find the good man (a man who himself should be open and frank), they, like him, refrain from using underhand, crafty or dishonest methods of argument. What these philosophers do, then, is take a closer look at the 'wise' man, and put forward the view that he is good not because goodness or justice automatically, or in themselves, offer him satisfaction, but, on the contrary, because a good man's life is free of fear, worry, anxiety and peril, whereas bad men always have something to feel uneasy about, and the prospects of trials and penalties are never out of their sight. No benefit or reward gained by injustice, these thinkers add, is substantial enough to

1. There was an allusion here to the Arcadians and Athenians, who claimed to be autochthonous, so that they were justified in holding the territory they occupied.

2. Cicero is referring to the Epicureans.

counterbalance perpetual fear, or the never-ending thought that some punishment or other is not far away.[1] . . .

Let us imagine that there are two men, one a paragon of virtue, fairness, justice and honesty, and the other an outrageous ruffian. And let us suppose that their country is so misguided that it believes that the good man is an evil, villainous criminal, and that the bad man, on the other hand, is a model of honourable propriety. Then let us go on to suppose that, since this is the unanimous opinion, the good man is attacked, seized, imprisoned, blinded, convicted, chained, branded, expelled and beggared, so that everyone feels, quite rightly, that he is the most wretched man alive. Whereas the bad man, on the other hand, is praised, courted and loved by one and all. Every kind of public office and military command is showered upon him, as well as riches and wealth from every quarter. To sum up, then, he will have the universal reputation of being the best man in the world, who deserves everything good that fortune can give him. Now, I ask you, who could be so mad as to doubt which of the two men he would prefer to be?[2]

The same applies to states, just as much as to individuals. No country would not rather be an unjust master than a just slave. I shall not range far ahead for the example I am going to quote. While I was consul, and you were on my council, the question of the treaty with Numantia came up before me.[3] Everyone knew that treaties had been made already, by Quintus Pompeius and then by Gaius Hostilius Mancinus.[4] Mancinus, a good man, went so far as to favour the bill which I myself had proposed in accordance with a senatorial decree, even though he was to be the sufferer. Pompeius, on the other hand, fought back strongly against an

1. About a page is lost here.

2. Cf. Plato, *Republic*, II, 361f.

3. The Spanish fortress city which led the Celtiberian resistance to Rome.

4. They were consuls in 141 and 137 respectively. Quintus Pompeius made a treaty with the Numantine rebels in Spain which was not accepted by the Senate, and which he himself repudiated. He was subsequently acquitted on a charge of extortion. Mancinus made another treaty, which was likewise disowned, on the younger Scipio's proposal, and Mancinus, with his own consent, was surrendered to the Numantines in expiation. They refused to accept him, however, and he returned to Rome and held a second praetorship. Numantia was finally captured in 133.

equally critical resolution directed against himself. If you are looking for self-denial, honour and integrity, those are the qualities that Mancinus displayed. But if you want rationality, good sense and prudence, Pompeius wins.[1] . . .

LAELIUS:[2] True law is in keeping with the dictates both of reason and of nature. It applies universally to everyone. It is unchanging and eternal. Its commands are summons to duty, and its prohibitions declare that nothing wrongful must be done. As far as good men are concerned, both its commands and its prohibitions are effective; though neither have any effect on men who are bad. To attempt to invalidate this law is sinful. Nor is it possible to repeal any part of it, much less to abolish it altogether. From its obligations neither Senate nor people can release us. And to explain or interpret it we need no one outside our own selves.

There will not be one law at Rome, and another at Athens. There will not be different laws now and in the future. Instead there will be one single, everlasting, immutable law, which applies to all nations and all times. The maker, and umpire, and proposer of this law will be God, the single master and ruler of us all. If a man fails to obey God, then he will be in flight from his own self, repudiating his own human nature. As a consequence, even if he escapes the normal punishment for wrongdoing, he will suffer the penalties of the gravest possible sort . . .

But a state is a more permanent thing than the individuals who form its parts. Individuals sometimes manage to escape the punishments which make an impression on even very stupid people – destitution, exile, imprisonments and beatings – by taking refuge in a speedy death. But even if death, on such occasions, seems to be offering individuals a way of escaping punishment, it actually, instead, amounts to precisely the opposite, indeed an absolutely fatal punishment if it descends upon a state. For a state ought to be so firmly established that it will last for ever. That is to say, whereas it is natural, and when the time comes necessary and desirable, that

1. The rest of Philus's report of the defence of injustice made by Carneades is lost.

2. This is the most famous and influential passage in the *Republic*: cf. *Cicero: Selected Works* (Penguin Classics), pp. 7f. It was preceded by a brief introduction, of which fragments survive – including a criticism of Carneades by Laelius.

human beings should die, for states to do so is not natural at all. Indeed, if we may compare things of very different dimensions, there is something in common between the overthrow and obliteration and extinction of a state and the death and dissolution of the entire universe.

Moreover, some states, and some individuals, have a right to control others.[1] Our own people have gained dominion over the entire world. For there is no doubt at all that nature has granted dominion to everything that is best – to the manifest advantage of the weak. And that, surely, explains why God rules over man, why the human mind rules over the body, and why reason rules over lust and anger, and the other evil qualities of the heart.

A war which is launched without provocation, however, cannot possibly be just. Only if it is undertaken either in retaliation or in self-defence does it qualify for insertion in that category. Nor can any war be regarded as just unless it has been officially declared and proclaimed, and unless reparation has first been demanded. It is by defending our allies that Rome has gained dominion over the whole world.[2]

But lawlessness in individuals must be deprecated with equal determination. Take Tiberius Sempronius Gracchus, for example. Certainly, he kept faith with his fellow-citizens. But he infringed upon the treaty rights of the allies and Latins.[3] Now, let us suppose that, as time goes on, this habit of disregarding legality begins to spread, and transforms our empire from the rule of law to the rule of force. When that happens, nothing will make those who have hitherto obeyed us remain obedient of their own free wills except fear. Our own generation have managed to stay safe, because they have kept on the alert. Yet in the situation I am forecasting I am

1. Cf. Aristotle, *Politics*, I, 1254 A–B.

2. This has been attacked as 'nauseating hypocrisy'. Other fragments, probably to be inserted at this point, reinforce the argument that certain nations and individuals are naturally fitted for, and benefit from, subjection to others. The deification of Hercules and Romulus, for their great services, is referred to, and the incorruptibility of Gaius Fabricius Luscinus (consul in 282 and 278), in the face of the wealth of Pyrrhus of Epirus, and of Manius Curius Dentatus (consul in 290), in rejecting the riches of the Samnites, and thus serving as a model for Marcus Porcius Cato the elder (censor 184).

3. Cicero refers to his confiscation of Italian land, to be distributed to poor citizens. Tiberius Gracchus was tribune in 133.

anxious about what will happen to our descendants – and anxious for the survival of our country, which can only continue to have a permanent future existence if the institutions and customs established by our ancestors remain intact.

After this declaration by Laelius, everyone expressed the greatest satisfaction with what he had said. And the most delighted of all was Scipio, whose enthusiasm knew no bounds.[1] Laelius had stressed that one state must not behave despotically to others. And Scipio, at this juncture, emphasized that it must not behave despotically to its own people either. Indeed, in his opinion, he said, a state which is ruled by a despot really does not deserve to be described as a state at all. For the word, he said, that defines a state is *res publica*, the property of the people, and obviously a country under a despotic regime is not the property of the people at all. On the contrary, it presents a situation in which the entire people is subjugated by the brutal authority of one single man, and there is no shared bond created by the law, so that those who live together in the community – that is to say, among its people – are united by no true partnership whatsoever.

That was the case, for example, in Syracuse. It was a place of the utmost distinction. Indeed, Timaeus[2] described it as not only the largest of all Greek cities, but also the most beautiful. Its citadel was a wonderful sight. And so were its harbours, which extended into the very heart of the town, where their waters lapped the ground floors of its buildings; and its wide streets, its colonnades, its temples and its walls. And yet, in spite of all these things, Syracuse was not what I call a state – while Dionysius I was its tyrant.[3] For the people owned nothing at all on their account, and indeed the people itself was owned by that one single man. When, therefore, a country is ruled by a despot, we ought not to pronounce that it is a bad kind of state – which is, I know, what I said yesterday – since logic requires us to conclude that it is no sort of state at all.

1. He said that neither the Roman orator Servius Sulpicius Galba, nor any of the Attic orators, could have expressed himself better. The two sentences that follow here are reconstructed from a missing passage.

2. The historian Timaeus of Tauromenium (*c.* 356–260).

3. 406–367.

LAELIUS: Very well said. And I now see what you were getting at earlier.

SCIPIO: So would you not go on to agree that, by the same token, when any single faction is completely in charge, once again one cannot accurately speak of a state?

LAELIUS: Yes, I certainly would.

SCIPIO: And you would be entirely right to do so. After the great Peloponnesian War, for example, when those Thirty governed the city of Athens in so outrageous a fashion,[1] the 'property of the Athenian people' had no significance or existence at all. Athens had its antique glory, its outstandingly beautiful buildings, its theatre, its gymnasiums, its colonnades, its noble Propylaea, its citadel, the superb works of Phidias, and the fine port of the Piraeus.[2] But none of those distinctions was enough to qualify it as a state any longer.

LAELIUS: I agree: because nothing was the 'property of the people'.

SCIPIO: And then think of the time when the Board of Ten governed Rome without being subject to any right of appeal, in that third year of their rule, when freedom had been deprived of all its defences.[3]

LAELIUS: Yes, once again there was no 'property of the people'. Indeed, the people rose in rebellion in order to get its property back.

SCIPIO: I will now pass to the third form of government, namely democracy. Here difficulties may seem to arise. Let us suppose that the people administers everything, and maintains total control. That means that the masses can inflict punishment on anyone they choose, and can manage things exactly as they wish, and plunder, possess and keep whatever they want. Then, certainly, everything will be the property of the people – and that is precisely what we have decided to be the definition of a state! So, in the circumstances that I have mentioned, Laelius, would you still describe that as a state?

1. The oligarchic revolution after the great defeat in the Peloponnesian War (404–403).

2. The Propylaea, the monumental gateway of the Athenian Acropolis, was designed by Mnesicles in *c.* 435 BC. Phidias, the director of Pericles's building programme, designed the gold and ivory statue of Athena in the Parthenon, and designed or supervised its metopes, friezes and pedimental figures. The Piraeus was, and is, the port of Athens.

3. The *decemviri legibus scribundis* (451–449 BC).

LAELIUS: No, I would not describe it as anything of the kind. On the contrary, there is no form of government to which I should more readily deny the definition of a state than one which is entirely under the control of the masses.

We decided that there was no true state at Syracuse or Agrigentum or Athens when those cities were ruled by despots,[1] or here at Rome when the Board of Ten were in charge. Well, I cannot see how the name of state can be regarded as any more applicable to a despotism exercised by the mob. For, to begin with, a people can only be said to exist at all when the individuals who comprise it are bound together in a partnership founded on law, according to your admirable definition, Scipio. But the sort of mass government to which you have referred is just as tyrannical as if a single person were the ruler, and indeed an even nastier despot, because there is nothing more disgusting than the sort of monstrosity which fictitiously assumes the name and guise of 'the people'.[2]

SPURIUS MUMMIUS: Yes, personally I prefer even monarchy to unmitigated democracy, which is the worst of all forms of government. But an aristocratic, oligarchic government is better than monarchy, because a king is a single individual, where a state will derive the most benefit if it comes under the rule of a number of good men, and not just one.

SCIPIO: I realize, Spurius, that you have always felt a particular dislike for popular power. My own feeling is that it might be more possible to endure than you have thought. Yet, all the same, I agree with you that it is the least desirable of all the three types of constitution.

But as to your suggestion that aristocratic rule is preferable to monarchy, that I cannot accept. For if wisdom is the dominant quality of the government, whether that wisdom is the possession of one man only, or of more than one, seems to me to make no difference one way or the other. Besides, our discussion is being led astray by a semantic point. 'The best men' – if that is the term we are going to use for aristocratic government – are obviously

1. The dictators referred to included Dionysius I (406–367) and Agathocles (317–289) at Syracuse, and Phalaris (*c.* 570/565–554/549) and Theron (488–472) at Acragas (Agrigentum).

2. About three pages are lost here.

preferable to everyone else, since 'the best' cannot help being better than anyone else! But when, on the other hand, we speak of a king, what we always have in mind is a *bad* king. Yet we are not speaking of bad kings in our present discussion, because the subject we are considering is kingship in general. Let us imagine, that is to say, that the king we are referring to is the good Romulus or Numa Pompilius or Servius Tullius.[1] Then in that case perhaps you will not feel so much distaste for monarchic government . . .

SPURIUS MUMMIUS: But to go back to democracy, what have you got to say in its favour?

SCIPIO: What about Rhodes, Spurius, which we visited together? Does that not seem to you to deserve to be called a state?[2]

SPURIUS MUMMIUS: Yes indeed it does, and by no means a contemptible one either.

SCIPIO: You are right. However, as you will remember, all the Rhodians were ordinary citizens at one time in their lives, and members of the city's Senate at another. That is to say, there was a system of rotation, whereby they served as private citizens for some months of the year, and as senators for others. In both capacities alike, they received payment for attending meetings. Moreover, both in the theatre and in the Senate-house, the same men decided not only capital lawsuits but cases of every other category as well. That is to say, senators and private citizens enjoyed exactly the same amount of power.

1. According to tradition, Numa Pompilius was the second king of Rome (715–673), and Servius Tullius was the sixth (578–535). The manuscripts read 'Tullus', i.e. the third king Tullus Hostilius (673–642), but he does not seem such a suitable example of a 'good' king.

2. Rhodes was one of the few important Greek Republics which flourished, in spite of the large empires elsewhere in the Near and Middle East, during the Hellenistic period. But Rome punished its equivocal attitude in the Third Macedonian War by proclaiming Delos a rival free port (167).

ON THE STATE (I, VI)[1]

The Roman state is founded firm, upon ancient customs and on men.[2]

Those words are both concise and true, and the poet who uttered them seems to me to have derived them from an oracle, that is to say from a divine source. For neither men by themselves, unless a state has customs as well, nor customs by themselves, unless they have men to look after them, could ever have sufficed to establish or to maintain, for so long, a state whose empire extends so far and wide as our own. Before our own lifetimes, our traditional customs produced outstanding men, and admirable men, thereafter continuing to maintain those ancient customs and the institutions of their ancestors.

When it came down to our own time, however, the state looked like a handsome painting which was already fading on account of its age. And this present age of ours has not only failed to restore its original fineness by renewing the colours, but has not even bothered to preserve its general form and outlines. For the 'ancient customs', upon which the poet declared that the Roman state was founded firm, are no longer to be found. They have sunk, as we can perceive, so completely into oblivion that they are not only no longer followed, but have actually disappeared from people's knowledge. And about the men, what shall I say? For the reason why our customs have died is that the men to carry them on are no longer available. It is a terrible disaster. As for ourselves, it is not only imperative for us to render an account, indicating why it has happened, but we ought to be prepared to defend ourselves against the accusation that this national collapse has occurred – just as if we were defendants in a lawcourt, on a capital charge. Moreover, the conclusion will be that the fact that our state only survives as a verbal concept, and has lost any practical reality at all, is not just an accident. We ourselves are to blame . . .

Let us compare what happens in the management of a private estate. The factor knows the character of the land, and the house-steward knows how to read and write. Both, however, employ

1. From the portions that have survived it seems that the qualifications and functions of the ideal statesman are the main subject of Book V, and the great value and noble reward of his labours the theme of Book VI.

2. From Ennius's *Annals*.

these skills, not merely for the sake of obtaining theoretical satisfaction, but in order to put them to practical use. And just the same applies to our statesman. Certainly, he will have taken the trouble to familiarize himself with the law, and with specific laws, and will have investigated how and why these laws came about. But it is not his duty to hamper himself by constantly having to give legal opinions, and doing all the reading and writing which that would require.

Because, you might say, he has to act as both the factor and the steward of the state, at one and the same time. True, he needs to have a complete understanding of the highest principles of justice, because, without such understanding, it is not within anyone's power to be just at all. And he must not be ignorant of the law of the land. But his awareness of it should be analogous to the knowledge of the stars that a ship's pilot possesses, or a doctor's knowledge of medicine. For both these professionals *use* their knowledge for their own practical purposes, without letting it divert or distract them from fulfilling those purposes.

The sort of state which we are considering is one in which the best men hope for commendation and glory, and want to avoid dishonour and disgrace. What prevents them from acting wrongly, however, is not so much fear of the penalties laid down by law as that sense of shame with which human beings are endowed by nature. This has the effect of making them afraid of incurring justified criticism. When a statesman is in charge of a country, he enhances this feeling among his citizens by whipping up public opinion. And he completes the process by establishing institutions and developing educational methods that fit in with his aims. The result of all this is that his public are deterred from wrongdoing by shame quite as much as by fear.

It is impossible to live well except in a good community, and the best guarantee of that goodness is a soundly constituted and structured state. The pilot of a ship wants a successful voyage, a doctor wants health, a general wants victory, and by the same token the man who is directing a state aims at a happy life for his citizens, supported by resources and material wealth, renowned and respected for integrity. That is the achievement which I want our statesman to bring to perfection: of all possible achievements that there could be, it is the greatest and noblest. What stimulated our ancestors to so many remarkable and splendid deeds was their desire for glory, and it is on glory that the leading man of a state must be nourished. At the same time, the state can only stand firm so long as respect is paid by one and all to their leader.

He must not, of course, be corrupt. And the element in state affairs which ought to be freest of all from corruption is the popular vote and expression of opinion. So it would be illogical for the man who corrupts the public by the employment of bribery to merit punishment, whereas the man who corrupts them by eloquence earns commendation! On the contrary, it appears to me that the person who corrupts a juryman by what he erroneously states in a speech is committing a graver crime than the man who does so by bribery. For even a virtuous man can be corrupted by oratory, though he cannot be corrupted by a bribe.

After Scipio had spoken in this vein, Spurius Mummius declared his complete approval, because rhetoricians inspired him with nothing short of hatred.[1]

1. This last sentence is one of the fragments that have survived. No doubt Mummius enlarged on this point of view. For Cicero's fuller opinions on oratory, see the *Brutus*, later in this book (Chapter 6).

CHAPTER 5

ON LAWS (III): How to Run the Ideal Government

On Laws *contains Cicero's second, and more practical, thoughts about how his ideal government ought to be conducted, turning to the force of law as the true cementing force of the state. The work appears to have been begun shortly after* On the State *was completed – or even before it received its final touches.* On Laws *was nearly but not quite ready by 52, and looks (in the form that has come down to us) like a finished product, though it may not have been published during Cicero's lifetime.*

Once again, the study takes the form of a discussion. It takes place at the orator's own home at Arpinum. He himself is the principal speaker, and his brother Quintus and his friend Titus Pomponius Atticus are the others. Their roles are subordinate (like those of Scipio's interlocutors in On the State*), but what they say is quite interesting, introduced to present not only agreement but also, sometimes, different, critical viewpoints. Originally the work contained six books, and possibly more.*[1] *The first three, to a great extent, have survived. The first deals with law and justice in general. The second considers the religious laws which ought to exist in the ideal state. The third, which is translated here, deals with another essential feature of government, the nature and functions of the state officials;*[2] *and much attention, also, is devoted to the legislative, judicial and executive functions of the government itself, on which Cicero's judgement, though not everyone will agree with it, is balanced and based on personal experience.*[3]

1. Books I, III and V were introduced by prefaces.

2. Including thinly veiled devices to give political power to the upper class (cf. Introduction). Cicero wanted to provide a firm legal basis for senatorial authority.

3. Cicero's Greek sources in *On the State* and *On Laws* have been much discussed. He also used Roman material, and added points of his own.

ON LAWS (III)

CICERO: So I shall again follow the example, as I did before, of that god-like personage, whose praises I perhaps utter more frequently than I ought to, such is my admiration for him.
ATTICUS: I suppose you mean Plato.
CICERO: Yes, Atticus, that is the man I mean.
ATTICUS: But you could never praise him too highly or too often, in my view! For even those people we know,[1] who do not like anyone to be praised outside their own group, nevertheless allow me the right to admire him unrestrainedly.
CICERO: And they are entirely correct in doing so. For I can think of nothing more appropriate to your own well-balanced life-style: you being a man who, both in what you do and what you say, seem to me to have successfully achieved that blend of humanity and serious purpose which is so very hard to bring about.
ATTICUS: If you think as favourably of me as all that, I am very glad I interrupted you! So continue, please, as you have begun.
CICERO: Our first task, then, is to offer praises to the law itself, in terms that are both accurate and appropriate.
ATTICUS: Yes, do just that, just as you did when you were speaking about the laws on religious matters.[2]
CICERO: Well, then, the function of a state official, as you know, is to govern, and to issue orders that are just and advantageous and in keeping with the laws. Indeed, it can truly be said that an official is the speaking law, and the law is a non-speaking official. Besides, government is something supremely in accordance with the prescriptions of justice and with nature; by which I mean that it is supremely in accordance with the law. For, without government, no household can exist at all, and no community, and no nation, and not the human race itself, or the world of nature, or for that matter the entire universe. For the universe obeys God, and is obeyed by the seas and lands, so that human life is governed by the law which is universally valid.

However, let us return to matters that are closer and better known to our own selves. Now, originally, all nations of antique origin were ruled by kings. This authority was, at first, entrusted to

1. The Epicureans.
2. This was the theme of the second book of *On Laws*.

men who were outstanding for their integrity and wisdom – and that was conspicuously the case of the early monarchy in our own country. Subsequently the kingship was handed down to the descendants of the earliest kings (which is still what happens in the monarchies that exist elsewhere today). At that stage, however, people who objected to the monarchical system wanted not, indeed, to be under no superior direction at all, but no longer to be invariably under one single man.

But what I am trying to do is to describe the legal system that a free people ought to possess. In my six earlier books *On the State* I presented my views about what the ideal government ought to be. And now what I intend to do is to outline the laws with which in my view that best kind of government ought to be equipped. And certainly it has to have officials as well, since without their good sense and careful attention no state can exist at all. In fact the entire nature of a state depends on the arrangements it has made regarding those officials.

First, they must be left in no doubt how far the limits of their authority extend. And the citizens, too, must be made fully aware of the extent of their obligation to obey the functionaries in question. It is worth remembering, in this connection, that the man who rules his country well will, obviously, have deferred to the authority of others in the past – and the man who has rendered this obedience conscientiously has thereby acquired fitness to become a ruler himself some time in the future. Indeed, this obedient subject has a right to expect that that is what he will one day become; and conversely the ruler will be well advised to bear in mind that he himself, quite soon in the future, may have to start obeying again.

We should also, like Charondas in his legal code,[1] make sure that the citizens not only obey their state officials dutifully, but that they actually respect them and love them. Indeed, our Plato[2] considered that people who revolt against their officials, as the Titans revolted against the gods,[3] deserve to be considered as no better than the Titans themselves.

1. Charondas, who probably lived in the sixth century BC, was the lawgiver of his home town Catana and other Sicilian cities.

2. *Laws*, III, 703C.

3. The Titans, children of Heaven and Earth, were older gods than the Olympians.

Now that that has been made clear, we can proceed, if you agree that this is the best procedure, with an examination of the laws themselves.

ATTICUS: Certainly, I agree, and indeed I agree, also, with the whole way in which you are conducting your argument.

CICERO: Orders, then, shall be just, and the citizens shall act upon them obediently and without protest. Citizens who are disobedient or harmful shall be liable to coercion, on the part of the officials, in the form of fines or imprisonment or beating, unless an equal or superior authority, or the Assembly, prohibit such courses of action. Citizens shall be entitled to appeal against these penalties. After the official has pronounced sentence, the final determination of the fine or other penalty shall be entrusted to the Assembly. Against orders given by a military commander in the field, however, there shall be no right of appeal; for the commands issued by those in charge of military operations shall possess the binding force of law.

There shall be lesser officials assigned to particular functions, with authority in their own fields.[1] In the army they shall command those placed under them, and act as their officers. In the city they shall have the care of public funds. They shall be in charge of the detention of criminals. They shall be responsible for carrying out capital punishment. They shall issue bronze, silver and gold coinage on behalf of the state. They shall pronounce the verdicts in lawsuits. They shall put the decrees of the Senate into effect.

The aediles shall look after the city and the food supply and the established Games. This post shall be the initial step in their promotion to higher office. The censors shall draw up lists of the citizens, providing details of their ages, children, households and resources. They shall supervise the temples, streets, aqueducts, treasury and taxes. They shall organize the distribution of the citizens among tribes, and divide them according to their financial positions, age and rank. They shall enlist recruits for the cavalry and infantry. They shall declare celibacy illegal. They shall control public morality. They shall check improper behaviour among senators. They shall be two in number, holding office for two years each, whereas other officials shall serve for a one-year term. The post of censor shall never be left unoccupied.

1. These six categories of lesser officials are, in the order given here: *tribuni militum* (military officers); quaestors; uncertain; *tresviri capitales; tresviri aere argento auro flando feriundo; decemviri litibus iudicandis.*

The praetor shall be the man who administers justice, and pronounces or guides the verdicts in private lawsuits. It is he who shall be guardian of the civil law. The praetors shall possess equal powers, and there shall be as many of them as the Senate decrees or the Assembly ordains.

There shall also be two officials with the power that used to belong to the kings. Since they lead (*praeire*), judge and give counsel (*consulere*), they shall be entitled praetors, judges and consuls; and it is 'consuls' that they will be habitually called. While on military service, they will be invested with supreme authority. There shall be no one above them. Their dominant preoccupation shall be the welfare of the people.

No one shall occupy the same office twice, except after an interval of ten years' duration. Age limits relating to annual terms of office shall be adhered to.[1] When, however, a serious war occurs, or civil strife, a single man shall be invested with the power that normally belongs to the two consuls, if the Senate so decrees. But this dictatorship shall not last longer than six months.[2] Favourable auspices shall be required, and then he shall rule the entire people. He shall have the services, under him, of a man to command the cavalry, who shall be equal in rank to the praetor who administers justice.[3] But on occasions when there are neither consuls nor a dictator, there shall be no other state officials either. In such a case the auspices shall revert to the Senate, which will appoint one of its members to organize the elections of consuls according to the proper procedure.[4]

Holders of *imperium*,[5] and other officials, and their assistants, and envoys of the state, shall move out of the city when the Senate so decrees or the Assembly so commands. They shall fight just wars, and fight them justly. They shall be careful to look after our allies.

1. The *leges annales* (the first was the *Lex Villia* of Lucius Villius, 180).

2. After a long lapse of time the dictatorship had been revived by Lucius Cornelius Sulla (81), and was to be revived again by Caesar (49), who was finally invested with the office in perpetuity (44).

3. The *magister equitum*.

4. The *interrex*. Mention has already been made elsewhere of the auspices, a form of divination taken by officials, and presided over by the priestly college of the augurs, at elections, inaugurations, etc.

5. The supreme official power, vested in the highest functionaries of the Roman Republic.

They shall keep themselves and their subordinates under control. They shall increase the glory of Rome. When they come home, they shall be received with honour.

No one shall be appointed as an envoy of the state when personal profit is his motive.

The ten tribunes shall be the men whom the plebeians appoint to defend them from forcible coercion. Their prohibitions, and decisions passed by the plebeians under their chairmanship, shall have binding validity. Their own persons shall be inviolable. They shall ensure that the plebeians never lack tribunes to protect them.[1]

All state officials shall be empowered to take the auspices, and shall enjoy judicial authority. The Senate shall consist of men who have held official posts. Its decrees shall be binding. If, however, an equal or higher functionary than the current presiding officer should veto a senatorial decree, its text should, none the less, be copied out and preserved. The senatorial order must be clear of any trace of impropriety, so that it can serve as a model for other sections of the citizen body. When voting takes place to elect officials, and pronounce the verdicts in trials, and pass laws, high-ranking citizens, the traditional governing class, shall be kept aware of what is going on, though the freedom of the ordinary person to vote as he wishes shall not be interfered with.

If any administrative actions over and above those performed by the regular state officials prove necessary, the Assembly shall elect additional officials to undertake them, and shall grant them powers for the purpose. Consuls, praetors, dictators, masters of the horse and officials whom the Senate may appoint to carry out the elections of consuls shall be entitled to take the chair at meetings of the Assembly and the Senate. The tribunes elected by the plebeians shall have the right to chair Senate meetings. But they shall also refer to the plebeian Assembly any points that may be necessary.

Moderate conduct shall be required at meetings of both Assembly and Senate. If a senator stays away from a meeting of the Senate, he must have good reason to have done so, or else shall be held to blame. A senator shall speak when his turn comes, and not for too long. He shall be required to have some knowledge of national affairs. There shall be no displays of violence at the Assembly's

1. The desirability of the tribunate (i.e. the civilian *tribuni plebis*, not the military *tribuni militum*) will be debated a little later on.

meetings. An equal or higher authority shall have the right to veto the Assembly's decisions. But the Assembly's presiding officer shall be held responsible for any disorders that may take place. Anyone who vetoes a measure that would have been harmful shall be deemed to have performed a valuable duty to the state. Presiding officers of the Assembly and Senate shall pay attention to the auspices, and submit to the decisions of the augurs. After a measure has been read out, they shall ensure that it is filed in the treasury. They shall not put more than a single measure up for the popular vote at any one time. They shall see that the Assembly is informed about matters that arise, and shall permit other officials, as well as private citizens, to offer them further information.

Personal exceptions shall not be countenanced. Cases in which the penalty is execution or deprivation of citizenship shall only be tried before the highest category of popular Assembly[1] and before men whom the censors have duly registered as members of the citizen body. No man who is candidate for an official post, or who occupies one or has done so, shall have a gift presented to him or shall accept it. The penalty for infringement of any of these regulations shall be adjusted to fit the gravity of the offence. The text of the laws shall be in the hands of the censors. When a functionary completes his term of office, it is to the censors that he shall submit an account of the official actions he has carried out. This shall not, however, exempt him from liability to prosecution.

The law has now been read! 'Go, and I will order the ballots to be handed round.'[2]

QUINTUS CICERO: You have offered a very concise formulation, brother Marcus, of what you propose regarding our various offices of state. Yet what emerges is virtually identical to the actual practices of our own Roman government, although what you have suggested does include a few novelties.

CICERO: That, Quintus, is an accurate assessment. What I have proposed is the balanced type of constitution which Scipio commends and warmly praises in that treatise of his. But without the sort of provisions I have indicated in connection with the various official posts it would have been quite impossible to maintain any such constitution at all. For a government, as you must realize,

1. The *comitia centuriata* which enacted laws and elected high officials.

2. A quotation from the proclamation of a presiding officer of the Assembly.

consists of its officials, the men who direct its administration, and what distinguishes different types of state, one from another, is the varying character of these posts. Well, it was our own Roman ancestors who designed the wisest and most sensible system. And that being so, there were no innovations, or at most a very few, which I believed ought to be introduced into the constitution they had devised.

ATTICUS: When you were dealing, earlier, with religious laws, you offered reasons, in response to my suggestion, why you considered these to be the best. What I should like you to do now, therefore, is to pursue exactly the same course with regard to the proposals you have made concerning the offices of state.

CICERO: Very well then, Atticus, I will do as you ask. My treatment of the subject will bear in mind the analyses and discussions made by erudite Greeks; but I shall also have something to say about our own laws, as I did before.

ATTICUS: Yes, that is the sort of treatment I am hoping for.

CICERO: In my previous work, *On the State*, I brought in a wide variety of material, since this had to be included when we were examining the character of the ideal form of government. But in this present examination of official posts let us concentrate on certain specific points which were raised first by Theophrastus and then, in more sophisticated fashion, by Diogenes the Stoic.[1]

ATTICUS: Are you saying that these are matters which the Stoics have dealt with?

CICERO: No, none of them except Diogenes, whom I have just mentioned, and subsequently the distinguished and learned Panaetius.[2] True, the older Stoics, too, had considered constitutions, and did so very acutely. But their theoretical analyses were not designed, like my own, to be of practical assistance to ordinary people and citizens.

This type of discussion, which I am undertaking, derives most of its material from that other philosophical school, of which Plato

1. Theophrastus of Eresus (*c.* 370–288/5 BC) was the successor of Aristotle as head of the Peripatetic school. Diogenes 'of Babylon' (not the Cynic) (*c.* 240–152) succeeded Zeno as head of the Stoic school. Both men wrote treatises on law.

2. Panaetius of Rhodes (*c.* 185–109) succeeded Antipater as head of the Stoic school.

was the leader. The men who came after him, Aristotle and Heraclides of Pontus, another follower of Plato, threw light on the whole topic of national constitutions through the inquiries they conducted.[1] Moreover, as you know, Theophrastus, Aristotle's disciple, specialized in this type of investigation; and another of Aristotle's pupils, Dicaearchus, was active in the same field of study.[2]

Later, also, one of Theophrastus's adherents, Demetrius of Phalerum, of whom I spoke before, enjoyed remarkable success in bringing erudition out of the scholarly recesses into the sunshine and the dust of daily life – and even, one might add, into the critical centre of the line of battle itself.[3] Certainly, one can also name many other important public men who have not been altogether lacking in scholarly knowledge. And one can name, on the other hand, numerous extremely learned men who have not been wholly inexperienced in political affairs. But I cannot think of anyone, except Demetrius, who excelled in both these activities at the same time – taking the lead not only in the pursuit of learning, but also in the actual government of his country.

ATTICUS: But I believe such men can be found. In fact you might say that one of us three fit into that category! However, carry on with what you were saying.

CICERO: Well, what these philosophers debated was whether it is desirable for a state to have *one single* official who is obeyed by everyone else. I understand that this was at first considered the most suitable course by our ancestors after they had got rid of the kings. The monarchy had in earlier days been well regarded, but was subsequently rejected, not so much because there was anything wrong with how things were run, as because it seemed discreditable to be ruled by a single individual. So, at the next stage, if one single

1. Heraclides Ponticus came to Plato's Academy in Athens as a pupil of Speusippus, after whose death he returned to his home town Heraclea in Pontus where he may have opened his own school.

2. Dicaearchus of Messana, who lived in the Peloponnese, was a contemporary of Theophrastus; his work on the mixed constitution of Sparta, the *Tripoliticus*, is lost. He was greatly admired by Cicero.

3. Demetrius of Phalerum, governor of Athens under Macedonian rule (318–307), whom Cicero, as he said, had mentioned before (in *II Laws*); and he was to revert to him again in the *Brutus* (Chapter 6). The orator found Demetrius uniquely relevant because he was the only philosopher who had practical experience of political leadership.

official was going to be selected to rule over all the others, it would have appeared that it was merely the royal title which had been abolished, while the institution of monarchy itself remained unchanged.

It was reasonable, therefore, that we established tribunes to check the consuls (just as King Theopompus set up ephors to oppose the kings of Sparta).[1] For the tribunes are the only officials from whom the consuls do not possess the legal right to exact obedience. And their posts were brought into existence, following the establishment of the consulships, precisely in order to make sure that what had happened before should never happen again. For the creation of officials who did not have to obey the orders the consul had given was the first step in the limitation of his power. The second step was taken when these same tribunes lent their support to other people as well, private citizens in addition to officials, who refused to obey the consul.

QUINTUS CICERO: Yes, and what you have just mentioned was a major disaster. For it was the tribunes' position that destroyed the influence of the traditional governing class, and increased the power of the masses.

CICERO: No, Quintus, I do not agree.[2] Surely it was unavoidable that the authority of the consuls, without any rivals, would be regarded by the Roman people as too overbearing and despotic. Since then, however, their power has been subjected to limitations – of a moderate and sensible nature.[3]

1. The ephors at Sparta (five in number in the fifth century BC) were high officials who shared power with the two joint kings. Theopompus, one of the kings (*c.* 720–?*c.* 670 BC), was believed to have founded the ephorate, although, in fact, it may have been of earlier origin, but became of increased importance during his reign.

2. The tribunes were officers of the Roman plebeians who first made their appearance, according to tradition, in 494 BC, after the first Secession of the plebeians (to the Sacred Mount). They were 'tamed' by the Senate, but during the later Republic recovered their position as an anti-senatorial force. Cicero strongly disapproved of the Gracchi, to whom this revival was largely due (although, as we shall see in the *Brutus*, he thought they were good orators), but here, with the aid of other persons in the discussion, he does present both sides of the question quite objectively.

3. The rest of Cicero's argument is missing; and when the work resumes he is commenting on laws.

'When he comes home, he shall be received with honour.' Yes, because when a good, honest official returns home, he brings nothing but honour, from enemy or ally alike.

'No one shall be appointed as an envoy of the state when something other than the national interest is his motive.' No, clearly, that would be thoroughly reprehensible. I do not propose to say anything about envoys who accept these jobs, or have accepted them in the past, in order to get hold of legacies or lucrative contracts for themselves. For to do such things, perhaps, is a weakness to which human nature is prone. But this I do want to stress. Nothing could possibly be more deplorable than the appointment of a senator as an envoy when he is given no official duties at all, no instructions to carry out, not the smallest governmental business to see to. Indeed, when I was consul,[1] I had hoped to abolish delegations of this kind altogether, and a packed Senate supported what I intended to do – though any measure of such a kind would have diminished the privileges of its members. However, an irresponsible tribune intervened to veto my measure. Nevertheless, I was still able to restrict the tenures of such appointments to a single year; their duration had previously been unlimited. So the disgraceful institution still exists, although now it is subject to a time limit.

But now, if you agree, let us leave the provinces and return to the city of Rome.

ATTICUS: Yes indeed, I agree – though others who go to the provinces may not be of the same opinion.

CICERO: And yet, Atticus, if they obey the laws I have in mind, the city of Rome itself, and their own homes, will seem to them very pleasant places indeed, and the provinces will appear tiresome and troublesome places in comparison.

Well, first of all, the law which establishes the power of the tribunes in our constitution does not need to be discussed.

QUINTUS CICERO: On the contrary, brother, I most certainly want to ask you what you think of that law.

My own opinion is that it is a disastrous law, which originated in civil strife and causes further disturbances. As to its origin, if we want to recollect how it came about, we see that the tribunate started at a time of violent dissension among our citizens, when

1. In 63.

parts of the city were in a state of siege and other parts had been forcibly occupied. Then, after the proposal to start such an office had been rapidly killed – very much in the same way as the Twelve Tables[1] enacted that gravely deformed children should be put to death – soon afterwards, nevertheless, it was somehow brought into existence again, in an even more disgusting and repulsive form than before.

For think of all the lamentable things for which this revived tribunate has been responsible! The first thing it did, which was entirely in keeping with its deplorable character, was to deprive the senators, totally, of the position they had formerly held. It made the lowest equal to the highest everywhere. It produced total confusion and disorder.

And even after fatally damaging the authority of our national leaders, this tribunate never stayed content. I will say nothing about the actions of Gaius Flaminius,[2] and other events that now seem to belong to the distant past because they happened so long ago. But take the tribunate of Tiberius Sempronius Gracchus:[3] he virtually left our leading men no rights at all. However, it was actually five years before Gracchus that another man, the mean and distasteful Gaius Curiatius, when he too held the office of tribune,[4] had already perpetrated an action wholly without precedent. For what he did was to arrest the consuls Decimus Junius Brutus Callaicus and Publius Cornelius Scipio Nasica Serapio, both men of exceptional merit, and throw them into prison. And consider, furthermore, that later tribune Gaius Sempronius Gracchus – and his overthrow.[5] That was the occasion, as he asserted himself, when he brought daggers into the Forum, so that citizens could use them to inflict wounds upon each other. And that, in turn, meant a national revolution – and the tribunate was responsible! After that, there is little reason to mention Lucius Appuleius Saturninus, and Publius Sulpicius, and all the other

1. 451–450.

2. Consul in 223 and 217. A 'new man' who initiated the late Republican challenges to the Senate by carrying popular measures directly through the Assembly – a precursor, that is to say, of the Gracchi.

3. In 133.

4. In 138.

5. In 121.

tribunes, whom our country could only ward off by resorting to the sword.[1]

However, there is no need at all to quote ancient instances, which affected other people altogether, who are no longer with us. Let us consider, instead, quite recent examples which we ourselves have experienced. There is not a single one of our most audacious enemies, men scheming to undermine our entire position, who has not, in order to achieve his aim, sharpened some tribune's sword-point against us. And when certain depraved criminals could find no amenable tribune in any family or clan, they felt it necessary instead, at a dark moment in our national history, to pervert the entire clan system so as to achieve their ends.[2] It is a source of legitimate pride, which will bring us fame for ever, that at that time not one single tribune could be persuaded, even by a promise of the most substantial reward, to act against us – except that one man, and one man only, and he had no right to become a tribune at all. Nevertheless, he caused appalling damage: damage that could only have been created by a desperate, irrational, filthy beast, inflamed by popular frenzy.

That is the sort of reason why I heartily support Sulla's laws in this field, since what they achieved was to deprive the tribunes of any capacity to do harm, leaving them only the right to provide assistance when needed.[3] And as for our friend Cnaeus Pompeius Magnus, in every other matter he always has my full and unqualified approval. With regard, however, to his attitude towards the tribunes I prefer to remain silent. For I do not wish to blame

1. Lucius Appuleius Saturninus (tribune in 103 and 101) was murdered in 100, largely because of his grain laws and proposed land distributions, which had encountered violent conservative opposition. Publius Sulpicius Rufus (tribune in 88) likewise proposed distributions of land, which were annulled, and he himself put to death, when Lucius Cornelius Sulla marched on Rome and made himself dictator (81).

2. A reference to the radical politician Publius Clodius Pulcher, who, although a patrician, induced a plebeian to adopt him with Caesar's support, so that he could become a tribune and attack Cicero (58).

3. Sulla's laws prohibited the tribunes from proposing laws to the Assembly without senatorial approval, and debarred former tribunes from standing for higher offices. Cicero disliked Sulla as the man who opposed his fellow-townsman Marius, but, in this respect at least, approved of his conservative measures.

him. But to praise him, in this connection, is more than I can manage.[1]

CICERO: You have pointed to the flaws in the tribunate, Quintus, very clearly indeed. But when one is criticizing an institution it is unfair just to list its faults, and to pick out the shortcomings its history has displayed, without also touching on the good it has done. If you are going to employ that sort of method, you can even abuse the consulship, once you have collected together the bad actions of certain individual consuls, whom I prefer not to identify. And as far as the tribunate is concerned, I admit that there is something wrong about the actual power it possesses. But it would be impossible to have the benefits which the tribune was designed to provide, without accepting that flaw as well.

'The tribunes have too much power,' you say. Yes, that is undeniable. But the power of the popular Assembly has a much more cruel and violent potential. Yet, in practice, that potential sometimes makes for greater mildness than if it did not exist at all – when there is a leader to keep the Assembly under control. And, when there is a leader, his behaviour is restricted by the recognition that he himself is at risk, whereas the impulses of the people care nothing at all about any risk that may be involved for themselves.

'Yes,' you object, 'but the tribunes sometimes stir up excitement among the people.' True, but they frequently have a calming effect as well. For no board of tribunes, surely, would ever be so outrageously constituted that not a single one of its members remained sane! Indeed, what caused the overthrow of Tiberius Sempronius Gracchus was the fact that he had an opponent on his own board, whose veto he brushed aside and whose powers he took away.[2] For that, indeed, is what brought about his downfall: his removal of one of his own colleagues from office, because he had exercised his right of veto against Tiberius Gracchus.

Note how wise our ancestors showed themselves to be in this matter. For once the Senate had, initially, granted the plebeians their tribunate, violence came to an end, and rebellion ceased. A

1. The restoration of the tribunes' powers, begun in 75, was completed during the consulship of Cnaeus Pompeius Magnus (Pompey the Great) and Marcus Licinius Crassus (70).

2. At Tiberius Gracchus's request, the Assembly deposed Marcus Octavius from the tribunate (133).

compromise, that is to say, had been devised, which enabled the masses to believe that they had been granted equality with the leading men of the state. And it was that compromise which saved our country. 'But since then we have had the two Gracchi,' you will protest. True, and you could go on to mention many other undesirable phenomena as well. Because when a board of ten tribunes is elected, you will always, at every period, find some of its members whose activity is damaging, and others, perhaps more numerous, who are, to say the least, bad and irresponsible influences. Nevertheless, the existence of the tribunes prevents the Senate from becoming the target of envious attacks, and the masses do not launch perilous struggles on behalf of their rights.

Had serious troubles occurred, it would have seemed justified to suppose, either that the kingship ought never to have been abolished, or, conversely, once it had been abolished, that the masses ought to have been given authentic freedom, and not just the pretence of freedom that they received. However, in fact, things have worked out differently, since the freedom that has been granted to them was, as I say, modified; so that they were induced, with the help of numerous judicious measures, to respect the authority of the leaders of the state.

But let me speak, my dear good brother, of my own personal case, and the impact of the tribunes' power upon myself.[1] It gave me no cause to complain against the institution of the tribunate as such. For although the prisons were opened, and the slaves were roused up against me, and I was subjected to the menace of military force, the free plebeian masses never responded to incitement or became my enemies.

Besides, what I really had to cope with was not just that rascally tribune Publius Clodius Pulcher, but the extremely serious national crisis with which I had to deal.[2] And if I had failed to respond to it firmly, my country would not have had the advantage of my services for very much longer. The outcome proved that I had calculated correctly. For every free citizen of Rome, and every slave, too, who was worthy of freedom, proved to have my safety very much at heart.[3] Yet even if the result of all I had done to

1. He is referring, once again, to the opposition of Publius Clodius Pulcher, who had arranged for him to be exiled (58–57).

2. The 'conspiracy' of Lucius Sergius Catilina (Catiline) (63).

3. So that Cicero was recalled from exile in 57.

preserve my country had not met with the universal applause which it, in fact, evoked; even if the hatred of an infuriated mob had not been stirred up to attack me and had driven me into exile; even if a tribune, by his power, had excited the people against me, as Gaius Gracchus excited them against Publius Popillius Laenas, and Lucius Appuleius Saturninus did the same against Quintus Caecilius Metellus Numidicus;[1] nevertheless, brother Quintus, I should have borne what had to be borne. Besides, I should have been comforted not only by past Athenian philosophers, whose function it was to provide such consolation, but also by other distinguished citizens of Athens, who were driven into exile and preferred to do without their ungrateful city rather than to remain while it persisted in its wrongful behaviour.[2]

In regard to this particular matter, you say, you cannot approve of Cnaeus Pompeius Magnus. But there is one point, it seems to me, that you have not sufficiently borne in mind. It is this: that he had to decide, not just what was theoretically best, but also what was practically necessary. For he realized that our government could not do without the office of tribune. Seeing that our people had so strongly desired the tribunate, when they did not even yet know how it was going to turn out, how could they be expected to dispense with it after it had become familiar to them, by experience? Besides, it was the duty of a wise citizen, in dealing with an office which was not evil in itself and which was so popular that resistance to it was out of the question, not to relinquish its defence to a representative of the masses – which would certainly have had highly unsatisfactory consequences.

Well, brother, you do realize, do you not, that in discussions of this kind it is customary to interject 'Absolutely right' or 'How true', in order to finish off one topic and pass to another.

QUINTUS CICERO: That is not quite the situation here, however, because as a matter of fact I do *not* agree with what you have been saying. By all means, however, go on to the next subject.

CICERO: But you do persist, then, in your previous opinion, about the tribunate, and have no intention of changing it?

ATTICUS: And as a matter of fact I, too, agree with Quintus, very definitely!

1. The two men were banished in 123 and 100 respectively.

2. e.g. Aristides, Themistocles, Cimon.

However, let us now hear what remains to be said.
CICERO: Well, then, the next law provided that the right to take the auspices, and judicial authority, should be vested in all state officials. The judicial authority is granted in order to ensure that the Assembly can retain the power to hear appeals. And the officials' right to take the auspices is designed to provide a convincing justification for suspending the many meetings of the Assembly that are not going to lead to any beneficial result. For recourse to the auspices has often given the immortal gods an opportunity to check undesirable moves on the part of the Assembly.

Another law, which provides that the Senate shall be entirely composed of former officials, is unquestionably democratic in character, since it ensures that no one is able to reach that elevated position unless they have previously been elected to an office by the Assembly (direct appointment to the Senate by the censors is ruled out). This might, I suppose, be described as a flaw in the system, owing to its democratic character. But if so, the defect is mitigated by our next provision, that the Senate's decrees shall be binding, since that establishes the Senate's authority on a proper legal basis.

For if the Senate is acknowledged as the leader of public policy, and its decrees are greeted by universal support, and if all the other orders of the state are content to allow this highest, senatorial order to direct the government by its decisions, then this constitutional compromise, by which the popular Assembly possesses the power but the Senate has the authority, will guarantee the preservation of the moderate and harmonious system of which, as I said, I am in favour.

And that will especially be ensured if the next law is obeyed. It ran as follows: 'that the senatorial order must keep clear of the slightest trace of impropriety, so that it can serve as a model for the other sections of the citizen body'.
QUINTUS CICERO: Yes, brother, that is indeed an admirable law. However, the requirement, that the order shall be free of impropriety, is so extremely general that it will need the services of a censor to interpret it.
ATTICUS: Although the senatorial order certainly approves of you yourself, Marcus, and retains the most grateful recollection of your consulship, I feel obliged to add, if you do not mind, that the task you mention would be enough to wear out not only the censors, but all the judges as well!

CICERO: Do not let that trouble you, Atticus. For we are not talking about this present Senate of ours, or the men of our own time, but about the people who will appear in the future: if any of them, that is to say, will ever have the inclination to obey these laws that I am proposing. For seeing that the particular law I have in mind insists that senators should be clear of impropriety, this means that no one who fails to meet this requirement will ever get as far as entering the senatorial order at all. Certainly, such a standard is difficult to reach, except through instruction and training. This is a matter, however, on which I may well have something further to say, if I can find room and time to do so.

ATTICUS: Since you are taking the entire range of our laws, one after another, the problem of finding room will surely not arise. As for time, there will be no lack of that either, since we have the whole long day for our discussion. But if you announce your intention of omitting this matter of instruction and training, I warn you that I shall insist that you revoke that decision, and deal with the matter all the same.

CICERO: Yes, Atticus, do just that, and call attention to anything else I leave out.

'The senatorial order shall be a model for the other sections of the citizen body.' If we achieve this, we shall have achieved everything. The state, as a whole, is constantly corrupted when its leading men display evil ambitions and vicious behaviour. But it assumes a correspondingly more praiseworthy character when they exhibit self-restraint. That great man Lucius Licinius Lucullus,[1] of whom we were all so fond, was once criticized because of the luxuriousness of his villa at Tusculum. The reply that he gave, however, was regarded as apt. For he answered that his house was adjoined by two neighbours, a Roman knight living above it, and a freedman below. Their villas, too, he said, were very luxurious, and he felt he was entitled to have the same life-style as those two neighbours, whose position in the state was inferior to his own. Yet you ought to realize, Lucullus, that if they desire luxury the fault is yours. If you had not gone in for luxurious living, it would not have been possible for them to do so either. Without your example before them, that is to say, the people would have found it unendurable to

1. Consul in 74; commander in the first stages of the Third Mithridatic War against Mithridates VI of Pontus (as described in *For Murena*, Chapter 2).

see those persons' mansions crammed with statues and paintings, some of which, in fact, were the property of the nation, while others were sacred objects, belonging to religious foundations.

To put an end, I am saying, to their covetous grasping would present no problem, if only the very men, whose obligation it was to put an end to such behaviour, were not just as grasping themselves. It is bad enough that leading figures in the state should do wrong. But what is much more damaging is that there are so very many people who want to follow their example. Recollect what happened in Rome's early history, and you will see that the character of our leading citizens was what moulded the shape of the entire community. Whatever alterations occurred in the life-styles of the leading men were reflected in the lives of the whole population.

This supposition is considerably more reliable than our friend Plato's theory. For he was convinced that a nation's character could be changed by transforming the nature of its music.[1] My own belief, on the other hand, is that a nation's character only changes when the customs and life-styles of its aristocracy undergo alteration. For that reason, national leaders who act improperly present a particular danger to the state, not only because of the undesirable practices in which they themselves indulge, but because they infect the whole community with this poison – not only, that is to say, because they are corrupt, but because they corrupt others. The examples they set to others do more harm than the bad things that they themselves are doing. This law applies to the whole senatorial order. Yet it can also be considerably narrowed down. What I mean is that the capacity either to corrupt the morals of the nation or to improve them rests, actually, with only a few people, in fact very few indeed, because of the lofty positions or reputations that they enjoy.

But I have dealt with this topic more completely in my earlier work,[2] and I have said enough about it here and now. So let us go on to what follows.

The next law deals with the subject of voting. What my decree proposed was that high-ranking citizens, the traditional governing class, should be kept aware of what was going on, but the freedom

1. *Republic*, IV, 424c.

2. The reference is to *On the State*, but the passage in question is lost.

of the ordinary people to vote as they wish should not be interfered with.

ATTICUS: I noted, certainly, what you said, but I did not entirely grasp what this law was supposed to mean, or understand the way in which you phrased it.

CICERO: I will explain, Atticus. The subject has often been dealt with before. But it is difficult, all the same. The question is this. When officials are being elected, or criminal cases adjudicated, or proposed laws voted upon, is it better for the process of voting to be conducted in the open, orally, or in secret?

QUINTUS CICERO: I cannot see that there is the slightest doubt about which of the two courses is right. I am afraid I am going to disagree with you once again!

CICERO: No, Quintus, I am certain you will not. For my view is the same as I know that yours has always been. That is to say, theoretically speaking, oral balloting, out in the open, is best. But we do have to reflect seriously: *is such a procedure actually practicable*?

QUINTUS CICERO: But, brother, may I, with your permission, object. The suggestion that certain measures, although right and proper, are 'impracticable' is likely to lead inexperienced people astray, and may very frequently cause damage to our national interests. For such a belief is based, all too often, on the opinion that the public will cannot be opposed. But it *can* be opposed, if the presiding officer is tough enough. And, in any case, it is better to fight for a good cause, and lose, than to give way to a bad one.

The fact is that, as everyone knows, the laws which provide for a secret ballot have deprived our national leaders of all their influence. Yet these laws were never sought after by the general public, as long as it remained free of external control. It was only after the people became tyrannized by powerful bosses that such legislation was demanded. (That, incidentally, is why oral voting produced severer criticisms of bosses than the secret ballot ever has.)

Ways should therefore have been thought out to prevent the people's Assembly from over-enthusiastically backing the bosses with their votes, however bad the proposed measures of those leaders may be. But what should *not* have been done was to provide the people with a method of concealment, whereby they could employ the secret ballot to hide the undesirability of the votes they were casting, while at the same time keeping the high-ranking citizens, the traditional governing class, in ignorance about what was going on in their minds.[1] For these reasons a law such as you are envisaging, which does not exclude the employment of the secret ballot, has never been proposed or supported by any statesman of integrity.

For look at the four such laws which have, in fact, been carried in the past. There was the Gabinian Law (139), introducing the secret ballot in the election of officials, of which the proposer was the tribune Aulus Gabinius – an unknown person, of undistinguished origin. Then, two years later, came the Cassian Law, making the same provision regarding trials before the Assembly. The tribune who proposed it, Lucius Cassius Longinus Ravilla, was a nobleman, but I have to add, without wishing to cause offence to his family, that he was at odds with his class, and spent his time promoting popular measures so as to hunt up cheap applause from the masses. The mover of the third law, the *Lex Papiria* – which extended the same practice to the adoption or rejection of proposed legislation – was Gaius Papirius Carbo,[2] an evil and seditious character, who failed to induce the conservative, governing class to safeguard his personal safety even when he resuscitated his adherence to their cause.

At that juncture oral, open voting seemed to have been completely abolished, with the single exception of trials for treason, which even Lucius Cassius had not included in his law about balloting. But the *Lex Coelia* of Gaius Coelius Caldus[3] imposed secrecy upon that category of trial as well – though he did feel regret, until the end of his days, because he had injured our country in this way, which he had done in order to ruin Gaius Popillius.[4]

In my own city of Arpinum, my own grandfather (whose name I bear), throughout his entire life, opposed a similar law, although his wife, our grandmother, was the sister of Marcus Gratidius, by whom the law was proposed. For Gratidius thereby stirred up a storm in a wine-ladle, as they say, which his son Marcus Marius Gratidianus subsequently did once again 'in the whole Aegean

1. The secret ballot, as Cicero remarks, had been established for elections in 139, and the principle was extended to judicial boards. The nobles and conservatives hated it. Cicero's proposed compromise, that ballots should be written but not secret, is curiously feeble, and one wonders if he was being ironical.

2. Tribune in 131.

3. Tribune in 107.

4. Gaius Popillius, who had capitulated to the Helvetian tribe of the Tigurini, was prosecuted by Gaius Coelius Caldus and banished.

Sea'.[1] When Marcus Aemilius Scaurus, the consul,[2] was told what our grandfather was saying, he commented as follows: 'Marcus Cicero, I wish you had chosen to devote the same spirit and courage, which you have dedicated to your home town, to the affairs of our whole country instead!'

Now, what I am concerned with at the moment is not just to enumerate the actual, current laws of Rome, but to revive old laws which have disappeared, or bring new ones into existence. That being so, I am convinced that you ought to propose, not merely the best measures that can be extracted from Roman institutions as they are at this present time, but instead those which are, objectively, the best. Your friend Lucius Cornelius Scipio Africanus the younger (Aemilianus) was blamed for the Cassian Law, since it was his support, people said, which got it passed. And, by the same token, if you propose a law about balloting, it is you who will have to take the responsibility for its enactment. As for myself, I shall not approve it. Nor will our friend Atticus, as far as I can judge from the look on his face.

ATTICUS: Certainly, no measure passed in the radical interest has ever received my approval. On the contrary, the best form of government, I believed, was the system established by Marcus Cicero here when he was consul: the sort of arrangement that gives power to the traditional leadership.

CICERO: Well, I see you have just brushed aside this law about balloting that I have just suggested – without having recourse to the ballot at all! In my previous work,[3] I gave Scipio Aemilianus the task of providing a sufficient defence of the ideas behind my proposal. But let me stress now, once again, that what I wanted to do is to grant the people liberty of action, but in such a way that the traditional leadership, nevertheless, shall retain its authority and be able to exert it. For the text of my law was going to be: 'that high-ranking citizens, the traditional governing class, should be kept aware of what was going on, though the freedom of the ordinary person to vote as he wishes shall not be interfered with'. This law

1. The reference is probably to Gratidianus's controversial plan to improve the coinage during his praetorship in 86. 'Storm in a wine-ladle': cf. our 'storm in a tea-cup'. The wine-ladle is Arpinum and the Aegean Sea is Rome.

2. In 115.

3. *On the State.*

implies the cancellation of all the supplementary laws which enforce total voting secrecy, ensuring that no one shall have the right to get a glimpse of a ballot, or question or hold up the voters. (The Marian Law even insisted that the gangways, from which ballots are deposited, should be made narrow so that no one could gain access to them.)[1]

Now, if the purpose of introducing such provisions is to prevent the purchase of votes by bribes, as is usually the case, I have nothing to say against them. But if, as I suggest, legislation has never, in fact, managed to put a stop to bribery, then I propose that, while the people should not be prevented from voting exactly as they wish – thus satisfying their claims to liberty – this should be accompanied by the provision that the resultant ballots must be freely displayed and exhibited to all our principal national leaders. And such an arrangement, indeed, would be another manifestation of liberty, in a particular sense: that is to say, the people would be granted the liberty to win the support of their leaders, by honourable means.

By these methods, Quintus, the result which you have in mind would be achieved. For the ballots in trials will, by this compromise, convict a smaller number of defendants than oral votes would convict – because the people have been given the power, and that makes them content. So let them keep that power; and in all else it will be possible for the authority and influence of the traditional governing class to direct what they do. I shall not be discussing, here, the corruption of popular voting by bribery. But let us assume that bribery does not intervene. Then you must see that, according to the system I have proposed, the people, when they vote, will seek the views of the leading men in the state. So our law, while conceding the appearance of liberty, will nevertheless preserve the authority of the leaders – and disputes between the classes will no longer exist.

The next law names the officials who are entitled to preside at meetings of the Assembly and Senate. This is followed by a particularly important law which I strongly commend: that moderate conduct shall be required at the meetings of Assembly and Senate alike. By moderate conduct I mean calm and decent behaviour. The

1. The *Lex tabellaria* introduced by Gaius Marius as tribune in 119 included this narrowing of the gangways (*pontes*), so as to reduce intimidation by keeping spectators out of the way.

presiding officer is the man who has the power to model and regulate the attitudes and wishes of the other members – indeed, one might almost say, he can even guide the expressions on their faces. True, in popular Assemblies, it is far from easy to ensure that this moderation prevails. But in the Senate it is not so difficult. Because a senator is not the sort of person who will base his views on the orders he receives from someone else; he wants to be respected as his own man.

To every member of the Senate I offer these three injunctions. First, he should attend the meetings, since a full house adds force to senatorial deliberations. Secondly, he should speak in his turn, that is to say when he is called upon. Thirdly, his speeches should be brief, and not run on for ever. For brevity in expressing what one has to say is a most valuable merit for a speaker in the Senate, or anywhere else for that matter. A long speech should never be made – except in two, different, circumstances. First, if the Senate is embarking on some harmful course of action – which happens often enough when some improper pressure is at work – and no state official is doing anything to prevent it; in which case it is desirable to spin one's speech out for the whole day. And, secondly, a long speech is once again justified when the subject of the debate is so important that the speaker has to go into the matter at length, either to win the Senate over or see that it is properly informed. (Our friend the younger Cato is very good at both these sorts of oration.)

I have also added this: 'He shall have some knowledge of national affairs.' Well, obviously a senator has to be adequately informed about our country's business. And this involves knowledge covering a very wide field. He must know Rome's military capacity, and the state of the treasury. He must know the names of our friends and allies, and of those who pay us tribute, and what laws and terms and treaties apply to them all. He must also be conversant with the normal procedure for passing a decree. And he must be familiar with the precedents we have inherited from our ancestors. All this will give you an idea of the extensive knowledge, hard work and good memory which are essential to a senator if he is to be equipped to carry out his duties.

Our next subject concerns the Assemblies of the people. Here, the first and most important requirement is this: there must be no employment of violence. In a state which has a regular, organized constitution, violence is more ruinous than anything else, being utterly out of keeping with legality and justice, and totally opposed to civic life and humanity. Another of my provisions requires that vetoes should be respected. This is particularly important. For I would even prefer that a desirable measure should be obstructed, rather than that a bad one should be passed.

My provision concerning the responsibility of the presiding officer is wholly derived from what the extremely acute Lucius Licinius Crassus proposed.[1] When the seditious acts fomented by Cnaeus Papirius Carbo[2] were reported to the Senate by Gaius Claudius Pulcher,[3] it passed a decree supporting Crassus's proposal. For it ruled that disturbances must not take place in an Assembly of the people in defiance of the presiding officer, since he is fully entitled to adjourn the meeting as soon as a proposed measure has been vetoed, and disorder begins to occur. For anyone who incites such disorder at a time after the conduct of business has come to an end is promoting violence, and the legislation to which I refer deprives a man who behaves in that way of any immunity from punishment.

The next law is: 'Anyone who vetoes a measure that is harmful shall be held to have performed a valuable duty to the state.' Surely everybody would be only too glad to come to the help of our nation, in the knowledge that his service will be commended by the unequivocal pronouncement provided by such a law!

The provision that follows already has its place in our national customs and laws. It prescribes that presiding officers of the Assembly and Senate shall pay attention to the auspices, and submit to the decisions of the augur.[4] Correspondingly, a good augur ought to realize that, when there is a major emergency, it is his duty to come to the rescue of the government. He enjoys the elevated status, he must remember, of interpreter and agent of Jupiter the Best and Greatest,[5] and that is the position, too, of his assistants whom he bids watch the auspices on his behalf. And, at the same time, he must bear in mind that the reason why these demarcated sections of

1. Consul in 95. More will be said about this orator in the *Brutus*.

2. Tribune in 92, Consul in 85 and 84.

3. Consul in 92.

4. The priestly college of augurs (diviners) was responsible for the auspices, as is described elsewhere.

5. Assemblies were under the protection of Jupiter, the god of light: meetings came to an end at sunset.

the sky have been assigned to him for divination is in order that they may enable him, whenever occasion arises, to come to the assistance of his country.

Next come the provisions regarding the moving of laws: they insist that no more than one law should be dealt with at any one time, and that private citizens and officials alike should be given the opportunity to speak.

Then we have two very good laws which I have taken over from the Twelve Tables,[1] one eliminating personal exceptions, and the other pronouncing that cases in which the penalty is execution or deprivation of citizenship shall only be tried before the highest category of popular Assembly.[2] For note that before the tribunes ever entered upon their seditious existence, or were even thought of, our ancestors had already framed excellent measures to safeguard the generations to come. What they ruled out was the proposal of any laws directed against particular individuals – any laws, that is to say, which authorized personal exceptions. For laws of such a kind would be against all the principles of justice, seeing that the very word 'law' signifies a measure or command which is of universal application.

Our forefathers also required that all decisions which affect the fates of individuals should be reserved for that same highest Assembly. For when, as there, the people are subdivided according to wealth, rank and age, they make more sensible decisions than when they meet, undivided, in the Assembly of the tribes.[3]

This was a further reason why the highly intelligent, talented Lucius Aurelius Cotta was accurate in his assessment of the measure sending me into exile.[4] For, since this was passed by the Assembly of the tribes, he concluded, the action thus taken against me lacked any proper legal basis. In addition, that is to say, to the damning fact that the presence of armed slaves directed the decisions that

1. The earliest Roman code of laws (451–450).

2. The *comitia centuriata*; see also the next note.

3. Whereas the *comitia centuriata* was the Assembly which enacted laws and elected senior officials, the *comitia plebis tributa* (*concilium plebis*), divided according to the tribes, elected more junior officials, including quaestors, curule aediles and certain army officers (*tribuni militum*). The tribes, which had become territorial, were divisions of the state into which all citizens were registered.

4. Cotta had been consul in 65, seven years before Cicero's exile.

were taken, no action of personal exception, singling out an individual in order to penalize him (by the infliction of the death penalty or loss of citizenship), could legitimately be pronounced by the Assembly of Tribes. This being so, Cotta concluded, since nothing had been properly enacted against me, I needed no further law to annul such a decision. But you and other distinguished men thought it preferable that the whole of Italy should pronounce its opinion of the man whom slaves and bandits claimed to have legally penalized.[1]

The next law relates to the acceptance of money – that is to say to bribery. And since the provisions I have in mind need to be enforced by sanctions that are more substantial than mere words, I have to add: the penalty for their infringement shall be adjusted to fit the gravity of the offence. This means that everyone will be paid in his own coin. Violence will be punished by the death penalty or loss of citizenship. Greed will be paid for by a fine. And excessive keenness to achieve public office will be penalized by public disgrace.

The last set of laws I want to propose have never been in force in this country. But it is in our national interest that they should be passed. What I am referring to is this. Our laws have no guardians to look after them, which means that they assume whatever form our clerks choose to give them. We go to official copyists when we want to see these laws; but we do not possess any state records in which their wording is incorporated. The Greeks took more trouble about this, because they appointed 'guardians of the laws', who not only maintained a watch on their texts – as, indeed, had once been done at Rome – but also kept an eye on how people were behaving, and made sure that they acted in obedience to what the laws told them to do.[2]

According to the law I have in mind, this would be among the duties of the censors, whose office, I insist again, must never be left vacant. And so, 'When a functionary completes his term of office, it is to the censors that he shall submit and explain the official actions he has carried out during his term of office.' And the censors shall

1. Cicero is alluding to the law of 57 BC which recalled him from banishment. Pompey had appealed to the Italians to take up his cause in their municipal Assemblies, or by coming to Rome.

2. These 'guardians of the laws' (*nomophylakes*) were apparently given special powers at Athens by Demetrius of Phalerum (317/315 BC).

publish their preliminary verdict concerning what has been done.[1] In Greece, on the other hand, this is the task of official prosecutors. However, you will not secure adequate severity from prosecutors, unless they are acting of their own free will, without external pressures. For that reason, it is better for the actions of an official to be submitted and explained to the censors; bearing in mind, however, that everything he has done must be subject to the law – and liable to prosecution before a court if it is out of order.

And so our discussion of state officials is now at an end – unless you have any questions to ask on the subject.

ATTICUS: But even if we remain silent, does not the very nature of the topic with which you have been dealing remind you that there is one theme which still remains for you to discuss?

CICERO: What do I still have to discuss? I imagine you are referring to the lawcourts, Atticus. But that is a subdivision of what I have already said about state officials.

ATTICUS: Do you not think, however, that something ought to be said about Roman law, as you originally planned to do?

CICERO: But on that subject, what do you consider has been left out?

ATTICUS: What I consider has been left out is something which it is quite deplorable that public men should know nothing about. You just referred to the fact that we have to apply to the state copyists for the text of our laws. And this means, as I have noticed, that many holders of official posts only know as much as their clerks want them to know, and remain completely unaware of the actual powers the law has conferred on them. Now, after you had enumerated your laws in the field of religion,[2] you thought it necessary to indicate how the right to perform religious ceremonies can be legally transferred from one official to another. And so, by the same token, having described the functions of secular governmental officers, you must surely go on to discuss the powers which they, too, possess in terms of law.

1. This was a suggested adaptation of the Athenian regulation according to which officials, at the conclusion of their tenure of office, underwent an examination (*euthyna*) of the actions they had performed. This strengthening of the venerable office of the censors is perhaps the most important of Cicero's proposed innovations.

2. *On Laws*, II.

CICERO: Very well, I will briefly do so, if I can. Marcus Junius Gracchanus dedicated to your father, who was his friend, a long treatise on the subject, which in my opinion was both erudite and meticulous.[1] Now, in dealing with this theme, we have to distinguish between two different things, natural law, which requires independent consideration and discussion, and Roman law, with regard to which we have to bear precedent and tradition in mind.

ATTICUS: Yes, I agree; and that is just the sort of treatment I am hoping for.[2]

1. This was his lost work *De Potestatibus*.

2. The rest of the book is lost. No doubt it contained Cicero's analysis of the legal bases and limits of the powers of state officials.

CHAPTER 6

THE BRUTUS:
THE IMPORTANCE OF ORATORY

In the Introduction it was pointed out that oratory was an absolutely vital, indispensable and all-important part of Roman government and politics, so that what Cicero, so superlative a speaker himself, and so experienced in government, has to say on the subject is of the greatest historical importance.

He said, in fact, a great deal about this activity. In his youth he wrote On Invention, *a largely technical treatise. Thirty years later, when the Second Triumvirate had removed him from political leadership, he turned back to theoretical handling of the subject once again – which gave him comfort*[1] *– and composed his three-book work* On the Orator *(55).*[2] *Then in 46 he wrote the* Brutus *(or,* On Famous Orators) *and the* Orator.[3]

The Brutus *offers a lively survey of Roman oratory from its earliest times, providing an epitome of the country's history from this significant point of view. Although showing signs of hasty composition,*[4] *it is a very thorough study, involving the names and relationships of a multitude of individuals of earlier epochs, and carrying on right down to the time of writing.*[5] *This, in itself, was a considerable achievement, since works of*

1. *Letters to Friends*, IX, 3, 2.

2. The first book is translated in *Cicero: On the Good Life* (Penguin Classics), pp. 236–336.

3. The *Brutus* was written between January and April 46, just before the receipt of the news of the battle of Thapsus, which shattered the Pompeian cause in north Africa. The treatise betrays signs of nervousness about the outcome (cf. *Letters to Friends*, V, 21), and seems to contain a few subsequent additions.

4. 'And lack of revision. It conveys the impression of rapid dictation, moving forward as one point suggests another, and frequently recalling itself to a sequence or a promised treatment overpassed' (G.L. Hendrickson, *Cicero: Brutus and Orator*, Loeb edition, p. 10). Hendrickson sees the work as a rapidly thrown off emotional defence of Cicero's own oratorical creed.

5. Some of the lesser names are here relegated to Appendix 2.

reference giving the necessary chronological assistance were lacking. As Cicero points out, the appearance of the Liber Annalis, *providing this framework, by Atticus himself, who is one of the participants in the discussion, made his task somewhat easier.*

But the Brutus *is also a self-conscious work, offering many valuable details of Cicero's own training as an orator and, despite his compliments to predecessors, suggesting, by implication, that the practice which he himself followed was better than anything else that had been achieved. This introduces a polemic against those of Cicero's younger contemporaries who called themselves 'Attic' but in fact cultivated, in his view, too bare a style.*[1] *Cicero resents them for disliking his own methods; but he politely assumes that Brutus was on his side on this point although, as a matter of fact, he was not.*[2] *The* Orator, *an attempt to sketch the perfect orator, continues to criticize the Atticists, while admitting that their principal opponents, the* Asiatici, *displayed 'superfluous fat'; although Cicero, while denying that he was one of the* Asiatici *himself, was more on their side (when they were at their best) than on the other, since he believed that to throw away the Grand Style was to throw away the best in Roman oratory.*

As is inevitable in any discussion of this subject, a lot gets said about government and politics. Cicero's attitude towards the men and deeds of earlier times has, by now, become pretty conservative, but he does recognize oratorical skill, and even sometimes statesmanlike ability, in people who had thought very differently, such as the Gracchi. When he looks, however, at the contemporary political scene, he is totally unreconciled to the dictatorship of Caesar, and emphasizes the despair which it inspires in him, as well as his fears for the future. He acknowledges Caesar's cultural gifts, but if we want to look for any recognition or gratitude, because, although Cicero himself had taken the other side in the Civil War, he had been allowed by Caesar to come back to Rome and the Senate, we shall not

1. The leader of these Atticist orators was Gaius Licinius Calvus (92–47?), who was also a distinguished poet, and a friend of Catullus. It has been suggested that Cicero's limited praise of Calvus dissatisfied Brutus.

2. Yet Cicero, as he asserts in this treatise, was greatly encouraged, during this time of adversity, by Brutus's treatise *On Virtue*, which stressed the moral considerations that made a man self-sufficient and serene. As we shall see in the next chapter, Cicero went on to hope that Brutus, after murdering Caesar, would succeed in restoring the Republic – with Cicero himself as his counsellor: though Brutus was never as cordial to the orator as Cicero would have liked (see also last note).

find it.[1] *Cicero makes out that Atticus and Brutus completely agreed with his gloomy assessment; though Atticus, in fact, remained neutral, and Brutus at the time was one of Caesar's chief henchmen, and governor of Cisalpine Gaul (north Italy) – not yet the man who would assassinate Caesar in 44,*[2] *although the dictatorship may already have caused him qualms, as Cicero's present picture of him suggests.*

THE BRUTUS

On leaving Cilicia I came to Rhodes, and there I was told of the death of Quintus Hortensius Hortalus.[3] The news upset me more than anyone imagined. I realized I had lost a friend with whom I had enjoyed an excellent companionship. And I saw that the death of such a distinguished member had caused our college of augurs to suffer a grave loss. Meditating on this, I remembered that it was upon Hortensius's initiative and sworn guarantee of my merits that I had been elected an augur,[4] and that it was he who had inducted me into its membership, so that in accordance with the college's tradition I was in duty bound to esteem him as my father.

I was also distressed for another reason as well. Wise and patriotic citizens were extremely scarce; and now, at a particularly unfortunate juncture in our national affairs, a first-class man had been lost to us. He was also a man who sympathized thoroughly with myself in every aspect of policy. And so Hortensius had left us to mourn the disappearance of his authority and brain power. I grieved to

1. In a letter to Atticus, however, Cicero stresses how tolerant Caesar (dead by this time) had been (*To Atticus*, XIV, 17, 6).

2. Indeed, when the Republican Marcus Porcius Cato the younger killed himself at Utica in 46, Brutus, while urging Cicero to write a eulogy of the dead man, also suggested that he should employ more cautious language than he had used in this treatise (written earlier in the same year). For the relations between Cicero and Brutus after Caesar's murder, see below, Chapter 7. Cicero had been opposed to Cato, though in quite a good-humoured fashion, in *For Murena* (Chapter 2).

3. Cicero was proconsul of Cilicia in 51–50. Hortensius had been consul in 69.

4. Cicero became an augur (official diviner) in 53, succeeding Publius Licinius Crassus, son of the triumvir.

have lost, not as some supposed, a hostile rival of my own achievements, but, instead, an ally and fellow-worker in our noble endeavours. Let us compare another (less distinguished) field of activity. Tradition records that illustrious poets have mourned when fellow-poets died.[1] So there is all the greater reason for me, in my own field, to sorrow for the death of a person with whom it was more glorious to compete than if there had been no competitors at all. All the more so because his career was never impeded by mine, or mine by his. The contrary was the case. By suggestions, pieces of advice and friendly support, he helped me, and I helped him.[2]

His life, at all times, was a good one. He departed from it at a time which suited himself well enough; though it did not suit his fellow-citizens. He died at a time when, if he had lived, he would have found it easier to lament the state of Rome than to put it right. He lived as long as it was possible for a man to live an honourable and praiseworthy life in this country. So if we must grieve for him, let us grieve for our own misfortune and loss. As for his own point of view, let us not view his death with commiseration, but rather with the grateful reflection that it came when he was content that this should be so. He was eminent and happy, and whenever we think of him let our thoughts be concentrated on the love we bore him, and not on our love for our own interests which have suffered by his death.

That we can no longer enjoy his presence among us is tragic. But it is a tragedy that we have to endure, with due restraint. What I mean is that we must take care, as I said before, not to harbour such a feeling because of the damage it inflicts on ourselves, rather than because (more fittingly) we have lost a friend. For if we choose to base our distress, instead, on the view that he, himself, has suffered some calamity, then we are failing to offer sufficient recognition of the good fortune which he continued to enjoy until the end. For if Hortensius were alive today, he, like other fine and patriotic citizens, would no doubt regret the loss of a great number of things. But one thing he would regret more than anyone else, or more than only a very few, at most. And that would be the sight of the Roman

1. e.g. Sophocles was said to have mourned the death of Euripides in 406 BC.

2. Cicero tactfully forgets that they had been on opposite sides in the Verres case (Chapter 1).

Forum, the stage of his talents, plundered and bereaved of the gifted eloquence that Romans, like Greeks, are entitled to listen to.[1]

That is what I find so painful in my own case. I am deeply hurt that my country feels no need for the capacity to give advice, and for the intelligence and authority that I had learnt to acquire and had become accustomed to apply – these being the weapons which a leading public figure, and a civilized, soundly based state, ought to have at their disposal. That was just the very moment, in the history of Rome, when the prestige and eloquence of a patriotic citizen was best qualified to disarm his angry opponents. And it was precisely the moment when, instead, the cause of peace was abruptly blocked; because of human error, or because people were afraid.

Certainly, there were other, general, aspects of the situation that were deplorable on a much greater scale. Yet to me there was one peculiarly distressing feature. I had had a distinguished career. I had reached an age when I was entitled to sail into port, and take refuge; not in order to be idle, and do nothing, but to enjoy respectable tranquillity. And, besides, my oratory had become mature – it had reached, you might say, a respectable age. What was peculiarly lamentable, therefore, then, was that that was the particular juncture when recourse was had to arms. And the men who had learnt to make successful use of those arms did not find a way of using them beneficially.

In other states, and most of all in our own, the men who, in my opinion, have led happy and fortunate lives are those who have been permitted full enjoyment of the authority owed to their glorious achievements and to the reputation their wisdom had earned them.

To recall that such men had existed, and to revive their memory, amid all the harrowing anxieties of the present time, proved a very pleasant relief, when we happened to come upon the subject in a recent conversation. I was at home one day, without any business on my hands, and was taking a walk in my garden, when Marcus Junius Brutus came to call on me, as he frequently did. He brought Titus Pomponius Atticus with him. The two men were close friends, and I was so fond of them and glad to see them that all the worries about our national situation that had been weighing me down disappeared. I greeted them, and asked:

1. The dictatorship of Caesar, and the outbreak of the Civil War (49), are criticized for hampering freedom of speech in politics and the courts.

'Well, Brutus and Atticus? Have you any news yet?'[1]

'No, nothing,' answered Brutus. 'Or at least nothing that you would want to hear, or that I should venture to call definite.'

Then Atticus intervened. 'Our purpose in coming to see you', he said, 'was precisely to get away from national affairs and to hear something from yourself, instead of distressing you with what we ourselves might say.'

'But, on the contrary, Atticus,' I replied, 'the very fact that you are here calms my worries. And indeed, when you were not here, you already provided me with a very real consolation. For your writings revived my spirits, and called me back to the studies in which I had been engaged before.'

'And I for my part was extremely glad', interposed Atticus, 'to read the essay that Brutus sent you from Asia.[2] It seemed to me not only to present you with comfort that came from the heart but also to offer sensible advice.'

'Yes, that is correct,' I answered. 'I had long felt extremely disturbed, which affected my whole state of health. But what Brutus had written made it possible for me to look at the light of day once again. It was like what happened after the disaster at Cannae.[3] The victory of Marcus Claudius Marcellus at Nola gave the Roman people new heart,[4] and from that time onwards successes followed, one after another. Well, in the same sort of way, after all the catastrophes that I myself, in common with our whole country, had suffered, nothing good had happened to me at all, nothing had in the slightest degree relieved my worries, until I received that communication from Brutus.'

'Certainly,' commented Brutus, 'that was what I hoped to achieve, and if at such a critical time I managed to do so I am very well rewarded. But I should also like to know which writing of Atticus brought you so much pleasure.'

'Indeed, Brutus, it was not only pleasure it brought me. It actually saved me!'

'Saved you?' he said. 'Then it must have been an extraordinary work. What was it?'

1. i.e. about the war in north Africa between Caesar and the Pompeians. The final defeat of the latter at Thapsus (46) was not yet known.

2. Brutus's treatise *De Virtute*.

3. In 216.

4. He gained two victories at Nola, in 216 and 214.

'I can assure you that no salutation – or salvation[1] – could possibly have given me greater pleasure, or could have been more appropriate to these times in which we live, than this work which Atticus addressed to me. There was I, lying on the ground, and it raised me up!'

'I deduce', observed Brutus, 'that you are referring to the book in which he offers a concise survey of all history – very faithfully, as far as I can judge.'[2]

'Yes, Brutus, that is the work. I repeat, it was my salvation.'

'That is extremely welcome praise,' said Atticus. 'But what exactly was it, in the book, that you found so novel or helpful?'

'A great deal of the book was novel,' I replied. 'And your comprehensive survey of the whole historical process, in chronological order, gave me just the help that I needed. I began to study what you had written very carefully; and the mere fact of doing so brought my health back. Furthermore, Atticus, it instilled in me the idea, not only, as I said, of taking something of yours for my own rehabilitation, but also of doing what I could to repay you.

'Certainly I am aware that no such repayment, however much you may appreciate it, can equal what you have given me! Learned people quote Hesiod's instruction to repay at the same rate as you have received, or at a higher rate still, if you can.[3] As far as goodwill is concerned, I will certainly repay you very fully indeed, but I do not yet seem able to repay you in the same literary medium as you yourself employed, and for this I ask your pardon. I cannot repay you out of a new crop, as farmers do, because no such crop exists: since all new growth has been crushed inside me, and all that fertility which was once so substantial has been burnt out by drought. Nor can I repay you from what is kept in my storehouse. For it just lies there, in the dark. I am the only person who has the power to bring it out, but I am unable to do so, because I cannot get near it. What I have to do, therefore, is to sow something in soil that has not so far been cultivated at all, but has been left alone. If I cultivate it meticulously, I *shall* be able to repay your generous gift – with interest. If, that is, my mind can operate as effectively as a

1. This is a play on the word *salus*, which means both.
2. Atticus's *Liber Annalis*.
3. *Works and Days*, 349f.

field: which after lying fallow for many years often provides a more abundant harvest than it ever did before.'

'I shall look forward to what you are promising,' answered Atticus. 'But I shall only require it at your convenience. And if you do pay back your debt in that way, I shall be grateful indeed!'

'And I too', added Brutus, 'shall look forward to what you are promising Atticus. However, I am Atticus's agent, and in that capacity, since you are his debtor, I may well be more peremptory than he is in demanding the repayment, which he says he will only require at your convenience.'

'All the same, Brutus,' I reminded him, 'I can assure you that I shall not pay *you* anything at all until you first pledge that your client will not try to exact payment twice over.'

'No,' said Brutus, 'I am afraid I can offer you no such pledge, since I can see that Atticus, although he denies it, will in fact claim back what you owe him, if not offensively, at least with determination and insistence.'

'I am afraid Brutus is perfectly right,' declared Atticus. 'Indeed, I already see myself on the verge of demanding repayment, now that today, for the first time, after so long a period of depression, I find you in a more cheerful frame of mind. In consequence, since Brutus has undertaken that he will recover what you owe to myself, I for my part, conversely, demand the repayment of what you owe him.'

'What do you mean by that?' said I.

'That you should do some writing. For it is a long time since you wrote anything whatever. Indeed since you produced those books *On the State* we have had nothing from you at all. That was the work which prompted and incited me to compile my own record of events and list of office-holders. But I only offer this request as and when you feel yourself able to meet it. As for now, if you feel free to do so, expound to us the matter which we came to ask you about.'

'And what is that?' I asked.

'The matter about which you began to speak to me recently at your house at Tusculum – concerning orators: when they first came into existence, and who they were, and what sort of people. When I reported that conversation to your friend Brutus, I should say our friend Brutus, here, he said he was very keen to hear about it. So we chose today for the purpose, knowing that you would be free.

If, therefore, it is not inconvenient, carry on with what you started on that occasion, for the benefit of Brutus and myself.'

'All right,' I replied. 'I will do what I can to satisfy you.'

'That you will certainly be able to do. But just relax a little first and, if you find it possible, set your mind free of other cares.'

'When we had that earlier discussion, Atticus, I believe I remember the point which gave rise to it. I had referred to the ample and well-rounded eloquence with which Brutus defended the case of that loyal and excellent monarch Deiotarus.'[1]

'Yes,' said Atticus. 'I remember that our talk began at that point. And I remember also how sad you felt about Brutus, and how you were almost in tears about the desolation of the lawcourts and the Forum.'

'That was certainly the case,' I said, 'and it often still is. For when I look at you, Brutus, it is you that I continually worry about. I worry about what career prospects remain available for your excellent natural talents and consummate education and remarkable capacity for work. For it was just at the very time when you were embarking on cases of major importance – the time when my own advancing age was making me lay down my sceptre and take second place to yourself – that public life collapsed. And in addition to its collapse in so many other fields, eloquence, the subject of our present discussion, fell silent.'

'For every reason that can be thought of,' replied Brutus, 'I share your distress, and regard it as wholly justified. But in regard to eloquence, it is not so much the rewards and fame which it offers that give me satisfaction, as the study and training which lie behind it. Nothing will take that away from me – and I look at the shining example of your own devoted activity. No one can be a good orator unless he is also a man of sound understanding. So whoever dedicates himself to true eloquence dedicates himself also to right thinking. For that is something which, even in the midst of mighty wars, no one can sensibly do without.'

'What you say is very true, Brutus,' I replied, 'and it makes me all the more happy about the reputation for eloquence which you

1. Deiotarus, a ruler (tetrarch) in Galatia (central Asia Minor), was a partisan of Pompey on whose behalf Brutus had spoken (unsuccessfully) before Caesar at Nicaea in Bithynia (47). Cicero also spoke for him: *Cicero: Murder Trials* (Penguin Classics), pp. 297ff.

yourself have acquired. Because as for the other rewards in public life which have always been valued most highly, any man, however humble, is able to convince himself that he can obtain them or has already done so. But no one has ever been made eloquent by war: of that I am perfectly certain.

'However, let us sit down, if you agree, so that our discussion can proceed more comfortably. And then we can carry on with what we want to talk about.'

They agreed, and we took our seats on the lawn, beside a statue of Plato.

'Well,' I began, 'what I am proposing to do is not to sing the praises of eloquence, to describe its power, and to list the high positions it brings to those who possess it; for there is no need to do so. But there is one point that I want to insist upon, without hesitation, and it is this. Whether oratory is a creation of rules, or of training, or of natural gifts, it is the most difficult of all things to achieve. It is said to consist of five elements.[1] And each of the five is a great art, in its own right. Just imagine, then, the potency of something that is made up of five great arts! And just imagine the problems involved!

'The Greeks bear ample witness that this is so. Fired with enthusiasm for eloquence, they have always excelled in it, beyond all other countries. And yet, all the same, they had invented and even perfected every other art that exists before they ever developed the power and abundance of eloquence.

'When Greece comes to my mind, Atticus, it is particularly your Athens of which I am thinking, for its eminence shines out with a great light. It was in Athens that orators first made themselves conspicuous, and it was there that their speeches were first set down in writings and records. Nevertheless, before Pericles, to whom some writings are ascribed, and before Thucydides[2] – and those are men who do not belong to the time of Athens's birth, but to its adult years – there are no Athenian speeches in writing at all, or at least none that display any finish or look like the work of an orator. And yet tradition maintains that Pisistratus, who had lived long before them, had been a very competent speaker, considering his

1. Invention, arrangement, diction, action, memory.

2. Pericles (*c.* 495–429) was leader of Athens for over thirty years. Thucydides (460/455–*c.* 400) is the historian.

epoch, and so was Solon who lived shortly before him, and Cleisthenes who emerged afterwards.[1] Some years later, as can be seen from Atticus's chronological accounts, was the lifetime of Themistocles, who is well known to have been outstanding not only for shrewdness but for eloquence as well. Then came Pericles, eminent in every field, but particularly as a speaker. And that was also the age of Cleon, who despite his violent behaviour in public life is known to have been a fine orator. Alcibiades, Critias and Theramenes were more or less his contemporaries.[2] So, too, was Thucydides, from whose writings the type of eloquence that prevailed in that period can best be reconstructed. The vocabulary of those men was imposing, and they expressed their thoughts acutely, but with a brevity that amounted to compression – for which reason what they said could at times be somewhat obscure.

'But when it came to be realized what power a carefully prepared and constructed speech could wield, then, suddenly, teachers of public speaking began to abound. Gorgias of Leontini, Thrasymachus of Calchedon, Protagoras of Abdera, Prodicus of Ceos, Hippias of Elis, were all regarded with respect.[3] They and many of their contemporaries professed, in distinctly arrogant terms, to demonstrate how the worse cause (for that is how they described it) could be made by eloquent speech into seeming the better. Against them stood Socrates, who regularly employed astute arguments to refute what they were teaching. His compelling discourses caused men of profound erudition to appear; and what they invented, we are told, was that type of philosophy which deals not with natural science – which was more ancient – but with ethical questions of good and evil, and with human life and customs. However, this branch of knowledge is not what we have set out to talk about today. So let us relegate our discussion of philosophers to some time in the future, and go back to orators – from whom I have digressed.

1. Pisistratus was tyrant of Athens from 561 to 556 and from 546 to 527. Solon, the Athenian statesman, was archon in 594–3, and Cleisthenes in 528–7.

2. Themistocles (*c.* 528–462) was the creator of Athens's fleet and the principal author of victory against the Persians (480). Cleon, assailed as a 'demagogue', was killed in battle against the Spartans in 422. Alcibiades (*c.* 450–404) was a maverick Athenian politician and commander, Critias (*c.* 460–403) was one of the Thirty Tyrants at Athens, and Theramenes was another, but was executed by their extremist wing.

3. They were all fifth-century sophists (popular philosophers and lecturers).

'When the Greeks of whom I have just been speaking were old men, Isocrates came to the fore.[1] His house became virtually a training school and workshop of oratory, accessible to numerous pupils. He was a fine speaker himself, and an admirable teacher, but he kept away from the bright light of public life, and inside the walls of his school perfected a distinction which, in my opinion, nobody else has achieved ever since. He wrote a great deal, very well, and taught extensively. He improved on his predecessors in many respects, and in particular he was the first to understand that even in the writing of prose, although strict metre should be avoided, it is nevertheless desirable to maintain a certain rhythm and cadence. Before Isocrates there had been no texture, linking words together, you might say, and no rhythmical terminations of sentences. Or if they had happened to occur, there was no evidence that they had been achieved intentionally. Perhaps that, in itself, deserved commendation, but in any case this rhythmical structure had only come about occasionally, as a natural process and by accident, rather than in pursuance of any rule or deliberate design. For natural instinct, at times, brings sentences to a close by a proper arrangement of material, disposing and marshalling the words in a rhythmical order. For what takes place is that the human ear itself decides what is complete and what is lacking, and the speaker's breathing, by some innate compulsion of its own, affixes the proper termination to the series of words which has constituted a sentence. If the breathing breaks down, or finds itself in trouble, the result is unsuccessful.

'A contemporary of Isocrates was Lysias.[2] He did not take part in forensic lawsuits himself, but wrote with remarkable subtlety and elegance. He was a man you would almost feel inclined to describe as the perfect orator. But as the *real* perfect orator, who was deficient in no respect whatever, you would inevitably have to name Demosthenes.[3] However sharp, however shrewd and cunning, your intelligence might be when you listened to him, you would never manage to find him guilty, in any of the speeches he wrote, of even the most insignificant oversight. The refinement, conciseness and directness of his language were as finished as could be; the

1. Athenian orator and educationalist (436–338 BC).
2. Athenian orator of Syracusan origin (*c.* 459–*c.* 380).
3. The greatest Athenian orator (384–322).

grandeur, the passion, the well-rounded forcefulness both of his vocabulary and of his general expression attained unequalled heights. Next after him, at Athens, came Hyperides, Aeschines, Lycurgus, Dinarchus, Demades (of whom no writings survive) and a number of others. Such was the prodigious fertility of that epoch's oratorical output. Down to that time inclusive, as it seems to me, the life-juice and blood of oratory remained without contamination, and kept its natural colouring, without the need for any dye to add supplementary tints.

'Their old age was followed by the young Demetrius of Phalerum.[1] He was the most learned of them all. But his methods were those of the training school rather than of the battlefield of public speaking. He did not so much stir up the Athenians' emotions as provide them with entertainment. For he had come into the light and dust of day not from a soldier's tent, but from the shaded retreat of the eminent philosopher Theophrastus.[2] Demetrius was the first to introduce modulations into oratory, and infuse it with softness and delicacy. He wanted to be charming (which he was) rather than grave; and the charm he employed was designed to pervade the hearts of his hearers without shattering them to pieces. His oratory left behind an atmosphere of harmoniousness. What it did not do was to leave, in addition to this pleasant impression, a powerful sting in the minds of his audience – which was what Eupolis[3] said of Pericles.

'So do you not see, Brutus, that even in that city of Athens in which eloquence was born and grew up, it was only at quite a late date that it came forth into the light of day? Before the time of Solon and Pisistratus, that is to say, there is no tradition of any significant orator at all. Certainly, those two men are early, in terms of Roman chronology. But in terms of all the epochs of Athenian history they must count as very young. True, they were already flourishing when Servius Tullius was king of Rome.[4] Yet even by that time Athens had already existed longer than the total existence of Rome down to the present day.

1. See p. 200, note 3.

2. Successor of Aristotle as head of the Peripatetic school (*c.* 370–288/5).

3. One of the leading exponents of the Athenian Old Comedy (later fifth century BC; fragment 94 Kock).

4. Traditionally the sixth king of Rome (578–535 BC).

'And yet I do not doubt that oratory had always been very influential, even before that. As long ago as Trojan times Homer would not have bestowed so much praise on Ulysses and Nestor for their speech-making – describing the forcefulness of the one, and the persuasiveness of the other[1] – unless eloquence, even at that early period, had already been held in honour. Nor indeed, if that was not so, would the poet himself have been such a skilful stylist – so completely, in fact, the orator. Homer's date is uncertain. Yet he certainly lived many years before Romulus. And he was not later than the first Lycurgus, who passed the laws that fixed the Spartan way of life.[2]

'But it was under Pisistratus, at Athens, that we can detect the full cultivation of oratory, and an increase in its influence. In the next generation he was followed by Themistocles. To us, once again, he seems early, but not to Athenians. For he lived when Greece was already a dominant power, at the time when our own state had only recently liberated itself from monarchic rule. For the most serious of the wars against the Volscians, in which Cnaeus Marcius Coriolanus took part while he was banished from Rome,[3] was more or less contemporary with Greece's Persian War.[4] And the destinies of the two famous men, Themistocles and Coriolanus, were not unlike. Both were leading men in their states. Both were unjustly banished by their ungrateful peoples. Both went over to the enemy. Both made plans for revenge against their home countries, but cancelled them by their voluntary deaths. Yes, Atticus, I know that in your book you tell Coriolanus's story differently. But let me be permitted, please, to describe his death in this way instead!'

Atticus smiled at this, and replied: 'As you wish – since rhetoricians are granted the privilege of fabricating history in order to give more point to what they are saying! Just as you have done in speaking of Coriolanus's death, Clitarchus and Stratocles both in-

1. Homer, *Iliad*, III, 221f., and I, 248f.

2. Lycurgus, if he existed, was the founder of the Spartan §§ (social and political system).

3. Coriolanus was said to have led a Volscian army against Rome (from which he had been exiled) in the early fifth century BC.

4. i.e. the battles of Marathon (490), Thermopylae and Salamis (480), Plataea (479).

vented a story of how Themistocles died.[1] But look at the version of Thucydides, an Athenian of distinguished birth and an eminent man, who lived only a little later than Themistocles. According to him, Themistocles merely died a natural death and was secretly buried in Attica. There were rumours, Thucydides added, that he had committed suicide by taking poison: whereas Clitarchus and Stratocles record that after sacrificing a bullock he drank its blood from a bowl, and after drinking it fell down dead. For that is the sort of death which gave them an opportunity to apply rhetorical and tragic colouring, whereas an ordinary natural end did not offer any similar opportunity. So if you feel the inclination to assign the two men comparable destinies, then I grant you permission to take the bowl – I will even give you a sacrificial victim – and make Coriolanus a second Themistocles.'

'Very well then,' I replied, 'as far as Coriolanus is concerned let it be as you wish. But from now on I shall be more cautious about historical matters when you are listening, since I know that you are a Roman historian of scrupulous accuracy – for which you deserve all praise.

'I was talking about Pericles, the son of Xanthippus. He was the earliest public speaker to make a study of oratory. Actually, there was at that time nothing to study, within the field. But since he had been trained by Anaxagoras, the natural scientist,[2] he found it a simple matter to transfer the same intellectual method from abstruse and esoteric matters to cases that come up in public life and the popular Assembly. The Athenians enjoyed the charm of Pericles's oratory, and admired its richness and fluency, and were intimidated by its forcefulness and the terrors it inspired.

'So that was the epoch which, unprecedentedly, produced an orator who was all but perfect. For when people are occupied with the creation of a new government, or engaged in the conduct of war, or tied up and shackled by monarchical domination, the urge to become a public speaker does not arise. Peace and tranquillity are the conditions which create eloquence as their comrade and ally; it is the product, one can say, of a state which is in good order. That is

1. Clitarchus of Alexandria was a third-century historian, and Stratocles probably the orator and politician who prosecuted Demosthenes for embezzlement (324).

2. Anaxagoras of Clazomenae (*c.* 500–*c.* 428), pre-Socratic philosopher.

why Aristotle says what he does about Sicily, after its tyrants had been expelled. After a long period of suspension, people were trying to get their private property back through the courts. That was why it came about that two Sicilians, Corax and Tisias, being persons of the acute and disputatious characters that their countrymen possess, were the first to write down some theoretical rules about oratory.[1] Before that time, although many had made speeches that were careful enough, and well arranged, no one had been accustomed to pursue a definite, regular method.

'Aristotle went on to recount that Protagoras organized and wrote down discussions of certain well-known topics, which we now know as "commonplaces". Gorgias also, he said, did the same, concentrating especially on commendation or censure of specific viewpoints, since he regarded it the particular function of orators to offer judgements, praising and magnifying, or condemning and belittling, the people they were talking about. Antiphon of Rhamnus, too, Aristotle added, wrote on similar subjects.[2] And Thucydides, who is highly reliable, declared that no one ever pleaded a case better than Antiphon, when, in the historian's hearing, he defended himself on a capital charge. As for Lysias, Aristotle maintained that it was only at the outset of his career that he professed to be a teacher of rhetoric, whereas thereafter, since Theodorus performed that function more skilfully (though he was somewhat arid as an orator),[3] he began to write speeches – for other men to deliver – and gave up teaching as a consequence.

'Aristotle also wrote that Isocrates changed his profession in the same way. At first Isocrates pronounced that no art of public speaking existed at all, although in spite of that he made a habit of composing speeches for others to deliver in the lawcourts. But then, more than once, he was prosecuted for having broken a law which was directed, like our own, against the criminal circumvention of justice.[4] And from that time onwards he stopped writing speeches

1. Corax of Syracuse (fifth century BC) was said to have been the first teacher of rhetoric. Tisias was his pupil.

2. Protagoras of Abdera (fifth century BC) was one of the earliest sophists. He taught at Athens, like Gorgias of Leontini (*c.* 483–376). Antiphon (*c.* 480–411) was an Attic orator, often confused with a sophist of the same name.

3. Theodorus of Byzantium (second half of fifth century BC).

4. Sulla's *Lex Cornelia de sicariis* (81) covered not only crimes of violence but bribery, conspiracy and perjury.

for others and transferred his entire attention to composing theoretical analyses of the subject instead.

'So you can see how oratory was born and originated in Greece, at an early period in comparison with our own Roman chronology, but from their point of view at quite a recent date. For long before Athens began to enjoy the glorious art of speaking, it had already accomplished many notable achievements in peace and war alike.

'As regards oratory, the rest of the Greek mainland did not share this process of development, which was peculiar to Athens. For there is no knowledge whatever of any oratory of Argos or Corinth or Thebes at that epoch – unless you want to propose the name of Epaminondas, who was, certainly, an educated man.[1] As for Sparta, I have never heard that it has produced one single orator, right up to the present day. True, Homer mentions that Menelaus was a pleasant speaker; though he adds that he did not say very much.[2] Brevity in oratory can, at times, be a virtue. But in eloquence taken as a whole it does not deserve to count as a merit.[3]

'Outside the mainland of Greece, on the other hand, public speaking was cultivated with enthusiasm, and the high honours which its practitioners were able to win gave oratory a distinguished name. For when eloquence had once sailed forth out of the Piraeus it passed through all the islands and pervaded the whole of Asia. Yet in the course of this expansion it became smeared with foreign ways and lost what you might call the wholesome sanity of Attic diction. Indeed, it almost forgot how people naturally speak. That was the source from which the Asiatic orators originated. Their fluency and abundance are by no means contemptible. Yet they lack conciseness, and are verbose. The school of Rhodes is healthier, and closer to the Attic orators.

'But that is enough about the Greeks. Indeed perhaps I have gone on about them at unnecessary length.'

'No,' said Brutus, 'on the contrary it was very necessary indeed – more so than I can easily tell you. I found it extremely interesting. No, your survey was not too long at all. I should have liked it to have been longer.'

1. The Theban political and military leader (died 362).

2. Homer, *Iliad*, III, 213ff.

3. Later on, Cicero returns to the point, in criticism of the Atticists; whom he praises, however, here (so long as they were not stylistic extremists).

'That is very good of you,' I said. 'But now let us come to our own early Romans. It is hard to learn anything more about them than what the historical records hint. It is impossible, however, to agree with the view that Lucius Junius Brutus, the founder of your noble family, lacked ready intelligence. On the contrary he interpreted the oracle of Apollo about kissing his mother with considerable cleverness.[1] Under the appearance of stupidity, he concealed extremely good sense. He drove a very powerful monarch, son of a famous predecessor, out of the country, and once he had liberated our land from the continuous domination of that despotic régime, he welded Rome together by establishing annual offices of state and creating laws and lawcourts. And he even deprived his own colleague of his job so that the memory of the royal name, which that colleague bore, should be erased.[2] All this could certainly not have been achieved without the persuasion that oratory was able to provide.

'Let us now pass on to a few years after the expulsion of the king. The plebeians had seceded to the third milestone, beside the River Anio, and had occupied the hill which from then onwards was called the Sacred Mount. At that point we find that Marcus Valerius, who was dictator,[3] calmed down the rift in our nation by his eloquence. Because of this success we are told that he was awarded honours of the utmost distinction. And for the same reason he was the first to be given the name of Maximus. I am also of the opinion that Lucius Valerius Potitus[4] must have been a competent orator. For he was the man who, after the strained relations caused by the decemvirs,[5] succeeded in appeasing the plebeians' wrath against the patricians. We can also suspect that Appius Claudius Caecus[6] was an able speaker, since he displayed the power to

1. According to tradition Lucius Junius Brutus, the founder of the Roman Republic, who drove out King Tarquinius Superbus (son of Tarquinius Priscus) and became consul in 509, had been told by Apollo's oracle that the supreme power at Rome would go to the man who first kissed his mother; whereupon, pretending to fall, he kissed the earth.

2. Lucius Tarquinius Collatinus.

3. Or he may have been called Manius. He was believed to have been dictator in 494.

4. Consul 449.

5. The *decemviri legibus scribundis* (451–449), who drew up the Twelve Tables.

6. Consul in 307 and 296.

reverse the Senate's inclination to make peace with Pyrrhus of Epirus.[1] And the same was surely true of Gaius Fabricius Luscinus,[2] since he was sent as an envoy to Pyrrhus in order to get our prisoners back; and of Tiberius Coruncanius,[3] since the records of the college of priests[4] reveal his exceptional intellectual gifts. Moreover, the same can be said, too, of Manius Curius Dentatus.[5] He was tribune of the people at the time when Appius Claudius Caecus, an eloquent man as I have said, was presiding over an election to consulships.[6] Appius, in defiance of the law, had refused to accept a plebeian candidate for the office. But Manius Curius opposed him, and compelled the senators to agree in advance that they would ratify the result of the election that was about to take place. It was a remarkable achievement to have got such a measure through before the Maenian Law was passed.[7]

'It is also legitimate to conjecture that Marcus Popillius Laenas[8] possessed oratorical gifts. While, in his capacity as consul, he was engaged in the performance of a state sacrifice, wearing the robes of his priesthood of Carmenta,[9] news came to him that the plebeians had risen against the patricians, and had revolted. Still in his priestly vestments, just as he was, he proceeded to the Assembly, and by his words, as well as his authority, quelled the disturbance.

'But that these men were considered orators, or that in those days there were any rewards for eloquence, I cannot remember ever having read. I can only suspect and guess that this was so. It is also reported that Gaius Flaminius, the tribune of the people who passed the law distributing the Ager Gallicus and Picenum,[10] and who as consul for the second time was killed in the battle of Lake

1. Pyrrhus (297–272) invaded Italy and Sicily. The peace plan was in 279/8.

2. Consul in 282.

3. Consul in 280.

4. The *pontifices*, of whom the chief priest (*pontifex maximus*) was the leader.

5. Consul in 290.

6. As *interrex*, in 298.

7. The *Lex Maenia* of Marcus Maenius (287) reaffirmed that the Senate had to ratify decisions of the Assembly before they became valid.

8. Consul in 359.

9. The priest was the *Flamen Carmentalis*. Carmenta, in myth, was a prophet and nymph, the mother of Evander; and she was also a goddess of water.

10. In 232.

Trasimene,[1] spoke effectively in the Assembly. Quintus Fabius Maximus Verrucosus Cunctator,[2] too, was, according to the standards of that period, regarded as an orator. And so was Quintus Caecilius Metellus, who was consul during the Second Punic War with Lucius Veturius Philo as his colleague.[3]

'The earliest Roman, however, about whose eloquence, and its recognition, a positive tradition survives is Marcus Cornelius Cethegus.[4] When I say this, I am speaking on the authority of the poet Ennius; an adequate authority in my opinion, especially as Ennius had, personally, heard Cethegus speak – and, moreover, was writing about him after his death, so that any favouritism on grounds of friendship is ruled out. I believe the relevant passage is in the ninth book of Ennius's *Annals*:

'"To his colleague Publius Sempronius Tuditanus was added the sweet-tongued orator Marcus Cornelius Cethegus, the son of Marcus." So Ennius calls him orator,[5] and calls him sweet-tongued as well. That is a quality that you do not find in most speakers nowadays, since they often seem to bark rather than speak. But what Ennius then goes on to say is a noble eulogy of eloquence:

> He used to be described by his contemporaries at that time,
> The men who lived then and spent their troubled days,
> As the choice flower of the people.

That was well said; since, as reason is the glory of humankind, so the lamp that lights reason is eloquence. For distinction in eloquence, therefore, the citizens of that time did well to describe such a man as the "flower of the people". And Ennius also describes him as "the marrow of Persuasion". Now, persuasion is the activity which it is the function of every orator to bring into effect. It was personified by the Greeks as *Peitho*, who according to Eupolis[6] always sat on the lips of Pericles. It was of this, then, that Cethegus was the marrow.

'Now Cethegus was consul, with Publius Sempronius Tuditanus

1. In the Second Punic War, against Hannibal (217). Cicero, elsewhere, censures Gaius Flaminius as one of the originators of anti-establishment radicalism.
2. Consul in 233 etc.
3. In 206.
4. Consul in 204.
5. But Ennius had meant *orator* to mean ambassador, rather than orator.
6. Dramatist of the Athenian Old Comedy, later fifth century BC.

as his colleague, in the course of the Second Punic War, during the year when Marcus Porcius Cato the elder (Censorius) was quaestor,[1] one hundred and forty years before I myself became consul. And if it were not for the fact that Cethegus's eloquence is known to us by the testimony of Ennius, and Ennius alone, the passage of time would have plunged him into oblivion: which is, no doubt, what many others have suffered.

'The language employed at that epoch can be reconstructed from the writings of Naevius. For it was during those two men's consulships, as early documents record, that Naevius died; although our friend Marcus Terentius Varro, keen investigator of early history as he is,[2] believes that date to be mistaken, and prefers to extend Naevius's life. He justifies this by the fact that Plautus, Naevius's contemporary, did not die until the consulship of Publius Claudius Pulcher and Lucius Porcius Licinus,[3] twenty years after the consulships of the two earlier men, when Marcus Porcius Cato the elder was censor.[4] Well, it was Cato, chronologically speaking, who followed Cethegus, becoming consul nine years after him.[5] Cato seems to us very early. He died when Lucius Marcius Censorinus and Manius Manilius were consuls,[6] precisely eighty-six years before my own consulship.

'Before that, I am unable to name any orator at all who could be classified among writers: unless some may find pleasure, perhaps, in that speech of Appius Claudius Caecus about Pyrrhus to which I have referred, or in certain funeral encomia. For some of these, sure enough, are still extant. The families of the dead men have preserved them as trophies and memorials to be brought out when later members of their houses die, in order to recall the past glories of their ancestries, and support their own claims to noble lineage. However, these eulogies have had the effect of falsifying our history. For they include numerous things that never occurred,

1. In 204.

2. The polymath Varro of Reate (116–27). St Jerome ascribed Naevius's death to 201.

3. In 184.

4. The death of Plautus, the comic dramatist, may have occurred later than 184, which refers (as frequently) to the last record of his production of a new play.

5. In 195.

6. In 149.

fictitious triumphs, multiple consulships, non-existent relationships, and fabricated transfers from patrician to plebeian status, in which men of undistinguished origins claim a blood-link with a noble family of the same name, although in fact no such link existed: as if I, for example, should claim descent from the patrician Manius Tullius Longus, who was consul with Servius Sulpicius Camarinus Cornutus ten years after the expulsion of the kings.[1]

'But to return to Cato and Lysias. Cato's speeches are almost as numerous as those of the Athenian (to whom, however, I believe that some are wrongly attributed). I call Lysias Athenian because he was certainly born and died at Athens, although Timaeus,[2] by a sort of Licinian and Mucian law,[3] ascribes him to Syracuse instead. Between Lysias and Cato there is a certain resemblance. Both are penetrating, elegant, clever and concise. But as regards reputation the Greek has been considerably more fortunate. He has a very definite body of supporters. They are men who cultivate a slim rather than an ample oratorical structure and, within the bounds set by good health, even favour leanness. True, Lysias himself often displays an effective muscular vigour. Yet his style as a whole belongs to the plain variety. And, as I have said, he has his admirers, who derive satisfaction from this stark style.

'As for Cato the elder, surely none of our orators today reads him, or knows anything about him at all. And yet, heavens above, what a man! To Cato as citizen, senator, general, I am not now referring. All we are considering here is Cato the orator. I can think of no one who deals out a more impressive compliment, whose words of censure, conversely, are more biting, who expresses what he thinks more penetratingly, who presents a demonstration or an explanation with greater acuteness. He delivered more than a hundred and fifty speeches – judging by those that I myself have discovered and read. Both in style and content, they are packed with brilliance. Choose from them the passages that seem to you most worthy of note and praise. You will find in them everything that is best in an orator. And take his *Origins*, too: they display

1. In 500.

2. Timaeus of Tauromenium (*c.* 356–260), Greek historian.

3. The *Lex Licinia Mucia* of Lucius Licinius Crassus and Quintus Mucius Scaevola Pontifex (95) set up an inquiry into aliens who were claiming to be citizens, relegating to the place of their birth non-Roman Italians who by long residence had assumed Roman citizen rights.

every ornament and splendour of eloquence that you could wish. Yet Cato is short of admirers. Many centuries ago, the same was true of Philistus of Syracuse,[1] and even of Thucydides. For they displayed an epigrammatic and sometimes too pointedly concise brevity which became eclipsed by the lofty, high-flown manner of Theopompus.[2] The same thing had happened to Lysias, whom Demosthenes superseded. And in just the same way the excessively elevated diction of subsequent writers has overshadowed Cato.

'Some people find the early period of Greek literature deeply satisfying, and admire its simplicity, which they describe as Attic. That the same quality is to be found in Cato, however, they are completely unaware. Their models are Hyperides[3] and Lysias. Excellent, but why do they not model themselves on Cato? Their admiration for the Attic style makes excellent sense – though I only wish they imitated its life-blood, and not just its bones! However, their intention deserves praise. But I still say, why, in that case, do they adore Lysias and Hyperides, while they know nothing about Cato at all? True, his phraseology is rather archaic, and some of the words he uses are somewhat uncouth. Yes, because that is how people spoke in those days. Change that – which he could not have done at his time – insert rhythm, and rearrange his words and fasten them together to make what he has to say run more smoothly (which even the early Greeks never managed to do), and you will not be able to find anyone whom you can set above Cato.

'The Greeks believe that language is beautiful if you modify your terminology by what they call "tropes", and employ the forms of epigrammatic expression which they describe as figures of speech. Now Cato was quite remarkably rich and distinguished in both these kinds of ornament. Certainly, I realize that he did not yet possess the polish an orator ought to have, and that a higher degree of perfection has to be aimed at. Nor is that so remarkable, seeing that from the standpoint of our own epoch he is so outstandingly antique that nothing of an earlier date which is worth reading exists at all. But the fact is that in ancient periods every other form of art was held in greater honour than this single art of eloquence.

'Look at those other, lesser arts, and everyone can realize that the

1. Historian (*c.* 430–356).
2. Historian from Chios (born *c.* 378).
3. Athenian orator (389–322).

statues made in Greece by Canachus are too stiff to be regarded as realistic. The figures of Calamis, too, still have a rigid look, although less so than those of Canachus. Even Myron's sculpture falls short of complete naturalism, although one would have no hesitation in describing it as beautiful. The statues of Polyclitus are more beautiful still, and indeed in my opinion are nothing short of perfect.[1] In painting you can see the same evolutionary process. We praise Zeuxis, Polygnotus and Timanthes, and admire their drawing and their outlines; but they only employed four colours.[2] In Aetion on the other hand, and Nicomachus and Protogenes and Apelles a zenith of achievement is reached.[3] And I rather think that the same applies to all the other arts as well. Nothing reaches its ideal form in the first stages after its invention. We can be sure, for example, that poets existed before Homer, performing at the banquets of the Phaeacians and the suitors.[4]

'And what about our own early verses, "which Fauns and bards used to sing, when no one had yet scaled the cliffs of the Muses, and no man before me was attentive to the form of his utterances"? That is what our poet Ennius writes about himself,[5] and his boast is fully justified: the facts are just as he says, for Livius Andronicus's *Latin Odyssey* is as primitive as a statue by Daedalus, and the dramas which he also wrote are not worth reading twice.[6] This Livius produced his first play during the consulships of Gaius Claudius Cento (son of Appius Claudius Caecus) and Marcus Sempronius Tuditanus, only a year before the birth of Ennius, in the five

1. Canachus was a Sicyonian sculptor of *c.* 500 (often confused with his namesake of *c.* 400). Calamis, perhaps a Boeotian, was of fifth-century date, and so were Myron of Eleutherae and Polyclitus of Argos, the sculptors of the Discobolus and Doryphorus respectively.

2. White, black, red, yellow.

3. These painters are Zeuxis of Heraclea in Lucania, Polygnotus of Thasos, and Timanthes of Cythnos and Sicyon (all fifth century BC); and the fourth-century artists Aetion, Nicomachus of Thebes (?), Protogenes of Caunus, and the famous Apelles of Colophon and Ephesus.

4. Homer, *Odyssey*, VIII, 44f., 62ff., 72ff., XXII, 330ff.

5. Ennius, *Annals*, VII. The 'cliffs' are Parnassus or Helicon.

6. Lucius Livius Andronicus of Tarentum adapted Homer and, as stated here, produced his first play (probably a tragedy) at Rome in 240. Daedalus (to be distinguished from the mythical inventor) founded a school of sculpture at Sicyon in *c.* 580/577 (?).

hundred and fourteenth year after the foundation of Rome. Or that is what the source which I follow records; writers disagree about the chronological sequence. But Accius described how Livius was taken prisoner at Tarentum by Quintus Fabius Maximus Verrucosus Cunctator during his fifth consulship,[1] thirty years after Livius had produced his first play. This information I derive from Accius, and I have found it in our early records as well. Accius goes on to report that this first play of Livius was produced eleven years after his capture at Tarentum, when the consuls were Gaius Cornelius Cethegus and Quintus Minucius Rufus, at the Youth Games which Marcus Livius Salinator had vowed at the battle of Sena Gallica.[2] Accius has made a big mistake here, because during that year Ennius was already forty years old. But assume, for argument's sake, that Livius *was* Ennius's contemporary. Then in that case it has to be concluded that the "first man to produce a play at Rome" was rather younger than Plautus and Naevius – who had already, in fact, produced numerous plays before that date.

'And, Brutus, if that digression does not seem very relevant to the subject we are discussing, you must put the blame on Accius, who has made me enthusiastic about tracing the dates and chronologies of famous men.'

'No, not at all,' answered Brutus. 'I find this kind of chronological analysis extremely interesting, and I regard this kind of careful investigation which you have undertaken as highly appropriate to the task you have set yourself; the classification, that is to say, of the various kinds of orators, according to the times in which they lived.'

'That was what I had in mind, Brutus, as you rightly say. I only wish that those songs recorded by Cato in his *Origins*, which many centuries before his time the guests at dinner-parties used to sing in turn in praise of famous men, had survived! As for Naevius, it is true that Ennius ranks him among antique bards and Fauns.[3] All the

1. The poet and dramatist Lucius Accius was born at Pisaurum in *c.* 270, and Fabius's fifth consulship was in 209.

2. i.e. the battle of Metaurus (207) in the Second Punic War, in which Hasdrubal, the brother of Hannibal, was defeated. Livius's play was produced in 197.

3. i.e. mythological figures: Faunus being identified with Pan; the Fauns were sylvan deities.

same, his *Punic War* still gives pleasure – like a sculpture by Myron. We must admit that Ennius is more polished, for he certainly is. But if Ennius had really thought little of Naevius, as he alleged, he would not, when setting out to tell the stories of all our wars, have chosen to omit that very savage conflict, the First Punic War.[1] He tells us himself why he did so. "Others", he says, "have dealt with the subject in verse." Yes, and they did so splendidly, though with not so much polish as you yourself, Ennius. And you ought to think the same, considering how much you have taken from Naevius – if you are prepared to admit that; or if you are not, then we must say, how much you have stolen.

'Among the older contemporaries of Cato was Publius Licinius Crassus Dives, who was consul with Publius Cornelius Scipio Africanus the elder.[2] We are told that Scipio himself was not inarticulate. And his son Publius Cornelius Scipio, the man who adopted as his son the younger Scipio (Aemilianus) – the son of Lucius Aemilius Paullus Macedonicus[3] – would have ranked among the very best speakers if he had enjoyed good health. Some minor speeches of his that have survived confirm that this was the case, and so does a historical piece he wrote in Greek, which is very attractive. A member of the same group, too, was Sextus Aelius Paetus Catus,[4] an extremely erudite civil lawyer who was also a competent speaker.

'Cato died at the age of eighty-five, and in the very year of his death[5] delivered a violent attack on Servius Sulpicius Galba[6] before the Assembly, a speech which he also left in writing. During his lifetime, many younger orators flourished.[7] Quintus Caecilius Metellus Macedonicus,[8] whose four sons all became consuls, was regarded as one of the most eloquent men of his age. He defended Lucius Aurelius Cotta[9] against prosecution by the younger Scipio

1. 264–241.
2. In 205. Cicero mentions him together with six others (see Appendix 2).
3. Consul in 182 etc.
4. Consul in 198.
5. In 149.
6. Consul in 144.
7. Cicero lists four of them here (Appendix 2).
8. Consul in 143.
9. Consul in 144.

Africanus.[1] Other speeches of his, too, are extant, in addition to his oration against Tiberius Sempronius Gracchus, which is copied down in the *Annals* of Gaius Fannius.[2] Lucius Cotta himself was regarded as a practised speaker. As for Gaius Laelius and the younger Scipio Africanus, they were exceptionally fine orators. One can judge their oratorical talents from the actual texts of their speeches, which have survived.

'But among all the rest of them, though a little earlier than the others in point of time, Servius Sulpicius Galba[3] was the man who unquestionably stood out as the most eloquent. Indeed, he was the earliest Latin orator to make use of the techniques which an orator should employ – and is entitled to – such as digression for the sake of embellishment, entertainment of his listeners, appeal to their emotions, embroidery of his theme, the introduction of pathos and the insertion of appropriate generalizations. Yet for some reason or other, although his pre-eminence as a speaker is generally recognized, his speeches nowadays sound drier and more archaic than those of Laelius or Scipio, or even of Cato himself. They have become so faded, in fact, that it is hard to appreciate them at all!

'Laelius and Scipio, as I said, were both renowned. But it was Laelius whose reputation as an orator was the higher of the two. All the same, his discourse about the priestly colleges is no better than any of Scipio's speeches. True, Laelius's oration is particularly pleasing, and what he has to say about religion carries unique authority. But he is much more old-fashioned and uncouth than Scipio. Tastes in regard to speaking vary, and it seems to me that Laelius showed a greater leaning towards antique fashions, and a more marked inclination to use an archaic vocabulary.

'But human beings do not like the same man excelling in a number of different fields. Thus no one could compete with the younger Scipio Africanus in regard to military glory (although Laelius, we may observe, did very well in the war against Viriathus[4]). In respect of literature, eloquence and philosophy, on the other

1. Scipio successfully blocked Cotta's appointment to the command against the Spaniard Viriathus (*c.* 147–140). (Cicero refers to Laelius's role in this war below.) Cotta's speech against Tiberius Gracchus was in 133.

2. Fannius, consul in 122, was an annalist opposed to Gaius Gracchus.

3. Consul in 144.

4. Leader of the Lusitanian rising against the Romans (147–140).

hand, although both were rated as first-class, people were willing enough to assign the first place to Laelius. Indeed, I suspect that this distribution of roles was not what others decided, but was agreed between the two men themselves! For there was a way of thinking, at that time, which was distinctly superior to the habits that prevail now, and was especially civilized in its application to this matter we are discussing. I refer to the general willingness to allow every individual his own personal, particular merits.

'I remember a story I heard from Publius Rutilius Rufus at Smyrna.[1] In his youth, he said, the two consuls of the year,[2] Publius Cornelius Scipio Nasica Serapio and Decimus Junius Brutus (I believe), were ordered by a senatorial decree to investigate a major, horrible crime. In the Sila forest,[3] murders had been committed. The men who had been killed were well known. Slaves of their households were accused, as well as free men whose company had leased the local pitch pine production from the censors;[4] one of them had been the younger Scipio Africanus, and the other Lucius Mummius Achaicus.[5] The Senate had therefore decreed that the current consuls Scipio Nasica and Decimus Brutus should examine the charges and pronounce on them. The case on behalf of the company was set out by Laelius with his usual care, and very neatly he did it. After listening to what was said the consuls, on the advice of their council, decided to postpone their sentence for further inquiries. Then, after a few days' recess, Laelius spoke again. This time his oration was even better thought out, and more effective still; whereupon the consuls deferred their decision once again. The members of the company escorted Laelius to his house, and expressed their gratitude, and appealed to him not to relax his efforts. But this is how Laelius, thus appealed to, replied. Out of sympathy for them, he said, he had done what he was able to, as conscientiously and meticulously as he could. But he now believed, he added, that their case could be defended, with greater weight and effectiveness, by Servius Sulpicius Galba, because Galba had a more spectacular and pungent delivery.

1. For Cicero's visit to the area, see the first sentence of this treatise. Rutilius was consul in 105.

2. 138.

3. In Bruttii (the toe of Italy).

4. In 142.

5. Consul in 146.

'Taking Laelius's advice, the company transferred its case to Galba. But he only took it on with modest hesitation, because of the quality of the man whom he was succeeding. Only one day was due to elapse before the final hearing took place, and Galba spent the whole of it thinking about the trial and preparing what he would say. When the day of the hearing arrived, Publius Rutilius himself, at the request of the company's partners, called at Galba's home in the morning, to remind him, and accompany him to the court in good time. But Galba, until he was told that the consuls had actually appeared in the court, still continued to apply himself to the case. He sat working in a vaulted room, from which everyone was shut out except a group of educated slaves, to each of whom he simultaneously dictated memoranda, which is what he was accustomed to do.

'Presently word was brought to him that it was time to go to court. He came out into the hall, red in the face and with flashing eyes. You would suppose from his excited demeanour that he had finished conducting the case, and had not merely been getting it ready. Rutilius added, what he considered a further relevant fact, that the scribes who came out with Galba were in a state of collapse! This illustrated the violent vehemence, Rutilius pointed out, which Galba displayed not only in speaking in the lawsuits in which he was engaged but even in preparing them. But let me make a long story short. Expectations were at their highest pitch. The audience was enormous. Laelius himself was there. And Galba delivered his speech with such formidable forcefulness that scarcely a passage in it was greeted with silence. After all the moving, tragic appeals that he poured forth on that day, the company's partners won their acquittal, amid universal acclamation.

'Rutilius's story prompts the following conclusions. There are two principal qualities that an orator ought to possess. One is a capacity for convincing argument, presenting the facts. The other is consummate skill in kindling the emotions of his hearers. What Rutilius's account shows is that the speaker who arouses his audience's emotions is far more effective than the man who merely seeks to instruct it. Laelius, then, was a fine speaker, but Galba had power. That power of his was very remarkably demonstrated on another occasion, too,[1] when Servius Galba was accused of

1. In 149.

massacring Lusitanians during the time of his governorship of Further Spain,[1] in violation, it was alleged, of his promise not to do any such thing. As a result Lucius Scribonius Libo, tribune of the people, worked up the feelings of the Assembly, and brought forward a bill which, in effect, was directed personally against Galba. Whereupon, as I mentioned before, Cato, now a very old man, supported the proposal, attacking Galba in vigorous terms (he incorporated the speech in his *Origins* only a few days or months before he died). In reply, Galba asked for no exoneration as far as he himself was concerned. But he begged for the support of the Roman people, and with tears in his eyes commended his boys to their protection, and commended to them the son of Gaius Sulpicius Galus as well. The presence of this weeping orphan aroused a great deal of sympathy, because of the recent memory of his distinguished father.[2] And that was how Galba saved himself from a conflagration that would have burned him up, by exciting the crowd's compassion for children. Cato wrote about this, and has left us what he wrote. Libo, too, it should be added, was a by no means incompetent orator, as can be seen from his speeches.'

After saying all this I paused for a little.

'Why is it then,' inquired Brutus, 'if Galba was such a skilful speaker, that this does not emerge at all from the surviving texts of his orations? Certainly, if people have left nothing whatever in writing, one cannot expect any such evidence, but that is not the case with Galba.'

'The reasons why people do not write at all, Brutus' – I replied – 'and why they do not write as well as they speak, are not by any means identical. The reason why orators have left nothing in writing is, in some cases, sheer laziness; they cannot summon up the energy to add another task, in the home, to the exertions they have already undertaken in the Forum. Because, of course, most speeches are written down *after* delivery, not before they have taken place. Other orators however, although nothing improves speaking more than writing does, have no interest in improving their style. For they cherish no ambition to leave posterity a record of their talents; they are satisfied with the reputation they have gained from their

1. In 151/150.
2. While, consul in 166.

oratory – and conclude that it will become larger still, if they produce nothing in writing that critics can examine!

'Others, again, refrain from writing because they understand that they speak better than they could ever write. That is particularly the case with men of authentic talent but inadequate training. Galba was just such a person. Certainly, his brain-power was considerable, but it appears that when he spoke a sort of emotionalism, that was part of his nature, gained control of him. This produced an oratorical manner that was animated, emphatic and vehement. But later on, when he subsequently took up his pen in tranquillity, and all that gale of excitement had subsided, his language flagged. A man who employed a more controlled method of speaking would not have that experience. For an orator does need a certain amount of common sense, and using it to guide him he can write in the same way as he speaks. But emotion dies down after a bit, and when it has done so all the fiery forcefulness that it had lent the orator is snuffed out. That is why Laelius's intellectuality still seems to breathe out from what he has written, whereas Galba's force has perished.[1]

'Gaius Sempronius Tuditanus,[2] in his whole life-style and behaviour, was a man of culture and refinement, with which his polished oratorical style corresponded. And another man in the same category was Marcus Octavius, who after injurious treatment at the hands of Tiberius Sempronius Gracchus persisted until he destroyed him:[3] a citizen of unswerving fidelity to the patriotic cause. As for Marcus Aemilius Lepidus, known as Porcina,[4] a slightly younger contemporary of Galba, he was rated a first-class orator, and as his speeches show he was also a writer of considerable distinction. He was the first Latin orator, it seems to me, to display that fluency which was so characteristic of the Greeks, and their mastery of period structure, and indeed, in general terms, to possess an artistic style. His devoted listeners included two talented young men of about the same age, Gaius Papirius Carbo and Tiberius Sempronius Gracchus, about whom I shall find an opportunity to speak after I have said a little about their elders . . .[5]

1. At this point Cicero mentions seven orators 'of moderate ability' – including Lucius Mummius the conqueror of Corinth (146) (Appendix 2).

2. Consul in 129.

3. In 133.

4. Consul in 137.

5. Cicero mentions a number of further orators here (Appendix 2).

'Some writings by Sextus Pompeius have come down to us; although reminiscent of an earlier age, they do not suffer from excessive dryness, and are full of good sense. Of about the same period was Publius Licinius Crassus Dives Mucianus.[1] He enjoyed, we are told, a high reputation as a speaker. He had intellectual gifts, augmented by careful study, to which he added the appropriate background with which his family connections could not fail to endow him. For in the first place a family relationship linked him with the outstanding orator Servius Sulpicius Galba, to whose son Gaius[2] he had given his daughter in marriage, and secondly, as the son of one Publius Mucius Scaevola and brother of another,[3] he had learnt Roman civil law in his own home. Crassus was, by general repute, an outstandingly industrious man, and very popular as well: a man who was frequently invited to provide legal advice and plead in court. To the same period, too, belonged the two Gaii Fannii, sons of Gaius and Marcus.[4] Gaius (the son of Gaius), who was consul with Cnaeus Domitius Ahenobarbus, has left one speech – which is very good, and widely known – concerning the allies and the rights of the Latins, and directed against Gaius Sempronius Gracchus.'[5]

'But wait,' interposed Atticus. 'Is that speech really by Fannius? I remember that when I was a boy there were various opinions on the subject. Some maintained that it was written, instead, by the scholarly Gaius Persius, whom Gaius Lucilius describes as a man of great erudition;[6] while others held that the speech was the work of a number of nobles, who each contributed what they were able to.'

1. Consul in 131.

2. More will be said about him later.

3. The father had been consul in 175, and the son (Crassus's brother) in 133.

4. Cicero is wrong: there was, in fact, only one Gaius Fannius in the younger generation, one of the consuls of 122, who, as stated above, was an annalist, though his speech against Gaius Gracchus also became famous.

5. Gaius Fannius and Ahenobarbus were consuls in 122. According to one version, Fannius, on behalf of the conservatives, asked the voters what room would be left for them at the Games and festivals if Gaius Gracchus's proposal to give citizenship to the Latins was accepted. It is possible that Gracchus proposed to extend citizenship to other Italians as well.

6. Although Gaius Persius, Cicero records elsewhere, did not want the poet Lucilius (died 102/101) as a reader.

'Yes,' I replied, 'I have heard those stories from our elders, but I have never quite believed them. My guess is that the suspicions arose because Fannius was only regarded as a mediocre speaker, while the recorded speech is, on the contrary, the very best of its time. Moreover, it does not possess the characteristics that one would expect to find in a composite production, since its whole tone and style remain homogeneous throughout. And, besides, Gaius Sempronius Gracchus would never have refrained from mentioning the imputation about Persius when he himself was being similarly criticized by Fannius for mobilizing the assistance of Menelaus of Marathus and others. Besides, Fannius himself was well known to be by no means inarticulate. He defended a number of cases in the courts, and his tribuneship of the people,[1] conducted under the authoritative patronage of Publius Cornelius Scipio Africanus the younger, was certainly not lacking in distinction.

'As for the other Gaius Fannius, son of Marcus and son-in-law of Gaius Laelius, he was a man of greater austerity, both in his way of life and in his performance as an orator. He did not feel any particular affection for his father-in-law Laelius, who had failed to nominate him for the college of augurs (diviners), and, in particular, had preferred his other, younger son-in-law Quintus Mucius Scaevola Augur[2] to himself (excusing his choice on the grounds that he had made it on behalf, not of his younger son-in-law, but of his elder daughter who was Scaevola's wife!) And yet, all the same, this second Gaius Fannius followed Laelius's example, and attended the lectures of Panaetius.[3] His gifts as a speaker can be deduced from the historical work of which he was the author. It is written with a good deal of competence, not exactly eloquent but also not excessively simple. As for Publius Mucius Scaevola Augur, he could speak well enough to defend himself in court, as he showed in his reply to Titus Albucius on a charge of extortion.[4] He was not, it is true, classified among the ranks of the orators. But his understanding of civil law and general statesmanlike intelligence were outstanding. With Lucius

1. In 142?
2. Consul in 117.
3. Head of the Stoic school (*c.* 185–109).
4. In 120 or 119.

Coelius Antipater you are, of course, familiar.[1] He was a man of considerable eminence in his time – very learned in the law, and the teacher of many pupils, including Lucius Licinius Crassus.

'I only wish that Tiberius Sempronius Gracchus and Gaius Papirius Carbo[2] had possessed political intentions as good as their oratorical talents. If so, their renown would have been the most splendid in the world. Instead, however, Gracchus's tenure of the tribunate[3] was thoroughly turbulent. He took the office because he was so infuriated with the nobility, owing to their rejection of the treaty with Numantia.[4] And then he was killed – by official action. Carbo too paid the penalty for his unfailingly shallow behaviour in support of the radical cause, and committed suicide; which rescued him from a heavy sentence in the courts. Yet both those men were first-rate orators. I base that assertion on what I have been told by our fathers, who heard them. As for the surviving speeches both of Carbo and Gracchus, their style is not particularly brilliant, but all the same they are acute, and full of thoughtful material. Gracchus, thanks to the care of his mother Cornelia, had been well trained from boyhood and was thoroughly acquainted with Greek literature. He had always been taught by the most respected Greek professors, of whom one, while he was still a very young man, had been Diophanes of Mytilene, the most eloquent man in Greece at that period. But Gracchus had little time to develop and display his gifts.

'Carbo lived longer. He became well known for his contributions to numerous legal cases and suits. Discerning men who had listened to him, such as my friend Lucius Gellius Poplicola[5] – who was accustomed to describe himself as Carbo's assistant during his consulship[6] – called him a melodious, fluent and distinctly vigorous orator, who tempered his vehemence with a good deal of charm

1. He wrote after 121 BC, and introduced the historical monograph to Rome.

2. Consul in 120.

3. In 133.

4. The Senate, on Scipio Africanus the younger's recommendation, had rejected the treaty which Tiberius Gracchus had been influential in arranging so as to save the defeated army of Gaius Hostilius Mancinus (consul in 137).

5. Praetor in 94.

6. In 120.

and a sense of humour. Gellius also said that Carbo had been a hard-working and painstaking man, who never failed to pay meticulous attention to oratorical exercises and preparatory studies. He was regarded as the outstanding pleader of his day.

'During the period when he was pre-eminent in the Forum the number of trials conducted there began to increase. This was partly due to the creation of the standing criminal courts when he had been young. They had not existed previously, for it was Lucius Calpurnius Piso Frugi[1] who first passed the extortion law, while he was tribune during the consulships of Lucius Marcius Censorinus and Manius Manilius.[2] Piso himself conducted cases and spoke for and against numerous bills, and left speeches, which are now forgotten, as well as *Annals* (written in a distinctly arid manner). And another reason why lawsuits increased was that trials before the Assembly, in which Carbo participated, increasingly required the services of professional advocates, now that secret ballots had been instituted, a measure which Lucius Cassius Longinus Ravilla pushed through during the consulships of Marcus Aemilius Lepidus Porcina and Gaius Hostilius Mancinus.[3]

'The poet Lucius Accius used to tell me, also, that your relation, Brutus, I mean Decimus (Callaicus) the son of Marcus,[4] had been an orator of considerable polish, and that he was, for his time, very well informed about Latin and Greek literature alike. Accius also bestowed similar praise upon Quintus Fabius Maximus Allobrogicus, the grandson of Lucius Aemilius Paullus Macedonicus;[5] and he recorded that, before Maximus, Publius Cornelius Scipio Nasica Serapio[6] – the man who, as a private citizen, led the killers of Tiberius Sempronius Gracchus – was as vigorous a speaker as he was violent in everything else . . .[7]

'Marcus Livius Drusus,[8] too, who as tribune repressed his colleague Gaius Sempronius Gracchus during the latter's second

1. Consul in 133.

2. In 149.

3. In p. 137. Cicero has discussed these ballots in his treatise *On Laws* (Chapter 5).

4. Consul in 138.

5. Consuls in 121 and 182.

6. Consul in 138.

7. Cicero inserts a list of further orators here (Appendix 2).

8. Consul in 112.

tribunate,[1] was not only a person of influence but an impressive orator as well. His brother Gaius (which was also the name of their father) was his close associate. And, Brutus, your relation Marcus Junius Pennus, too, did well as tribune, but then, after becoming aedile, died when the highest offices were within his reach.[2]

'Linked with these men were Gaius Scribonius Curio,[3] Marcus Aemilius Scaurus, Publius Rutilius Rufus[4] and Gaius Sempronius Gracchus. About Scaurus and Rufus I need not say very much. Neither was considered a first-class orator, although both acted in numerous lawsuits. Then, as now, there were men who enjoyed a good reputation, because, even if not particularly talented, they displayed a praiseworthy capacity for hard work. I do not mean that the two men I am speaking of were altogether lacking in talents, but their talents did not lie in the direction of oratory. For it is not sufficient to realize what has to be said. You also have to be able to say it, fluently and pleasingly. Indeed, even that is not enough, either, unless what you say is spiced by some qualities of vocal and facial expression and gesture. Theoretical training, too (I need hardly add), is indispensable. True, without it one may manage, with nature's help, to say something worthwhile. But if so, that depends on chance; and so you cannot rely on it always being at your disposal.

'Scaurus was a wise man and a good one, and whenever he spoke he spoke with dignity and a certain natural authority, so that when he was defending a client you had the impression that he was not so much pleading a case as making an objective statement. Indeed, this manner of speaking hardly seemed appropriate to a pleader at all, although for delivering his views in the Senate, of which he was chairman, it was just what was required. What he said not only sounded wise but sounded trustworthy as well: and that is what matters most of all. In his case, it was a gift of nature, for which no amount of artistry could easily have provided a substitute; although, as you know, the textbooks offer precepts for such requirements. We have speeches of his, and he has also left three autobiographical writings, addressed to Lucius Fufidius.[5] They are useful enough

1. In 122.
2. Pennus was tribune in 126 and aedile in *c.* 123.
3. Praetor in 121.
4. Consuls in 115 and 105.
5. Praetor in 81?

works, but nobody ever reads them. They prefer to read, instead, about the life and education of Cyrus,[1] an excellent book certainly but not very well suited to the times in which we ourselves live – and much less desirable than Scaurus's defence of his own record. (Fufidius too, to whom he dedicated the book, had a certain position among speakers at the bar.)

'The oratorical style of Publius Rutilius Rufus[2] was rough and austere. Like Scaurus, he had impetuous, vehement feelings. These showed when the two men were candidates for the consulship at the same time. For not only did Rutilius, who lost, charge his successful competitor Scaurus, now consul elect, with bribery, but Scaurus, after he himself had been acquitted, brought a similar accusation against Rutilius. Rutilius was a very busy man and a very industrious one, which the public had good reason to appreciate, because he was generous with his services as a legal consultant. His speeches are bare. But they contain a great deal of valuable matter about the law, and Rutilius was a learned man, well versed in Greek literature. He was also a pupil of Panaetius, and his knowledge of Stoic doctrine was virtually perfect. The style of oratory favoured by those Stoics, as you know, is ingenious and full of devices, but it is dry and not well adapted to winning public support.

As for Rutilius, he displayed the doctrine of self-sufficiency, which is so typical of the Stoic school, in a very emphatic and unequivocal form. So much so, indeed, that when he became the defendant in that trial[3] which, as we know, exercised such a shattering effect on our state, he refused – although completely innocent – to call in the assistance of either of the two outstanding orators of the time, Lucius Licinius Crassus and Marcus Antonius. Instead, he himself spoke in his own defence. Gaius Aurelius Cotta, too, the son of his sister, added a few words, already adopting the role of an orator, although he was still a very young man. And Quintus Mucius Scaevola Pontifex also addressed the court, in the plain but polished fashion that characterized his speeches, yet without a trace of the fire and amplitude which a trial of that nature and importance demanded.

1. Xenophon's *Cyropaedia*, a fanciful biography of Cyrus II of Persia (559–529).
2. Consul in 105.
3. In 94?

'So we have to rank Rutilius as a Stoic sort of speaker, and Scaurus as an old-fashioned one. But let us praise them both all the same, for letting us see that neither of these two types of speaking have lacked a distinguished place in our public life. What I have been aiming at, in describing them, was to do for the Forum what is done for the stage. That is to say, I have sought to allocate praise not only to the actors who engage in rapid and complicated movements, but also to those who are described as "quiet", whose performances display a straightforward naturalism, without exaggerations or excesses.

'Since I have been speaking of the Stoics, mention ought to be made of Quintus Aelius Tubero of the same epoch,[1] the grandson of Lucius Aemilius Paullus. He could not, it is true, be ranked as an orator. But his life-style was severe, and harmonized with the philosophical school that he followed, although actually exceeding it in rigidity. It was typical of him that, as one of three joint presidents of the court, he ruled against his own uncle Publius Cornelius Scipio Africanus the younger when the latter argued that augurs were not entitled to exemption from service as jurymen. But Paullus's language was as harsh, as uncultivated and as rough as his life itself, so that he never attained the high official positions that his ancestors had occupied. Yet he was an unswerving, courageous citizen, and one of the most adamant opponents of Tiberius Sempronius Gracchus, as Gracchus's speech against him makes clear. Speeches that Tubero delivered against Gracchus also exist. As an orator, however, he was only mediocre, although he could argue with skill.'

'Yes, among our own countrymen', commented Brutus, 'I see the same phenomenon that characterized the Greeks. That is to say, if they are Stoics, they are almost invariably good at argument. They operate according to set rules, and are architects, you might say, in building up structures of words. But transfer them from arguing to oratory, and they turn out poorly. I make only one exception. That is the younger Marcus Porcius Cato.[2] Thoroughgoing Stoic though he is, his first-class eloquence leaves nothing to be desired. This was something which Fannius, as far as I can see, only possessed to a limited degree, Rutilius not to any great extent, and Tubero not at all.'

1. Tribune in 130?
2. Praetor in 54.

'I can tell you why that is, Brutus,' I replied. 'For those are men who concentrate entirely upon dialectic. Wide ranges of style, or fluency or variation, do not interest them in the least. Your maternal uncle Cato, as you are aware, took over from the Stoics what they had to offer.[1] But he also learnt to be an orator, from experts in oratory, and made use of their training methods. If, however, someone wanted, instead, to base his education entirely on the philosophers, his style as a speaker would derive greater benefits from what the Peripatetics have to teach.[2] I feel, however, that the course which you have adopted, Brutus, is particularly praiseworthy; because you have followed a philosophical school which possesses both of these two merits at one and the same time:[3] I mean not only logical methods of discussion, but also an agreeable, ample style.

'All the same, the manner in which both Peripatetics and Academics proceed, in regard to methods of speaking, makes it impossible for them ever to produce an orator themselves. And yet, on the other hand, the perfect orator could never come into existence without them. While Stoic speaking is too concise and compact for the ears of the public, the oratory of the Peripatetics and Academics is, by way of contrast, more uninhibited and prolix than the conventions of the lawcourts and Forum will allow.

'As for other philosophers, you could never find a more eloquent writer than Plato. Jupiter himself, men of that occupation declare, would speak like Plato, if he spoke Greek. Nor could you find a more incisive style than Aristotle's, or a writer more beguiling than Theophrastus. Demosthenes, it is said, used to read Plato with great care, and was actually his pupil. And that emerges from the nature and splendour of his vocabulary. In fact, he himself reports that this was so, in one of his letters.[4] But his manner, I venture to say, if transferred to philosophy, would seem too aggressive. Theirs, on the other hand, transferred to the lawcourts, sounds too placid.

1. Marcus Porcius Cato the younger was the half-brother of Brutus's mother Servilia.

2. The school of Aristotle (the Lyceum).

3. The Old or Fifth Academy of Antiochus of Ascalon (*c.* 130/120–68), which broke away from the New Academy of Carneades, and claimed to revive Plato's original Academy (although it incorporated Aristotelian and Stoic ideas).

4. The author of the Fifth Letter attributed (wrongly) to Demosthenes claims to have been a pupil of Plato.

'But now, if you will permit me to do so, I will go on to mention the remaining Roman orators in respect to the periods in which they lived and with reference to their various merits.'

'Indeed, that', said Atticus, 'is very definitely what we want. And I know I am speaking for Brutus as well as for myself.'

'Well, Gaius Scribonius Curio[1] was an orator of about the same period, and quite an eminent one too. We can judge him from reading his speeches themselves. A number of them are extant: and in particular there is his well-known oration in defence of Servius Fulvius Flaccus on a charge of incest.[2] When I was a boy, this was regarded as exceptionally good, though it has almost vanished from view among the mass of new writings that we have amongst us today.'

'As to this mass of new writings you are speaking of,' remarked Brutus, 'I have a very good idea who is responsible for them.'

'And I too,' I said, 'know whom you are referring to – that is to say, myself. For I do like to think that I have been of some help to today's young people, by showing them a more elevated and elaborate style of speaking than they had known of before. All the same, it is also quite possible that I have done them harm! Because older speeches, superseded by mine, have ceased to be what most people read. They have not stopped being read by myself, however, because I prefer them to my own orations.'

'Place me', declared Brutus, 'among that majority! Although I do now realize, in view of what you have told us, that I have a great deal still to read – writings that I previously despised.'

'Well,' I said, 'that much-praised speech of Curio about incest is, at many points, childish. Much of what he says about love, about torture, about rumour, is fatuous. And yet to our ears, at that time, which were quite inexperienced, and to the taste of a public which was still entirely untrained, all that seemed perfectly tolerable. Besides, Curio wrote a number of other works as well. He made many quite important speeches, and was a pleader of some reputation. Indeed one is compelled to wonder, since he lived for a long time and was by no means out of the public eye, why he never became consul.

'But next we come to a man of outstanding intellectual gifts, and

1. Praetor in 121.
2. Possibly a case in 113, in which Lucius Licinius Crassus also appeared.

ardent industriousness, and thorough training from his childhood onwards: Gaius Sempronius Gracchus. You could not believe, Brutus, that there was anyone in the world more abundantly and lavishly equipped for a career as a public speaker than he was.'

'I entirely agree,' replied Brutus. 'And indeed he is almost the only one of our earlier orators whose speeches I have read.'

'And how right you were, Brutus, to have read him. His premature death was a disaster for Rome and its literature. If only he had displayed as much loyalty to his country as he showed to the memory of his brother![1] Had his life lasted longer, how easily, with the remarkable gifts that he possessed, he would have rivalled the glory of his father and grandfather![2] As far as eloquence was concerned, I doubt if he would have found anyone to equal him. His diction was sublime, his ideas penetrating, his entire style impressive. His writings, one must admit, lacked the final touch – full of brilliant sketches, but missing ultimate perfection. Nevertheless he, Brutus, if anyone, is the man whom our young people ought to read. He can both sharpen their minds and give them intellectual sustenance.

'To the years that came next belonged Gaius Sulpicius Galba, son of the outstandingly eloquent Servius, and son-in-law of Publius Licinius Crassus Dives Mucianus,[3] who was himself a good speaker as well as a significant jurist. Our fathers thought highly of Gaius Galba; and they looked favourably upon him because they remembered his father. But he fell in the race. For he was brought to trial under the bill proposed by Gaius Mamilius Limetanus,[4] which stirred up hatred against men accused of conspiracy with Jugurtha. Galba spoke in his own defence. But he was found guilty. The concluding portion of his speech, known as the *Epilogue*, is still available. When I was a boy it was so highly regarded that we learnt it by heart. In the whole of Roman history he was the first member of a priestly college to be convicted by a public lawcourt.

'Publius Cornelius Scipio Nasica Serapio, who died during his

1. Cicero, as he stresses elsewhere, disapproves of the 'radical' tribunates of Tiberius and Gaius Sempronius Gracchus (the latter was killed in 121).

2. His father was Tiberius Sempronius Gracchus (consul 177), the son of a certain Publius.

3. Consul in 131.

4. Tribune in 109.

consulship,[1] did not speak a great deal, or very often. But his Latinity was as good as anyone's, and his wit and sparkle were unequalled. His fellow-consul Lucius Calpurnius Bestia possessed a keen brain and was something of an orator. He had begun well as a tribune, for he brought in the bill which recalled Publius Popillius Laenas,[2] exiled by the brutal initiative of Gaius Sempronius Gracchus. But Bestia's consulship came to a grim end. For under that unfair law of Mamilius a court made up of jurymen who were supporters of Gaius Gracchus annulled the civil rights not only of the priest Gaius Galba, as I have said, but also of Lucius Bestia and three other men of consular rank as well, Gaius Porcius Cato, Spurius Postumius Albinus and the laudable Lucius Opimius,[3] who had been the killer of Gaius Gracchus – and, although he took this action against the radical cause, had been acquitted by the Assembly.

Gaius Licinius Nerva[4] had behaved quite differently from Bestia during his tribuneship: and in every other aspect of his life as well. Indeed, he was a disreputable citizen, though not a bad orator. Gaius Flavius Fimbria[5] was approximately contemporary with these men, although he lived on until a later date. He was what you might call a violent speaker, harsh and vituperative, and in every respect excessively excitable, and too worked up. Yet his industry and integrity and life-style gave him a considerable reputation in the Senate. As a pleader he was adequate, and he knew quite a lot about the law; besides, his way of speaking was as open and frank as his life. When we were boys we used to read his speeches. But now they are hardly to be found.

'Another man who had a lively brain was Gaius Sextius Calvinus.[6] He spoke attractively, but his health was poor. He took part in lawsuits when his gout was not too painful, but only infrequently. So although people were able to get his advice whenever they needed it, they could only get him to plead for them in court on rare occasions. Marcus Junius Brutus belonged to the same period.

1. In 111.
2. Consul in 132.
3. Consuls in 114, 110 and 121.
4. Tribune *c.* 120?
5. Consul in 104.
6. Possibly identifiable with the man of that name who was consul in 124.

He was a great disgrace to your family, Brutus. For like the politician Lycurgus at Athens[1] he made a career of prosecution – in spite of his distinguished name and distinguished father, who was such a good man and such an able jurist.[2] The son never sought an official position, but was a sharp-tongued and formidable prosecuting counsel. You could see how the natural virtues he inherited had been corrupted by the depravity of his chosen profession.

'Another prosecutor of the same time, a man of humble social class, was Lucius Caesulenus. I heard him speak once, when he was an old man. He was demanding an indemnity, under the Aquilian Law.[3] I should scarcely have mentioned such an insignificant person were it not to record that he showed greater skill than anyone I have ever known in planting suspicions and insinuating guilt. To pass to Titus Albucius,[4] he was a person who possessed an erudite knowledge of all things Greek. In fact a Greek is what he practically was. That is my personal view, which I pass on to you. But you can form your own opinion from his speeches. When he was a young man he lived at Athens, and emerged as the complete Epicurean – which is a school ill adapted to public speaking.

'Next I come to Quintus Lutatius Catulus.[5] He was not trained according to the old Roman methods, but according to the modern style that we nowadays favour, which he carried to perfection. He had read very widely, and displayed a natural graciousness in his manner of living as well as in the impeccably pure Latinity of his diction. This can be seen in his speeches, but especially in his memoirs relating to his consulship and the actions he had performed, written in a flowing style reminiscent of Xenophon,[6] and dedicated to his friend the poet Aulus Furius Antias;[7] although the work in question is no better known than those three autobiographical books by Marcus Aemilius Scaurus, which I mentioned before.'

1. Statesman (*c.* 390–*c.* 325/4), famous for his savage invective.

2. The Brutus criticized by Cicero was known as a prosecutor after 114. His father of the same name (praetor 140?) was one of the founders of Roman legal learning.

3. This may be the *Lex Aquilia de damno* (for damages and restitution) of Gaius Aquilius Gallus (66 BC), but the reading is uncertain.

4. Titus Albucius (propraetor in Sicily in *c.* 105/104) spoke successfully against Quintus Mucius Scaevola Augur in 120/119.

5. Consul in 102.

6. The Greek writer and commander (*c.* 428/7–*c.* 354).

7. Writer of an epic poem, the *Annales* (*c.* 100).

'I personally don't know it', said Brutus, 'any more than I know Scaurus's books. None of them has ever happened to come into my hands – though I confess that that is my own fault! Now, however, stimulated by what you say, I shall make a greater effort to hunt for them.'

'As I remarked' – I went on – 'Catulus spoke very pure Latin, a considerable stylistic asset, to which the majority of authors pay too little attention. His melodious voice and elegant enunciation you will not expect me to describe, since you knew his son personally.[1] True, the son was never considered an orator, although when he put forward his views in the Senate he showed excellent sense and expressed himself in a polished and cultivated fashion. But his father too, Catulus himself, did not rank foremost among orators. Indeed, when you were listening to speakers who did enjoy that reputation, you would scarcely have regarded him as their competitor. But when you heard him alone, without any such comparison arising, you would give him high praise, and would not think of asking for anything better.[2]

'Lucius Aurelius Cotta, the one who became praetor,[3] was rated as a speaker of only second-rate ability, and did not advance very far along the road to oratorical eminence. But he deserved to be recorded, all the same, because of his deliberate attempt to reproduce and imitate antique models, by means of his terminology and adoption of a more or less rustic accent. In speaking of this Cotta, and certain others as well, I realize that I have classified as orators men who did not speak with any particular ability, and I shall go on doing the same. For what I am trying to do is to summarize the people whose function it was, in public life, to deliver speeches. How well they succeeded and how difficult it is, as in every other art as well, to achieve oratorical perfection can be judged from what I have to say about their qualities.

'But what a lot of orators I have already mentioned! And what a long time it has taken me to list them! And yet, all the same, despite all this laborious effort, just as earlier we got as far as Demosthenes and Hyperides, so now we have only reached Marcus Antonius and

1. Consul in 78.

2. At this point Cicero lists a number of other orators (Appendix 2).

3. Praetor in 95? This is stated in order to distinguish him from the consul of the same name (119).

Lucius Licinius Crassus.[1] To compare them with those two Greeks is legitimate, because in my view both the Romans were outstanding orators, in whose persons, for the first time, Latin eloquence equalled the glory of Greek.

'As for Antonius, no relevant arguments ever evaded his attention – and he invariably produced them at the points where they would carry the most effective weight. Like a general deploying his cavalry and infantry and light troops, he distributed all the materials at his disposal in whatever parts of his speeches would suit them best. His memory was superb. There was never any suggestion that he had rehearsed what he had to say beforehand, and whenever he came forward to make a speech it always sounded as if he was performing impromptu: although, in fact, when he spoke, he was so thoroughly well prepared that it was very often the jurymen, rather than himself, who had to make an effort to keep on their guard. He did not use elegant language, and for that reason was not ranked as a particularly polished speaker. I do not mean that his diction was excessively impure, but his employment of words did not display a truly oratorical quality. To speak good Latin, as I said before, is a fine thing, but not so much for its own sake as because so many people neglect it. It is not so glorious to know Latin well as disgraceful to lack that knowledge – and, indeed, to know it well is not so much, I feel, the sign of a good orator as the sign of a true Roman!

'But to go back to Antonius. In selecting words – which he chose more for emphasis than for charm – and in arranging and knitting them compactly together, Antonius proceeded according to a carefully thought-out, premeditated plan. And the same procedure was even more noticeable in the embellishments and rhetorical devices which he employed to develop his thought. It is because, in respect of these qualities, Demosthenes outstrips everyone else that experts have judged him the greatest of all orators. The principal ornaments of oratory are what the Greeks call figures of speech. Their significance does not so much lie in their capacity to add colour to language as in their power to present ideas with increased vividness. Antonius excelled at all this, and, in addition, his delivery was exceptionally effective. If we subdivide delivery under two headings, gesture and voice, his gestures did not attempt to reflect what he

1. Consuls in 99 and 95.

was actually saying, but mirrored the direction of his thinking: hands, shoulders, flanks, foot stamping, postures, gait, every kind of movement, all corresponded with the thoughts he was voicing: while his voice remained strong throughout, although it was a little hoarse by nature. If this was a defect, he possessed the skill, better than anyone else, to convert it into an asset. For when the moment came for pathos he spoke with an emotional force that was well adapted to win sympathy and attract compassion. Antonius's achievement illustrates the truth of the saying attributed to Demosthenes. He was asked what came first in oratory, and what he replied was this: first delivery, second delivery, third delivery. For that, more than anything, is what penetrates the hearts of listeners, and moulds and shapes and converts their feelings and thoughts, and makes the orator seem the man he wants to seem.

'Some ranked Lucius Licinius Crassus equal to Antonius. Others placed him higher. But on one point everyone was in agreement: that no one who had the opportunity to employ either of them as his counsel needed the assistance of any other man's abilities at all. I personally, although I ascribe to Antonius all the talents that I have indicated above, maintain that Crassus attained a degree of perfection that it was impossible for anyone else to equal. He possessed great natural dignity, but was capable of adopting, also, an affable and witty manner, and of displaying a kind of charm that was not mere buffoonery but suited an orator excellently. His Latin was accurate, meticulous and elegant, but quite unaffected. His expositions were admirably lucid. His handling of the civil law or equity or morality was rich in convincing arguments and analogies.

'Antonius displayed an astonishing gift for establishing probabilities and creating or allaying suspicions among his listeners. But where Crassus was unsurpassable was in interpreting, defining and explaining the implications of equity. I could illustrate this by various examples. But I will record, for the purpose, the case of Manius Curius before the Board of One Hundred.[1] Crassus spoke against the written word in support of the principles of equity and morality. And he did so with such brilliance that Quintus Mucius Scaevola Pontifex, despite all his cleverness and expert knowledge of the law – upon which this case hinged – was overwhelmed by

1. The *centumviri* dealt with civil suits, especially those relating to inheritances. The *causa Curiana* of 92 related to a will; the plaintiff was Marcus Coponius.

the abundance of arguments and precedents that he brought forward. The contest between these two advocates of the same age and the same consular rank, each bringing forward legal arguments but from wholly opposed points of view, meant that Crassus came to be described as the greatest jurist among orators, and Scaevola as the finest orator among jurists.

'Scaevola possessed a remarkable capacity for getting down to the truth or falseness of concepts relating to equity and law. And, at the same time, he showed extraordinary skill in expressing what he had to say without deviating from relevance, or failing to be concise. So let us acclaim him as a marvellous speaker – marvellous beyond anything else that I have ever seen, in respect of his resources of interpretation, explanation and demonstration. In amplifying his material, on the other hand, in embellishing it, that is to say, and in refuting his opponents, I should describe him as a person whom you would not like to have speaking against you, rather than as an orator who inspired admiration. But let us return to Crassus.'

'I thought I knew Scaevola Pontifex fairly well,' commented Brutus, 'from what I used to hear from Gaius Rutilius,[1] whom I used to come across at the house of our friend who was likewise called Quintus Mucius Scaevola.[2] But I was quite unaware that Scaevola Pontifex was such a notable orator. And it gave me satisfaction to learn that we had such an accomplished person, of such eminent intellectual gifts, in our public life.'

'Yes, our country, Brutus, in my opinion, has never produced anyone more distinguished than those two men, Crassus and Scaevola Pontifex. Just now I remarked that the former was the finest orator among jurists, and the latter the greatest legal expert among orators. In other respects, too, you could weigh up, and distinguish, their respective qualities. So much so that you could find it hard to conclude which of the two you would prefer to resemble! If you take people of taste, Crassus was the most austere man they could produce. If you take people who practised austerity, Scaevola had the best taste. Crassus was very agreeable, but added a touch of severity. Scaevola was distinctly severe, but could be agreeable as well. One could go on endlessly in the same vein! Though I am afraid it may look as if I am inventing all this, to create an effect.

1. Perhaps the son of Publius Rutilius Rufus (consul in 105).
2. Tribune in 54.

However, that is how it was. All virtue, according to your Old Academy,[1] Brutus, consists of the Mean. And it was the Mean, the middle course, that both Crassus and Scaevola set out to follow. But what in fact happened was that while each of them enjoyed a share of the talent that was characteristic of the other, each also retained his own particular quality in full, undivided measure.'

'What you have just said', interposed Brutus, 'has given me, I feel, a pretty good understanding both of Crassus and of Scaevola. And when I think of you and Servius Sulpicius Rufus[2] I have the impression that much the same resemblance can be said to exist between you and him, as existed between Crassus and Scaevola.'

'How do you mean?' I asked.

'Because', he replied, 'it looks to me as if you have aimed to learn as much about the civil law as was necessary for an orator, whereas Servius made it his business to acquire as much eloquence as was needed to enable him to ensure respect for civil law. Moreover, you are much the same age as he is, which was also the case with Crassus and Scaevola.'

'There is no need to say anything about myself,' I replied. 'But your observation about Servius Sulpicius is sound, and I will give you my view. I cannot think of anyone who has studied oratory and all the humanities more thoroughly than he has. When we were young, he and I shared the same training courses here, and subsequently he went to Rhodes with me, to increase his qualifications and learn more. When he got back, my impression is that he deliberately chose to be first in the second art than second in the first. My own belief is that, as an orator too, he could have been in the very first rank. But he may well have preferred, instead, what he did in fact attain: which was to be the foremost expert in civil law – foremost not only in his own epoch, but of all time.'

'Do you mean', asked Brutus, 'that you would rank our Servius even before Scaevola Pontifex?'

'Yes, Brutus; I would put the matter like this. Scaevola, and many others too, had extensive practical experience of civil law.

1. Cicero means the recent Fifth Academy of Antiochus, which, as stated earlier, revolted from the 'New Academy' of Carneades and Philon, and professed to revert to the original Academy of Plato.

2. Consul in 51. Principally famous as a lawyer. Cicero had been opposed to him in the Murena case (Chapter 2), but praises him in the Ninth Philippic.

Servius, however, has been the only man to have made it into an art. Now, that is something that he could never have brought about merely by knowledge of the law. For, in order to do that, he also needed, and acquired, an additional technique as well. By this I mean the branch of oratorical study which instructs how the whole can be subdivided into its component parts, which shows how to bring out and define what has hitherto been obscure, which demonstrates how to detect and then pin down ambiguities, which applies (in short) a standard making it possible to distinguish between what is true and what is false, and to determine which conclusions follow logically from which premises, and which do not. And Servius's achievement was to apply this art, the greatest of all arts, so as to illuminate all the legal opinions or lawsuits that had hitherto merely received unsystematic treatment from others.'

'I suppose you are referring to dialectic or logic,' interposed Brutus.[1]

'Yes, I am. But Servius also possessed literary knowledge, and spoke in a polished style, as can be easily seen from his writings, which are like nothing else in the world. In order to learn his job he had called on the services of two leading experts, Lucius Lucilius Balbus and Gaius Aquilius Gallus.[2] Gallus was a keen and highly trained man, a sharp, well-prepared pleader and consultant. But Servius outdid him in acuteness and accuracy. Balbus possessed learning and erudition, but, by the same token, he was a reflective person who took his time. Servius was quicker off the mark, and got things done more expeditiously. So he possessed the qualifications of Balbus and Gallus alike, and supplied what each of them, singly, lacked. And here I suggest another way of measuring Servius against Crassus and Scaevola Pontifex. Crassus had been the more prudent of the two, because whereas Scaevola was willing to undertake court cases in which Crassus eclipsed him, Crassus refused to offer legal consultations at all, since he did not want to invite unfavourable comparisons with Scaevola. So Servius, following Crassus's line of thought, and realizing that these occupations, legal consultancy and the courts, were the two careers leading to fame

1. Cicero stresses the pre-eminence of dialectic in his work *On the Orator*. Aristotle was said to have called it 'the art of arts, the science of sciences'.

2. Balbus was a pupil of Quintus Mucius Scaevola Pontifex. Gallus, praetor in 66, had originally been a Roman knight.

and popular esteem, sensibly concentrated on the attainment of supremacy in the latter, only borrowing from the former as much as was necessary to keep the civil law intact, and secure his own advancement to consular rank.'

'That', said Brutus, 'is exactly the view that I myself had already adopted. For only lately at Samos,[1] when I was engaged in learning to what extent our priestly law is related to civil law, I listened frequently and carefully to what Servius had to say. And the assessment you have offered now enables me to reaffirm, with greater confidence, the impression I formed at that time. Moreover, one thing in particular gives me pleasure. This is the fact that while you and Servius are of much the same age, and rank equally in official status, and are so closely linked in your professional occupations, this closeness, which so often produces bad relations and envy, has in your cases by no means poisoned your regard for one another, but has actually increased it instead. For I know very well that he feels the same friendly sentiments towards yourself as you feel towards him. The current situation, therefore, in which the Roman people has so long been deprived of his counsel, and of your voice, causes me quite particular distress. It is a deplorable situation on its own account, and more particularly so when one sees into whose hands these functions, I can hardly say have been transferred, but at any rate have landed.'

At this point, however, Atticus had a point to make. 'I said at the beginning', he reminded us, 'that we should not speak about politics. Do let us stick to that! For if we proceeded otherwise, and went on to enumerate all the things we have lost, we should never come to an end of our complaints and lamentations.'

'Well then,' I resumed, 'let us go on to what still has to be said, and continue with the survey we began. When Crassus arrived in court, he was always well prepared. His arrival was eagerly awaited. He was carefully listened to. From their outset his speeches, so meticulously prepared, rewarded his audience's expectations in full measure. Abrupt movements of the body, tricks of vocal variation, walking up and down, repeatedly stamping his feet, were things

1. Brutus visited Samos during his return journey from the province of Asia in 47. Servius Sulpicius Rufus had been with Pompey at the battle of Pharsalus (48), and after its disastrous outcome withdrew to Samos, where he stayed until he received Caesar's pardon.

that he avoided. Yet his language was vigorous and sometimes angry – full of justified indignation. A lot of wit emerged; but it never meant that dignity was sacrificed. Moreover, he achieved the most difficult thing of all. For although what he said was never unattractively plain, it remained brief. And his cross-examinations displayed outstanding skill.

'He appeared in lawsuits of almost every kind – and became one of our foremost orators at an early age. While he was still extremely young, he prosecuted Gaius Papirius Carbo,[1] famed for his eloquence. The case caused Crassus's abilities to be greatly respected, and earned him widespread admiration. Subsequently, at the age of twenty-seven, he defended the Vestal Virgin Licinia in court. In his defence of her he showed exceptional eloquence, and he has left a written version of parts of his speech. Furthermore, while he was still a young man he chose to take the radical side in a case relating to the colony of Narbo, and set out to become the leader of the colonization of that town, which he achieved.[2] His speech on this subject – in favour of the law providing for the settlement – is, once again, extant, and it reads like the work of an older man than he actually was. Many other court cases then followed. However, Crassus's tenure of the tribuneship attracted such an insignificant minimum of attention that if he had not dined, during his term of office, with the herald Quintus Granius, and if Lucilius[3] had not told us the story of this occasion twice over, we should not know that he had ever been tribune of the people at all.'

'Yes, that is certainly so,' agreed Brutus. 'But I don't seem to remember hearing anything about Scaevola's tribunate either, and I assume that he was Crassus's colleague in that post.'

'No, that was true of every other office,' I replied, 'but Scaevola was actually tribune in the year after Crassus;[4] and it was while Scaevola was presiding on the rostrum that Crassus spoke in support of the Servilian Law.[5] (True, Crassus also became censor without having Scaevola as his colleague, because no Scaevola ever stood for

1. Consul in 120.

2. The *colonia Narbo Martius* was founded in 118.

3. The satirical poet, who died in 102/101 BC.

4. In 106.

5. The *Lex iudiciaria* of the consul Quintus Servilius Caepio giving senators a large share of the seats on criminal juries. Crassus's speech was unsuccessful.

the censorship.) But the recorded speech of Crassus when he was tribune, which I am sure you have frequently read, was delivered when he was thirty-four years of age – and he was thirty-four years older than myself. For he spoke for the Servilian Law in the year of my birth, while he himself was born during the consulships of Caepio's father of the same name and Gaius Laelius,[1] which made him three years younger than Antonius. I am recording this point for a special reason, so that the time when Latin oratory first came of age can be noted: and indeed this, it must be understood, was the juncture when it had almost been brought to perfection. After that, it was hardly possible to add anything that could make our oratory better – unless someone might turn up who had a deeper knowledge of philosophy, civil law and history.'

'Will such a man indeed turn up,' said Brutus, 'or is the man you are waiting for already here?'[2]

'I have no idea,' I said. 'But to go back to Crassus. We also have, from his consulship,[3] his eulogy of the younger Quintus Servilius Caepio[4] which formed part of a speech in Caepio's defence – long enough for its eulogistic purpose, though the whole speech was not long. And finally we have his oration as censor, which he delivered in his forty-eighth year.[5] All these discourses display a certain natural colouring of their own, without any artificial aid. Even the groupings and collocations of words, for which we use the Greek term "periods", are concise and succinct in Crassus's speeches, and he preferred to divide his sentences into the shorter elements which the Greeks call "colons".'[6]

At this point Brutus interrupted. 'In view of the high praise you accord to these two orators,' he said, 'it is regrettable that Antonius did not leave anything in written form except his slender treatise on the art of speaking,[7] and that Crassus too did not choose to write more. If they had done so, they would have bequeathed a monument for everyone, and would have left ourselves valuable instructions

1. In 140.

2. i.e. Cicero himself.

3. In 95.

4. Praetor in 90, son of the consul of 106.

5. In 92.

6. Aristotle, *Rhetoric*, III, 9, 5, describes the 'colon' as the clause of a sentence.

7. The second rhetorical treatise in Latin after the elder Cato's, apparently incomplete.

about how to attain eloquence. As regards Scaevola, on the other hand, the fineness of his oratory is sufficiently well known to us from the speeches that he did, in fact, leave.'

'As far as I myself was concerned,' I went on, 'from my boyhood onwards, that oration made by Crassus in favour of the Servilian Law was a fundamental model. It emphasized the majesty of the Senate, to which his words were dedicated with compliments. It sought, also, to whip up feelings against the faction of knights, from which both the jurymen and the prosecuting counsel were drawn; and in order to achieve the diminution of their excessive power it was necessary to appeal to the feelings of ordinary people. There was a great deal of gravity in Crassus's words, though a lighter touch appeared as well. There was no lack of harshness, but also quite a lot of humour. He said more, in his speech, than the written version has recorded, as can be deduced from certain headings in the latter, which indicate themes he went on to dwell upon, but do not reproduce his spoken words in full. Similarly, his discourse during his censorship, directed against his colleague Cnaeus Domitius Ahenobarbus,[1] is not really a speech at all, but more of a summary, or a fairly full outline. That he said a good deal more is evident, since no disputation between orators was ever received with louder applause. For the way in which Crassus spoke was very well suited to ordinary listeners. Antonius's oratory, on the other hand, was better adapted to the lawcourts than to Assemblies.

'I spoke of Domitius, and I do not want to leave my reference at that. He did not, it is true, count as an orator. But he spoke well enough, and was competent enough, to live up to his elevated position as a public official of consular status. I can say the same about Gaius Coelius Caldus.[2] He was a very industrious man, possessing remarkable qualities. His eloquence, in dealing with private affairs, was sufficient to come to the aid of his friends, and in public life it was good enough to do justice to his rank. During the same period Marcus Herennius, though he took trouble over his speaking and his Latin, was only ranked among orators of mediocre capacity. And yet, in competition for the consulship,[3] he succeeded in defeating Lucius Marcius Philippus, despite the latter's noble

1. Consul in 96.
2. Consul in 94.
3. For 93.

birth, family and guild and college connections, and outstanding talents as an orator.

'Another man of that time, Gaius Claudius Pulcher,[1] although principally distinguished for his aristocratic origins and for the influence he wielded, was also not too bad as a public speaker. Gaius Titius, a knight, was of about the same age. He went, it seems to me, as far as any Latin orator was able to go without any knowledge of Greek literature, and without extensive practical experience. Yet his speeches are so lively, so full of illustrative anecdotes, so richly packed with charm, that they almost have an Attic ring. His tragic dramas display the same animation; it makes what he writes look clever, but scarcely tragic. A man who tried to model himself on Claudius Pulcher was the poet Lucius Afranius, a dexterous writer whose plays, as you know, attain authentic eloquence.[2] There was also Quintus Rubrius Varro, whom the Senate bracketed with Gaius Marius as a public enemy.[3] As prosecuting counsel he displayed sharpness and vehemence, and in that capacity was a speaker of some note.

'My relative Marcus Gratidius could be described as a born orator. Extremely knowledgeable about Greek literature, he was a close friend of Marcus Antonius, under whom he served in Cilicia, where he was killed.[4] It was he who was the father of Marcus Marius Gratidianus, and who prosecuted Gaius Flavius Fimbria.[5]

'Among the allies and Latins there were likewise men who enjoyed a reputation as orators.'[6]

'What are the qualities', inquired Brutus, 'that you regard as characteristic of such speakers, who could be described as foreigners?'

'Just the same qualities', I replied, 'as are attributable to Romans,

1. Consul in 92.

2. He was the most prolific writer of *comoediae togatae*, relating to domestic life in Italian towns.

3. In 89.

4. While fighting against Cilician pirates (102).

5. Marcus Marius Gratidianus (praetor in 85 and 84) was Cicero's second cousin. Fimbria, the son of a new man of the same name (consul in 104), was a friend of Gaius Marius; he committed a number of murders and was defeated in Asia by Lucius Cornelius Sulla, and forced to commit suicide (85).

6. Cicero lists a number of them (Appendix 2).

with the single exception that their oratory lacks a certain sophistication.'

'What exactly do you mean by that?'

'I cannot define it; but I only know that it exists. You will understand what I mean, Brutus, when you arrive in Gaul.[1] You will hear some words, there, which are not familiar at Rome: though you can forget them, and supersede them by standard terms. What is much more important is that our authors here employ a certain intonation and accent which reflect city sophistication. These characteristics are to be detected not only in orators, but in others as well. I remember hearing Titus Tinca of Placentia, an entertaining person, engaged in a witty exchange with our friend Quintus Granius the herald.'

'You mean the person about whom Lucilius writes so much?'[2]

'Yes, that is the man. What Tinca said was just as amusing, but Granius completely defeated him by what you might call the local, metropolitan Roman flavour of what he said.

'So the story told about Theophrastus[3] causes me no surprise. He asked an old woman in the market what the price of something was. She told him, and added: "Yes, not a penny less – stranger." He was annoyed that she had realized he was a foreigner, although he spent his life at Athens and was the best speaker of his time. I believe that the same is true here, and that our city people have their own peculiar way of talking, like the Athenians.

'But let us come back home, and return, I mean, to our own orators. Crassus and Antonius, then, were at the top, but next to them came Lucius Marcius Philippus[4] – though next after a considerable interval. Certainly, no one else could be said to rank before him. Yet, even so, I would not place him second – or even third. In a chariot-race I would not name as second or third the chariot which had scarcely crossed the starting line when the winner had already won the race and been awarded the prize. And, similarly, as regards orators, I would not extend the same compliment to a man

1. Before leaving for north Africa late in 47 Caesar had appointed Brutus as governor (*pro praetore*) of Cisalpine Gaul (north Italy).

2. Gaius Lucilius, the satirical poet, referred to earlier.

3. Aristotle's successor as head of the Peripatetic School (Lyceum) (*c.* 370–288/285 BC).

4. Consul in 91.

who is so far behind the leader that he hardly seems to be competing in the same race. Now Philippus, if we steer clear of comparisons with those two, did possess merits which have to be recognized as by no means insignificant. He spoke fluently, and he could be very funny. His imagination was fertile, and his expositions easy and relaxed. For his time, he knew Greek literature very well. And as a debater he displayed notable wittiness, not unmixed with a certain malicious pungency.

'Lucius Gellius[1] was their approximate contemporary. He was not particularly admired as an orator, although you would find it difficult to say what he lacked. He was not an uneducated man, his thought processes were quite rapid, he knew his Roman history, and he was reasonably articulate. But that was an age of great orators. All the same, Gellius helped his friends frequently and usefully. And he lived so long that he had dealings with speakers of a number of successive generations . . .[2]

'But now let me come back from men who just made speeches, and were not really orators at all, to others who truly deserved to be described by that term.'

'Yes, I agree that that is what you ought to do,' said Atticus. 'For your intention, I thought, was to provide a survey of the men who were truly eloquent, and not merely those who worked hard at it.'

So I went on. 'In gaiety and wit,' I continued, 'Gaius Julius Caesar Strabo Vopiscus, son of Lucius, outdid all his contemporaries and his predecessors as well.[3] His oratory was totally deficient in forcefulness, it is true, but its polish and charm and attractiveness gave it a flavour all of its own. Some of his speeches are extant, and from these, as from his tragedies, you can gain an impression of his smooth and rather unvigorous style. Among his contemporaries was Publius Cornelius Cethegus, who was a good enough speaker for political purposes.[4] For he had a thorough knowledge of politics,

1. Consul in 72.

2. Cicero lists a number of his contemporaries who made speeches (Appendix 2).

3. A supporter of Gaius Marius, and the uncle of Julius Caesar the dictator, he is the principal speaker on wit and humour in Cicero's work *On the Orator*. He was aedile in 90 and was killed in 87. He was given the nickname Sesquiculus (with buttocks one-half too large).

4. He fled from Italy with Gaius Marius but later joined Sulla and took an active part in the proscriptions.

and understood what they were about, so that in the Senate his influence was equal to that of any former consul. In criminal cases, on the other hand, he was negligible; though for the handling of private suits he had managed to acquire sufficient skill . . .[1]

'Now we come to the category of orators, or one should rather say just loudmouths, men who possessed neither education nor manners or were positively uncouth. Within their ranks, I would claim that Quintus Sertorius among us senators,[2] and Gaius Gargonius of the equestrian (knightly) order, take the prizes as far as fluent delivery and brain-power are concerned. A man who was a ready and easy speaker, and whose grand life-style and intellectual gifts earned admiration, was Titus Junius, son of Lucius. It was he who was the prosecutor who got the praetor designate, Publius Sextius, convicted of bribery. Junius only reached the office of tribune,[3] but would have gone on to higher office but for his weak health and illness.

'I realize perfectly well that I have concerned myself with the enumeration of many people who were never reputed to be orators and, in fact, were not orators at all, while at the same time I may have passed over certain earlier figures who deserved to be mentioned in favourable terms. But if so, I plead ignorance. For it is impossible to write anything about men of ancient epochs when they themselves have left us nothing, and no one else has left any records about them. As to those, on the other hand, whom I have personally seen, I am missing out practically no one whom I have ever heard speak. For what I want to make clear is that in our own great and antique country, which has granted such rich records to eloquence, all men have had the ambition to become speakers, but not a very great many have ventured to make the attempt, and few have succeeded. But I will say something about them all: so as to let you know which of them I consider to have been a mere ranter, and which a genuine orator . . .

'The individuals who were contemporary with Gaius Julius Caesar Strabo Vopiscus, but slightly younger than he was, included as rich a crop of orators as any in our history.[4] But among these personages,

1. Here Cicero inserts a further list of speakers of the time (Appendix 2).
2. Leader of the revolt against the Roman government in Spain (81–73/72).
3. Before 80.
4. Cicero gives the names of eight of them (Appendix 2).

in my opinion and the opinion of the public, Cotta and Sulpicius easily ranked first.'

'When you say, however,' asked Atticus, '"in my opinion and the opinion of the public" what exactly do you mean? Can it always be pronounced that, as regards the favourable or unfavourable assessment of an orator, the opinion of the ordinary public is the *same* as the opinion of experts? Or should it not rather be stated that some orators win the approval of ordinary people, whereas others are approved of by the people who are qualified to judge?'

'That is a good question, Atticus,' I replied. 'Yet the answer you will get from me will very possibly not be one that everybody will accept.'

'But what I am really driving at is this,' pursued Atticus. 'Why are you interested in the approval of the public at all provided that you can get Brutus here to approve?'

'Well, certainly,' I agreed, 'in this discussion which we are now engaged upon, about the reasons for considering an orator good or bad, it would be much more important for me to secure agreement from yourself and Brutus, than from the public in general. But when we come to the actual speaking that I myself undertake, what I need is that it should be well received by the public. For the fact is that a speaker who wins a good reception from his ordinary listeners *does* inevitably, also, win approval from the experts. What is right or wrong about the way men have spoken I will allow myself to judge, assuming that I possess the ability and knowledge to do so. Yet the real quality of an orator can only be deduced from the *practical results* that his speech-making attains. Now the three things a speaker ought to achieve, as I see the matter, are these: he should instruct his listeners, win their sympathy, and vigorously move their emotions.[1] By what qualities in the orator each one of these results can be produced, or by what faults on his part he fails to produce them or slips and falls in the process, an expert is entitled to judge. But – to turn to the third point – whether or not the orator manages to arouse in his audience the emotions that he wishes them to feel can only be decided by their mass reaction and approbation.

'As a matter of fact, however, the experts have never differed

1. Cf. *On the Orator*, II, 115: the three *officia oratoris*. 'Instruction' means proving what is true.

from the general public about whether an orator was good or bad. You must surely agree that, during the careers of the men I have been speaking about, the experts did not rank the orators any differently from the way in which the public ranked them. If you had asked any member of the public whom he considered to be Rome's greatest orator, he might have hesitated between Antonius and Crassus, or one person might have put Antonius first, and another Crassus. I myself, deliberately applying theoretical standards, placed Philippus, with all his attractiveness, dignity and humour, next after them. And would any of the public have disagreed, and placed him *before* them instead? No, they would not. For that is the distinctive mark of the supreme orator: that the public realizes his supremacy.

'When they gave one of his pupils a chilly reception, the flautist Antigenidas[1] is supposed to have said to him, "Perform for myself and the Muses." But to Brutus here, when he is speaking, as he usually does, before a large crowd, I would prefer to say, "Brutus, my friend, perform for myself *and the public*." Your eloquence will have its effect on them. And I shall understand why it is having that effect. When someone is listening to an authentic orator, he believes what he hears, he is sure that it is true, he agrees and applauds: the orator has convinced him. An expert, surely, need ask for nothing more. The listening multitude is delighted, finds itself carried along by what he says, is pervaded by a sort of pleasurable excitement. There is nothing you can take exception to in that. They feel joyful, they feel sorrowful, they laugh, they cry, they are moved to show sympathy or hatred, contempt, envy, pity, shame, disgust. They are angry, or amazed, or hopeful, or terrified. And all of this happens because the minds and hearts of these listeners are worked up by the words and sentiments and delivery of the orator.

'Obviously, there is no need to wait for the verdict of an expert! It is quite evident that what the crowd approves must gain the expert's approval as well. I say once again that experts and the public have never, in fact, disagreed on such a matter. And in support of this assertion, I have one final question to ask. There have been many orators, and they have spoken in many different fashions. But among all these men has there been a single one, adjudged outstanding by mass opinion, who has not likewise gained

1. Flautist and composer, active *c.* 400–370.

a favourable verdict from the experts? In our fathers' time, for instance, if a man was free to choose who was to speak for him in court, surely there was never the slightest doubt that he would choose either Antonius or Crassus. Many other advocates, as well, were available; and, as between the two of them, one might certainly hesitate which to select. But concerning the fact that either one or the other of the two had to be chosen, to the exclusion of all others, there would never have been the smallest hesitation at all. And the same was true of Gaius Aurelius Cotta and Quintus Hortensius Hortalus, when I was young. Every potential client, if he had freedom of choice, would have selected one or the other of them rather than anybody else.'

'But why', said Brutus, 'do you speak of others rather than of yourself? We have frequently had occasion to note how clients were determined to have *your* services; and we have seen that Hortensius felt exactly the same. When you and he were acting together on a case – and of this I am able to say from personal experience, because I was often there – he always left the concluding speech, which carries the greatest weight, to yourself.'

'Yes, that is true,' I replied. 'His friendly feelings, I realize, caused him to treat me with exceptional kindness. What the public think of me I have no idea. But one thing I can state confidently about other speakers. Those whom the public believed to be the best are identical with those who have gained the warmest approval from the experts. Demosthenes could never have made the assertion attributed to the famous poet Antimachus.[1] While Antimachus was reading aloud that long poem of his, which you know, before an assembled audience, in the middle of his recitation every one of his listeners walked out – except only Plato. Whereupon Antimachus remarked: "I shall continue reading all the same. Plato, by himself, is as good as a hundred thousand listeners as far as I am concerned." That was perfectly right, in regard to an abstruse poem, which only a small number of people could have appreciated. But a speech delivered to the public must be of a character that will win public approval. If Demosthenes, that is to say, had had no other audience but Plato, and everyone else had abandoned him, he would have been reduced to silence. And what about you, Brutus? If the entire

1. Antimachus of Colophon, the epic poet, was probably born in *c.* 444 and died early in the fourth century.

Assembly had deserted you, as it once deserted Gaius Scribonius Curio,[1] would you have been able to go on?'

'I must admit', replied Brutus, 'that even in cases in which I have to deal only with jurymen, and not with the general public at all, if my listeners got up and left me, I should find myself reduced to complete silence.'

'Yes, that is how things are,' I said. 'It is like blowing the flute. If the musician blows it, and the instrument does not make a sound, he knows it has got to be thrown away. An orator's flute, you might say, is the ear of his audience. If he blows on it and this has no effect, if his hearers fail to respond like a horse that fails to respond to the reins, he may as well cease his useless efforts. There is one qualification, however. The public does sometimes applaud a speaker who has not deserved any such praise. But, when it does so, it is not comparing him with anyone else. When people are pleased with someone who is mediocre or actually bad, they are merely satisfied by his current performance, and it does not occur to them that there could be something better. They are approving, that is to say, just what they hear, and not awarding marks for quality. For even a mediocre orator can gain attention, if he has any ability at all. Let him produce a well-arranged and polished speech, and there is nothing in the world more capable of arousing human emotions.

'Any ordinary person, for example, who listened to Quintus Mucius Scaevola Pontifex defending Marcus Coponius – in that case I mentioned before[2] – could never have expected, or even thought it possible, to hear a more highly finished or elegant performance. Manius Curius had been named as heir to an inheritance in the event that a posthumous son (whose birth was said to be about to take place) should die before reaching his majority. What Scaevola had to set out to prove was that Manius Curius could not become the heir, because no posthumous son was born after all. In his discussion of testamentary law, antique formulas, and the way in which the will ought to have been framed to provide for Curius's recognition as heir in the event of no posthumous son being born, Scaevola said everything that there was to be said.

'Morever, he emphasized, very cogently, how deceptive it would

1. Consul in 76.

2. The case of Manius Curius before the Board of One Hundred (*centumviri*) (92).

be for the public if the exact phraseology of the will were set aside, so that its intentions had to be arrived at by pure guesswork: a situation in which the written words of ordinary people could be twisted by the interpretations of experts. And Scaevola also had a lot to say about the authority of his own father,[1] who had always been against this sort of thing, and argued in favour of the strict, literal interpretation of wills. What he was stressing, in fact, was the importance of maintaining, intact, the traditions of civil law that had been handed down. He spoke with expert knowledge, but also briefly and concisely, and yet at the same time with a good deal of polish; and his speech was very attractive. I cannot imagine, that is to say, that any of his ordinary listeners could have been disappointed that he had not produced something better, or even believed it would have been possible to do so.

'When Crassus began to argue against him, he told the story of an imaginative boy who, while walking along the sea-shore, came upon one of the thole-pins to which the oars of boats are fastened; and this made him long to be able to build an entire boat. Scaevola, he said, was like this boy: basing himself on nothing larger than a sophistical thole-pin, he had built it up into a whole inheritance case submitted to the Board of One Hundred. From this beginning, making use of other equally entertaining pieces of wit, he won over the sympathies of all his listeners and diverted them from any serious analysis to plain enjoyment of the way in which he was talking – the second of the three things which, as I said, an orator ought to achieve. At that point he suggested what, in his view, the real intention and wish of the testator had been. He had intended, Crassus maintained, that in the event of no son of his surviving to adulthood (either because no such son was born, or because he died before reaching that stage), his heir was to be Curius. Most people, Scaevola commented, wrote their wills in this fashion; it was a valid way of proceeding, and always had been. With these arguments, and many others of the same sort, he got his listeners to accept what he had to tell them – which is the second, as I said, of the three functions of an orator.

'Next he passed on to considerations of equity and morality. His argument was that the court should carry out what had been the dead man's wish and intention. He stressed how deceitful words can

1. Publius Mucius Scaevola (consul in 133).

be, in wills as in everything else, if intentions are ignored. But what he was in fact contesting was the autocratic idea that nobody, in time to come, should ever make a will at all except in the way that Scaevola thought he should! Expounding all this, with a good deal of seriousness and profuse illustration, accompanied by numerous amusing witticisms, he moved the emotions of his audience, to such an extent that it seemed that nobody could be against him. This was an example of what I named as the third of the functions of the orator – but in significance it comes foremost and first.

'Now a juryman who was one of the ordinary people, who had admired Scaevola's opponent when he was heard by himself without comparison, would, on hearing Scaevola, just jettison his first conclusion as contemptible. But the expert on the other hand, listening to Scaevola, would have concluded at once that his oratory lacked a certain element of richness and polish. If, however, when the case was over and done with, you would have asked both the expert and the juryman which of the two orators was the better, I am sure you would find that the expert's verdict invariably coincided with the verdict of the ordinary person.

'One must ask, therefore, in what respects the expert is superior to the other. Well, he is superior in one very important way, although it is difficult to explain. Important it certainly is, because it is obviously important to understand how an effect which ought to be achieved by eloquence, and ought not to be missed, does in fact either come off or fail to do so. Well, one advantage that the expert enjoys, over the person who has not received the same training as he has, is this. When two orators, or more, receive a favourable reception from the public, it is the expert who is generally best fitted to recognize which of them has the best oratorical style. When, however, we are talking of a type of speech-making which does not succeed in gaining public approval, then the expert, too, will not be impressed. You can tell how skilful a harpist is from the sound he conjures up from the harp-strings. And in just the same way you can tell how effective an orator may be, in his attempts to move an audience, just by seeing how much they are, in fact, moved.

'An expert who understands the principles of oratory does not need to sit down and listen attentively to what is being said. Instead, by a single passing glance at the audience, he can usually tell how good the speaker is. Let us imagine he sees one of the jurymen yawning, talking to one of his colleagues, perhaps even chatting to a group of them, sending out to discover what time it is, asking the presiding officer to declare an adjournment. When the expert notes all this, he realizes that this is a lawsuit in which the speaker is not capable of playing on the hearts of the court, as the hand of a musician plays on his strings.

'But if, on the contrary, he notices that the jurymen are concentrating attentively, and look as though they are trying to learn what the case is about, or are visibly displaying their assent by their facial expressions, or hanging upon the words of the speaker like birds entranced by the siren song of a catcher, or, what is most essential of all, if he observes that they are moved by pity or hatred or some other emotion – all he has to do is to note these things with a passing glance, without listening to a word, and he will already be able to understand perfectly well that an authentic orator is in action in that court, and that the job an orator ought to do is being done, or has been done already.'

Both Atticus and Brutus expressed their agreement with what I had been saying. So I resumed my survey.

'It was from Cotta and Sulpicius', I recalled, 'that this discussion began; it was they, I indicated, who were ranked as the best orators by experts of the kind I have been speaking about, as well as by the general opinion of their time. So I will now return to considering those two personages once again. And then I will go on to speak of the others in turn, as I set out to do. There are two sorts of good orators[1] (and it is *good* orators we are considering now). Those of one sort speak plainly and succinctly, and the others display a more elevated and fuller style. This second manner is the better of the two – because it is more brilliant, and more impressive. Certainly, other qualities need to be considered as well, qualities which are good and outstanding in their own way, and consequently deserve to be praised. But the concise orator needs to steer clear of aridity and meagreness, and the more ample performer has to guard against becoming overblown and tasteless.

'To go back to Cotta, he possessed a rich imagination, and his language was fluent and pure. Since his lungs, however, were not powerful, he had very sensibly dispensed with any kind of aggressive

1. The different types of style are usually referred to as *three* in number, the plain, the middle (mean) and the grand, but here Cicero reduces them to two.

approach, and adapted his manner of speaking to his physical shortcomings. Yet everything he said was sincere, straightforward and sane. And what was the most noteworthy of all was this. He could scarcely expect to sway the jurymen by vehement methods. Indeed, he never tried. But he pushed them gently, and by this technique succeeded in arousing their emotions, just as Sulpicius aroused them by his own more energetic methods.

'For of all the orators I have ever listened to, Sulpicius had the most grandiose and melodramatic style. His voice was robust but agreeable and noble. His gestures and movements were graceful, and better adapted to the Forum than they would have been to the stage. His language flowed easily and rapidly, without ever becoming prolix or verbose. He modelled himself on Crassus – while Cotta preferred Antonius. But Cotta lacked the forcefulness of Antonius. And Sulpicius did not have Crassus's charm.'

'So what a remarkable art oratory is,' commented Brutus, 'when one reflects that these were its supreme practitioners, and yet each of its two most important ingredients was deficient in one of them!'

'Yes, and the same two men remind us of another thing as well, which is that orators can be supreme and yet extremely different. It would have been impossible to be more different from one another than Sulpicius and Cotta were, and yet you can bracket them together as vastly superior to all their contemporaries. Their contrasted qualities recall that what an intelligent teacher has to do is to discern the particular characteristics of each of his pupils, and to direct the training methods he applies to them accordingly. Thus Isocrates, whose students included the lively Theopompus and the placid Ephorus, remarked that to the former he employed the rein, and to the latter the spur.[1]

'The extant speeches that bear the name of Sulpicius are believed to have been written after his death by Publius Cannutius, who is a contemporary of mine and the best orator, in my opinion, outside the ranks of our senatorial order.[2] No speech written by Sulpicius himself is in existence. I often heard him remark that he had never

1. Isocrates, Athenian orator and rhetorician (436–338); Theopompus of Chios, historian (born *c.* 378); Ephorus of Cyme, historian (*c.* 405–330).

2. Publius Cannutius was also remembered later by Tacitus, *Dialogue on Orators*, 21.

formed the habit of writing, and found he was no good at it. The speech entitled "Cotta's defence under the Varian Law"[1] was likewise not his own work, having been composed at Cotta's request by Lucius Aelius Stilo. This Aelius was a remarkable man. A Roman knight of high principles, he knew a great deal about Latin as well as Greek literature. Indeed, in our own early traditions he was expert, possessing a profound knowledge not only of the writings but of historical origins and facts as well. Our friend Marcus Terentius Varro took over all his erudition, with additions of his own, being a man of outstanding ability and scholarship, who was able to expound the same themes in works which were both more numerous and more distinguished than those of Aelius.[2]

'Aelius set out to be a Stoic, but an orator was something he never wanted to be, and he did not become one. However, he did write speeches for others to deliver; for example for Quintus Caecilius Metellus, Quintus Servilius Caepio and Quintus Pompeius Rufus;[3] though Quintus Pompeius also wrote speeches in his own defence, though not without the assistance of Aelius. I, too, had some part in these compositions, because as a young man I used to go to Aelius's house, where I listened very attentively to what he said. But his public speeches were trivial and insignificant, and I am surprised that Cotta, who was himself a first-class orator and by no means lacking in taste, should have been willing to let them be thought of as his own.

'Next to Cotta and Sulpicius, none of their contemporaries really deserves even to be ranked third. However, Cnaeus Pomponius[4]

1. The *Lex Varia de maiestate* (90 BC) of the tribune Quintus Varius Hybrida, setting up a special court with knights (*equites*) as jurymen. Stilo was the first Roman philologist, who made his name by researches into the genuineness of Plautus's plays.

2. We know the titles of fifty-five of Varro's works, of which two (on language and agriculture) have wholly or partially survived.

3. This Metellus could be either Quintus Caecilius Metellus Nepos (consul in 98) or Quintus Caecilius Metellus Numidicus (consul in 109). Quintus Caecilius Metellus Balearicus (the father of Nepos, whose name is tentatively restored here, in a gap in the manuscript, as the patronymic of the Metellus referred to) had been consul in 123. Caepio (quaestor in 100?) has already been referred to by Cicero as the object of an encomium by Lucius Licinius Crassus during the latter's consulship (95). Quintus Pompeius Rufus was consul in 88 with Lucius Cornelius Sulla, whose daughter married his son.

4. Tribune in 90.

pleased me most – or displeased me least, I should rather say. In the most prominent legal cases, however, there was, in fact, no room for anyone except the men I have already spoken about. Antonius was in the greatest demand; and he was always ready to take a case on. Crassus was rather more selective, but he was, on occasion, prepared to take part in a lawsuit. People who could not get either of them usually applied to Lucius Marcius Philippus or Gaius Julius Caesar Strabo Vopiscus. Next they went on to Cotta and Sulpicius.

'All the more important lawsuits, then, were handled by these six pleaders. In those days, not so many trials came to the courts as come now. And the present practice of employing several counsel for a single case had not been introduced. It is, in fact, a deplorable custom, requiring us to respond to speeches that we have not even heard: moreover, the versions of them that are reported to us are often quite different from what was actually said. Besides, it is, I believe, essential that I myself should see, with my own eyes, exactly how my opponent is presenting every aspect of his case, and, most of all, see how all his points are received by his listeners. But the very worst result of the new practice is this: although a defence ought to be one homogeneous unit, after one speaker has brought a case to a close, it then has to be opened up all over again. For every case has its natural beginning and its natural conclusion; while the remaining portions of the argument have their own force and value when they are located as integral parts of the whole picture. Even a single speaker, in his own lengthy oration, sometimes finds it hard to avoid contradicting himself. So how much harder it is to avoid saying something that contradicts another speaker who has spoken before! However, we have accepted this multiplicity of speakers quite happily. We have done so because presenting an entire case means so much more work than presenting only part of it, and because if you speak on behalf of several clients instead of only one you enable a greater number of people to feel an obligation towards you without spending any additional time.

'It was maintained, however, in certain quarters, that there was a good third after Cotta and Sulpicius: namely Gaius Scribonius Curio.[1] This seems to have been because he used rather spectacular

1. Consul in 76; the son and father of orators.

language and spoke quite a decent Latin; probably he was used to doing so at home. His literary education, however, was non-existent. The type of person one listens to every day at home clearly makes a considerable difference – the men and women one has been talking with since boyhood, how one's father speaks, or the slave who looks after one, one's mother. We have read the letters of Cornelia, the mother of Gracchi.[1] They indicate clearly that the boys were not only nursed at their mother's breast, but by her conversation as well. I quite often heard Laelia speak, the daughter of Gaius Laelius.[2] It was evident that her father's elegant diction had left its mark on her. Moreover, the same was true of her two daughters, the Mucias, both of whom I have heard speaking, and of her two granddaughters, the Licinias, whom I have likewise heard. One of them, the wife of Publius Cornelius Scipio Nasica,[3] you must have listened to, Brutus, as well.'

'Yes,' said Brutus, 'and I was very glad to – especially as she was the daughter of the orator Lucius Licinius Crassus.'[4]

'Well, what do you think of the son of this Licinia, Lucius Licinius Crassus Scipio, who assumed the name of Crassus by adoption according to his grandfather's will?'[5]

'He is said to have been a very brilliant man,' replied Brutus. 'And his brother Quintus Caecilius Metellus Pius Scipio,[6] my colleague in the priesthood, seems to me not only an excellent talker but also a very able public orator.'

'That is an accurate estimate,' I said; 'and the reason was that his forebears had stood in the very roots of wisdom itself. For his grandfathers were Publius Cornelius Scipio Nasica[7] and Lucius Licinius Crassus, of whom we have spoken, and his great-

1. Cornelia, the famous model of womanly excellence, was the daughter of Scipio Africanus the younger, and the wife of Tiberius Sempronius Gracchus (consul in 177 and 163).

2. She was married to Quintus Mucius Scaevola Augur (consul in 117). Gaius Laelius had been consul in 140.

3. Praetor in 94.

4. Consul in 95.

5. He is unknown, and may have died young. His father was Publius Cornelius Scipio Nasica Serapio, and his grandfather was the orator Lucius Licinius Crassus.

6. Consul in 52.

7. Consul in 111.

grandfathers included Quintus Caecilius Metellus Macedonicus,[1] Publius Cornelius Scipio Nasica Serapio, who as a private citizen liberated the state from the domination of Tiberius Sempronius Gracchus,[2] and Quintus Mucius Scaevola Augur,[3] who was not only an extremely learned lawyer but a very agreeable man. And to turn to Metellus Scipio's great-great-grandfathers, we come to the eminent Publius Cornelius Scipio known as Corculum, who was twice consul,[4] and we come, also, to that paragon of wisdom Gaius Laelius.'

'What an extraordinarily distinguished genealogy!' said Brutus. 'Just as, upon one single tree, one can see various fruits grafted, the wisdom of many ancestors has been grafted and incorporated in his single house.'

'Yes, and in the same way, I imagine – to compare a minor with a major example – the home of Gaius Scribonius Curio,[5] although he was left an orphan, was accustomed to the pure Latin which had become the rule under his father. What convinces me particularly of this is the fact that of all the orators who have amounted to anything at all I have never known anyone so totally uneducated and ignorant of the humanities. He knew no poet, he had read no orator, about history he had learnt nothing; public, private and civil law alike were wholly unfamiliar to him. Certainly, this was a defect of other orators as well, including very important figures, notably Sulpicius and Antonius, for neither of them was at all well acquainted with the liberal arts. Nevertheless, there was one other quality which they did possess: and that was a highly developed mastery of the art of speaking.

'This, as everyone knows, can be divided into five parts.[6] In none of these parts can an orator be entirely deficient. For if he proved wholly lame in regard to any one of them he could not be an orator. However, it is perfectly possible for one man to excel in one

1. Consul in 143.

2. Serapio (consul in 138) led the charge of senators and their clients against his cousin Tiberius Gracchus, who was killed (133).

3. Consul in 117.

4. In 162 and 155.

5. Consul in 76.

6. Collecting the material (invention), arranging it (disposition), putting it into words (style), memorizing it, and finally delivering it: as Cicero also observes elsewhere.

of the five parts, and another to excel in a different one. Thus Antonius was very good at tracking down what needed to be said, and preparing the way for it and understanding in what part of a speech to locate it; and his memory never played him false. But his greatest strength was his delivery. In respect of some of the five parts he was Crassus's equal, and in others he was superior; but Crassus's manner of speech was the more sparkling of the two. When we pass on to Sulpicius and Cotta, or indeed any other capable orator, it would be impossible to say that they were wholly lacking in any of the five cardinal parts of which rhetoric consists.

'As for Curio, the point which he illustrates very forcibly is this: what wins an orator the highest praise of all is the excellence and fluency of his vocabulary. Curio's argumentation, on the other hand, was feeble, and his arrangement muddled. As for his delivery and his memory, they earned him jeering and mockery on both counts. His physical movements were branded for ever by a comment from Gaius Julius Caesar Strabo Vopiscus. Curio was swaying his entire body from side to side, and Julius asked: "Why is that fellow talking off a boat at sea?" And Cnaeus Sicinius,[1] too, a coarse man but distinctly funny – the only oratorical merit that could be credited to him – made a similar joke. As tribune, it was his job to present the consuls Curio and Cnaeus Octavius to the Assembly. Curio spoke at great length, while Octavius sat swathed in bandages and smeared with a variety of cures for his gout. Then Sicinius addressed Octavius with these words: "You will never be able to thank our colleague enough! Because if he had not flung himself about as he did today, the flies would surely have eaten you alive where you are sitting."

'When we come to Curio's memory, it was so totally defective that sometimes when he had said he would mention three points he would add a fourth as well, or miss out the third. Moreover, in an important private lawsuit, when I was speaking for Cotta's client Titinia[2] and had finished what I had to say, and Curio was arguing in favour of Servius Naevius against me, he suddenly forgot altogether what the case was about, and pronounced that it was all a matter of magic potions and spells arranged by Titinia. These were convincing signs of how shaky his memory was. Worse still, when

1. Tribune in 76.

2. This was during Cotta's consulship (75). The speech has not survived.

he was writing something he would often forget what he himself had just written slightly earlier. In one of his treatises, for example, he records walking out of the Senate after a meeting over which Caesar as consul[1] had presided, and talking with my young friend Gaius Vibius Pansa Caetronianus[2] and his own son Gaius Scribonius Curio[3] as they went with him. In fact, however, the treatise had originated from the questions the son asked about what had taken place at the Senate's meeting – at which he had not been present. What had happened was that his father had delivered a lengthy attack on Caesar, and the text of the essay took the traditional form of a dialogue incorporating this attack. Moreover, as I said, the discussion was dated to the aftermath of a senatorial session which Caesar had convoked during his consulship. Yet, in spite of that, Curio in his dialogue criticizes Caesar for administrative actions that he took in Gaul a year *later*, and during the years that followed thereafter!'[4]

Brutus expressed surprise at this. 'Could Curio's memory really have been so bad', he said, 'that in an actual written description he failed to notice, on reading it through, what a blatant anachronism he had committed?'

'Yes, that is what happened,' I said, 'and, intending, as Curio did, to voice the criticisms which, in fact, he then proceeded to express, it was stupid of him not to assign his dialogue to a date when the events to which it referred had actually taken place. But he went even more wrong than that, because in the same treatise he observed that Caesar, during his consulship, did not go into the Senate. And yet he also, as I have said, depicted himself leaving a Senate meeting over which Caesar as consul had presided! Now, memory is the custodian of a man's general intelligence, and, if Curio's memory was so bad that even in a written work he could not remember what he had just written down before, it is hardly surprising that he also, on many occasions, suffered from lapses of memory when he was speaking extemporaneously.

'As a result, although he had a sense of duty[5] and was very keen

1. In 59.
2. Consul in 43.
3. Tribune in 50.
4. Caesar only started his *Gallic War* in 58.
5. Or: enjoyed influential connections.

to go in for public speaking, very few cases got entrusted to his care. Nevertheless, his contemporaries ranked him next to the best, because of his excellent language, as I said, and the fluent rapidity and smoothness of his style. So in spite of their defects I am of the opinion that his speeches deserve attention. True, they sound a bit slack, but their study does increase and strengthen our impression of his merits, which we must admit that he possessed, to a certain degree – and, indeed, they are significant merits, sufficient, in themselves, to justify regarding Curio as some kind of orator. But let me go back to the rest of my theme . . .[1]

'Among the radicals who came after the Gracchi, the best was, apparently, Lucius Appuleius Saturninus,[2] though he attracted the public more by his appearance and his physical movements and even his clothes than by any real oratorical talent or even a moderate allowance of good sense. As for Gaius Servilius Glaucia,[3] he proved the most outrageous figure since humankind began, but was very clever and cunning all the same, with a great capacity for raising a laugh. In spite of the squalor of his life-style and his whole career, he would have been elected consul during his praetorship if his candidature had been regarded as valid; because he had the support of the populace, and had won the allegiance of the knights as well, owing to his law.[4] But instead, while still praetor, he was put to death by a governmental decision, on the same day as Saturninus, during the consulships of Gaius Marius (for the sixth time) and Lucius Valerius Flaccus.[5] Servilius was like the Athenian Hyperbolus, whose scandalous behaviour was denounced in Attic comedies.[6]

'One of the supporters of those men was Sextus Titius,[7] a voluble speaker and quite sagacious, but so languishing and soft in his gestures that a kind of dance came into existence called "the Titius".

1. At this point, Cicero lists a considerable number of other orators (Appendix 2).

2. Tribune in 103 and 100.

3. Praetor in 100.

4. The *Lex Servilia de repetundis* (of 101 or 100), transferring the extortion court from the senators to the knights.

5. In 100.

6. 'Demagogue' during the Peloponnesian War, murdered by oligarchs in 411.

7. Tribune in 99.

His example is a warning to keep your delivery or diction free of any mannerisms which could be imitated and thus excite ridicule. But now I have gone back to a slightly earlier epoch. Let me return, then, to the period which I was talking about before.

'Publius Antistius Rufus belonged to about the same period as Sulpicius. He was a ranter of some considerable skill. For a long time he had not spoken at all, and was generally despised and laughed at. But then, while he was tribune,[1] he gained popular favour, by rightly condemning the illegitimate candidacy of Gaius Julius Caesar Strabo Vopiscus for the consulship. This was all the more impressive because, although Sulpicius himself, who was his fellow-tribune, took part in the same case, Antistius's arguments were fuller and more convincing. As a result, after he had ceased to be tribune, many cases began to be referred to him, and eventually all the most important cases that came up, whatever their nature. He got down to the essential points very acutely, arranged his material with care, and possessed a reliable memory. His language was not elaborate, but it was not flat either. His style was free, and ran easily, and his manner, in general, was not without a certain polish. But his delivery gave rather a lame impression, because of some vocal defect, and tasteless gestures.

'The period in which he flourished was between the departure of Lucius Cornelius Sulla from Italy and his return, when law and respectability were no longer to be seen in the country.[2] This meant that the Forum was more or less empty, so that Antistius was able to attract all the more attention. Sulpicius had fallen, Cotta and Curio were out of the city,[3] and the only advocates of the time who were still alive were Gaius Papirius Carbo Arvina and Gnaeus Pomponius,[4] both of whom Antistius easily surpassed.

'In the next generation his closest competitor was Lucius Cornelius Sisenna.[5] Sisenna was a learned man, devoted to the humanities. He

1. In 88.

2. i.e. between Sulla's departure for Asia Minor to fight the First Mithridatic War against Mithridates VI of Pontus, and his return to defeat the Marians and become dictator (88–81).

3. Sulpicius was executed as an adherent of Marius in 88, and Cotta had been exiled under the Varian Law (on *maiestas*, treason) of Quintus Varius Hybrida in 90.

4. Carbo and Pomponius were tribunes in 90.

5. Praetor in 78.

spoke good Latin, was well informed about politics, and could be witty. But he did not work hard enough, and possessed too little legal experience. His career came, in point of time, between those of Sulpicius and Quintus Hortensius Hortalus. But he did not manage to rival the older man, and had to give way to the younger. Sisenna's qualities can be seen from his *History*. In its substance, it easily surpasses all its predecessors. Yet it also demonstrates how far short of the highest excellence this type of writing is, and how it has failed, so far, to win a truly distinguished place in Latin literature.

'I mentioned Hortensius. His talent was like a statue of Phidias.[1] It only had to be seen to be admired. He began his career in the Forum during the consulships of Lucius Licinius Crassus and Quintus Mucius Scaevola Pontifex,[2] and in their presence, as presiding officers, gained the approval not only of everyone who heard him, but of the consuls themselves, who greatly exceeded the rest of the audience in their ability to judge such matters. At that time he was only nineteen years of age. He died when Lucius Aemilius Paullus Lepidus and Gaius Claudius Marcellus were consuls.[3] We can see from this that Hortensius's career as an advocate lasted for forty-four years. About his achievements as an orator I shall say something more a little later. Here it has only been my intention to insert him in his proper age-group between orators of different generations.

'When men have a long life, they invariably get compared with people who are much older than themselves as well as with those who are a good deal younger. Thus Accius tells us that he and Pacuvius each produced a play, under the same aediles,[4] when he himself was thirty and Pacuvius was eighty.[5] The same applied to Hortensius. He had links not only with his contemporaries but also with your era and mine, Brutus, as well as with men who were a good deal older than himself. For he had already embarked on his career as a public speaker when Lucius Crassus was still alive, and continued with even greater success in the time of Antonius. In the

1. The fifth-century Athenian sculptor. Cicero began this treatise with a tribute to Hortensius, who had just died.

2. In 95.

3. In 50.

4. One of the responsibilities of the aediles was to supervise the Public Games, at which plays were performed.

5. Accius was born at Pisaurum in 170, and Pacuvius at Brundisium in 220, so that the play to which Cicero refers was produced in 140.

case concerning the property of Cnaeus Pompeius Magnus (Pompey the Great),[1] although still very young, Hortensius was the principal speaker on Pompeius's behalf, along with Lucius Marcius Philippus,[2] who was by that time an old man. Among those whom I have mentioned as belonging to the generation of Sulpicius, he came to occupy an unchallengeable position. Among his own contemporaries,[3] his total superiority was recognized. He and I encountered one another when I was very young, eight years younger than himself, and we competed for the same rewards for many years.[4] But we also worked together, on behalf of numerous clients; and in the same way he and you became associated, on behalf of Appius Claudius Pulcher,[5] shortly before Hortensius's death.

'You see that this discussion has now reached the chronological point, Brutus, when you yourself became an orator. Yet what a lot of other orators there were, between the time when I began to speak and you did! In this survey, however, I decided not to mention anyone who is still alive; because I do not want you to display too much curiosity and extort my opinion about this or that living individual! So I only propose to mention those who are dead.'

'The reason', said Brutus, 'which you give for deciding not to speak about those who are still living is not, in fact, your real one.'

'So what is my real reason?' I asked.

'I suspect', he said, 'that you are afraid that this discussion will leak out, and that men whom you fail to mention will take offence.'

'Can't you keep a secret, then?'

'Yes, certainly we can, without any difficulty at all. All the same, I have an idea that what you want to do is to keep your own mouth shut, rather than see whether *we* can.'

'Well, I'll tell you something frankly. I never expected this discussion to become extended right down to our own time. But this process of moving ahead from one period to another has led me

1. This was a lawsuit brought for the restitution of property seized by Pompey's father Cnaeus Pompeius Strabo (consul in 89).

2. Consul in 91.

3. Cicero mentions four of them (Appendix 2).

4. This is perhaps a reference to their opposition to one another in the case of Verres (Chapter 1).

5. Consul in 54.

on – to such an extent that I have actually come as far as speakers who are younger than myself.'

'Right, then,' said Brutus, 'bring in the name of anyone you want to. And when you have done so, let us return to you and Hortensius.'

'To Hortensius, certainly,' I replied. 'But as for myself, others will speak about me, if they choose to.'

'No, that is not good enough,' he objected. 'Although I have found everything you have said very interesting indeed, all the same your account does strike me as having been rather long drawn out – because I am impatient to hear about yourself! I do not mean that I want to hear about the merits of your oratory, because of course I am well aware of these, as everyone else is as well. But I should like to hear about the successive measures you took, and the processes you underwent, in order to bring this gift of yours to maturity.'

'I will do what you ask,' I said, 'since you do not want me to proclaim my own talents, but only all the hard work I have done. However, I will begin by recording certain other speakers, as you have agreed that I should, and I will start with Marcus Licinius Crassus Dives, who was Hortensius's contemporary.[1]

'Crassus had only had a mediocre cultural education, and possessed little natural talent for making speeches. However, by working industriously, and, most of all by the careful dispensation of his influence in order to win cases, he was for a number of years one of our principal pleaders. Among the features of his oratory were pure Latin, a by no means banal vocabulary, and meticulous arrangement of material. But of ornament and brilliance there was not the slightest sign. His thinking was lively enough, but the same could not be said of his voice, since his delivery, at all times, was uniform and monotonous.

'As for his contemporary and enemy Gaius Flavius Fimbria,[2] he went in for vigorous self-assertion, but did not succeed in keeping it up for very long. He bellowed out everything at the top of his voice, and although his vocabulary was adequate he poured out

1. Marcus Crassus, consul in 70 and member of the First Triumvirate, appeared with Cicero to defend several people. He was killed by the Parthians near Carrhae in 53.

2. Fimbria, mentioned earlier, fought against Mithridates VI of Pontus but lost his army to Sulla and committed suicide in 85.

such a raging torrent of language that one wondered how the public could be so feckless as to rank such a lunatic among orators at all. Cnaeus Cornelius Lentulus Clodianus,[1] too, gained a higher reputation from his manner of speaking than his abilities warranted. He was not, in fact, a very intelligent man, though his face and features made it look as though he was, and his terminology was not extensive, although, once again, it gave the contrary impression. For his employment of dramatic pauses and exclamations was so effective, the sound of his voice so pleasing and melodious, the whole manner of his delivery so warm, that the qualities he lacked were never missed.[2] In consequence, just as Curio's fluent diction gave him the status of an orator although he was without any other qualification whatever, in the same way Lentulus's effective delivery covered up the mediocrity of his other oratorical abilities. In much the same way, too, Publius Cornelius Lentulus Sura[3] distracted attention from the slowness of his imagination and speech by his impressive appearance. His gestures were harmonious and graceful, and his voice agreeable and strong. Delivery, in fact, was all he had. In all other respects he was inferior to the other Lentulus as a speaker.

'Any merits that Marcus Pupius Piso Frugi Calpurnianus[4] was able to muster he had acquired from his education. None of his predecessors was as well informed about Greek theory as he was. He also possessed, it is true, a certain natural adroitness; and he had polished it by training. It showed itself in a shrewd and ingenious way of criticizing other people's choice of language, which meant that what he said was often ill-tempered, and sometimes went too far, but could also be amusing. The tough race of Forum life, however, he did not succeed in enduring for very long; because his physical condition was weak – and he could not put up with the human stupidities and fatuities which we advocates have to swallow! He found such annoyances intolerable, and angrily refused to accept them, either because he had a peevish character, as people supposed, or just out of high-principled disgust. As a young man he did well, but later on his reputation began to flag. Subsequently, however,

1. Consul in 72.
2. The text here is uncertain.
3. Consul in 71.
4. Consul in 61.

his successful handling of the Vestal Virgins' case earned him a great deal of praise,[1] and it seemed that he had been called back to the race. Indeed, from that time onwards he kept his position – as long as he was willing to face the hard labour that it involved. After that, as his application waned, so did the esteem in which he had been held.

'Publius Licinius Murena did not possess any great ability, but he was a keen historian, studious and not unscholarly, a man who laboured with persistent diligence. Gaius Marcius Censorinus knew quite a lot about Greek literature. His presentation of his material was efficient, and his delivery by no means ugly, but he was slothful, and disliked the Forum.[2] Lucius Turius[3] was not very clever but an assiduous worker, who employed such gifts as he possessed to speak on numerous occasions. In consequence he only failed to win the consulship by a small margin of votes.

'Gaius Licinius Macer was always a lightweight, but became one of the most active court lawyers. If his life, and his personality, and even his very features, had not militated so strongly against any appreciation of his abilities, his fame in this respect would have been more conspicuous.[4] The language at his disposal was not richly abundant, but it was not meagre either. His voice and gestures and delivery were entirely lacking in charm. Yet his use of original material, and his arrangement of what he had to say, were carefully thought out. Indeed I have never known anyone else who surpassed him in these respects. However, you might regard such devices as professional routine rather than oratory. Macer gained a reputation in criminal suits. But it was in civil cases that he was thought of most highly.

'Gaius Calpurnius Piso[5] was an orator of the relaxed type. His

1. In one of his speeches against Catilina (III, 4.9) Cicero refers to 'the acquittal of the Vestal Virgins' (priestesses of Vesta) during his consulship (63), but nothing is known about the case. See *Cicero: Selected Political Speeches* (Penguin Classics), p. 114.

2. Murena and Censorinus both lost their lives to Sulla in 82. Murena was perhaps the uncle of the Lucius Murena defended by Cicero (Chapter 2).

3. It has been suggested, however, that the correct reading is 'Lucius Furius' (praetor in 75).

4. As tribune in 73 he agitated for popular rights. He became praetor in 68 but was convicted for extortion in 66 and committed suicide. He wrote a *History of Rome*.

5. Consul in 67.

speeches were filled with conversational expressions. Although he was by no means deficient in imagination, his facial expression seemed to promise greater intelligence than he in fact possessed. His contemporary Manius Acilius Glabrio (consul in the same year) had received an excellent training from his grandfather Quintus Mucius Scaevola Pontifex,[1] but laziness and negligence slowed down his career. Lucius Manlius Torquatus[2] was an accomplished speaker, and a man of sound judgement – altogether a cultivated person. Cnaeus Pompeius Magnus (Pompey), my contemporary,[3] was destined by nature for a splendid career. His eloquence would have earned him greater fame than it did if ambition for even more conspicuous glory had not diverted him to a life of military renown.

And there were others too . . .[4] There was, for example, Publius Autronius, whose only quality was a raucous voice. And there was Gaius Staienus, who got himself adopted into another family, and so became an Aelius instead of a Staienus. His style of speaking was intense, petulant and frenzied. Yet many people liked it, and he would have climbed to high rank if he had not been caught out in a manifestly criminal action and convicted in court, as the law required.[5] Quintus Arrius Secundus,[6] who was Marcus Crassus's lieutenant, ought to be a lesson to all of us: since he demonstrated the value, in our city, of making one's time available to a whole host of people, and helping them in their careers or in the lawsuits that threaten them. Such were the methods by which Arrius, himself of the humblest origins, rose to high office and riches and influence, and although wholly lacking in training and ability alike gained a place among pleaders. But one may use the analogy of boxers, when they, too, are insufficiently trained. Their keenness for victory in the Olympic Games enables them to stand up to fists and to blows. Yet the full force of the sun may turn out to be too much for them. And the same may be said of Arrius. After doing extremely well, and exerting himself vigorously, he found that the

1. Or possibly he was Quintus Mucius Scaevola Augur.

2. Consul in 65.

3. They were born in the same year (106).

4. Cicero lists a number of them (Appendix 2).

5. As quaestor in 77 he led a mutiny against the consul Mamercus Aemilius Lepidus Livianus. After his adoption he had become known as Gaius Aelius Paetus.

6. Praetor in 73.

court restrictions imposed in the year of Pompeius's consulship could not be borne.[1] For him, they were the lethal noonday sun.'

But at this point Atticus interrupted. 'You're drawing from the dregs now,' he said, 'and have been for some time. I didn't say anything; but I was really surprised that you descended as far down as the Staienuses and Autroniuses.'

'You did not imagine, I hope' – I replied – 'that I went down to their level out of a desire to win favour – especially when they are no longer alive! But as I proceed with my chronological arrangement it is inevitable that I should mention some people who are known to me personally and are my contemporaries. Moreover, I have a particular purpose in mind. This is to make the point that, when all the names of those who have ventured to speak in public have been listed, only very few of them deserve to be remembered, and the number of those who have achieved any reputation whatever has been small.

'But let me go back to what I was saying, and carry on with my plan. Titus Manlius Torquatus (the son of the man of the same name) had acquired a good deal of learning at Molon's school on the island of Rhodes. He was also, by nature, such a fluent and ready speaker that, if he had lived, he would have profited from the law against bribery and secured election to a consulship.[2] But his ability as an orator exceeded his ambition, so that he did not really dedicate himself to public speaking. Nevertheless, he never failed to respond to appeals from his dependants, and was always capable of expressing his views in the Senate.

'My fellow-townsman from Arpinum, Marcus Pontidius, took an active part in many private lawsuits. He spoke with great speed, and was by no means slow-witted as a speaker – indeed, "by no means slow-witted" is hardly an adequate description, since when he made a speech he positively boiled with burning indignation and anger! He was a man who frequently quarrelled not only with the counsel on the other side, but also with the judge himself, whom speakers are well advised to conciliate.

1. One of the *Leges Pompeiae* of Cnaeus Pompeius Magnus (Pompey) during his consulship in 52 restricted the plaintiff's speech to two hours and the defendant's to three.

2. The *Lex Pompeia de ambitu* of Cnaeus Pompeius Magnus (52) penalized bribery. Molon had also greatly influenced Cicero.

'Marcus Valerius Messalla Niger,[1] who is younger than I am, was by no means incompetent, but his choice of words was not particularly distinguished. However, he was a sensible, acute and prudent pleader, who worked hard to master and organize the numerous cases that came his way. Cnaeus Cornelius Lentulus Marcellinus, too, was always regarded as an able speaker, and displayed particular eloquence during his consulship.[2] He thought quickly, never found himself at a loss for words, possessed a melodious voice, and had quite a sense of humour. Gaius Memmius, son of Lucius, had an excellent knowledge of literature, but only Greek, because he had a contempt for what was written in Latin.[3] He was an ingenious orator, and had a pleasant way of speaking, but shirked the effort it required, and indeed even shied away from the effort of thinking. His failure to work at such pursuits meant a corresponding deterioration of his capacity to perform them.'

'But I do wish', interposed Brutus, 'that you would also feel inclined to speak about the orators of today! Not about the rest of them so much, but at least about two whom I know you esteem highly, Gaius Julius Caesar and Marcus Claudius Marcellus.[4] I would find hearing about them every bit as interesting as what you have said about those who are dead.'

'I don't quite understand why,' I answered. 'Why should you be interested in my views about men whom you know as well as I do?'

'That applies', he said, 'to Marcellus, but not to Caesar. Marcellus I have often heard, but ever since the time when I was first old enough to form an opinion Caesar has been away from Rome.'

'Well, what is your judgement of Marcellus, whom you have actually heard?'

'What do you suppose that I could think? – only, surely, that he is a mirror of your own self, as you surely must see!'

'If that is really so,' I replied, 'then I hope that you approve of him highly!'

'Yes, I do,' Brutus answered. 'I like Marcellus's speaking very

1. Consul in 61.

2. In 56.

3. Nevertheless, this was the man to whom Lucretius dedicated his poem *De Rerum Natura*. His father had been praetor in 58.

4. Marcellus, consul in 51, led the senatorial opposition to Caesar, but did not like Pompey either.

much indeed. And I have good reason to do so. For he has studied the subject with care, has pursued it to the exclusion of everything else, engaging, with determination, in daily practice exercises. You can see the result in his carefully selected vocabulary and abundant expression of ideas. Moreover, his imposing voice and dignified gestures add impressiveness and distinction to what he is saying. All these assets add up to a total which makes one feel that he has every quality an orator ought to possess. And what I regard as particularly admirable is the fact that at this present time, he finds whatever consolation the disastrous malignity of our common fate permits in two things: the awareness that his own attitude has been beyond criticism, and the resumption of his scholarly activities. I saw him at Mytilene a short time ago – a real man if ever there was one.

'As regards my comparison between yourself and him, I had noticed the resemblance of his oratorical style to yours earlier on. And now that he has benefited from the instruction, in various fields, of the erudite Cratippus[1] – who is a friend of yours too, I discovered – I felt that he was more like you than ever.'

'To hear you praising so fine a man and so good a friend', I said, 'gives me pleasure. But it does remind me painfully, too, of the miseries which we all share – and it was precisely in order to forget those miseries that I have extended this discourse of mine to such a length. But to come back to Julius Caesar, I should like to hear what Atticus thinks of him.'

'As to your own opinions,' said Brutus, 'you have certainly made it clear that you mean to stick to your purpose of remaining silent about men who are still alive. If, on the other hand, you *did* deal with the living, as you have dealt with the dead, you would find no lack of Autroniuses and Staienuses. But whether you deliberately avoided referring to our present gang of pleaders, or you were afraid that someone would complain that he had been omitted or inadequately praised, you might in any case have said something about Julius Caesar, especially as your opinion of his talents is very well known already, and his opinion of your own is no secret either.'

'My own view about Caesar, Brutus,' Atticus put in at this point '– and I have very frequently heard the same from our acute judge

1. Cratippus of Pergamum was a Peripatetic philosopher who met Cicero at Mytilene (51).

of oratory who is with us here today – is that, out of almost all the speakers whom we possess, he speaks the purest Latin. It is a custom he has inherited from his family, as we heard just now about the Laeliuses and Muciuses. And heredity, certainly, is a significant factor. Yet, in addition, he himself has striven to perfect this gift of fine speaking by his own extensive, minute and recondite studies, which he has pursued with the greatest determination and industry.

'And more than that,' continued Atticus, turning to me, 'while deeply engaged in other, highly exacting, activities he found time to write, with meticulous care, his treatise on the art of correct Latinity; which he dedicated to yourself.[1] In its first book, he pronounced that the selection of words was the basis of eloquence. And our friend Cicero here, Brutus, who, I think, prefers that I rather than he himself should speak about Caesar, received a singular compliment in that essay. For after naming him in the dedication this is what Caesar said: "There are certain men who have devoted intense study and practice to producing oratory which gives brilliant expression to their thoughts. In this connection we must recognize that you, as virtually the pioneer and founder of formal eloquence, have been a credit to the name and glory of the Roman people." (Not that that entitles us, by any means, to treat the ordinary, conversational manner of speaking – in contrast to the formal oratorical style – as something we need no longer take into account.)'

'That is indeed, I feel, a most friendly and conspicuous compliment,' said Brutus; 'when he declares that you have been the pioneer and founder of formal eloquence, and a credit to the name and glory of Rome. For it means that the only thing in which conquered Greece was, instead, our conqueror[2] has either been taken away from them altogether or at least we now share it with them. Such a testimonial coming from Caesar is in my view a more eminent distinction, I will not say than the public thanksgiving which was also voted in your honour,[3] but certainly than the military triumphs that have been awarded to so many others.'

1. *De Analogia* (55 or 54 BC – after the date at which this treatise is staged!)

2. Later echoed by Horace, *Epistles*, II, i, 156: 'captive Greece made its fierce conqueror captive'.

3. The *supplicatio* voted after the suppression of the 'conspiracy' of Catilina (63).

'I agree, Brutus,' I said: 'if only that is what Caesar really thinks, and is not merely a friendly gesture of goodwill! For the man – whoever he is, and if such a man truly exists – who not only spread a knowledge of the art of formal eloquence in this city, but actually founded it, unquestionably made a greater contribution to the glory of the Roman people than some individual who managed to capture Ligurian fortresses,[1] actions which, as you know, have been the pretexts for numerous triumphs.

'There have, I know, been instances of superhuman inspiration, in which the brilliance of our leaders has more than once saved our country by military action, just as much as in peacetime. But leaving these exceptions aside, if you will bear with me, a great orator is far more important than an insignificant general.[2] You may object that the general is of more practical use. I do not deny it. Still – and I am not afraid of your protests, since here one can say freely what one thinks – I should myself give preference to that single speech of Lucius Licinius Crassus, in defence of Manius Curius, over any two of those triumphs over Ligurian forts. Contradict me, if you wish, by asserting that the capture of a Ligurian fort was more useful for our country than that able speech in favour of Manius Curius. All right: but you could equally say that it was more useful for the people of Athens to have solid roofs over their houses than to possess that magnificent ivory statue of Minerva (Athena). Well, I personally would rather have been Phidias than even the best carpenter who made roofs! What I mean is that in judging a man's significance the point is not the uses his work can be put to, but how valuable he is in himself. There is no risk of a shortage of porters or labourers; but able painters and sculptors are few.

'But go on, Atticus, about Caesar (and complete the repayment of your debt).'

'Well, the basic requirement of oratory', continued Atticus, 'is, as you know very well, pure Latin diction. Those who have possessed this qualification, up to now, have not acquired it as a result of systematic study, but because they had got into the excellent habit of employing this pure language when they talked. There is no

1. Liguria (north-east Italy and south-east Gaul) was gradually subjugated by the Romans during the second century BC.

2. This is hardly what Cicero said in *For Murena* (Chapter 2).

need for me to refer to Gaius Laelius, or Lucius Furius Philus,[1] or Scipio Africanus the younger. Good Latin, just as much as integrity of character, was a feature of their time; though it was not universal, since their contemporaries Caecilius Statius and Marcus Pacuvius, as we can see, used inferior language.[2] Still, almost everyone who belonged to that epoch, unless he lived outside the city or was corrupted by some barbarous influence in his home, spoke correctly. But the passage of time has caused this situation to deteriorate, in Rome as in Greece. For our own city, just like Athens, has received, from various places, a large influx of people whose speech is impure. This has created a state of affairs which imperatively demands a purification of language, and the establishment of a solid, immutable criterion – a sort of touchstone – to make it possible for the degraded adulterations of common usage to be avoided.

'I remember, as a boy, seeing Titus Quinctius Flamininus, who had been consul with Quintus Caecilius Metellus Balearicus.[3] His Latin was admired, although his literary culture was non-existent. As for the elder Quintus Lutatius Catulus,[4] he was not deficient in training, as you remarked, but what gave him the name of being a good speaker was his attractive voice and pleasant elocution. When we turn to Cotta, it is true that the broadness of his vowels made his pronunciation the very reverse of Greek, and in contrast to Catulus he spoke in a somewhat rustic and countrified fashion. And yet he, too, by this rural, woodland route likewise achieved a reputation for pure speaking. Then, as you said, there was Lucius Cornelius Sisenna, who set out to be a reformer of current linguistic usage. Even the observations of the prosecuting counsel Gaius Rusius did not deter Sisenna from introducing unfamiliar words.'

'What are you referring to?' asked Brutus. 'And who was this Gaius Rusius?'

'He was a veteran prosecutor,' answered Atticus, 'who was speaking against Gaius Hirtilius at the time. The defending counsel

1. Consul in 136.

2. Both playwrights: Caecilius Statius was an Insubrian Gaul from Mediolanum taken prisoner in 223/222. Pacuvius of Brundisium, mentioned earlier, lived from 220 until *c.* 130.

3. In 123.

4. Consul in 102.

was Sisenna, who in the course of his speech described certain of the accusations as *sputatilica* – spittable upon.[1] Whereupon Gaius Rusius intervened. "I can't go on, members of the jury," he cried out, "unless you come to my help. I haven't the slightest idea what Sisenna is saying – and I suspect he is trying to trap me. *Sputatilica!* What on earth is that? *Sputa*, spit, I understand, but I haven't a notion what *tilica* means." Everyone laughed. But my friend Sisenna was genuinely convinced that the way to speak well was to employ unfamiliar words.

'Caesar, by way of contrast, seeks to remedy degraded and corrupt usage, and restore pure, uncorrupted language, by the application of rational principle. First, he chooses his Latin vocabulary with precision – which is a thing every free-born Roman citizen ought to do anyway, even if he is not an orator at all. Then Caesar adds the stylistic ornaments that oratory requires. The effect he produces by such means is that of a well-painted picture seen in a good light. With this achievement to his credit, in addition to the qualities that are common to orators in general, he seems to me unequalled. His manner of speaking is superb, and without a trace of routine dullness. Voice, gesture and bearing alike are all impressive and noble.'

'Yes,' said Brutus, 'his speeches seem to me very pleasing indeed. I have read a number of them, as well as the *Commentaries*, which he wrote about his own actions.'[2]

'Pleasing they certainly are,' I agreed. 'They are like nude figures, plain and beautiful, stripped of all stylistic ornamentation, like a bare body stripped of its clothes. His modest aim was to provide others with the facts they would need, in order to write history themselves. His attempt to carry out this task proved welcome, I am sure, to third-class writers, who see an opportunity to brighten up what he wrote with curling irons of their own. But sensible would-be authors are deterred from competing with his brilliance; since clear and straightforward brevity, such as his, must surely be the supreme quality a history can possess.

'But now, if you do not mind, let us go back to men who are no longer living. Gaius Sicinius, son of the daughter of Quintus

1. An adaptation of the Greek word *kataptusta*.

2. The *Gallic War* and *Civil War*: an anachronism because both were written after the literary date of this dialogue.

Pompeius,[1] died when his last post had been the quaestorship. He was an orator who deserved approbation, and had, indeed, already received it. He was a product of the school of Hermagoras,[2] which, although weak in regard to embellishment, is adept in creating original material. The school lays down fixed oratorical rules and precepts, which although they do not help to produce a more ample style – since their keynote is dryness – nevertheless have the merit of imposing order and fixing lines from which one must not deviate. Keeping to the lines in question, preparing himself carefully before he embarked on his cases, and enjoying a natural fluency of speech, Sicinius's adherence to these methods and principles had enabled him, by the time of his death, to establish a place for himself among orators.

'One of his contemporaries was my scholarly cousin Gaius Visellius Varro, who after holding the curule aedileship died while serving as president of a criminal tribunal.[3] With regard to him, I confess that my own estimation differed from the view of the public, because his oratory made no appeal to them. True, his manner of speaking was abrupt, and indeed unclear, because it contained so much close argumentation. Moreover, what he said was obscured by the fact that he spoke so fast. Yet in choice of words and richness of thought I cannot readily think of anyone who outclassed him. He was also well informed about literary matters; and he possessed a mastery of the civil law as well, inherited from his father Gaius Visellius Aculeo.[4]

'While I am on the subject of the dead, two men still remain to be mentioned. One was Lucius Manlius Torquatus.[5] He was quite an able speaker, but you would not call him a trained orator. He was more what the Greeks describe as *politicus*, a citizen who speaks on state affairs when he has to. He was widely read, not in popular literature, but in subjects of a more recondite and esoteric kind. His memory was marvellous, his choice of words precise and impressive,

1. Censor and consul in 141.

2. Hermagoras of Temnos (second century BC) was the leading rhetorical theorist of the Hellenistic age.

3. *Iudex quaestionis*; a non-elective post held by an ex-aedile. Varro had been curule aedile in *c.* 59.

4. A Roman knight, married to Helvia, the sister of Cicero's mother.

5. Praetor in 49.

and all this received a further adornment from the seriousness and integrity of his character. I also admired the speeches of Gaius Valerius Triarius, which in spite of his youthful years displayed the maturity of a cultivated older man. His facial expression, too, was dignified, and his language effective; and every word he uttered had been carefully weighed.'

Brutus was moved by these references to Torquatus and Triarius, of both of whom he had been fond. And now he had this to say: 'There are, I know, a very great many other reasons, as well, for thinking the sad thoughts that have come into my mind at this juncture. But recalling these two men makes me grieve once again that your own continual endeavours in favour of peace did not achieve their aim! For if things had gone otherwise our country would not have lost those admirable personages, and numerous other distinguished citizens as well.'[1]

'But let us not talk about that, Brutus,' I said. 'It would only make us even sadder than we are. And it is not just a question of remembering the past. That, indeed, is distressing enough, but dread of what the future may bring is more distressing still. So let us set our lamentations aside, and I will instead continue to assess the gifts of the various Roman orators, since that is the purpose of our inquiry.

'One of those who lost his life in the same war was Marcus Calpurnius Bibulus.[2] He wrote a great deal with considerable care, and engaged persistently in legal cases, although he was by no means an orator. Another speaker was your father-in-law Appius Claudius Pulcher, who was my colleague as augur, and a friend.[3] He was quite an erudite person, and a knowledgeable, experienced orator, and well-informed about augural and public law and history. Lucius Domitius Ahenobarbus,[4] on the other hand, was wholly untrained in public speaking, but used good Latin, and expressed himself freely. Then there were the two Lentuli, who had both gained consulships. One was Publius Cornelius Lentulus Spinther,

1. They were killed at the battle of Thapsus (46), so that this reference probably only dates from a subsequent, revised version of this treatise.

2. Consul in 59; a persistent but unsuccessful opponent of Caesar: he died in 49/48.

3. Consul in 54.

4. Consul in 54.

who avenged the wrongs that I had suffered.[1] Study had made him the orator he was, since he had no natural talents in that direction. Yet his fine brain and character enabled him to aspire, perseveringly, to all the honours that fall to a distinguished figure, and to live up to them with dignity. Lucius Cornelius Lentulus Crus[2] was an energetic orator – if you could describe him as an orator at all. But he found that the effort of thinking a case out was too much of a bore. His voice was agreeable, and his style not too crude. But the manner he adopted was vehement, and positively menacing.[3] For the lawcourts one might hope for something better. As far as political life was concerned, however, his methods were adequate. Titus Postumius, too, was a by no means contemptible orator.[4] Speaking on public affairs with the same vigour that he displayed as a soldier, he adopted an unrestrained and distinctly fierce manner. About the laws and institutions of the state, however, he was knowledgeable.'

'If you had not explained your plan,' Atticus intervened to say, 'and if all these people whom you have been mentioning were still alive, I would suspect that you were trying to ingratiate yourself with them. Another point: you have named almost everyone who has ever ventured to get on his feet and speak, so that I feel that it may have been by an oversight that you omitted to mention Marcus Servilius Geminus.'[5]

'No, Atticus,' I said, 'I do realize that there have been many such men who never uttered a word in public, yet had the capacity, nevertheless, to speak better than some of the orators whom I have enumerated. But one of my reasons for offering you the list to which you referred has been to show you, first, how, if you take the whole total of those who might have chosen to speak, the number of those who actually ventured to do so is small, and, secondly, I have wanted to point out how few of them have deserved commendation. This being my plan, I ought just to give the names of two Roman knights, friends of mine who have

1. As consul (57) he was active in securing Cicero's return from exile.

2. Consul in 49.

3. He violently attacked proposals conciliatory to Caesar before the Civil War.

4. Titus Postumius was praetor in 57. According to a variant reading, however, the reference is to a certain Lucius Postumius.

5. Identity disputed.

recently died. One was Publius Cominius of Spoletium, who was the prosecutor I opposed on behalf of Gaius Cornelius.[1] His material was well arranged, and his diction pointed and fluent. The other knight I have in mind was Titus Accius of Pisaurum, against whom I defended Aulus Cluentius Habitus.[2] Titus Accius was a careful speaker, and reasonably eloquent. Furthermore, he was instructed in the doctrines of Hermagoras.[3] These are precepts that do not furnish oratory with lavish ornamentation. Nevertheless, they do provide ready-made debating points which can be applied to this or that type of case: spears, you might compare them with, to which thongs are already attached, so that a light-armed soldier can throw them whenever he wants to.

'Now take my son-in-law Gaius Calpurnius Piso.[4] I have never known anyone who surpassed him in diligence and industriousness, or in ability either, for that matter. In every moment of the day he was busy either pleading in the Forum or writing or thinking at home, in preparation for cases that lay ahead. He operated with such speed that he seemed more like a flier than a runner. His vocabulary was chosen with discrimination, his periods were appropriately organized and rounded. He employed diversified and well-thought-out arguments; and his ideas were convincing, consistent and to the point. His gestures and bodily movements, which looked like artificial products of training, but were not, displayed a natural poise. I detect a danger that my affection for Piso might induce me to ascribe him greater qualities than he actually possessed. But that is not, actually, the case, since I could go on to praise him for other and even more outstanding qualities than those that I have so far mentioned. In respect of self-control, for instance, or sense of duty, or any other virtue that you may like to mention, I do not believe that there was any other member of his generation to compare with him.

'Marcus Caelius Rufus was another man whom I ought not to pass over – whether it was bad luck or deliberate suicidal intention that brought about his end. So long as he paid attention to my advice, while he was tribune, so long he stood with exemplary

1. Tribune in 67.
2. In Cicero's speech *For Cluentius* (*Cicero: Murder Trials*, pp. 111 ff.) in 76.
3. The second-century rhetorician.
4. The first husband of Cicero's daughter Tullia. Quaestor in 58.

firmness on the side of the Senate and the best of our citizens against the lunatic, criminal violence of the radical faction.[1] But what served him best in maintaining this praiseworthy line of conduct was a splendid, imposing, witty and sophisticated oratorical style. He delivered a number of notable public addresses and three penetrating orations as prosecuting counsel, all concerned with national political disputes. Speeches he made on behalf of clients, and in his own defence, were inferior to those I have just mentioned, but were by no means negligible all the same, indeed not at all bad. When he was elected to the curule aedileship he had conservative support, but to my great regret, after my departure,[2] he abandoned his earlier principles and fell, imitating people whom he himself, previously, had undermined.[3]

'But now let me say something about Marcus Calidius as well.[4] He was not just one of the crowd of contemporary speakers. On the contrary, he stood out among them, as a unique figure. For his speaking was characterized by a flexibility and sensitiveness that were perfectly moulded to express his intentions, and I know of no other orator who could match this achievement. His style was pure and lucid, and flowed so easily that nothing held it up. Every word, as you could see, was located in its proper place like the pieces in the pattern of a mosaic, to which Lucilius refers.[5] Besides, none of Calidius's utterances were harsh, or discordant, or banal, or far-fetched. And, in addition, far from restricting himself to literal expressions, he introduced numerous metaphors, in such a manner, however, that they did not seem irrelevant intrusions but gave the impression of having been inserted at precisely the point to which they belonged.

'Calidius also employed sequences of words in such a way that

1. Cicero had defended him in *For Caelius* (56), and he, in return (as tribune), had backed Titus Annius Milo, for whom Cicero spoke in 52. *For Caelius* and *For Milo* are translated in *Cicero: Selected Political Speeches*, pp. 165ff. and pp. 215ff.

2. Cicero is referring to his departure for Greece in 49.

3. He was captured and killed while helping to lead an insurrection in south Italy in 48. He had been curule aedile in 50.

4. Calidius, praetor in 57, was a friend of Cicero who went over to Caesar's side.

5. Gaius Lucilius, the satirical poet already referred to. The phrase (84 Marx) is cited again in *Cicero: Orator*, 149.

they never seemed unattached to one another, or lacking their appropriate connection. On the contrary, they were bound together by rhythmical linkages, though these were not effected in any obvious or monotonous fashion, but were variegated and well disguised. In addition, he made use of those figures of speech and thought which the Greeks call *schemata*; his speeches were studded with them like a series of decorated designs. He was also very good at detecting the main point at issue, that essential theme of judicial formulation.[1] Added to that was an organization of subject-matter based on correct rhetorical theory, and a gracious delivery, and a relaxed and reasonable manner. So if speaking in a pleasing fashion is the ideal sort of oratory, you would say that you need not look for anything better than Calidius. But as I mentioned before, there are three things which the orator ought to achieve. He ought to instruct, and please, and move. Well, Calidius possessed the first two of those qualifications in the highest degree. That is to say, he expounded with great lucidity, and he charmed his audience by the attractiveness of his language. But the third qualification, which consists of stirring and arousing the emotions of his audience, he failed to display. And that, as I have said, is what, above all, makes an orator successful. Calidius showed no force or passion at all. That may have been intentional, on the grounds that a more exalted way of speaking and a more excitable delivery would have denoted mental imbalance and frenzy. Or it may have been due to a natural disinclination for that sort of thing, or to habit; or because he just could not do it. That is the one quality which was missing in his oratory. If it was unimportant anyway, just call it something he did not bother about. But if it meant that an essential element was not there, you must call it a defect.

'In his prosecution of Quintus Gallius,[2] I remember, he accused Gallius of attempting to poison him. He had detected the plan, Calidius said, and had submitted proofs of it to the court, in the form of writings in Gallius's own hand, as well as evidence from witnesses, and examinations under torture. He set out his charge

1. The *formula* was the praetor's exposition to the *iudex* who was going to conduct the trial.

2. Gallius had been aedile in 67, and was known as a supporter of Catilina in the following year, when this trial took place. Gallius was acquitted, and became praetor in 65.

with meticulous exactness and care. I was speaking for the defence, and after putting forward such arguments as the case required, I used this very defect I have mentioned as a weapon against Calidius. He was claiming, I pointed out, to have uncovered a threat against his life, and to have acquired proofs of a plot to assassinate him. And yet he had presented this assertion in the most flat and emotionless fashion, practically yawning. "Come, Marcus Calidius," I protested, "are you putting your case in this unconvincing way because you have just made it up? You have always used that eloquence of yours energetically enough when you were arguing in favour of some defendant. So is it believable that you would not do the same when you are speaking on a matter that actually concerns yourself? I see not a sign of any distress, of that fervent indignation which arouses even people who have no capacity for speaking at all to vociferous complaints when they think that they have been wronged. But you, on the other hand, show no trace whatever either of mental or of physical agitation! I have not seen you smiting your brow, slapping your thigh, even stamping your foot. So totally unexcited were we all by what you said that we almost went to sleep where we sat!" Calidius was a distinguished orator, but that was how I dealt with his restrained, or faulty, manner of speaking – using it as an argument to contradict his accusation.'

'But surely there is no doubt at all', said Brutus, 'whether we should describe it as restraint or a fault! Everyone in the world will agree that of all the talents an orator can have at his disposal by far the greatest is his power to arouse the emotions of his hearers and turn them in whatever direction the case requires. If an orator does not possess that power, he lacks his most indispensable qualification.'

'That is certainly the case,' I agreed.

'But now let us return,' I went on, 'to the one man who still remains to be described: and that is Quintus Hortensius Hortalus. Afterwards, I will add a few words about myself, since that, Brutus, is what you demand. But before doing either of those things I do think that first I ought to mention two young men who, if they had lived longer, would have become very famous public speakers.'

'I imagine', said Brutus, 'that you are referring to Gaius Scribonius Curio and Gaius Licinius Calvus.'[1]

1. Curio, the son of a consul of 76 (who supported Verres and was often

'Yes, they are the people I want to discuss. Curio spoke with an easy freedom which gave ample expression to thoughts which flowed abundantly and were, at times, penetrating. Greater elegance and fluency could not be imagined. He had received little instruction from teachers, but had a wonderful natural talent for speaking. Whether he was industrious or not I cannot say, but he was certainly enthusiastic. If he had chosen to listen to what I had to tell him, he would have gone after high office rather than just after power.'

'What do you mean by that?' said Brutus. 'And how do you distinguish between the two?'

'Like this,' I replied. 'High office is a reward for merit bestowed by the judgement and favour of the citizen body. So I maintain that the man who has achieved it by their votes is entitled to be regarded as a good and justly honoured person. But when someone, profiting from an accidental circumstance, and actually against the wishes of his fellow-citizens, has risen to a post of command, he has only achieved the semblance of honour, and not true honour itself. That is what Curio tried to do. But if, on the other hand, he had listened to my point of view instead, he would have risen through the successive grades of public office just as his father and other eminent men had risen before him, finally attaining the highest posts the state has to offer, and winning favour and renown in the process.

'When Publius Licinius Crassus, the son of Marcus, became my friend at an early age,[1] I remember that I frequently advised him in the same sense, urging him earnestly to follow the same path to fame that his forebears had trodden and prepared for his benefit. For he had been excellently brought up, and had received a thorough education. His brain was active enough, and his vocabulary quite rich and well chosen, and although not a pretentious person he was not lacking in dignity. He was reserved, but not lazy. Yet he too was devoured by a passion to make a name for himself, which was inappropriate for a person of his youthful years. Because, as a soldier, he had fought under a general, he wanted to become a

---

hostile to Cicero), was tribune in 50, served under Julius Caesar in the Civil War – hoping, in vain, to win Cicero to Caesar's cause – but then, after occupying Sicily, crossed over to north Africa, where he was killed by the pro-Pompeian King Juba of Numidia (49). Calvus was an orator and poet (82–47?).

1. He was killed, like his father the triumvir, by the Parthians at Carrhae (53).

general himself, straightaway – a rank for which, by tradition, a certain age is required. However, things do not always turn out well for such persons, and Crassus came to a disastrous end. He had intended to be like Cyrus and Alexander,[1] whose careers had so speedily achieved success, but instead, as became clear, his achievements fell far short of those of his uncle the orator Lucius Licinius Crassus[2] and many other members of his family.

'But now let us get back to Calvus, as we planned to do. He was a speaker of much more extensive literary knowledge than Curio, and his oratorical style was more careful and discriminating. But for all his scholarly refinement, a continual self-examination and meticulous fear of committing some fault meant a loss of vitality. Through over-scrupulousness, that is to say, his language sounded thin. Erudite and attentive listeners appreciated its distinction, but the crowd in the Forum, who had to swallow it down, failed to digest it – and it is for them that eloquence exists.'

'Our friend Calvus', observed Brutus, 'wanted to be known as an Attic orator. That was the reason for his stylistic bareness, which he went in for deliberately.'

'Yes, that was the line he selected. But he was wrong, and he forced others to make the same mistake.[3] If you choose to maintain that everyone whose way of speaking avoids fatuousness and pedantry or affectation is Attic, then you will be quite right to pronounce that no one who is not Attic has any merit at all. For you will then be able to insist that tastelessness and extravagance are forms of oratorical mania, whereas sanity and purity of style are what every scrupulous, conscientious speaker ought to aim at. And if meagre simple aridity is classified as specifically Attic, subject of course to the proviso that polish and refinement and finish must also be present, so far so good. But Atticism has also included better qualities than those, and one must never forget that Attic speakers have in fact belonged to various categories, not at all the same as one another – and in addition to this diversity have also been by no means deficient in forcefulness.

1. Cyrus II (559–529 BC), founder of the Achaemenid Persian Empire, and Alexander III the Great of Macedonia (336–323).

2. Consul in 95.

3. Cicero implies that it was Calvus who introduced the name 'Atticism' to describe the new, bare style which reacted against the more ample traditional manner.

'You may declare that it is your ambition to imitate Attic models. But which? Because, as I say, they are by no means homogeneous. Demosthenes, for example, was totally unlike Lysias. Again, both of them were utterly different from Hyperides. All three bore no resemblance whatever to Aeschines. Whom, then, are you going to imitate? If you name only one of them, that might seem to be implying that the others did not speak pure Attic. If, on the other hand, you say "all of them", what you propose is impossible, because they differ so markedly one from another. And in this connection I should like to ask a question: did the famous Demetrius of Phalerum speak good Attic? I would answer, myself, that his speeches are redolent of the very perfume of Athens itself. You may say that he is more highly coloured than Demosthenes or Lysias. But that, I suppose, was the way he was made. Or perhaps it was his deliberate choice.

'While on this theme, let me record the names of two other Greek orators who had been contemporaries, and were both Attic, but spoke in totally contrasted fashions: Charisius and Demochares. Charisius, who wrote numerous speeches for other men to deliver, seems to have aimed at imitating Lysias. Demochares, the nephew of Demosthenes, likewise wrote speeches – as well as composing a history of contemporary Athens which seemed a good deal closer to oratory than to historiography. It was Charisius, incidentally, whom Hegesias took as a model.[1] Hegesias considered himself such a perfect Atticist that he regarded authentic members of that category as practically rustic in comparison with himself. Yet the carefully balanced manner in which he expressed himself strikes us as a fractured, puerile, mincemeat of a style.

'"We want to be Attic." Good. "Are Charisius and Demochares Attic orators?" Yes, without question. "Then those are the men on whom we model ourselves." But how, when they are so unlike one another, and unlike all the rest as well? "Well, then, we take Thucyides as our model." Excellent, if you are intending to write history, but if the pleading of cases is what you propose, not so good. Thucydides was a trustworthy and impressive recorder of

1. Charisius lived in *c.* 300 BC. Demochares (*c.* 360–275) rose to power after the expulsion of the representatives of Cassander of Macedonia in 307. Hegesias of Magnesia ad Sipylum was a third-century historian and orator, regarded as un-Attic and Asianic, despite his own alleged view of himself.

historical actions. But these forensic courtroom disputations of ours were not his field. Certainly, he introduced speeches into his history, and quite a number of them too. And I have always thought highly of them. But I should not have the ability to use them as models, nor would I want to, I think, if I could. I can be compared, in this respect, to a man who likes Falernian wine,[1] but does not want to drink it if it is only last year's product. But the Falernian equally does not, on the other hand, need to be so old that it has to date from the consulships of Lucius Opimius or Lucius Anicius Gallus.[2]

'But those vintages, you will object, are recognized to be the best. Yes, I realize that, but wine that is too old does not have the taste we enjoy, and is, in fact, hardly drinkable any longer. All right, but even if one agrees that that is so, one does not need to go, by way of contrast, to an absolutely new press to find a wine that one can drink. No, what one should do instead is choose a wine that is just reasonably old. And the same applies to oratory. On the one hand your friends, I maintain, are perfectly right to reject this novel sort of speech-making that is still raw, like unfermented wine straight from the vat. Yet, conversely, they ought not to try to reproduce the style of Thucydides, which is certainly noble, but, like Anicius's vintage, too old. Thucydides himself, if he had lived at a later epoch, would surely have been less crude and harsh.

'"Then let us make Demosthenes our model." There, in heaven's name, you are perfectly right. We could aim for nothing better! But the trouble is that we do not achieve it. True, our would-be Atticists believe that their attempt to do so is successful. But what they do not appreciate is the incontrovertible historical fact that when Demosthenes was due to speak people flocked from all over Greece to hear him speaking. When these Atticists of ours, however, make a speech, they are abandoned not only by the audience, which is humiliating enough, but even by the people who are warmly in favour of the client the speakers are endeavouring to defend. Well, if speaking in a cramped and meagre way is Attic, let them call themselves Atticists! And indeed, when they come to the Assembly, they may speak exactly as they wish if they only have to address the praetor, standing in front of them. But if they are going to harangue the benches, they will have to talk more loudly and fully.

1. The *Falernus ager* was a section of northern Campania famous for its wine.
2. In 121 and 160 respectively.

'I will tell you the sort of situation I hope my orator will create. When it is reported that he is about to speak, I shall want the benches not to have one single empty place, the jurymen's tribunal to be equally packed, the clerks devoted to the task of helpfully assigning places or getting them vacated, a large crowd milling about, the judge alertly listening. When the orator gets to his feet, I should like to see the crowd insisting that everyone should hold their tongues so that they can hear him, and then repeatedly shouting out their approval, and applauding vociferously. This speaker of mine will arouse laughter whenever he seeks to, or tears if that is his aim. As a result, anyone looking on from a distance, even if he has not the slightest idea what the case is all about, will see quite clearly that he is winning his audience's favour, like Quintus Roscius Gallus on the stage.[1] If *that* is how things turn out, you can be sure that you have a man who is speaking like an authentic Attic orator: like Pericles, as we have heard, or like Hyperides, or Aeschines, or like Demosthenes most of all.

'Our Roman Atticists may however, I realize, prefer a manner of speaking which, while acute and sensible and straightforward and dry, does not make use of any effective embellishments. And they may maintain that this is what is meant by saying a style is Attic. If that is their interpretation, I shall not object to it. Because in an art that is so comprehensive and diversified as oratory, there is room even for plainness, somewhat meagre though it may be.

'My conclusion, then, is this. It is not true that everyone who speaks in the Attic fashion speaks well. But everyone who speaks well is entitled to call himself Attic.

'However, let us return to Hortensius.'

'All right, do so,' said Brutus, 'though I have found your digression very enjoyable.'

But at this point Atticus had a remark to make. 'On a number of occasions,' he said, 'I have felt inclined to break in. But I did not want to interrupt. Now, however, since you look like winding up your own observations, I will let you know, if you do not mind, what I think.'

'Yes, Atticus, please do.'

'I want to bring up the subject of irony,' he said. 'We are told that Socrates employed this device; it is attributed to him by Plato,

1. Roscius of Solonium was the most famous actor of Cicero's time.

Xenophon and Aeschines. I admit that it is a neat and clever way of speaking. It makes a man look modest, and at the same time humorous, when, for example, in a discussion of wisdom, he denies that it is a quality he possesses himself, but concedes it mockingly to others, who claim, unlike him, that they possess it. That is how Socrates, according to Plato, loads the Sophists Protagoras and Hippias and Prodicus and Gorgias and the rest with praises, while declaring that he himself is totally uninformed and ignorant. This sort of disclaimer somehow seems appropriate to Socrates, and I do not agree with Epicurus who condemns it.[1] But in a historical survey, such as you have been professing to undertake in your analysis of orators, I do want you to consider whether irony of this kind is not just as reprehensible as it would be in the witness-box.'

'What are you getting at?' I inquired. 'I don't understand.'

'My point is this,' he said. 'To begin with, you have praised certain orators in a manner likely to mislead people who are not well informed about the subject. In some instances, in fact, I could scarcely help laughing. One moment when I felt like that was when you compared our Cato[2] to Lysias. Certainly, Cato was a fine man, indeed one of the finest, quite exceptional. Nobody could deny it. But as an orator how could you possibly compare him with Lysias, whose word-pictures were so uniquely brilliant? Amusing irony, if we are joking. But if we are talking seriously, we surely ought to be as scrupulous as if we are giving evidence on oath. Your Cato I admire, as citizen, senator, general, in fact as a man of first-class integrity, industriousness and every good quality you can think of. His speeches, too, I estimate highly – for their time. They show distinct signs of talent. But they are crude and unpolished. So when you credited his *Origins* with every oratorical merit, and compared Cato with historians of the calibre of Philistus and Thucydides, did you really imagine that Brutus or I would be convinced by what you were saying? Those Greeks were writers whom nobody has been able to rival. And yet you compare with them a man from Tusculum who had not the slightest idea how to infuse his speeches with the fullness and grace that an orator ought to have.

1. Epicurus of Samos (341–270), founder of the Epicurean school of philosophy at Athens.

2. Cato the elder, consul in 195, censor in 184.

'Another man you praise is Servius Sulpicius Galba.[1] If you are praising him as the leading man of his epoch, I agree with your estimate. That, indeed, is what we have learnt to be true. But if you are praising him as an orator, let us look at his speeches; for it is possible to get hold of the texts. And then tell me whether you would really like Brutus here, whom you claim to love more than you love yourself, to speak in that sort of fashion! You also express approval of the speeches of Marcus Aemilius Lepidus Porcina.[2] I am prepared to go along with you, but only up to a point – that is to say, if you are praising his orations as antiques.

'Next, you bring up Publius Cornelius Scipio Africanus the younger and Gaius Laelius. You describe their language as attractive, and indeed august. But what you are doing is seducing us with the names of great men, and the distinction of their life-styles, which were certainly very noble. But set those factors on one side, and I am afraid you will find that the attractive language to which you refer is such a minor consideration that it hardly deserves a glance.

'As for Gaius Papirius Carbo[3] I am well aware that he has been reputed one of the greatest orators. But in oratory, as in everything else, people make a habit of praising whatever is supreme in its own day, whether it is objectively valuable or not. I could say the same of the Gracchi, although your observations regarding them seem to me right. All the others I will pass over, but I do want to comment on the two men whom you regarded as having attained the perfection of eloquence, Marcus Antonius and Lucius Licinius Crassus. I heard them speak myself, and they were unquestionably eminent orators. So when you praise them, I welcome what you say. But I do not entirely agree with the way that you put it. You indicated that Crassus's speech in support of the Servilian Law had been your teacher and guide. But I imagine you meant that in the same way as Lysippus used to declare that the Doryphorus of Polyclitus had been his model – which could not be taken seriously, but was, in other words, ironical.[4]

1. Consul in 144.

2. Consul in 137.

3. Consul in 120.

4. Lysippus of Sicyon, sculptor of the Apoxyomenus, and Alexander the Great's favourite portraitist.

'Why I think this I shall not say, in case you should accuse me of flattery. Your remarks about Cotta, Sulpicius and just now Julius Caesar I shall pass over without any objection. For they, at least, were authentic orators. How great, and what sort of orators, I must leave it to you to say. But as regards all that collection of mere hack performers that you got together, I take your opinions less seriously. Some of them, it seems to me, would have willingly given their lives for the privilege of finding themselves included in your list of orators at all.'

After listening to what he said, I went on. 'You have touched on a topic, Atticus,' I said, 'which it would take us a long time to deal with, and which deserves a whole new discussion on its own account; but we shall have to leave it for another occasion. We should have to consult a number of books by a number of people, starting with the elder Cato. When we do so, you will see that he produced, to use painters' language, wonderful outlines, lacking nothing except a certain liveliness of tinting that had not yet been discovered. Turning to that speech by Crassus, I hold the view that he himself might perhaps have written it better; but that nobody else could have done so. And when I called it my teacher do not suppose that I was being ironical. You are kind enough, it appears, to rate my own abilities, here and now, more highly than his. All the same, when I was young, Crassus was the best Latin model one could follow. You also comment on my packing in so many names. But this I did, as I said before, with a set purpose: my aim was to emphasize that, although everyone wanted to distinguish himself in this oratorical field, very few succeeded in achieving this. Gaius Fannius tells us in his *History* that the younger Scipio Africanus was not averse to using irony. But I for my part would not wish to seem to be doing so.'

'As you say,' replied Atticus. 'But I am surprised, I confess, that you should so completely disclaim a practice in which both Scipio Africanus and Socrates were prepared to indulge.'

'Let us talk about all that later,' interjected Brutus. 'For what I want you to do now', he told me, 'is to go back to some of those early speeches to which you were referring, and to say something about them.'

'I should very much like to do so, Brutus,' I answered. 'But on some other occasion, at my house at Cumae or Tusculum, at both of which we are neighbours. As regards our present discussion, however, let me now return to the point from which this digression started.

'We were talking about Hortensius. When he was still very young, he began to speak in the Forum, and soon afterwards was called upon to undertake more significant cases. He inaugurated his career when Cotta and Sulpicius were ten years older than himself, and when Crassus and Antonius, and then Lucius Marcius Philippus and subsequently Gaius Julius Caesar Strabo Vopiscus, were at their zenith. Yet Hortensius's fame as an orator constantly aroused comparisons with these masters. First of all he possessed a memory such as I have never known in anyone else. Once he had prepared some material in private, he could reproduce it without written assistance in precisely the form in which he had framed it. This naturally excellent memory he employed to such effect that he was able to remember not only the exact terms of what he himself had previously written, or had even merely composed in his mind, but also, without prompting, he could recall everything that had been said by the other side.

'Hortensius was so eager to succeed that his dedication to his profession exceeded anything I have ever seen. He never allowed a day to pass without either making a speech in the Forum or practising his oratory elsewhere. Often, indeed, he did both, on one and the same day. Moreover, he introduced a style of speaking that was wholly singular. It included two features which were unique to himself. One was the inclusion of headings indicating what he was about to say; and the other was the recapitulation of the arguments which both his opponents and he himself had already put forward. His choice of words was impressive, the structure of his speeches felicitous, and his style admirably well rounded. These were advantages which he owed partly to his own exceptional gifts and partly to assiduous exercises. He invariably knew by heart what he was going to say in his speeches, and kept their successive sections clearly divided in his mind. He hardly ever allowed anything relevant to proving or refuting his case to escape his attention. His voice was melodious and pleasant to listen to; though possibly his method of delivery, and his gestures, were a little more artificial than an orator needed.

'Hortensius's career began to flourish at the time when Crassus died, Cotta was exiled, the lawcourts were suspended owing to the Social War,[1] and I myself first appeared in the Forum. In the first

1. 91–88.

year of the war Hortensius served as an ordinary soldier, in the second as a junior officer. Sulpicius was a senior officer at the time. Marcus Antonius, too, was away from Rome. The only lawcourt still in action was occupied, exclusively, with cases under the Varian Law.[1] The rest were in the state of suspension to which I referred. I was constantly in attendance at that one court which was active, and although the persons accused, speaking in their own defence, were not first-class orators – men such as Lucius Memmius and Quintus Pompeius Rufus[2] – still they were orators of a kind. And there was one really eloquent individual, Lucius Marcius Philippus,[3] whose evidence in support of the accusations he brought forward displayed all the force and fluency of an able prosecutor . . .[4] This was a time when Gaius Julius Caesar Strabo Vopiscus, as curule aedile,[5] delivered carefully prepared speeches every day.

'I myself was an eager listener to what these men were saying, but the first discouragement I received was the banishment of Cotta.[6] However, I went on listening to the speakers who were left. I also trained very assiduously, writing every day and reading and practising. And I did not confine myself to rhetorical exercises, either. In the next year Quintus Varius Hybrida was exiled, a victim of his own law. Meanwhile I made it my business to study the civil law under Quintus Mucius Scaevola Augur[7] (who bore the same name as his father). He was a man who, although he did not undertake any formal teaching, nevertheless provided instruction to those who were interested when they were present at the delivery of his legal opinions to the persons who consulted him. In the next year Lucius Cornelius Sulla and Quintus Pompeius Rufus were consuls.[8] Publius Sulpicius, who was one of the tribunes, gave public addresses every day, so that I got to know his style of speaking very fully. At that time Philon, who was head of the

1. The *Lex Varia de maiestate* of Quintus Varius Hybrida (90) – occupying the attention of the *quaestio maiestatis*.

2. Tribune in 89 and consul in 88 respectively.

3. Consul in 91.

4. Cicero now lists several other speakers.

5. In 90.

6. Under the Varian Law (*Lex Varia de maiestate*), mentioned in note 1 above.

7. Consul in 117.

8. In 88.

Platonic Academy at Athens at the time,[1] had fled from that city because of the war against Mithridates VI of Pontus, together with a number of other leading Athenians, and had arrived in Rome. Deeply interested in philosophy as I was, I devoted myself completely to his teaching. The diversity and splendour of his treatment were a joy to me. But I listened to him with all the more attention because it seemed, then, that the entire procedure of the lawcourts had been abolished for ever. Sulpicius met his death in that year, and in the year that followed three orators of three different generations were brutally killed, Quintus Lutatius Catulus,[2] Marcus Antonius and Gaius Julius Caesar Strabo Vopiscus. (Another man under whom I studied in the same year was Molon of Rhodes, eminent as pleader and teacher.)[3]

'This information, I realize, may not seem relevant to the plan I proposed for this talk. However, I have provided it all the same, so that you can see how my career developed, which was what you wanted, Brutus (for Atticus knows all about it already). And, in particular, you can see how closely I followed Quintus Hortensius Hortalus step by step.

'For about three years the city was free from the threat of warfare. But because so many orators were dead, or away, or in exile – for even younger men like Marcus Licinius Crassus and the two Lentuli[4] were not in Rome – Hortensius was the principal pleader at the time.[5] Throughout the whole of this period I spent all my days and nights studying a wide variety of subjects. I worked under Diodotus the Stoic, who lived in my house and my company, and it was at my home that he recently died.[6] From him, in addition to other subjects, I received a thoroughgoing education in dialectic, which can be regarded as a concise, condensed form of

1. Philon of Larissa (160/159–*c.* 80) was the last undisputed head of the Academy (110/109) before it split up. In 88, when the First Mithridatic War broke out, he left Athens for Rome.

2. Consul in 102.

3. Here Cicero has got the year wrong: he corrects himself later on. Or he means to refer here to Apollonius *the son of* Molon.

4. Cnaeus Cornelius Lentulus Clodianus (consul in 72) and Publius Cornelius Lentulus Sura (consul in 71). The latter, accused of being a member of Catilina's conspiracy, was executed by Cicero's orders in 63.

5. Cicero mentions five others.

6. In *c.* 60, making Cicero his heir.

eloquence. For your Stoic school of philosophy, Brutus, tells us that that is what eloquence is, an amplified version of dialectic, without which, according to you, it cannot be authentically attained.[1] But although I applied myself intensely to Diodotus's teaching on a wide range of themes, I never let a day pass without also undertaking oratorical exercises. I delivered practice declamations, as they are now called, on every single day, often in the company of Marcus Pupius Piso Frugi Calpurnianus[2] or Quintus Pompeius Bithynicus,[3] though with others as well. I sometimes conducted these exercises in Latin, but more frequently in Greek. This was partly because it was Greek, with its larger store of stylistic adornment, which got me accustomed to the employment of similar techniques in Latin. But another reason was the fact that Greek was the only language the leading teachers knew, so that unless I used that tongue they could not correct my shortcomings, or, indeed, communicate their instruction at all.

'Meanwhile, while political stability was being re-established, disturbances broke out,[4] and three orators were brutally killed: Quintus Mucius Scaevola Pontifex, Gaius Papirius Carbo Arvina and Publius Antistius. And other orators, too, were no more: Cnaeus Pomponius, Gaius Marcius Censorinus, Publius Licinius Murena.[5] However, others came back to Rome: Cotta, Curio, Lucius Licinius Crassus, the two Lentuli and Cnaeus Pompeius Magnus (Pompey). The legal system came into force once again, and the courts were revived. Orderly government had been restored . . .

1. Zeno of Citium, founder of Stoicism, emphasized their relationship (and difference).

2. Consul in 61.

3. In offering a list of orators in an earlier chapter (Appendix 2), Cicero describes him as ambitious, well trained and very industrious, but pronounces that his oratory was charmless. The orator corresponded with his son Aulus in 44.

4. When Sulla returned from Asia Minor in 83 he defeated the supporters of Marius at the Colline Gate (82), before becoming dictator (81).

5. Scaevola Pontifex, consul in 95, and Carbo, tribune in 90, were killed in 82 by Lucius Junius Brutus Damasippus, the Marian. Antistius had been described by Cicero as a man whose reputation increased daily. Pomponius had been tribune in 90. Gaius Marcius Censorinus, lucid and graceful but lazy, was executed on the orders of Sulla. Murena was industrious and had studied history; perhaps he was a son of Lucius (praetor not later than 101), and the uncle of Cicero's client (Chapter 2).

'That was the time when I first began to take on both private and public cases in court. For what I had in mind was not to learn my profession in the Forum itself, as most people do, but in so far as this was possible to arrive in the Forum with my training already done. (At this time, too, I was studying under Molon, who had come to Rome during the dictatorship of Sulla as one of a deputation applying to the Senate about the reimbursement of the Rhodians.)[1] My first criminal case was the defence of Sextus Roscius Amerinus.[2] It won me so much praise that thereafter I was regarded as capable of handling every sort of case. So a great many followed. I worked on them very carefully, burning the midnight oil in order to do so.

'Now, you seem to want to know all about me, not merely by the birthmark or the rattle which they show in plays,[3] but through and through, so I will now supply certain details which might have seemed unnecessary. I was very thin in those days, and my physical condition was by no means robust. My neck was long and scraggy. In fact I had the type of physique for which hard work and lung-strain are regarded as practically fatal. People who cared for me were all the more concerned because I was accustomed to speak without pausing or changing my tone, at the top of my voice, with my whole body tensed up. Indeed, my friends and my doctors urged me to give up pleading altogether. But I decided that I was prepared to run any risk, however great, rather than abandon my ambition to achieve fame as an orator. However, I did come to the conclusion that I should adopt a more relaxed delivery and not speak so energetically, since this change of approach would avoid the danger to my health, as well as providing me with a more moderate oratorical style. So that was why I left for Asia Minor.[4] At the time when I left Rome, I had been active in court for two years, and was already well known in the Forum.

'First I went to Athens, where I spent six months with Antiochus,

1. In consequence of the war against Mithridates VI of Pontus.

2. In 80. Translated in *Cicero: Murder Trials* (Penguin Classics), pp. 31ff.

3. Marks of identification or recognition, which play a part in the plots of many ancient plays.

4. It was alternatively believed, however, that Cicero left Rome because he was afraid of Sulla, whose freedman Chrysogonus he had attacked in his speech *For Sextius Roscius Amerinus* (see note 2, above).

that famous, sagacious philosopher of the Old Academy.[1] With him to guide and instruct me, I resumed the study of philosophy, which I had pursued from my earliest youth and had never entirely abandoned, making continual progress in the subject as time went on. Moreover, during my stay at Athens at that time, I also continued industriously with my rhetorical exercises, under the Syrian teacher Demetrius, who had long and distinguished experience as a speaker.[2] After that, I travelled through the whole of the province of Asia, keeping company with the most eminent orators of the country, who generously allowed me to practise under their direction. The leading figure among them was Menippus of Stratonicea. He was, in my view, the best orator in the whole of Asia at that time. And he was an orator who could truly be regarded as Attic, if speaking unaffectedly and in good taste is what Attic means. But for most of the time I was with Dionysius of Magnesia beside Sipylus. And I also attached myself to Aeschylus of Cnidus and Xenocles of Adramyttium.

'These were the men who at that period were regarded as the principal instructors of rhetoric in Asia. However, they were not enough for me, and so I went to Rhodes and enrolled under Molon, whom I had also heard at Rome. He had distinguished himself as a pleader in court cases, as well as composing speeches for others to deliver. But he also showed a particular talent for noting and criticizing the faults of others; and indeed he was, in general, an excellent teacher. He set himself to do what he could to check the excessive exuberance of my style, which at that time displayed a juvenile lack of restraint. As a result, when I returned to Rome, after having been away for two years, I was much better trained – hardly the same man at all. My voice was no longer over-extended, my language, you might say, had gone off the boil, my lungs were much stronger, and I weighed a good bit more.

'At that period there were two pre-eminent orators on whom I wanted to model myself. They were Cotta and Hortensius. Cotta was calm and relaxed, expressing his thoughts easily and fluently in straightforward terms. Hortensius was ornate and vigorous, and not at all like the man whom you knew later on, Brutus, when his

1. Antiochus of Ascalon (born *c.* 130/120) was head of the Fifth (Old) Academy in 79–78 when Cicero attended his lectures.

2. Unknown.

powers were declining, but much more energetic in expression and delivery alike. When I compared the two of them, it was clear that Hortensius was the man I had to compete with: he was closer to me in point of age, and his stylistic animation, too, was more comparable to my own style. Besides, I had noticed something in the lawsuits in which both were employed, for example in the cases of Marcus Canuleius, or of Cnaeus Cornelius Dolabella, who had formerly been consul.[1] What I had observed was that although Cotta was taken on as the leading counsel, it was Hortensius who played the more prominent part. Because what a great gathering demands, amid all the hubbub of the Forum, is an orator who is lively and fiery, and possesses a compelling voice.

'During that first year after my return from Asia,[2] I spoke in a number of important cases. I was a candidate for the post of quaestor at the time, Cotta for that of consul, and Hortensius for the aedileship. Next followed my year in Sicily as quaestor. Cotta, after his term of consular office, left for Cisalpine Gaul. Hortensius stayed in Rome, as the principal pleader, and that is how he was regarded. But when I came back from Sicily a year later I had the impression that whatever gifts I possessed had reached their fullest point of development, and could be described as mature. However, I am afraid too much is being said about myself, especially as I am the one who is saying it! – though my intention in doing so is not to boast of my talents or eloquence, which is very far from my purpose, but only to tell you how hard and industriously I worked. Nearly five years passed, during which I occupied myself with many lawsuits and was associated with the leading advocates of the day, before finally I came up against Hortensius. I was aedile elect and he was consul elect. I was speaking in defence of the Sicilians. It was a momentous confrontation.[3]

'However, this discussion in which we are engaged is not merely to offer a list of orators, but to convey some lessons as well. So I ought to indicate briefly the respects in which I find it legitimate to criticize and find fault with Hortensius. When he had finished his

1. Dolabella, consul in 81, was unsuccessfully prosecuted by Julius Caesar (77) for extortion while governor of Macedonia (80–78).

2. In 76.

3. The prosecution of Verres (Chapter 1).

consulship,[1] he must have seen that no other ex-consul could be ranked as his equal, and I imagine that he regarded all those who had not yet held that office as negligible. So he allowed his ardour, which had driven him on since boyhood, to die down. His explanation was that he wanted to get more pleasure out of life. Or, at any rate, he wanted to take things more easily. One, two, three years spent in this state of mind did something to diminish his eloquence. It was like the way in which the colours of an old picture fade. An ordinary person might not have noticed it. But a trained, intelligent observer could detect what was happening. And as the process continued, every aspect of his eloquence weakened – in particular, the swift complexity of his language slowed down – and you could see, every day, that he was no longer what he had been before.

'Meanwhile I, on the other hand, persisted continually in my endeavours to increase such abilities as I possessed by constant practice, and especially by writing. What took place during this period, and in the years that followed my aedileship, I shall mainly pass over. I was made praetor, coming first on the list, and then an extraordinary wave of popular support secured my election to the consulship.[2] For people had begun to notice me. This was partly because I was such a hard-working and indefatigable pleader. And it was also because of my novel style of speaking, which was worked out with a meticulous care that the public was not used to, and which in consequence, I like to think, was out of the ordinary.

'But I shall not say anything more about myself. For what I propose to do is to speak about the others. Not a single one of them seemed to have a better acquaintance with literature than the ordinary man in the street, although reading is the very well-spring from which first-class eloquence flows. Nor had any of them acquired any understanding of philosophy, the mother of all good deeds and sayings. Not one of them, again, possessed any mastery of civil law, which is an absolute necessity for private lawsuits, and is needed by an orator to enable him to judge between right and wrong. Nor was there a single speaker who had a thorough knowledge of Roman history, from which he could have summoned, as occasion required, convincing witnesses from the dead; or who was able to bring out a concise and witty epigram at his

1. In 69.
2. In 63.

opponent's expense, in order to refresh the court and transform its seriousness, for a moment, into amusement and laughter; or who had the capacity to generalize and convert a problem relating to a particular person and time into a universal truth; or who could divert his listeners by introducing a brief digression; or who had the power to make jurymen feel fiercely indignant, or move them to tears, or arouse in their hearts, in fact, whatever feelings the case may demand – which is the main thing an orator has to achieve.

'Well, by now Hortensius had practically vanished from the scene. And I, in the earliest year sanctioned by the law, six years after him, had been elected consul. At this juncture, he began to take up his work once again. My career was now equal to his, and he seemed afraid that, in some respects, I might look like his superior! However, during the twelve years immediately following my consulship, we collaborated very closely in important lawsuits, in which I sometimes deferred to him, and he sometimes to me. My election as consul had, at first, caused him a little irritation. But in the end it proved a link between us, because he admired what I achieved during my consulship, and praised me for it. Our cooperation became particularly notable just a short time before this profession of ours, Brutus, bowing to the menace of force, suddenly fell silent and went dumb. According to the Pompeian Law, only three hours each were conceded to pleaders for the defence.[1] When this enactment came into force, Hortensius and I both appeared every day in cases which, although we treated each one of them differently, were in fact extremely similar, or indeed identical.

'Hortensius's life was shorter than it ought to have been. Yet, all the same, his career had started ten years before you, Brutus, were born.[2] And in his sixty-fourth year, only a few days before his death, you joined forces with him in the defence of your father-in-law Appius Claudius Pulcher.[3] Posterity will be able to judge his and my respective styles from our speeches.

'If we ask why Hortensius did better as a speaker when he was young than when he was older, we can find convincing reasons.

1. One of the *Leges Pompeiae* of Cnaeus Pompeius Magnus during his sole consulship (52). Speeches for the prosecution were limited to two hours.

2. Brutus was born in 85.

3. Pulcher, consul in 54, had been governor of Cilicia in 53–51 (Cicero's predecessor).

One was his employment of the Asianic style of oratory, which wins greater approval when a young man employs it than when the speaker is old. This Asianism can be divided into two categories. The first is epigrammatic and artificial, characterized not so much by serious and profound thinking as by elegant symmetry of expression. Timaeus the historian exemplified this manner.[1] So too, when I was a boy, did the orator Hierocles of Alabanda, and to an even greater extent his brother Menecles, both of whose speeches are fine specimens of this version of the Asianic style.[2] The other version does not concentrate so much on sententious epigram, but favours, instead, a swift and speedy outpouring of language – the predominant feature of Asianic oratory today – in which this torrential flow is accompanied by a choice and refined vocabulary. That is how Aeschylus of Cnidus spoke, and my contemporary Aeschines of Miletus. The headlong movement displayed by their speeches aroused admiration, but the thinking these discourses contained was not presented with any sort of elegant elaboration.

'Both these types of Asianism, as I said, are better suited to youthful speakers. Employed by older men, they lack dignity. Hortensius was an equally skilful exponent of both types of speaking. When he was young, therefore, he was greatly applauded, because he had Menecles's taste for sparkling epigrams and produced them in abundance. But his utterances, like the Greek's, were often little more than attractive and melodious, and did not touch on the things that needed to be said, or would have served a useful purpose; although the rapid vivacity of his language did not mean that polish and finish were necessarily sacrificed.

'Older men did not always look upon this sort of thing with favour – I often saw Lucius Marcius Philippus[3] listening to Hortensius with a mocking smile on his face, or even with downright indignation and anger. But young people were entranced, and the general public felt greatly moved. In their view Hortensius, in his youth, was pre-eminent, and easily came first. True, his style of speaking was lightweight, but it seemed appropriate to his juvenile years. His natural talents showed a brilliance of their own, which he

1. Timaeus of Tauromenium (*c.* 356–260).

2. Hierocles and Menecles are elsewhere described by Cicero as 'the leading figures among Asiatic orators' (*Orator*, 231).

3. Consul in 91.

had enhanced by careful training; and the structure of his periods was rhythmical, accomplished and compact. For these reasons he earned enormous admiration. But when the progress of his career, and the authority of advancing age, demanded something more solid, he still kept to exactly the same manner, although it no longer suited him. He had relaxed, by now, for some time past, the hard practice and industriousness which had been such a feature of his previous activity, and although his powers of neatly balanced expression, and his fertile thinking, did not abandon him, they no longer assumed the same sumptuous forms as before. Perhaps that was why, Brutus, he gave you less satisfaction than he would have if you had heard him at the time when he was still full of enthusiasm and at the height of his powers.'

'I appreciate the force of your criticisms of Hortensius,' said Brutus, 'and yet, all the same, I have always regarded him as a great orator. I took a particularly favourable view of the speech he delivered in defence of Marcus Valerius Messalla,[1] while you were away.'

'Yes, they say it was good,' I went on; 'and the written version of the speech, which corresponds exactly, I am told, with what he said, confirms that verdict. Well: Hortensius pursued a successful career which spanned the entire period lasting from the consulships of Lucius Licinius Crassus and Quintus Mucius Scaevola Pontifex down to those of Lucius Aemilius Paullus Lepidus and Gaius Claudius Marcellus.[2] My career accompanied his from the time when Lucius Cornelius Sulla was dictator[3] down to approximately the same date. But then, in that last year, the voice of Hortensius was extinguished by his death, and mine by the death of our country.'[4]

'Please, do not say things that sound so ill-omened!' said Brutus.

'Have it your own way,' I replied, 'and in any case I was thinking not so much of myself as of you. Hortensius's end, I might add, was fortunate, because he did not live to see the future that he had foreseen. We often lamented the impending catastrophes together, when we saw individuals' personal ambitions launching the threat

1. Consul in 53.

2. i.e. from 95 to 50.

3. In 81.

4. The civil war between Pompey and Caesar broke out in 49, and Caesar became dictator.

of civil war, and were fully aware that our national policy proved incapable of responding to hopes of peace. As for Hortensius, however, he enjoyed, throughout his life, a special sort of felicity; and in the end it intervened, one must feel, to protect him from the miseries that have followed – by bringing his life to an end.

'And so it is we, Brutus, who since the death of Hortensius are left to be the wardens of eloquence, which his disappearance has so gravely bereaved. Let us keep her safe in our homes, protected by the guardianship which her glory deserves. Let us repel these vulgar and impudent suitors of hers, and protect her chastity as we should come to the defence of a virgin staving off the advances of lecherous admirers. It causes me the deepest distress that I have entered upon my life at so late a date that, before my journey is finished, night has fallen upon this country of ours. Yet I am cheered by the consolation, Brutus, which your very welcome letter has bestowed on me.[1] Writing this, you asserted that I ought to take courage. This was because, you said, I had performed deeds which, even if I remain silent, will speak for me, and will live on after I am dead. And you also declared that the preservation of our country, if it survives, and its downfall if it does not, will confirm that what I did for the state was right.[2]

'But it is when I think of you yourself, Brutus, that I feel the deepest grief. Your youthful career earned applause. But in the very midst of the race the malign ill-fortune of our country stood in its way and put a stop to its progress. This is the sadness and anxiety which most profoundly affects and upsets me, and not myself only but my friend here who loves and esteems you as much as I do. We wish you well, we want you to reap the reward of your great qualities, we desire that our national affairs will enable you to revive the glory of two magnificent families, and even add to their distinction. The Forum was yours, its platform was yours, and you brought to its service not only a tongue sharpened by training but very real eloquence, enriched by knowledge of many important subjects. Through studying them you had amplified the reputation for eloquence which you already possessed, by the addition of all the splendour that philosophical learning can bestow. On your account, we feel a double distress. You have lost your country. And your country has lost you.

1. As mentioned earlier, this was Brutus's treatise *De Virtute*.

2. i.e. during the Catilinarian 'conspiracy', when Cicero was consul (63).

'For the grim disaster that has overtaken our state has arrested the development, Brutus, of your talents. All the same, I pray you to persevere with your career, from which, indeed, you have never desisted. And make sure – though this you have nearly, or wholly, accomplished already – that you distance yourself altogether from the multitude of pleaders whom I have crowded together in this present discussion.

'The intellectual resources you needed were not available at home. So you went to seek them out at Athens, which has always been hailed as the centre of scholarship; and you furnished your mind very amply with what they had to offer. And now that that has been done, it would not be becoming for you just to allow yourself to remain one of the common herd of advocates. If you were content with that, even the training of Pammenes, by far the most eloquent man in the whole of Greece, would not have been any use to you. Nor would the instruction of that Old Academy of yours, and my friend and guest Aristus its inheritor,[1] if, in any case you were not going to surpass the average pleader.

'In any and every period, we can see, one can scarcely find a couple of orators who have really attained distinction. Galba had many contemporaries, but he was the only one of them who excelled. Even Cato, who was older than he was, yielded his place to him, and so did all his juniors as well. After Galba came Marcus Aemilius Lepidus Porcina, then Gaius Papirius Carbo.[2] Nor do I need to remind you of the Gracchi, whose speeches delivered to the public showed a much freer and looser manner of speaking, though even right down to their epoch the art of eloquence was still not entirely satisfactory. Then came Antonius and Crassus, next Cotta and Sulpicius, and Hortensius. And now I have nothing more to add – except this: to be reckoned just one more among a multitude of pleaders would have been something that I myself was not prepared to accept.'

1. The brother of Antiochus of Ascalon who founded the Old (Fifth) Academy.

2. Consuls in 137 and 120 respectively.

CHAPTER 7

THE PHILIPPICS (IV, V, X): AGAINST RULE BY ONE MAN

Cicero's fourteen passionate, rancorous, brilliant speeches against Marcus Antonius (Mark Antony), of which two were addressed to the Assemblies[1] *and the others to the Senate, were given, by himself – half in jest – the name of* Philippics, *after the speeches delivered by the equally eloquent Athenian Demosthenes against Philip II of Macedonia, nearly three centuries earlier.*

Cicero was a passionately convinced Republican, and had deplored the dictatorship of Julius Caesar, even though (mainly on the basis of their shared literary interests) the two men maintained polite social relations. But after Caesar had been assassinated it seemed to the orator intolerable that a second-rate character like Marcus Antonius (Antony) should aspire to carry on the same sort of autocracy.[2] *To recapitulate what was said in the Introduction, Cicero was not a courageous man, but at this critical juncture he risked his life (and eventually lost it) by these speeches which tried to block Antonius's path to despotism. They were his ultimate and most splendid contributions to the art of government, and the bravest expressions of his adamant belief that dictatorial rule could not be endured. He had put up with Caesar, but he was not prepared to put up with Antonius, and he risked everything, fatally, in order to say so.*[3]

During the first few days after the murder of Julius Caesar (15 March 44) a compromise between the assassins and supporters was reached, and the

1. Speeches to the Assemblies (the assembled people in one of its forms, mainly *centuriata* or *tributa*) were *contiones*; the only ones that have survived are seven orations by Cicero. *Contio* could also mean a less regular sort of public meeting at which officials reported questions that were going to be asked in the Assemblies proper.

2. Cf. also *Letters to Friends*, X, I, XII, 2. Cicero was, arguably, somewhat unjust to Antony.

3. At the same time he urged his case in a vigorous correspondence with governors and commanders.

dead man's acts were ratified. Early in April his adopted son and principal heir Octavian (whose adoption gave him the name of Gaius Julius Caesar) landed in Italy from Illyricum, thus proclaiming his rivalry to the claims of Antonius to supremacy. Antonius, who was consul[1] *(he had been Caesar's colleague in the office), proceeded to southern Italy to enlist Caesar's ex-soldiers. In June, back in Rome, he summoned the Senate to a meeting in the Temple of Concord, and put into effect a number of 'acts' of Caesar which his enemies believed were fictitious. In July Sextus Pompeius (the son of Pompey the Great), who had continued to hold out against the government despite the defeat of his cause at Munda in southern Spain in the previous year, laid down his arms as a result of the mediation of Marcus Aemilius Lepidus, who had become chief priest in Caesar's place and was governor of Narbonese Gaul and Nearer Spain.*

Cicero, who had started out for Greece on 17 July, abandoned his voyage and returned to Rome on 31 August.[2] *On 1 September, however, he stayed away from a meeting of the Senate, and Antonius criticized him for his absence. On 2 September, Cicero came to the Senate and replied in the First Philippic, a general attack on Antonius's recent political record. On the 19th Antonius answered him in violent terms, but Cicero was not there. On 9 October Antonius set out for Brundisium to take command of four legions from Macedonia. There, and at Suessa Aurunca, he ordered that a number of Roman citizens should be put to death. In November, Antonius returned to Rome with an army, and summoned the Senate for the 24th and 28th, with a view to the declaration as a public enemy, and prosecution, of Octavian, whose actions and ambitions had aroused his distrust. When he heard, however, that the Martian and Fourth Legions had defected from him, he left hastily for Alba Longa. Refused admission into that town, however, he moved instead to Tibur, where he distributed a donation among the troops to secure their allegiance. He then moved north towards Cisalpine Gaul (northern Italy) to confront and dislodge Decimus Junius Brutus, one of the assassins of Caesar, who was in control of that province.*[3]

1. Cicero contested the legality of this consulship (*III Philippic*, 12).

2. During summer and autumn 44, Atticus tried to dissuade Cicero from action, advising that he should write history instead (*Letters to Atticus*, XVI, 13, 2).

3. In June 44 Marcus Antonius (Antony), ignoring the Senate, had instigated legislation allotting Cisalpine Gaul, as well as Narbonese Gaul, to himself, in exchange for Macedonia, although he had been allowed to keep the Macedonian

It was at about this time that Cicero published the formidable Second Philippic (which was never delivered).[1] *Then, on 9 December, he returned to Rome. The tribunes convened a meeting of the Senate on the 20th to take measures for the safety of the state. Cicero delivered his Third Philippic at this meeting, and on the same day delivered the Fourth to the Assembly in the Forum. His speech, emphasizing that the Senate had already declared Antonius a public enemy 'in fact, if not in word', is translated here.*

THE FOURTH PHILIPPIC

Your unbelievably large attendance at this Assembly, Romans, larger than any that I can remember, inspires me with the keenest eagerness to protect our state, in the hope of making it once again what it was. At earlier moments, I never lacked the will to achieve just that. But the time was not yet ripe. As soon, however, as our circumstances seemed to offer some gleam of light ahead, I took the lead in protecting your freedom. If I had launched my efforts before, I would not be in a position to do the same now. For today is the day, Romans, on which the foundations have been laid of what still has to be undertaken in the future. Do not imagine, however, that what has already been achieved is just a minor matter. For even if the term has not been actually used, Antonius has, in fact, been judged by the Senate to be an enemy of the state. And what has happened here in the Assembly, too, I find more encouraging still. For you, also, have unanimously and loudly confirmed that an enemy is what he is.

For I must tell you, Romans, that there are only two possibilities. Either the men who have raised armies against a consul are unpatriotic, or the man against whom these hostilities have been launched is an enemy. But there was never the slightest doubt which of these answers is correct: It is the second. All the same, just in case any such doubt could conceivably have arisen, the Senate has ruled it

---

legions. This had torpedoed Cicero's conciliatory achievement in sponsoring a general amnesty. The older of Antony's younger brothers, Gaius, then set out for Macedonia.

1. *Cicero: Selected Works* (Penguin Classics), pp. 101–53.

out today. Gaius Caesar (Octavian), whose devotion and policy, not to speak of his personal financial resources, have defended and are defending the state and your own freedom, has been honoured with emphatic praise by the Senate. And I praise you too, Romans, I compliment you most warmly, because of the conspicuous gratitude which you are showing towards this distinguished young man, or rather boy – for that is all he is by age, though his actions are ageless.[1]

There are many exploits of past times, Romans, that I can remember, and have heard about, and have read about. But out of all the exploits that have been performed throughout the ages, I have never known anything equal to his. Slavery was crushing us. Things were getting worse every day. Help could not be found. It was the time when we were terrified by the destructive, murderous prospect of Antonius's return from Brundisium. And that was the moment when Gaius Caesar formed his plan, which nobody had ventured to hope for, and nobody, indeed, had known anything about. He was going to levy an invincible army of his father's soldiers and use it to frustrate the savage designs of the frenzied Antonius: thus rescuing the state from annihilation!

For it must be clear to everyone that if Gaius Caesar had not collected his army together, the imminent return of Antonius would have meant the end of us all. He was coming back blazing with hatred against yourselves, and red with the blood of the Roman citizens whom he had massacred at Suessa and Brundisium; all he could think of, it became clear, was wiping out the Roman people altogether. If Gaius Caesar's army, consisting of his father's intrepid soldiers,[2] had never existed, how do you suppose that your own lives and liberties could possibly have been saved? His services have been superhuman and immortal, and they deserve honours and praises on a superhuman, immortal scale. I have moved that he should receive those honours. The Senate agreed, and it has just now decreed that the acceptance of my motion should be placed on its earliest agenda.

Everyone can see what this means: it means that Antonius has

1. Octavian (born 63) had 'come of age' in October 49 (and strongly objected to being called a boy). For the lamentably mistaken trust Cicero placed in the Republicanism of Octavian, see the Introduction.

2. i.e. the soldiers of his adoptive father, Julius Caesar.

been judged a public enemy. For when the Senate decrees that those who lead armies against a man should be singled out for conspicuous praise, what else but an enemy can that man be? And think of the Martian Legion, named, it seems to me, by divine inspiration, after the very god from whom, we are told, the Roman people itself had its earliest origins. For this legion had by its own decision, even before the Senate had formed the same view, decreed that Antonius was an enemy.[1] And if that had *not* been the case, those who are against Antonius, those who acted against the so-called consul, would have had to be the enemies – which they are not!

By acclamation, Romans, by well-timed, rousing acclamation, you show clearly how what the Martian legionaries have so nobly accomplished enjoys your approval. They have safeguarded the authority of the Senate, and safeguarded the liberty of yourselves. In fact, they have safeguarded the very existence of the state itself. And it is by deserting that public enemy and brigand, that patricide son who has murdered his own fatherland, that they have performed this great task. Moreover, they acted not only with spirit and courage, but with wise deliberation as well. For Alba Longa, where they stationed themselves, is a strategically located, fortified city, not at all far distant from Rome, filled with a courageous population of loyal, excellent citizens. And then the Fourth Legion, too, under the command of Lucius Egnatuleius, followed this admirable example set by the Martians, and likewise acted as Gaius Caesar's army had, thus earning the commendation which the Senate has just recently awarded to its commander.

These events, Marcus Antonius, as you must surely see, add up to the severest possible criticisms of yourself. Gaius Caesar, who has mobilized an army against you, is lauded to the skies because of what he has done. Legions which you yourself have summoned – and which would have been yours if you had behaved like a consul, and not like an enemy of Rome – have deserted you; and their desertion wins them superlative praise. For these courageous, correct decisions which the two legions took have received ratification by the Senate, and the approval of the entire Roman people. Unless

1. As was mentioned in the Introduction to this speech, the Martian and Fourth Legions had gone over to Octavian from Antony, who was planning to declare him a public enemy.

maybe, Romans, you *still* think of Marcus Antonius as a consul rather than as your national enemy! But it seems to me, on the contrary, that you have shown what you think: and it is not that. Moreover, we also have every reason to suppose that the Italian citizen communities, and colonies, and districts, take exactly the same view. The entire human race unanimously agrees that this plague must be opposed by every single weapon that those who want our world to survive are able to raise.

Besides, ask yourself, Romans, whether you could possibly suppose that the judgement of Decimus Junius Brutus,[1] which you can assess by the edict he has pronounced today, is something that ought now to be despised. Romans, you say it should not, and what you say is right and true. For it is by the generous gift of the immortal gods, one is entitled to believe, that the family and name of the Brutuses has been granted to our state, for the purpose of establishing, or re-establishing, the freedom of the people of Rome.[2] Let us consider, then, what Decimus Brutus has decided about Antonius. He shuts him out of his province. He opposes him with an army. And in order to oppose him he whips up the whole of Cisalpine Gaul, which is, indeed, already roused to that action, on its own account and initiative. If Antonius is a consul, then Brutus is an enemy. But if Brutus is our country's saviour, then the enemy is Antonius. As to which of these alternatives is the correct one, can we have the slightest doubt whatever?

And indeed you yourselves, with one mind and one voice, declare that the smallest hesitation on the subject can be set aside. And so does the Senate, which has just decreed that Decimus Brutus has performed a very great service to the state, by standing up for the authority of the Senate and the freedom and empire of the Roman people. Standing up for them against whom? Against their enemy of course, because that is the only sort of standing up that deserves to be praised. Next, too, the province of Cisalpine Gaul

1. One of the assassins of Julius Caesar, although Caesar had given him the governorship of Cisalpine Gaul (he had previously governed Narbonese Gaul), and had designated him consul for 42. In April 44 he went to his province, and now he had refused to hand it over to Antony, who claimed it by virtue of a law he had passed in June. More will be said of Decimus Brutus in the Fifth and Tenth Philippics.

2. This is a reference to Lucius Junius Brutus, the traditional founder of the Roman Republic and consul in 509.

receives commendation, and is deservedly honoured by the Senate in very complimentary terms – because of its resistance to Antonius. Now, if that province accepted that he was a consul, and nevertheless refused to receive him, it would be guilty of a serious crime; since all provinces should be under the jurisdiction and command of the consul. But Decimus Brutus – general, consul elect, citizen born to serve his country – denies that Antonius is a true consul at all. And Cisalpine Gaul denies it, too, and so does the whole of Italy, and so does the Senate, and so do you yourselves.

One must conclude, therefore, that the only people who accept him as consul must be complete outlaws. Yet even they themselves do not really believe what they say. Criminal and disloyal though they may be, and indeed that is just what they are, they could not, all the same, one would think, disagree with something maintained by the entire human race. Yet goods lavished upon these individuals, and allocations of land, and that auction which goes on for ever,[1] have failed to sate their desire for more: and they are still blinded by hopes of plunder and loot. What they have determined to plunder is Rome itself, and the properties and fortunes of its citizens. They are the sort of men who believe that if only there is something for them to rob and take away then everything will turn out all right! And these are the people – immortal gods, I beg you, avert and ward off the omen! – these are the people for whom Antonius has promised to carve up the city.

So may your prayers be answered, Romans, and may the punishment for this man's lunatic fury rebound on himself and his own family! And that is what I am sure is going to happen. Because I believe that not only human beings, but the immortal gods themselves, have joined together in alliance to preserve our country. For if the gods send us portents and prodigies to prophesy the future, these have been so unmistakably declared, in the present case, that Antonius's retribution, and our own liberation, must indeed be near at hand. For we are entitled to conclude that, when everyone is so completely of one mind, this unanimity must have some divine impulse behind it. And indeed we cannot have the slightest doubt about where the will of heaven lies.

It remains for you, Romans, to continue to maintain the attitude which you are now so unequivocally displaying. I intend, therefore,

1. Of the property of the defeated Pompeian party.

to behave as generals habitually do when their troops are drawn up for battle. They may see that the soldiers are completely ready for the fight; and yet they utter words of exhortation all the same. And that is what I am doing, even though you yourselves are already poised and burning to win your liberty back.

Your enemy Antonius, Romans, is a person with whom any terms of peace are out of the question. In his frenzy he is not just eager to enslave you, as he was before, but he is after your blood. The most agreeable sport in the world seems to him to be bloodshed, butchery, the massacre of citizens before his own eyes. The creature you have to deal with, Romans, is not just a villainous crook but a monstrous, loathsome wild beast. He has fallen into the pit, and let that be the place where he sinks. For if he ever escapes out of its depths, there is no limit to the brutal tortures to which we shall be inescapably condemned. As it is, however, the forces that we already possess are keeping him in check, harassing him and pressing him hard. And in a few days' time the new consuls[1] will be levying new troops to keep up the pressure.

Romans, put your backs into the struggle! Indeed, that is what you are doing. You have never been in such complete accord, one with another, as you are on behalf of this cause; or in such complete agreement with the Senate. And that is not surprising. For the issue is not the nature of the conditions under which we shall live our lives, but whether we shall go on living at all, or perish in humiliation and torment.

Certainly, nature has decreed that all men should die. But it still needs courage to resist a death that is cruel and dishonourable. And courage is an inborn quality of the Roman race and stock. What I ask of you is this. Hold fast to the legacy that your ancestors handed down to you. For while everything else is false and uncertain, precarious and shifting, courage alone stays fixed; its roots lie deeply in the ground. There is no force in the world that can ever upset it, or move it from where it stands. *This* was the quality which enabled your ancestors first to conquer the whole of Italy, and then to obliterate Carthage, and destroy Numantia;[2] which prompted them to subject the most powerful of monarchs and the most warlike of nations to this empire of ours.

1. Gaius Vibius Pansa Caetronianus and Aulus Hirtius.

2. Carthage was destroyed at the end of the Third Punic War (146), and Numantia in Spain after prolonged Celtiberian resistance (133).

And another point, Romans: the foes against whom your ancestors had to deal owned states and Senates of their own, treasuries, united and single-minded citizen bodies, even the machinery, if things turned out that way, for establishing peace and setting up a treaty. But this enemy of yours, on the other hand, is attacking *your* state while he himself possesses nothing of the kind himself. He is eager to destroy *your* Senate, which is the council of the entire world, while again he himself entirely lacks any council of his own whatsoever. And he has drained *your* treasury dry, while, once more, he himself has got nothing of the kind. As to 'single-minded concord among citizens', it is something which he just has not got the power or right to promote, seeing that he is no longer a Roman citizen himself. Nor is there the slightest point in talking about peace with a man of such unbelievable savagery and total lack of good faith.

So the fight, Romans, is quite simply between the Roman people, conqueror of all the nations of the world, and an assassin, a bandit, a Spartacus.[1] He likes to boast that he resembles Catilina. Well, he does measure up to him in wickedness. But in energy he falls behind him. For Catilina, when he had no army, quickly got one together;[2] whereas Antonius was given an army, but lost it. As for Catilina, by my own exertions,[3] and the authority of the Senate, and your own enthusiasm and courage, he was crushed. And now, by the same token, you will hear that your unprecedented cooperation with the Senate, and the good fortune and courage of your generals, will in a very short time have put an end to the abominable robberies of Antonius as well. For my own part, in so far as taking trouble, and working, and keeping my eyes open, and using my influence, and giving advice, will enable me to get something done, I shall not fail to take every possible step that seems conducive to the protection of your liberty; since to fail to do that would be criminal, in view of the enormous kindnesses you have shown to myself.

And already today the motion of Marcus Servilius here[4] – a

1. The Thracian gladiator who had led the Third Slave Revolt in Campania (73–71).

2. In 63.

3. As consul in 63: see Chapter 2.

4. He was to become a tribune in 43.

valiant individual who is your very good friend – and of his loyal and distinguished colleagues, put forward with my support and under my leadership, has for the first time, after so long an interval of time, fired us with the hope that we shall be free!

THE FIFTH PHILIPPIC

This first of January, senators, has seemed to me to take a longer time arriving than any other date in my life. And during these last days I have had the impression that every one of you, too, has felt the same.

For the men who are fighting a war against our country did not bother to wait until this day arrived. Whereas we, on the contrary, at a time when it was particularly imperative for us to devote our advice to the rescue of our country, were not even summoned to any Senate meeting at all. However, whatever complaints we might have wanted to make about the days that are now past have been erased by the orations of the consuls for the coming year, Gaius Vibius Pansa Caetronianus and Aulus Hirtius, who have spoken in terms which make the first of January seem not just unduly late, but the day we have been longing for. These speeches by the consuls have raised my spirits and brought hope, not merely that we shall be kept safe but that we shall be able to regain the dignity that once was ours. All the same, the contrary opinion of the senator who was first called upon to speak[1] would have worried me, if I did not have full confidence in your courage and your tenacity.

For this day has dawned for you, senators, this opportunity has been granted to you, so that you can be given a chance to demonstrate to the Roman people how much bravery, tenacity and seriousness of purpose is truly to be found in this senatorial order of ours. Remember that time just thirteen days ago[2] when you displayed such unanimity, such courage and such tenacity and gained so much applause and glory and gratitude from the people of Rome. And the decisions that you made on that day, senators,

1. Quintus Fufius Calenus (consul 47), regarded by Cicero with hostility (*To Atticus*, XIV, 8), though he elsewhere describes him as a 'friend' (*VIII Philippic*, 11). See also *X Philippic*, translated here.

2. 20 December 44.

have left you only two acceptable alternatives: an honourable peace, or a necessary war.

Is it peace that Marcus Antonius wants? In that case, he must lay down his arms, make his petition, appeal for our pardon. He will find nobody fairer than myself – even though he preferred, while ingratiating himself with disloyal citizens, to be my enemy instead of my friend. To someone who is actually fighting against you there is no concession that can be made. To someone, on the other hand, who appeals to you for mercy it may perhaps be possible to offer some concession. But to send envoys to the man against whom, thirteen days ago, you pronounced the severest and most critical censure is not only frivolous but, if I may express my opinion frankly, demented.

Earlier on, you commended the generals who on their own private initiative had undertaken to make war on Antonius. And you commended the ex-soldiers who, although Antonius had planted them in colonies, rated the liberty of the Roman people above what he had done for them. Think of the Martian Legion, and of the Fourth Legion[1] – and ask yourselves why they are being praised. For the person whom those men deserted was their consul; blame is all they are entitled to. But if, on the other hand, the man they deserted is a national enemy, then it is right to offer them praise. Well, what you decreed (although you did not have any consuls)[2] was that a motion should be brought forward at the first possible moment assigning rewards to the soldiers, and honours to their general. And how while decreeing rewards for the men who have taken up arms against Antonius, you can propose, at the same time, to send him envoys, I do not understand! The result, I fear, is to make one feel ashamed that the legions' decisions are more honourable than the Senate's; seeing that the legions have decided to defend the Senate against Antonius while what the Senate does is to dispatch envoys to visit him!

One wonders if the effect of this will be to strengthen the soldiers' determination – or will it not, rather, serve to dampen

1. See the Fourth Philippic on these legions' abandonment of Antony for Gaius Caesar (Octavian).

2. One of the consuls for 44, Publius Cornelius Dolabella, had left for Asia Minor on his way to Syria, and the other, Marcus Antonius, to Cisalpine Gaul – where Decimus Junius Brutus was hostile to him – and the consuls for 43, Gaius Vibius Pansa Caetronianus and Aulus Hirtius, had not yet taken office.

their courage? For this, it appears, has been the outcome of the last twelve days: that the man for whom no one (except Cotyla)[1] felt inclined to speak up can now boast that he numbers even former consuls among those who sponsor his cause. I would have liked them all to have been asked to give their opinions before I was called on myself, since it would have been easier for me, then, if necessary, to point out where they were wrong – although I have a good idea of what some of these men, who will be called upon after myself, are in fact likely to say.

For it is understood that someone is going to propose that Antonius should be given the governorship of Gallia Comata, which is now held by Lucius Munatius Plancus.[2] But what this means is that everything Antonius needs to fight a civil war will be lavished upon a man who is our national enemy, first of all the very sinews of battle, unlimited funds, of which he now stands in need, and cavalry, too, as much as he wants. I say 'cavalry', but you need not suppose he will shrink from importing entire barbarian peoples if he feels he needs them. Anyone who does not see this is an idiot. If somebody does see it, on the other hand, and then proposes that Antonius should be given the governorship of Gallia Comata that he wants, then he is a traitor. You cannot be keen to hand over the money, infantry and cavalry of Gaul and Germany to a criminal ruffian! Those excuses of yours, 'he is my friend', are no use. Let him be his country's friend first. Or, 'he is my relative'. But surely the closest relationship a man can have is with his fatherland, of which even his parents form part. 'He has given me money.' I look forward to meeting the man who has the nerve to admit that!

But let me now explain what I believe to be at stake, because it will then be easy for you to decide what opinion to pronounce or follow. What is at stake is whether Marcus Antonius is to be given the opportunity of obliterating the Roman state, of slaughtering good Romans, of cutting up the city, of distributing land among his brigands, of reducing the Roman people to a condition of the most oppressive slavery; or whether, con-

1. Or Cotylo? A nickname ('half-pint') of Lucius Varius, a friend and envoy of Antony.

2. To look ahead, he eventually stopped backing Decimus Junius Brutus in Cisalpine Gaul and joined Antony and Lepidus (late summer 43).

versely, he is not going to be permitted to do any of these things at all.

You find it hard to make up your minds what to do. What I have been saying, you object, is not what Antonius actually intends to do. But that is something which even Cotyla would not venture to assert. For surely my words apply only too thoroughly to the man who declares that he is defending the acts of the late Julius Caesar, and yet at the same time actually overthrows those of Caesar's laws which we had been willing to support. Caesar proposed to drain the marshes.[1] Marcus Antonius, on the other hand, has placed the whole of Italy in the hands of his 'moderate' brother Lucius, to be parcelled out.[2] Yet this piece of legislation, I am certain, has never received the Roman people's approval. Surely the auspices would have been invoked to prevent it from ever being brought forward. Our augur Antonius keeps quiet, since he is too modest to interpret the auspices without consulting his colleagues.[3] And yet, in this case, the auspices do not need any expert interpretation at all. For it is universally known that, when Jupiter thunders, the Assembly is debarred from carrying out business.

The tribunes, in the Assembly, made a proposal about the provinces which contradicted the acts of Julius Caesar. For he had established a two years' tenure for governors, and they altered it to six. Once again, the proposal was never accepted by the Assembly itself. Indeed, it was never made known in advance, and was proposed before it had even been drafted. The deed was done, we saw, before anyone had the slightest idea of what it was going to be. The Caecilian–Didian Law was totally forgotten,[4] including the provision that advance notice should be given on three market days, and the penalty on the subject introduced by the Junian–Licinian

1. The Pomptine (Pontine) marshes south-east of Rome.

2. Lucius Antonius (consul 41) was the younger of Marcus's younger brothers.

3. Cicero sarcastically implies that Antony was too conscious of his own lack of proficiency to make a pronouncement without his fellow-augurs' support. The auspices, for which the augurs were responsible, were commented upon in the treatise *On Laws* (Chapter 5); (p. 198; cf. p. 108).

4. The *Lex Caecilia Didia* of the consuls Quintus Caecilius Metellus Nepos and Titus Didius (98) established procedures for valid legislation, imposing an interval of three market days (*nundinae*) between promulgation of a law and voting on it.

Law was forgotten as well.[1] So the ratifications of these measures of yours, Antonius, could only be regarded as having taken place if every other law was abolished. But nobody, as we shall see in a moment, was in a position to steal into the Forum and pass any regular legislation at all.

Besides, there was that terrible thunder, that storm. Granted, therefore, that the auspices made no impression on Marcus Antonius, yet all the same it would have been astonishing if such a violent storm and rain and hurricane did not seem to him an insurmountable impediment. And yet, all the same, this augur declares that he passed this law not only when Jupiter was thundering but when there was such a noise in the heavens that it was practically impossible to proceed. In these circumstances I cannot see how he is going to fail to admit that the measure was passed in defiance of the auspices. Again, I do not understand how this good augur of ours can dismiss as irrelevant to the auspices the fact that he proposed the measure in association with a colleague whose tenure he himself had disqualified by his own augural report.[2]

We are his colleagues in the augurate, and so our interpretation of his auspices must carry some weight. Searching for people who can interpret his use of armed force is another matter. In the first place, he had barricaded all the approaches to the Forum. This meant that there was no possibility of getting into the place at all except by knocking the barricades down. It was like the forts and fortifications that a city erects to prevent an enemy from getting in! And that was the situation even if Antonius's armed supporters had not barred the way as well. But in fact groups of these armed men were planted there, with the result that you could see the population of Rome, including even tribunes, pushed back from entering their own Forum.

For these reasons I take the view that the people of Rome are not bound at all by these laws which Marcus Antonius is said to have passed, because they were all put through by violent means and in disregard of the auspices, so that the people of Rome are not bound

1. The *Lex Junia Licinia*, proposed by the consuls Decimus Junius Silanus and Lucius Licinius Murena (after his defence by Cicero, Chapter 2) in 62, ordered that a copy of promulgated laws should be lodged in the treasury.

2. Publius Cornelius Dolabella. Antony's report was mentioned in *II Philippic*, 81 (*Cicero: Selected Works*, Penguin Classics, p. 137).

by this legislation at all. And even if Antonius has, we are told, put through some more defensible laws – to confirm Caesar's acts, or to abolish the dictatorship for evermore, to found colonies – the best thing would be if those laws could be passed all over again, with proper regard for the auspices, so that the public can regard them as valid. For some of his laws, on their own account, deserve approval, but they were carried by irregular and violent methods and cannot therefore be regarded as legally binding at all. And it is up to ourselves, with our authority as senators, to repudiate the brazen doings of a man who is no better than a lunatic gladiator.

Moreover, the way in which he has squandered public funds is unendurable. By false entries, and gifts, he has made away with seven hundred million sesterces.[1] That so much money belonging to the Roman people could have disappeared in so short a space of time seems wholly irregular. Nor, once again, can we be expected to tolerate the monstrous profits which have been gobbled up by Marcus Antonius's household. He sold forged decrees; and he arranged for presentations of whole kingdoms, conferments of citizenship, immunities from taxation to be officially recorded – in return for bribes. He was taking these actions, he said, in accordance with the memoranda of Julius Caesar. But it was only he himself who had vouched for the authenticity of the memoranda. Inside his house there was an animated buying and selling of matters of all kinds, everything relating to national affairs. His wife, who did better for herself than for her husbands,[2] was putting whole provinces and kingdoms up for auction. Exiles were being brought back from banishment with what was said to be legal correctness, but was, in fact, nothing of the kind. But now that we have entered a new period in which there are hopes of re-establishing our government, these are measures which the Senate will have to exert its authority to cancel. For if it fails to do so, not even a semblance of a free country will be left to us.

Yes, Antonius declared that he was proceeding on the basis of the acts of Julius Caesar, when, instead, what he had embarked upon was the falsification of Caesar's memoranda and the sale of his

1. To pay his debts Antony had forged papers, alleged to be Caesar's, authorizing the transfer of funds to his creditors.

2. Fulvia's previous husbands, Publius Clodius Pulcher and Gaius Scribonius Curio, both died violent deaths.

handwritten notes. By means such as those an enormous sum of money got piled up in that house. And he also accepted bribes for recording forged decrees of the Senate: bonds were sealed, and senatorial decrees that had never been decreed at all were filed at the treasury. Even foreign nations were witnesses of these deplorable proceedings. At the same time, too, treaties were agreed upon, kingdoms given away, peoples and provinces exempted from tribute, and fraudulent records of these transactions were posted up all over the Capitol; while the Roman people groaned. These, then, were the ways in which vast sums were accumulated inside that one single residence. If only such enormous sums of money could be transferred to the treasury! Once that was done, the government would never find itself short of funds again!

Antonius also passed a law about judicial affairs, pure and upright pillar of the lawcourts and the law that he was. As members of juries, he appointed élite fighting men,[1] ordinary soldiers, members of the legion of the larks.[2] And the other people he enrolled were gamblers and exiles and Greeks. A distinguished body of jurymen, indeed, and a court of remarkable dignity – a court in which I simply long to plead a defendant's case! Take Cydas from Crete, the island's monster[3] – an outrageous and abominable figure. All right, suppose that he is not as bad as all that. But I am sure, all the same, that he does not know Latin, that he is not the sort and type of juryman that we are used to, and, what is most important, he does not know our laws and customs, or, for that matter, our people. For you know Crete better than Cydas knows Rome. Even when our own citizens are being considered for jury service, there is customarily some prior investigation, some process of selection. But who knows, or could possibly know, a juryman from Gortyna?

Now Lysiades of Athens, on the other hand, most of us do know. For he is the son of Phaedrus, a well-known philosopher.[4] And he is a festive sort of person, so that his relationship with Curius, his assessor and fellow-gambler, presents no problem. But what I want to know is this. When Lysiades, summoned as a juryman, fails to respond, offering his membership of the Athenian Areopagus as a

1 *Antesignani*, who fought in front of the standards.

2. The *Alauda*, a legion raised by Julius Caesar in Gaul, at his own expense.

3. A reference to the Minotaur.

4. Epicurean (*c.* 140–70).

reason,[1] on the grounds that he cannot be expected, at one and the same time, to sit in one law court at Rome and another at Athens, will the presiding officer of the Roman court accept this excuse offered by a Greekling juryman who alternates between wearing a Greek cloak and a Roman toga? Or will he, on the contrary, brush aside the very ancient regulations of the Athenians on the subject?

Anyway, heavens above, what a bench that will be! A Cretan juryman, and a thoroughly bad type. How a defendant is going to approach such a man I do not like to think.[2] They are a tough lot of people, the Cretans.[3] Ah, but the people of Athens, it can be said, are compassionate; and even Curius, who puts his fortune at risk every day of his life, is not, I suppose, particularly cruel.[4] But another point is this. Some of the jurymen who have been selected may very well have to be excused from serving. For they will be able to present the legitimate explanation that they altered their domicile because they were exiled, and have not been subsequently recalled. Yet we are called upon to note that these are the sort of person whom this deranged Antonius deliberately chose, recording their names at the treasury: these the men to whom he was keen to entrust a major part of our national affairs! If, that is to say, he could possibly have imagined that any semblance of our nation was still in existence at all!

Now, the jurymen I have spoken of were at least people of whom you have heard. There are others whom you know less, and I hardly like to mention them. But you must be aware that dancers, harpists, the whole debauched Antonian gang have been propelled into the third panel of jurymen.[5] *That* is the reason why this brilliant, wonderful law was brought forward in the middle of a downpour of rain, while storm and gale were raging, amid tempest and hurricane, lightning and thunder. They were people whom no one would have wanted to accept as guests in their houses. But we had to have them as jurymen. It was the gravity of Antonius's

1. The ancient criminal court of Athens.

2. Cicero is suggesting that shady jurymen of this sort are open to bribery.

3. They were famous as pirates – and their culture was proverbially 'Spartan'.

4. i.e. he would be sympathetic enough to the bad luck of defendants before the court. As we shall see, however, Cicero heard that these jurymen might be *too* compassionate.

5. Properly only open to people with a certain amount of money.

crimes, his consciousness of all the evil he had done, his embezzlement of all that money that appeared in the accounts at the temple of Ops,[1] that explained why a third panel of this kind was devised. It was only when he had lost hope of getting honest jurymen to exonerate guilty defendants that dishonest ones were recruited in their place. What shameless impudence it was, what a disgusting scandal, to choose them for the job! Their choice branded the government with a twofold disgrace. First, that persons of so degraded a type should be appointed as jurors. And, secondly, that it became openly known how many low characters we had in the community.

So I maintain that this law and the others like it – even if some of them were passed by non-violent means, and in accordance with the auspices – should be repealed. Or rather, why should I express the view that they should be repealed, when I am convinced that they were never legitimately passed at all?

And let us note another deeply dishonourable thing, so dishonourable that this senatorial order should record its existence for posterity. That is to say, Marcus Antonius is the only man in this city, ever since it was founded, to go about openly escorted by an armed guard. It is something that even our kings never did, and not even those who, after the expulsion of the kings, attempted to seize kingly power. I remember Lucius Cornelius Cinna.[2] I have seen Lucius Cornelius Sulla.[3] Lately I have seen Julius Caesar. Those were the three men who, since the liberation of our country by Lucius Junius Brutus,[4] concentrated greater power in their own hands than the entire Roman state. Certainly, I cannot assert that they had no weapons about them. Yet this I can say: that those weapons were not numerous, and that they were concealed. But this pestilential Antonius, on the other hand, was attended by a whole array of men bristling with arms. Cassius, Seius Mustela, Numisius Tiro, brandishing their swords, led a gang of individuals of their own stamp through the Forum. Barbarian archers[5] marched in regular columns. And when they came to the temple of Con-

1. Goddess of Plenty, whose oldest shrine was in the Regia in the Forum.
2. Consul in 87.
3. Dictator in 81.
4. Legendary founder of the Roman Republic (509).
5. From Ituraea (in Lebanon).

cord,[1] Antonius's men packed the steps, and the sedan chairs were set down on the ground. It was not that he felt the men's shields ought to be hidden. But he did not want his associates to become exhausted by carrying them any further.

But the most disgusting thing of all was this: disgusting not only to witness, but even to hear about. Armed men, thugs, murderers were actually stationed within the shrine of Concord itself. The temple became nothing less than a prison. And when its doors were closed, senators started giving their votes while gangsters roamed around among their seats. And if I myself failed to turn up here on September the first, Antonius declared, he threatened that he would dispatch workmen to pull my house to pieces! For he was proposing to bring forward on that occasion, he said, a motion for a public thanksgiving. A matter, no doubt, of special importance!

On the next day, I did attend the Senate – though he did not. I spoke about our country's situation, less freely, indeed, than I am accustomed to speak, but more freely than was safe in the light of his menaces.[2] For he threatened hostile action against me and bade me attend the Senate's meeting on the nineteenth of September; displaying a ferocity and violence designed to eliminate the freedom of speech which we customarily practise – and which had been most creditably utilized by Lucius Calpurnius Piso Caesoninus thirty days previously.[3] In the meantime, for seventeen days on end, Antonius pronounced harangues against me in the villa of Quintus Caecilius Metellus Pius Scipio[4] at Tibur. His purpose was to stimulate his own thirst. Indeed, that is his usual reason for uttering declamations of that kind.

When the day on which he had bidden me to attend the Senate had arrived, he himself came into the Temple of Concord surrounded by his armed guard, and vomited a torrent of rhetoric out of his filthy lips. I was not there. Indeed, on that day, if my friends had allowed me to come to the Senate – which myself I wanted to – he would have murdered me, as the opening scene of a general massacre. For that is what he planned. And if he had once begun to

1. Beneath the Capitoline hill.

2. The First Philippic (*Cicero: Selected Political Speeches*, Penguin Classics, pp. 295 ff.).

3. Actually, thirty-three days previously (1 August 44). Piso had attacked Antony. He had been consul in 58.

4. Consul in 52.

dip his criminal sword in blood, there would have been no end to the killing he would have embarked upon, until he was sated and too tired to go on.

For his brother Lucius was there, that Asiatic gladiator, who had once fought to the death in the arena at Mylasa.[1] He was thirsting for our blood. Much of his own he had lost in that gladiatorial encounter. And he was totting up *your* property, noting town and country possessions. So our fortunes were at risk from this pauper's greed. He was distributing lands, whichever caught his fancy, and to anyone he wished. No ordinary citizen could obtain access to him, so pleas on grounds of fairness were out of the question. All that any man still possessed was what Lucius Antonius had left him after his hand-out. The actions that he performed, of course, will be cancelled if you rule that those laws are invalid. Meanwhile, they should, in my view, be taken careful note of, every one of these doings, individually. And we should also pronounce that the entire land commission is annulled,[2] and that none of the measures that it has taken should be given official sanction.

As for Marcus Antonius, everyone, surely, has to think of him not as a citizen, but as an enemy, and a horrible, brutal one at that. For he is the man who sat in front of the temple of Castor, and in the hearing of the Roman people declared that no one should be left alive – with the exception of those who were the winners! And you have no justification for supposing, members of the Senate, that these threats exaggerated what he was planning to do. He had the audacity to remark, at a public meeting, that even after he had ceased to be consul, he would still be close to the city with an army, and would enter it as often as he liked – a statement that could only be described as an open threat that he intended to reduce the people of Rome to slavery.[3]

Consider also his journey to Brundisium, and the haste with which he undertook it. Clearly what he was hoping for was to bring an enormous military force up to Rome itself and indeed inside its walls. Remember that gathering of the centurions, and the

1. As a *myrmillo*, armed like a Gaul, with a fish on the crest of his helmet. This was probably during Lucius Antonius's quaestorship in Asia in 50–49.

2. A commission for distributing lands to ex-soldiers.

3. It was illegal for a commander, at the head of his army, to enter Rome, except to celebrate a triumph.

unrestrained ferocity he displayed. When the legions courageously shouted their rejection of his promises, he ordered the centurions whom he had recognized as true patriots to come to his house; and there he had them assassinated before his feet and those of his wife, whom this august commander had brought with him to meet the soldiers. You can imagine what his attitude would have been towards ourselves whom he detested, when he had displayed such cruelty to men he had never seen before! And think of the greed he would have shown for the wealth of the rich, when he had been so determined to shed the blood even of the poor! As for their property, such as it was, his cronies and drinking companions got it; for he immediately distributed it among the lot of them.

Now, this lunatic was already moving the standards of his army up from Brundisium, with hostile intent towards his country, when Gaius Caesar (Octavian), by the gift of the immortal Gods and his own heaven-sent greatness of heart and mind and judgement, took action. No doubt he was doing so on his own initiative, being an outstandingly courageous young man, although he also had the support of my authority behind him. What he did was to move into the colonies his father[1] had founded, call together the ex-soldiers, raise an army in the space of a few days, and block the precipitous onslaught of Antonius's bandit gang. And once the Martian Legion had seen that splendid commander, it kept one single objective in mind, namely that we Romans should finally be set free! Then the Fourth Legion, too, followed its example.

Marcus Antonius had, by this time, summoned a meeting of the Senate, and put up an ex-consul[2] to pronounce that in his opinion Gaius Caesar was a public enemy. But now he suddenly caved in. But although he was wearing his general's cloak he omitted to offer the usual sacrifices and vows, and did not set out on any military expedition. Instead you might suggest that he just ran away. But where did he run to? He ran to a province filled with loyal and courageous citizens.[3] He came with the intention of fighting against them, but even if that had not been what he had in mind they could still never have endured him. For he showed what a violent, angry

1. i.e. his adoptive father, Julius Caesar.

2. Probably Quintus Fufius Calenus (consul in 47), of whom Cicero would have more to say in the Tenth Philippic.

3. Cisalpine Gaul.

creature he is, abusive and arrogant, grasping and looting all the time, and continually drunk as well. Even in peacetime he is a man whose evil-doing no one could tolerate. And now he has made war, against the province of Cisalpine Gaul. He has placed Mutina, a steadfast and noble colony of the Roman people, under siege. And he is attacking Decimus Brutus,[1] a general, consul-elect, a citizen who from his birth has dedicated himself not to his own advantage, but to the service of ourselves and our country.

If Hannibal was an enemy,[2] how can Marcus Antonius be ranked as a citizen? There is nothing for which Hannibal, our enemy, was blamed which Antonius, too, has not either done, or is doing, or is planning and scheming to do. That entire journey of the two Antoniuses can be summed up as a series of depopulations and devastations and massacres and plunderings. Even Hannibal himself did not commit such deeds. True, he kept a lot for his own use. But these two Antoniuses have appropriated the resources and possessions of Roman citizens without giving the matter a thought. Moreover, living as they did merely from one hour to the next, they did not even think of what was really going to be for their own advantage.

Heavens above, is this the man to whom we are deciding to send envoys? I wonder if those prospective envoys of yours have any true understanding of the character of our national constitution, of the laws of war, of the precedents set by our ancestors. I wonder if they realize what the majesty of the Roman people and the dignity of the Senate demand. Are you actually proposing a delegation? If you are doing so in order to appeal to Antonius, he will despise you. If your intention, on the other hand, is to issue him orders, he will take no notice. Moreover, however strict your instructions to the envoys may be, the mere fact that they have been sent at all will damp down the ardent determination of the Roman people, and will weaken the spirit of Italy and its towns. That is serious enough. But there is something else, too. The dispatch of this proposed delegation will prolong hostilities and delay their end. Some people, I expect, will object: 'Let the envoys start out: we can get on with preparing for warfare just the same.' Yet the fact remains that the very existence of the envoys will undermine the spirit of the population and slow down the effective conduct of the fighting.

1. Already praised in the Fourth Philippic.
2. The Carthaginian invader of Italy in the Second Punic War (218–204).

In times of crisis, senators, little influences produce large changes. This applies to public affairs of every kind. But it applies most of all to war, and especially to civil war, which is usually guided by opinion and rumour. No one will ask what instructions we gave the delegation when we ordered it to go. The mere fact that something called a delegation was dispatched, and dispatched unsolicited, will make it look as though we were afraid. No, Antonius must retreat from Mutina, he must stop attacking Decimus Brutus, he must evacuate Cisalpine Gaul. He must not be invited to do these things by words of mouth. He must be compelled to do them by military force.

Hannibal, once upon a time, was sent envoys by the Senate ordering him to withdraw from Saguntum, Publius Valerius Flaccus and Quintus Baebius Tamphilus.[1] And they were instructed, if Hannibal did not act in accordance with their request, to move on to Carthage itself. Yet where should we tell our envoys to go if Antonius does not comply? But, anyway, what we are doing, if we dispatch envoys to talk with him, will not be at all the same thing as we did then. For what we will be doing is to send envoys to a fellow-citizen of our own, to urge him not to attack a general and a colony of his own Roman people. It seems strange that that is the sort of thing that we have to send envoys to request! For, heaven knows, attacking a colony established for the protection of the Roman people, a fortification, you might say, defending Rome, is just as deplorable as attacking the city of Rome itself.

The cause of the Second Punic War, which Hannibal fought against our ancestors, was his assault on Saguntum. To order envoys to go *to him* was a justified action. For they went to a Carthaginian, for the purpose of protecting his enemies, who were allies of ours. Between what happened at the time, and the present circumstances which we are discussing today, there is no comparison at all. If we send envoys to Antonius now, it is, instead, to a fellow-citizen of our own that we are sending them – and a fellow-citizen, what is more, whom it will be their duty to ask to stop besieging and assailing a Roman general, a Roman army, a Roman colony, and to desist from depopulating that colony's lands: from making himself, in the most real sense, our enemy!

Suppose he obeys. Have we, in that case, either the will or the

1. In 220/219.

power to treat him as a citizen? On December the twentieth, by your decrees, you condemned him.[1] You decided that January the first should be the day when this motion should be brought forward, concerning the honours and rewards to be allocated to those who by opposing him have deserved, and deserve, well of our country. And foremost among these you placed, correctly, Gaius Caesar (Octavian), who warded off Marcus Antonius's attacks on the city, and diverted him to Cisalpine Gaul. Next, you praised the ex-soldiers who were the first to support Gaius Caesar, and you also praised those heaven-sent, divinely inspired legions, the Martian and the Fourth. They had not merely deserted Antonius, who claimed to be their consul, but were actually fighting against him, and you promised that they would be rewarded. Then, on the very same day, when an edict of that admirable citizen Decimus Junius Brutus had been brought before you and proposed for acceptance, you commended what he had done, and employed your national authority to approve of the war which he had undertaken on his private initiative.

Clearly, your one and only objective on that day was to declare Marcus Antonius a public enemy. After these decrees of yours, how can he possibly look at you with equanimity, or how can you, on the other hand, look at him with anything but the utmost indignation? He has been excluded from the state, dragged outside its boundaries into complete isolation. The causes of this were his crimes. And I cannot help feeling that the good fortune that blesses Rome was also responsible.

If, by any chance, he chooses to obey the envoys, and returns to the city, you can be sure that the worst type of citizens will then see his standard as one to which they can rally. Not, however, that this is my principal fear. There are other things that I worry about with even greater anxiety. What I mean is that he will *not*, in fact, obey the envoys' instructions at all. For I know what an arrogant madman he is. I know the sort of evil advice his devoted friends offer him. The leader of the gang is his brother Lucius, a man with experience of combat, since he has fought abroad.

Grant, for a moment, that Marcus Antonius himself may actually show some signs of sanity; though that, in fact, would never be an accurate estimate – and in any case his friends could never allow him to be anything of the kind. But what will happen meanwhile,

1. When the Third Philippic was spoken.

on that assumption, is that time will be wasted, and the preparations for fighting him are bound to cool down. Slowness and delay – those are the factors which have caused the war, already, to become so protracted.

From the very first moment after the bandit Antonius left, or, rather, fled in despair, from the moment when it first became possible to hold an unimpeded meeting of the Senate, I have constantly pressed that a meeting should be held.[1] And then it was.[2] On that day, as the consuls-elect were not present, it was I myself who put forward my views; you completely agreed with them, and thus were laid the foundations for our national recovery. This, I admit, happened a good deal later than it ought to have. I had not been in a position to make the move before. All the same, if from that time onwards not a single further day had been lost, we should certainly have no war now. Every evil is easily suppressed at its birth. It is when it has had time to remain in existence that it gathers strength. When our meeting was held, however, everything was postponed until January the first. Perhaps not wisely.

But let us turn our eyes away from the past. What we must consider now is whether we shall add this *further* delay, until the envoys set out and return. While we wait, doubts about the entire war are going to flourish. And, amid such doubts, it cannot be supposed that recruitment will proceed with any energy.

For these reasons, senators, I propose that there should be no further mention of envoys. I am convinced that we should get on with our task, and move with all speed, and without any postponement whatsoever. A state of civil war should be formally proclaimed.[3] The courts of justice should be declared shut. Men should put on their uniforms. A recruitment drive should be conducted. All exemptions from service should be suspended in Rome and in Italy as well, except Cisalpine Gaul. If all this is done, the widespread consciousness that we have taken such rigorous action will make this unhinged, criminal gladiator think again. For he will realize that he has got himself into a war against his country.

Yes, the strength and power of a unanimous Senate will make an

1. Antony left Rome on 28 November and Cicero returned on 9 December.

2. 20 December 44.

3. *Tumultus*, a sudden perilous war in or near Italy – usually relating to Cisalpine Gaul.

impact on Antonius. It is *not* unanimous, he is saying at present, since there are two conflicting parties. But what parties is he referring to? One side has been defeated.[1] The other side comprises the partisans of the late Julius Caesar, whom Antonius might have hoped would support him, but are, in fact, siding against him (and it would hardly be right that the consuls Aulus Hirtius and Gaius Vibius Pansa Caetronianus, and Julius Caesar's own Octavian, should be classed as anti-Caesarians).[2] However, in any case, it is not a struggle between two parties that has brought about this war. It has been brought about by the criminal hopes of evil citizens. Our goods, our properties have been listed and, indeed, already distributed among these ruffians, according to what each of them fancies.

I have read a letter Antonius wrote to one of his colleagues among the land commissioners, a person guilty of capital crimes. 'See that you get whatever you want,' he said. 'Whatever you like the look of, you shall certainly have.' Here, then, is the man to whom we are to send envoys, against whom we are to delay launching hostilities! If he had entrusted our fortunes to a lottery, we should have been better off. But instead he has handed us over to the covetous acquisitiveness which any and every character might care to display. Indeed he has not even left anything over, intact, for his own self. For he has promised everything to someone else.

What is needed to deal with this man, senators, is war. And at the first possible moment. Delays created by the sending of envoys must be wholly rejected. And so that is why I am now offering a proposal that will avoid passing new decrees day by day. What I propose is that our national welfare should be entrusted into the hands of the consuls, and that they be charged to protect the state, and ensure it comes to no harm.[3] And I add the further suggestion

1. The Pompeians – who having been defeated hardly constituted a party. It has alternatively been suggested that Cicero is referring to the partisans of Antony in the Senate, who were 'defeated' by its decision on 20 December, but it seems more probable that he is ignoring the Antonians, as enemies of the state.

2. Since Hirtius and Pansa had both been officers of Julius Caesar, and Octavian, though not Caesar's son by birth, was his adoptive son. Cicero's argument is somewhat convoluted here, but he is making the point that Antony's 'two conflicting parties' do not exist.

3. The terms of the *senatusconsultum ultimum* – the traditional emergency decree.

that anyone in Antonius's army who deserts him before February the first should be exempted from any penalty. If you adopt these proposals, senators, you will be able to restore the freedom of the Roman people and your own authority, and quite soon at that. If, on the other hand, you decide to act less decisively, you will still be forced to pass the same measures in the end. But by then it may be too late.

So far as your reference to the Senate concerns our national interests,[1] I think it is adequately answered by my motion. We now come to the question of honours, since I understand that is the next thing we have to discuss. And as regards this matter of honouring courageous men, I will keep to the order of proceedings which is normally observed when senators' opinions are asked for. Let us therefore, in accordance with custom, begin with the consul-elect, Decimus Junius Brutus.

His earlier services are great,[2] but have been fully appreciated by public opinion, even if not, so far, by any official commendation. However, I shall not speak of them now. What we have to consider now is the manner in which our praises for what he is doing at this present time ought to be framed. For praise and glory are the only rewards which merit of this calibre looks for; although, even if no such rewards materialized, merit of such a kind would rest content enough with what it had itself achieved, which could not fail, even without formal recognition, to be lodged in the memories of his grateful fellow-citizens; and they would make sure it saw the light of day. Nevertheless, it is up to us to bestow our commendation upon Decimus Brutus, recording the judgement and testimony that his actions demand. Here then, senators, are the terms of the decree which I propose:

'Seeing that Decimus Brutus, general, consul-elect, is maintaining the province of Cisalpine Gaul as a possession of the Senate and Roman people; and seeing that in so brief a period, with the enthusiastic support of the municipalities and colonies of the province, a province which has deserved and continues to deserve excellently of our country, he has mobilized and gathered together

1. Cicero is here addressing the new consuls, Hirtius and Pansa, who had consulted the Senate on the situation.

2. Especially his part, Cicero means, in the assassination of Julius Caesar.

such a substantial army, we decree that these actions of his were entirely right and proper, and in the interests of the nation, and that his outstanding services to our country earn, and will continue to earn, the gratitude of the Senate and Roman people. For the Senate and the Roman people are of the opinion that by the endeavours and planning and courage of Decimus Brutus, and owing to the wonderful determination and unanimity of the province of Cisalpine Gaul, our nation has been rescued at a critical time.'

As a reward for these noble actions performed by Decimus Brutus, senators, and his outstanding services towards Rome, no honours could be too great. For if Cisalpine Gaul had lain open to Marcus Antonius, if he had crushed the municipalities and colonies there, and had been permitted to penetrate into Transalpine Gaul, our country would indeed now be threatened by a terrifying menace. For clearly this demented creature, impetuous and erratic in all his decisions, would not have hesitated to make war on us. He would be launching his army against us with the full force of his barbaric ferocity, so that even the Alps would not have availed as a barrier against his frenzied onslaught. That is why we owe Decimus Brutus so much gratitude. For here was a man who, without waiting until he had your authority behind him, by his own decision and initiative refused to accept Antonius as consul, but treated him as an enemy who must be kept out of Cisalpine Gaul, and preferred to be besieged himself rather than see this city of ours in a state of siege. So I urge that his outstandingly fine conduct should receive everlasting recognition from the decree that we shall pass. And I urge also that Cisalpine Gaul, which always protects and has protected our empire and the freedom that we all share, should be granted just and truthful commendation for refusing to surrender itself and its resources to Antonius, and mobilizing them against him instead.

Moreover, I also propose that the highest honours should be decreed to Marcus Aemilius Lepidus for his great services to our country.[1] It has always been his ambition that the Roman people

1. Lepidus had been consul in 46, and was 'master of the horse' (*magister equitum*) of Julius Caesar as dictator (46–44). After Caesar's death, he succeeded him as chief priest, and left to govern the provinces Caesar had assigned to him (Narbonese Gaul – the old province of southern Transalpine Gaul – and Nearer Spain).

should be free. And of this wish, and of his determination, he offered a most convincing demonstration upon that day when Antonius placed a diadem upon Julius Caesar's head.[1] Whereupon Lepidus turned aside, and made it clear, by his melancholy sighs, that servitude was something which he hated, that he desired the Roman people to be free, and that he had endured what he endured not from choice, but because of the inexorable pressure of the times.

Nor can any of us forget the moderation that Lepidus displayed during the national emergency that followed Julius Caesar's death. That was fine behaviour indeed. But I have even nobler conduct to speak of now. What I am talking about is that exceptionally wonderful action that he performed, wonderful, heaven only knows, in the eyes of every nation, and extraordinarily welcome to the Roman people. For at the height of the Civil War, of which we all dreaded the outcome so strongly, it was Lepidus who brought the hostilities to an end by his wisdom and mercifulness, rather than allow them to be decided by violence and force of arms.

It had been a ferocious and miserable war, and if Caesar had been as sensible as Lepidus about it, then we should still have the two sons of Pompeius (not to speak of the father), unharmed, in our midst.[2] It was wrong that their filial dutifulness should have counted against them. How I wish Marcus Lepidus had been able to save them all! He made it clear that he would have done just that, if he had had the power to do so, when he restored Sextus Pompeius to his fellow-citizens, to be not only a conspicuous ornament of the state but a glorious memorial to the clemency of Lepidus. What a dreadful business all that was for Rome, what a horrible misfortune! For when Cnaeus Pompeius Magnus (Pompey the Great) died, the light that had illuminated Rome's empire was extinguished. And then his elder son Cnaeus perished as well – the son who so closely resembled his father. However, the immortal gods granted us a compensation for these disasters when Sextus Pompeius was preserved for our country.

1. On 15 February 44, at the festival of the Lupercalia, Antony publicly offered Caesar a diadem, which he refused, preferring his dictatorship (although it had been ominously made 'perpetual') to the unpopular role of monarch.

2. The older of them, Cnaeus Pompeius (from whose violence Cicero was saved by Cato in 48), was captured and executed after the battle of Munda in Spain (44), and Sextus was to be recognized by the Senate (on Lepidus's initiative) in April 43 but then outlawed in August, whereupon he occupied Sicily.

For this compelling reason, and because Marcus Lepidus by his humanity and wisdom transformed a large-scale, perilous civil war into peace and concord, I propose a senatorial decree in these terms:

'Whereas our country has on many occasions been efficiently and successfully directed by Marcus Aemilius Lepidus, general and chief priest, and the Roman people has understood that he feels a particular distaste for autocratic power; and whereas by his endeavours, courageous acts, and decisions, and by his outstanding clemency and leniency, a very savage civil war has been brought to an end, and Sextus Pompeius, the son of Cnaeus, has obeyed the authority of this senatorial order by laying down his arms, and with the most cordial agreement of the Senate and Roman people has been restored to his fellow-citizens, let it be decreed that, bearing in mind Marcus Lepidus's numerous, mighty services to our nation, the Senate and Roman people invest their highest hopes of peace, tranquillity, concord and liberty in his courage, authority and good fortune, and record that they will never forget his services to our country, and signify their decision that a gilt equestrian statue representing him shall be erected upon the rostra, or on any other site in the Forum that he may choose.'

Senators, these are, I know, conspicuous honours. The most important thing about them, however, is that they are thoroughly well deserved. Nor are they only granted because of what we hope for in the future, but because of immense services already rendered. I cannot remember that such outstanding honours have ever been conferred before, by a Senate that was acting by its own free, unfettered will.

Now, senators, I come to Gaius Caesar (Octavian). If he were not living, you must agree that none of us, either, would be alive any longer. Speeding towards the city from Brundisium, you will remember, was Antonius. He was a man of ungovernable violence, burning with hatred, deeply hostile to every patriotic citizen. And he had an army with him. Now, what on earth could we have mobilized to withstand his criminal fierceness? Up to that time, we had no commanders, no military forces. We had no council representing the state, no freedom of action. Our necks were at the mercy of his brutal designs. The intention of every one of us was to get ourselves away, but even getting away did not ensure that we would escape. It must have been some god, at that moment, who presented to us, presented to the Roman people, this heaven-sent youth Gaius Caesar. It was a time when there was absolutely nothing to stop that poisonous Marcus Antonius from obliterating us. But then suddenly, unexpectedly, this young man emerged and got together an armed force to oppose Antonius's savage malevolence before anyone imagined that he intended anything of the kind.

Cnaeus Pompeius Magnus, too, had received great honours when he was still a young man; and rightly so, because he came to the aid of the government. But he had been a good deal older and stronger – and better placed because his soldiers were looking out to find a commander. Besides, his war was of a different sort. Or take Lucius Cornelius Sulla. His cause did not please everyone. You only have to look at the number of the men who were proscribed, and the disasters that overtook so many towns.[1] Gaius Caesar, on the other hand, is many years younger. The ex-soldiers he has armed want nothing better than to retire. Yet the cause which he has chosen to support is one which appeals very strongly indeed to the Senate and Roman people, and the whole of Italy, and to gods and men alike. To go back to the comparison, and contrast, with Cnaeus Pompeius Magnus. What Pompeius had done was to attach himself to the powerful commander Sulla, and his conquering army – whereas Gaius Caesar did not have anyone to attach himself to. Instead, he, personally, took the initiative in raising an army and organizing defences. Again, Pompeius controlled the territory of Picenum, which was hostile to his enemies. Gaius Caesar, on the other hand, had to raise his army from men who were friendly to his enemy Antonius. However, they were more friendly still to the cause of freedom, so he found it possible to raise them against Antonius all the same. Pompeius helped Sulla to become an autocrat. Gaius Caesar, by way of contrast, provided the means of removing the autocracy of Antonius from the scene.

So let us entrust the command to Gaius Caesar. Without it, no military affairs can be conducted, no army can be held together, no war carried on. Make him a propraetor,[2] so that he can have the fullest powers. Certainly, that is a considerable distinction for someone of his youthful years. But the purpose of such a conferment is

1. Cicero is referring to Sulla's return to Italy in 83 and the horrors that accompanied the battle of the Colline Gate against the Marians (82).

2. i.e. rank equivalent to that of praetor.

not merely to enhance his personal dignity but to make it possible for what needs doing to be done. So that is what we should ask for. And that is all we are likely to gain today. I very much hope that this will not be by any means the only occasion on which we senators and the Roman people will have the opportunity of decorating this young man with honours and distinctions. At the present juncture, however, I am content to move that our decree should be in these terms:

'Whereas Gaius Caesar, the son of Gaius, priest, propraetor, has at this highly critical time for our country encouraged the ex-soldiers to rally to the defence of the Roman people, and has mobilized them for this purpose; and whereas the Martian and Fourth Legions, with great zeal and admirable patriotic unanimity, under the command and leadership of Gaius Caesar, are defending and have defended the government and liberty of the Roman people; and whereas Gaius Caesar, propraetor, has with his army set out for the defence of the province of Cisalpine Gaul, has brought its cavalry, archers and elephants within the authority of himself and the Roman people,[1] and has preserved the people's lives and dignity in a period of extreme national crisis: for these reasons it is the pleasure of the Senate that Gaius Caesar, son of Gaius, priest, propraetor, should become a member of its order, and speak from the benches reserved for praetors; and if he seeks office, whatever it may be, his candidature will enjoy the same degree of legal eligibility as if he had been quaestor in the previous year.'

For there is no reason whatever, senators, why we should not be in favour of Gaius Caesar's election, at the earliest possible moment, to the most senior offices of state. True, the laws governing the minimum ages at which offices could be held fixed a later age than his for the consulship,[2] because they were afraid of the rashness of youth. But Gaius Caesar, while certainly still very young, has already demonstrated that merit of the highest quality does not need to await the oncoming of age. And that was why our ancestors, in the distant past, had no laws laying down the minimum ages for offices. It was rivalries between candidates, many years later, that led to the introduction of such laws, so that those who

1. They were auxiliaries who had probably been brought by Julius Caesar from north Africa.

2. Forty-two, under the *Lex Villia annalis* of Lucius Villius (180).

were competing to achieve higher offices should be of the same age. That meant, very often, that a great talent was lost altogether, before it could be of service to our country.

When we think, however, of ancient epochs, men like Quintus Fabius Maximus Rullianus[1] and Publius Decius Mus[2] and Marcus Valerius Corvus,[3] and many others too, were elected consuls at a very early age.[4] More recently, too, early consulships went to Publius Cornelius Africanus the elder[5] and to Titus Quinctius Flamininus.[6] And these were men whose achievements were so noteworthy that we owe them the extension of our empire and its glory. Moreover, Alexander III of Macedonia, too, was only a very young man when he began to perform his extraordinary exploits. Indeed, he was only in his thirty-third year when he died:[7] ten years younger, that is to say, than the minimum age when, according to our laws here, a man can become consul. From this one can deduce that merit asserts itself without waiting for age.

Some people feel envious of Gaius Caesar, and pretend that they are afraid of what he may do. But there is no reason to fear that he will prove unable to exercise self-control, or that our honours will go to his head and he will employ his powers intemperately. Once a man has understood what true glory is, once he feels that the Senate and knights and people of Rome love him and see him as beneficial to our country, then he will realize, senators, that *this* is the glory most worth having.

How I wish that the other Gaius Julius Caesar, his father I mean, had equally endeared himself to the Senate, and to patriotic citizens, in his earliest years! Because he neglected to accomplish this, he squandered his entire brainpower, which was enormous, on the fickle public. And that was how, displaying not the slightest regard for the Senate and loyal Romans, he cleared the way for that enhancement of his power which the free and noble people proved unable to tolerate.

1. Consul in 322 and 310.
2. Consul in 340.
3. Consul in 348.
4. Cicero calls Rullianus Rullus, and calls Corvus Corvinus, although it was actually Corvus's son who took the name Corvinus.
5. Consul in 205 and 194.
6. Consul in 198.
7. In 323.

But the way in which his son proceeds is very different indeed. He is liked by everybody, and especially by the people who are most worthwhile. Our hopes of freedom depend on him. As for our own personal safety, he has given this back to us already. We have requested that he receive the highest possible honours; and that is already settled, and they await him. We admire his excellent judgement – there is no need to be afraid that he will do anything foolish. For it *would* be foolish to prefer empty power, envoy-provoking wealth, a hazardous, treacherous lust for despotism to authentic, stable, solid glory. Having realized this as a boy, surely he will continue to realize it as he grows older.

But he is hostile, some will object, to certain highly distinguished, reputable fellow-citizens. There is nothing to be afraid of there. Gaius Caesar has shelved his personal enmities and given them up – as a gift to his country. He has made his country his judge; he has entrusted everything he plans and undertakes to the guidance of Rome. For he has embarked on our nation's affairs in order to strengthen Rome, not to overturn it. I know what the young man is feeling; I know it through and through. Rome is what he loves more than anything else in the world. Your authority is what he values most highly. The favourable opinion of good men is what he desires above all. And true glory seems to him the sweetest thing that exists. So do not be afraid of anything he may do. On the contrary: you would be fully entitled to expect even greater and nobler actions in the future. And the fact that he has set out to rescue Decimus Brutus from his besieged condition shows there is no need to fear that family mourning[1] will remain in his heart to the exclusion of the safety of our country.

In this connection, senators, I shall make so bold as to offer a solemn pledge, to yourselves, and the Roman people, and our country. And that is something I should never have hazarded, unless force had absolutely compelled me to. For otherwise I should have seriously risked, when so vital an issue is at stake, incurring a damaging reputation for temerity. What I am promising then, senators, what I take upon myself to vow, is this: that Gaius Caesar will always be the sort of Roman citizen that he is today; and that we should particularly wish and pray that he should continue to be just like that.

1. i.e. for the death of his (adoptive) father the dictator, whom Decimus Junius Brutus had helped to murder.

In the circumstances, I shall regard what I have just said about Gaius Caesar as enough. But I do not think we should be silent, either, about Lucius Egnatuleius, a brave and steadfast citizen who is an excellent friend of our people. His admirable achievement in bringing over the Fourth Legion to Gaius Caesar, for the protection of the consuls, the Senate, the Roman people and our country, it is our duty to recognize. Because, therefore, of what he has done, I move that we confer upon Lucius Egnatuleius the right to be a candidate for government posts, and to accept them and hold them, three years before the age fixed by law. This is not just a question of conferring a practical benefit upon Lucius Egnatuleius. For the point is to honour him. For this purpose, it is necessary, and enough, to have your name named.

And regarding the army of Gaius Caesar I propose that we should decree as follows:

'The Senate decrees that the ex-soldiers who, placing themselves under the leadership of Gaius Caesar, priest, propraetor, have defended and are defending the freedom of the Roman people and the authority of our senatorial order, shall have exemption from further military service, and their children shall likewise be exempted; and that the consuls Gaius Vibius Pansa Caetronianus and Aulus Hirtius, one or the other of them or both of them, if they so decide, should find out what land there is in the colonies, land allocated to the settlement of ex-soldiers, which is held in violation of the Julian Law,[1] so that it can be distributed among Gaius Caesar's ex-soldiers; and with regard to land in Campania that they make a separate investigation,[2] and devise a means of increasing the financial advantages of the ex-soldiers in question. Furthermore, as regards the Martian and Fourth Legions, and those soldiers of the Second and Thirty-fifth Legions who joined the consuls Pansa and Hirtius, and enrolled under their leadership because of the loyalty they feel and have felt towards the authority of the Senate and the freedom

1. Julius Caesar's agrarian law during his consulship of 59, which provided state land for the ex-soldiers of Cnaeus Pompeius Magnus (Pompey) following his campaigns in the east, and for the poorer citizens of Rome.

2. Julius Caesar, during his dictatorship, had set aside state land in Campania for the settlement of ex-soldiers who fought for him against the Pompeians in the Civil War. Cicero accused Antony of distributing this land among his drinking and gambling companions (*II Philippic*, 101). Antony had gone there to supervise the allotments in late April 44.

of the Roman people, the Senate decrees that they and their children should be exempted from military service, except on occasions when civil war has been declared in Cisalpine Gaul or Italy. And the Senate rules also, that, when the war is over, these legions should be discharged; and that whatever sums of money have been promised to his soldiers by Gaius Caesar, priest, propraetor, should be handed over to them; and that Pansa and Hirtius, consuls, one or the other of them or both of them, shall, if they think fit, note the particulars of the land that can be divided, without causing personal hardship; and that the soldiers of the Martian and Fourth Legions to whom reference has been made shall be assigned and awarded lands equal to any that have ever been allocated to soldiers before.'

I have spoken, consuls, about all the proposals that you have placed before us. If they are passed rapidly, and without delay, you will find it that much easier to make the preparations which the necessities of this present time demand. But speed is imperative. If we had used it before, we should not, as I have said more than once, have a war on our hands at the present time.

Cicero's Fifth Philippic was only a partial success. That is to say, the Senate did agree to legitimize Gaius Caesar (Octavian) and honour Decimus Junius Brutus (in Cisalpine Gaul) and Marcus Aemilius Lepidus (governor of Narbonese [Southern Transalpine] Gaul and Nearer Spain). But it persisted, despite Cicero's arguments to the contrary, in sending a delegation to Marcus Antonius. Cicero, however, continued to make speeches against him, and the Sixth Philippic, trying to make the best of the Senate's not wholly favourable reception of the Fifth, was delivered before the Assembly on 4 January 43. Its peroration is famous.

'It is up to me to show foresight for my fellow-citizens. Day and night, it is my duty to plan for your freedom, and for the safety of our country. For I owe you everything, Romans. I can claim no ancestry, and yet you have set me above every nobleman in Rome in all the honourable posts that you have bestowed upon me, one after another. Am I ungrateful? Nobody could be less ungrateful than myself, who, after winning all these great offices of state, have worked just as hard in the Forum as when I was still a candidate for those same offices. Nor can you call me inexperienced in government affairs. Nobody has more experience of them than I have. For twenty years I have been fighting against citizens disloyal to our country.

'Moreover, I will continue in the future, Romans, to advise you to the best my powers, and to work for you, too, to the best of my powers – and almost beyond them. I will keep guard. I will keep watch, on your behalf. For I cannot imagine a citizen, and especially a citizen of the rank which you have been good enough to confer on me, who could be so forgetful of your kindness, so lacking in thought for our nation, so eager to undermine his own reputation, that he was not moved and fired by the wonderful way in which you have spoken with one voice. As consul, I convened many important public meetings. And I have attended many others as well. But never have I witnessed a meeting as important as this one today.

'You all feel the same, and share an identical objective. That objective is to preserve our country from the schemes of Marcus Antonius, to extinguish the flames of his frenzy, to suppress his brazen violence. Every order in the state has this one purpose, and that is the single purpose, too, of the municipalities and colonies, indeed of the whole land of Italy. The Senate already stood firm, on its own initiative. But you have made it stand firmer. Citizens, the time has come. It has come later, indeed, than befitted the dignity of the Roman people. But now it is ripe, so ripe, indeed, that a further hour's delay must be avoided at all costs.

'True, a catastrophe has overtaken us. Somehow or other it had to be endured. It was the work, you could say, of Destiny. But if another catastrophe overtakes us now, it will be by our own choice. That the Roman people should be slaves is not right. On the contrary, the immortal gods have granted Rome the rulership of all the nations of the earth. We have come to a moment of extreme crisis. The issue is whether we are going to be free men, or not. You must win, Romans. And surely your patriotism and unanimity will bring this about. You must do anything in the world rather than lapse into slavery. Slavery is what other peoples may have to endure. What belongs to the Roman people is freedom.'

Some time later in the same month of January 43 BC, *Cicero spoke again, delivering his Seventh Philippic to the Senate, which emphasized that peace with Antonius would be dishonourable and dangerous – as well as impossible. During the closing days of the same month the envoys (except for Servius Sulpicius Rufus, who had died) returned from Antonius, bringing his counter-proposals. However, they were not approved by the Senate, which in February, rejected a proposal that a second deputation should be sent to Antonius, declaring a state of civil war instead. On the next day Cicero, addressing the Senate in the Eighth Philippic, attacked Calenus and those of the senators who, he declared, lacked fighting spirit, and scorned the idea that peace should be made with Antonius.*[1] *He followed his address up with the Ninth, delivered to the same body.*[2]

It was probably in March that the older of Marcus Antonius's younger brothers, Gaius, after gaining control of Macedonia, was besieged in Apollonia in Illyricum by Marcus Junius Brutus, Caesar's assassin, who had retreated to the region in the face of Gaius's confrontation.[3] *In the Tenth Philippic Cicero proposed to the Senate that Marcus Brutus's command of all the troops in the area – in Illyricum, Macedonia and Greece – should be confirmed, in opposition to the claims of Gaius Antonius (although he was doubtless aware that Marcus Brutus had no incontestable legal right to such powers, any more than his fellow-assassin Gaius Cassius was entitled to the similar powers he had assumed in Syria, in opposition to Publius Cornelius Dolabella).*

The meeting at which Cicero delivered this speech had been summoned by the consul Gaius Vibius Pansa Caetronianus, who first delivered an oration himself, in which he praised Marcus Brutus warmly. But then Pansa's son-in-law Quintus Fufius Calenus, whose hostility to Cicero has been noted before, expressed a contrary view, proposing that Brutus should be deprived of his command. This was the opinion that Cicero had to answer.

THE TENTH PHILIPPIC

We all have to feel extremely grateful to you, Gaius Vibius Pansa Caetronianus; and we must place this on record. We never supposed that you would convene a meeting of the Senate today. But when

1. Who may now, it seems, have been prepared to give up Cisalpine Gaul.

2. Cicero also proposed honours to the late Servius Sulpicius Rufus (who had died while a member of the deputation to Antony), although, in fact, he had never held a great opinion of the jurist's political abilities: see *Against Verres* (Chapter 1).

3. Gaius Antonius had left Rome at about the end of November 44 to take over Macedonia, but the Senate had annulled his appointment (with legal correctness, according to Cicero) on 21 December.

you received that letter from the distinguished Marcus Brutus, you did not delay for a moment before giving us the opportunity of expressing our delight and congratulations on the contents of his report. Everyone will feel gratitude for what you did, and especially for the speech you made after you had read out the letter. For you thereby showed – and it is something that I have always felt myself – that no man who is conscious of his own merits need feel grudging about admitting them in somebody else!

My own association with Brutus is based on many mutual services and close personal friendship.[1] But after what you have stated I do not need to talk about him at length. For your speech has anticipated what I was going to say. Nevertheless, senators, I do feel obliged to make a somewhat longer oration than I had intended to, owing to the remarks that were made by the member who was called upon before me.[2] I disagree with him so frequently that I have begun to be afraid that these perpetual differences of opinion will weaken our friendship; though they ought to do nothing of the kind.

But what purpose or principle, Calenus, lies behind the fact that ever since January the first you have never once agreed with the consul who has been inviting you to speak first[3] I really fail to understand. And, indeed, although many senators have been present, there has never been a single one who has backed your views. I cannot see why you have to persist in defending people who are entirely unlike yourself! Your own life, your fortune, offer you every opportunity for the enjoyment of leisure and dignity. So why on earth do you approve, propose and support measures that are calculated to destroy the leisure and dignity of everyone else?

About earlier matters I am going to say nothing at all. But concerning one point, which seems to me particularly surprising, I cannot remain silent. What on earth is this war that you are fighting against the Brutuses?[4] I cannot follow why, all on your own, you attack them, when they are men whom we ought to admire; indeed, we ought to admire them almost to the point of veneration.

1. This somewhat complex relationship is discussed in the *Brutus* (Chapter 6). Brutus did not entirely reciprocate Cicero's approval.

2. Quintus Fufius Calenus: see just below.

3. Gaius Vibius Pansa Caetronianus, his father-in-law.

4. Decimus and Marcus Junius Brutus.

One of them is being besieged,[1] and it does not worry you at all. And what you are proposing for the other is to rob him of the forces which by his own labours, and at his own peril, and with no one to help him, he has collected together, not by any means with the purpose of saving his own life, but in order to preserve our country. The feelings and reasonings behind your disapproval of the Brutuses and approval of the Antoniuses I find entirely incomprehensible. It means that the men whom everyone else loves are objects of your hatred, and that those whom the rest of us bitterly hate are viewed by yourself with unremitting affection.

You have a very ample fortune. You have reached the highest offices in the state. You have a son[2] who is born to win success, and will win it, so I hear and hope, and I wish him well, for our nation's sake and yours. So I put it to you, whether you would wish him to be like Brutus; or, instead, like an Antonius – and I allow you to select whichever of the three Antoniuses you prefer. 'Heaven forbid!' you will say. Why, then, you fail to extend your favour and approval to those whom you would like your son to resemble I do not understand. For, by doing so, you would at one and the same time set him examples for imitation, and serve the interests of Rome.

And there is one particular point, Calenus, about which I want to complain to you, without, I again hope, damaging our friendship but as one senator differing from another. You expressed the view in your proposal – and I am quoting from a manuscript draft, since without that I should have suspected you had made a verbal slip – that Brutus's letter was written 'rightly and properly'. But that, surely, is praise of Brutus's secretary, not of Brutus himself.[3] By this time, Calenus, you ought to have, you are in a position to have, ample experience in state affairs. But I am sure you have never before seen a decree using language like that. There have been innumerable senatorial resolutions about this sort of matter. But when has the Senate ever decreed that a letter has been 'well

1. In Mutina, by Antony.

2. Called Quintus Fufius Calenus, like his father.

3. Cicero chooses to take Calenus's remark as referring to style or calligraphy, whereas Calenus had meant it to refer to the letter's content – showing that he did not want to display total disapproval of Marcus Brutus; but Cicero chooses to obscure this concession.

written'? Yet the term did not escape you by accident, as is apt to happen. You wrote it down, and it had been deliberately chosen.

Suppose that your habit of criticizing good citizens on every possible occasion could somehow be eliminated! Then you would still have every quality left that any man could desire. So pull yourself together, and now, finally, calm yourself down. You have many excellent friends. Pay attention to what they say. Talk with your father-in-law Pansa, who is a very wise man; talk with him more often than with yourself. Then, if you do so, your reputation will really become first-class. And there is one matter which I hope you do not regard as unimportant. Indeed, on account of our friendship, it is a matter that often causes me some personal distress. I refer to the word going round, and reaching the ears of the people of Rome, that the senator who first gave his vote, namely you yourself, found no one at all to offer him any support. And that, Calenus, is what I think is going to happen again today.

You want to take Marcus Brutus's legions away from him. Let us consider what legions you have in mind. You refer, of course, to those which he rescued from aiding the criminal projects of Marcus Antonius, and upon his own authority transferred to the service of the state. Evidently you would like him, for a second time, to become a defenceless, isolated exile from our country.[1] But senators, if you desert and betray Marcus Brutus, I cannot imagine how there could ever be any Roman citizen at all whom you would wish to honour or favour. Unless perhaps you believe that the men who placed the diadem on Julius Caesar's head ought to be cherished, but those who abolished autocracy altogether[2] should be abandoned.

I shall say nothing, today, of the god-like, immortal action that Marcus Brutus performed.[3] For it is preserved in the thankful remembrance of every citizen, although not ratified, yet, by public authority. Think, in heaven's name, of the patience and moderation Brutus showed, think of his calmness and self-effacement in the face

1. After their murder of Julius Caesar, both Marcus Brutus and Cassius had been compelled to flee from Rome, probably in April 44.

2. *Regni nomen*; or *regnum omnino*, 'those who totally abolished the autocracy'. Cicero had mentioned the diadem offered to Julius Caesar by Marcus Antony, at the Lupercalia of 44, on an earlier occasion.

3. By the murder of Julius Caesar.

of evil! He was city praetor[1], but he did not stay in the city. He had restored legality to the government, but he did not choose to administer the law. He could have been surrounded, every day, by a throng of all patriotic citizens – indeed, a remarkably large crowd continually accompanied him; and, furthermore, he could have had the whole of Italy as his bodyguard. Yet he preferred to be defended, from a distance, by the goodwill of all patriotic Romans, rather than have his actual person protected by military force. His Games in honour of Apollo had been planned on a scale which befitted his own dignity and that of the Roman people. Yet he stayed away from their actual celebration, in case, by attending them, he might have given criminals their chance to launch the nefarious designs they planned.

The days of the Games were occasions of a great deal of pleasure. In response to verses from a play,[2] the people of Rome greeted the memory of what Marcus Brutus had done with clamorous shouts of applause. The liberator was not present in person, but the recollection of what he had done to liberate them was there; and in that recollection the image of Marcus Brutus himself was plain to the eye.

During those days, while the Games were on, I myself saw him on the island[3] of the noble young Marcus Licinius Lucullus, his neighbour. The one thing in Brutus's mind was peace, and good relations between the citizens of Rome. I also saw him later at Velia – when he was sailing away from Italy, in order that he should not become the cause of the outbreak of a civil war. It was indeed a tragic spectacle, tragic not only for the men who stood around but even for the waves and seaboard that witnessed the scene, that the saviour of his country should be departing from its shores, whereas its destroyers still remained there! And Gaius Cassius's fleet followed a few days later. To return to the city, members of the Senate, from which those men had departed, made me feel ashamed. But you know why I returned, from the first of these speeches,[4] and since then you have had reason to test the accuracy of what I said.

1. In 44.

2. The *Tereus* of Accius, containing passages which seemed to have a contemporary application.

3. Or 'the Nesis estate' (between Puteoli and Neapolis).

4. See the Introduction to this chapter.

Marcus Brutus, then, has been waiting for his time to come. So long as he saw you were putting up with all that happened, he remained unbelievably patient. But when he realized you had alerted yourselves to defend your freedom, the protection of that freedom became the object of his endeavours as well as yours.

The opposition he had to encounter was poisonous. For if Marcus Antonius's brother Gaius had been able to carry out the intention he had in mind – and he could well have done so, if Marcus Brutus had not had the courage to block his evil endeavours – we should have lost Macedonia, Illyricum and Greece. Greece would, then, have become a place of refuge available to Marcus Antonius if he was defeated; or, worse, a base for launching an attack on Italy. As it is, on the other hand, the military command and authority and armed forces of Marcus Brutus have meant that the Balkan peninsula is ready and thoroughly equipped for war, so that it reaches out its right hand towards Italy, and promises protection. Anyone, therefore, who takes Marcus Brutus's army away from him is robbing our country of a powerful bulwark, a place we can fall back upon.

As for Marcus Antonius, in north Italy, I want him to learn of our support for Marcus Brutus at the earliest possible moment, in the hope of making him realize that it is not Decimus Brutus whom he is blockading with his palisade, but that it is he himself who is being blockaded. Marcus Antonius holds only three towns in the entire world.[1] Cisalpine Gaul is his bitter enemy, and that includes the people across the River Padus, who would, he thought, be his friends,[2] but who are now, instead, thoroughly hostile to his cause. The whole of Italy is against him. Countries outside Italy, too, from the nearest coasts of Greece as far as Egypt, are held by garrisons commanded by Romans of impeccable bravery and patriotism.

Antonius's only hope was his brother Gaius, who, in point of age, comes between his two brothers, but has proved the equal of both of them in viciousness. Gaius ran off from Rome with such speed that you might have imagined that the Senate had propelled him into Macedonia instead of forbidding him to go there, as in fact they had. God knows what a conflagration and devastation and plague would have consumed Greece had the marvellous, god-sent valour of Marcus Brutus not been there to check that madman and

1. Bononia, Regium Lepidi and Parma.

2. Because Julius Caesar had granted them Roman citizenship.

his ferocious activities! Brutus was speedy, resourceful and courageous. However, Gaius Antonius, too, was by no means contemptible as far as speed was concerned. If some lapsed inheritances, which he seized, had not delayed him on the way, his rapidity was such, you would have said, that he seemed to be flying rather than marching. When we want other men to leave Rome to conduct public business it is usually quite difficult to extract them and get them moving. But it was the opposite with Gaius Antonius. We wanted to keep him back; but the only effect of that was to push him out!

Actually, Gaius Antonius had no claim at all to Apollonia or Dyrrhachium or Illyricum, or to the army of that territory's governor, the general Publius Vatinius.[1] His appointed task was to succeed Quintus Hortensius Hortalus, the governor of Macedonia,[2] and he said so himself. Macedonia has clearly defined boundaries and a governorship of clearly defined tenure. And of its army, also, the same is true, if you can say that an army existed. But with Illyricum, with the legions of Vatinius, Gaius Antonius had nothing whatever to do. Now, some ill-intentioned person might say that this applies, also, to Marcus Brutus. But the answer is that all the legions and all military forces everywhere belong to the state. Those legions, for example, which deserted Marcus Antonius cannot be said to have ever belonged to him, rather than to the government. And a man who uses his military command and his army to *attack* the government has lost any right to have a command or army at all.

So, if the state itself is to pass judgement, if what is right and wrong depends simply on what the state decides, I ask you this: is it to Gaius Antonius or to Marcus Brutus that the state would assign the legions of the Roman people? As for Antonius, he had suddenly set out, on wings, with the aim of plundering and ruining our allies. Wherever he went, he devastated, looted and stole everything he could find. He launched an army of the Roman people against that very Roman people itself. As for Marcus Brutus, by way of contrast, he had made it his own personal rule that, wherever he

1. Cicero had attacked him in his speech *For Sestius* (56). Vatinius handed Illyricum over to Marcus Brutus.

2. The son of the orator, made governor of the province by Caesar in 44; a close relative of Marcus Brutus.

went, hopes of salvation should seem to shine bright. To sum up, Gaius Antonius looked for backing so that he could overthrow our country, Marcus Brutus so that he could preserve it. One does not always expect the wisest judgement from soldiers. But on this matter they saw the truth as clearly as we did.

Marcus Brutus writes that Gaius Antonius is at Apollonia with seven cohorts. Yet Gaius Antonius may, now, be a prisoner, and may the gods grant that this is so. Or alternatively, being such a modest man, he does not venture to move into Macedonia, so that it will not look as if he is acting against the Senate's decree. On the other side, a recruitment drive has been launched by the determination and energy of Quintus Hortensius, a man whose fine qualities, worthy of his ancestors and his own self, you have been able to assess from Brutus's letter. The legion which Lucius Calpurnius Piso, Antonius's legate, had been commanding, has transferred itself to my son Marcus.[1] When one comes to the cavalry, which was being moved to Syria in two squadrons, one squadron has left the quaestor, who was its commander, in Thessaly and has joined up with Decimus Brutus; and the other, in Macedonia, has been diverted from the legate in Syria by that valorous, high-principled, resolute young man Cnaeus Domitius Ahenobarbus.[2] And Publius Vatinius too, who has been justly praised by you before and now, once again, deserves your equally high praise, has opened the gates of Dyrrhachium to Marcus Brutus, and handed over his army.

So our state controls Macedonia, controls Illyricum, and guards Greece. Legions, light-armed troops, cavalry, are all ours. And ours, too, is Marcus Brutus, and always will be. Born, as he was, to serve his country, this was confirmed not only by his own exceptional merits, but by the destiny which gave his father and mother their origins and their names.[3]

Here, surely, is a man whom no one can suspect of being a warmonger. For before we were forced to fight, it was not success

1. He had left his studies at Athens to serve in Brutus's army.

2. In 43 he was condemned (perhaps unjustly) for taking part in the murder of Julius Caesar (but later joined Antony, and became consul in 32). The *legatus* in Syria, perhaps Lucius Cornelius Cinna, was a subordinate of the Caesarian Publius Cornelius Dolabella.

3. On his father's side, Brutus claimed descent from Lucius Junius Brutus, who expelled the monarchy (509), and on his mother's from Gaius Servilius Ahala, who killed the would-be despot Spurius Maelius (439).

in war that he wanted at all, but obscurity in peace; though it cannot be said that he was ever truly obscure, because it is impossible to apply the term to a person of such superlative merits. He was the man our nation longed for, the man everyone was talking about; his name was on everyone's lips. But he felt such detestation for the prospect of war that, although Italy was passionately longing for freedom, he preferred to stand aside from his fellow-citizens' enthusiasm rather than run the risk that they would have to fight. For that reason, those who feel inclined to censure his slowness – if such people exist – must also admire, at the same time, the moderation and patience that he displayed.

But he has other critics too, and I can see what they are saying; indeed they do not make it a secret. They are worried, they maintain, about how the ex-soldiers will react to Marcus Brutus's possession of an army. As if there was the slightest difference between the armies of Aulus Hirtius, Gaius Pansa, Decimus Brutus and Gaius Caesar on the one hand, and this army of Marcus Brutus on the other! For if those four armies that I listed before his own are praised for taking up arms in defence of the liberty of the Roman people, then the army of Marcus Brutus, surely, must also be included in the same category.

But Marcus Brutus's *name*, it is objected, is viewed with suspicion by the ex-soldiers. Not, surely, more than the name of Decimus. Indeed, although the deed was shared by both the Brutuses, and they have an equal partnership in its glory, those who deplored it were angrier with Decimus than with Marcus, because, they argued, it was less fitting for him to take part in it.[1] And yet, now, think of the number of armies, on the other hand, which are engaged in liberating Decimus Brutus from the blockade. And think of the commanders of those armies, who are most certainly not people who want Julius Caesar's acts to be upset and the cause of his ex-soldiers to be betrayed.

Indeed, if Julius Caesar were still alive, I cannot imagine how even he himself could defend his own acts with greater tenacity than the valiant Hirtius does. And, equally clearly, no one could be found more attached to Julius's cause than his own son.[2] Yet

1. Because of his close friendship with Julius Caesar, from whom he had received the governorship of Cisalpine Gaul. The 'deed' was Caesar's murder.

2. i.e. his adoptive son Gaius Caesar (Octavian).

consider what these two men are doing. Hirtius, although not yet recovered from a persistent and serious illness, has dedicated what strength he has to defending the freedom of the men whose prayers, he believed, saved him from death. Moreover Gaius Caesar, too, whose qualities outstrip his age, has taken these very same ex-soldiers with him to rescue Decimus Brutus from the siege that threatens him. Here, then, are two unmistakable, determined supporters of the acts of Julius Caesar. Well, who are they and what are they doing? They are fighting a war to save Decimus Brutus. These, then, are the leaders whom the ex-soldiers are following. For they realize that what they have to fight for is not their own personal advantage, but the liberty of the Roman people. When these men, therefore, champions of Caesar's acts, want to devote all their resources to the preservation of Decimus Brutus, it would be entirely wrong for them to suspect the army of the other Brutus, Marcus, either.

Besides, if there was any reason to feel afraid of Marcus Brutus, Pansa would perceive that this was so, and having perceived it would be anxious. For no one is wiser than he is in prophesying future events, or more diligent in warding off prospects of anxiety. Well, you have seen how friendly he is towards Marcus Brutus, and how eager to help him. It was Pansa who told us, in his speech, what we ought to decree concerning Marcus Brutus, and what our feelings should be towards him. And he was so far removed from regarding Marcus Brutus's army as a national peril that he held the exactly opposite opinion – that it is the firmest and most vital defence that our country possesses. To suppose that Pansa is not very clear in his mind about this – is not particularly bright, that is to say – could not be a serious suggestion. And to suppose, on the other hand, that he *does* realize the facts about Brutus's army, but chooses to disregard them, because he is not interested in the ratification of Julius Caesar's acts, would be equally absurd. For, as regards those acts, it is actually Pansa himself who intends, with the backing of our senatorial authority, to propose a law in the Assembly which will verify and confirm them.

Well, it is time for men who are not afraid at all to stop pretending that they are afraid, which they claim as an excuse for taking measures which they allege will protect our country. Or, alternatively, if they *are* afraid of everything, I suggest that they should stop being over-timid. Either way, we shall suffer, in the former instance because of what they are pretending, and in the latter case because they are cowards. This continual citation of the ex-soldiers as a reason for opposing the just cause will do nothing but harm. However much I might admire the bravery of those soldiers – as indeed I do – I would never put up with them if they started behaving haughtily and arrogantly. What we are trying to do is to shatter the bonds of slavery. In these circumstances, objections that this is not what the soldiers want must not be allowed to hamper us. For there are, I am quite sure, innumerable people who are fully prepared to take up arms on behalf of our universal freedom, and there are others, too, quite apart from what the ex-soldiers may think, who can be roused by the distressful situation of our citizen body as a whole to help it ward off slavery. Reliance on the ex-soldiers would, in any case, not be enough to save the state, unless it had the widespread support of young people in general. As far as the ex-soldiers are concerned, they deserve your welcome as people who could help us regain our freedom – although as supporters of slavery they should not have your backing at all.

And in this connection, last of all, I cannot refrain from blurting out something that I owe to myself – and it is something that comes from the heart! If the decisions of this senatorial order are to be directed by the nods of the ex-soldiers, if everything we say or do is to be governed by their will, I myself would rather die. For death would be better than becoming a slave. Slavery is, at all times, thoroughly disagreeable. However, let us admit that formerly we could not avoid it.[1] Now, on the other hand, I must ask you whether you do not surely contemplate getting your freedom back. That earlier catastrophe, as I said, was unavoidable; you might say that it was fated. But if we let a similar disaster overtake us once again, this time we shall be accepting it voluntarily, and that is something that I do not see why we should endure. The whole of Italy is blazing with a passion to be free. Our people can no longer be slaves. We have given the Roman people military uniforms, and we have given them weapons – long after they first demanded them, it is true, but at any rate we have done so.

We have taken up the cause of liberty with high hopes; hopes amounting, almost, to certainty. Yes, I know it is uncertain how

1. Under the dictatorship of Julius Caesar.

wars will turn out, I know Mars is capable of taking either side.[1] Yet for the sake of liberty it is worth risking our lives. For life is not a matter of just breathing. Life is something a slave does not have at all. Other states, it is true, can tolerate slavery. But ours cannot. The explanation is that other states are anxious to avoid toil and distress, and will tolerate everything to avoid them; whereas in ourselves, on the other hand, our ancestors have instilled and implanted the idea that all our decisions, all our acts should be measured by the standard of what is worthy and right. And the recovery of our freedom is such a glorious idea that in pursuing it we ought not to shrink even from death. Or imagine, for a moment, that we *did* shrink from facing our present peril, and by that means escaped death altogether and became immortal! Yet even immortality would be too dear a price to pay if it meant perpetual servitude. Every day and every night, hazards surround us on all sides, and it is not for a man, least of all for a Roman, to hesitate to give up his life, which nature has given him, to save his country.

People are crowding in from every side to put out the fire in which we are all engulfed. The ex-soldiers who were the first to support Gaius Caesar's initiative have repelled Antonius's designs. Next, the Martian Legion blocked his maniac plans, and then the Fourth Legion put an end to them. And so, condemned by his own legions, Antonius burst into Cisalpine Gaul, which he knew was his bitter foe, both in action and in feeling. The armies of Aulus Hirtius and Gaius Caesar went to chase him, and then Pansa's mobilization put Rome and the whole of Italy on full alert. Antonius is the man everyone hates. And he has with him his brother Lucius, whom the Roman people loves so greatly (I am, of course, joking), and whose continued absence the community finds it so painfully hard to endure! Actually, Lucius is an appalling, bestial character. The one purpose of his existence seems to be to show that there can be someone even nastier than his brother Marcus.

With Marcus, also, is Gaius Trebellius, who has become his friend again now that debts have been cancelled.[2] Titus Munatius

1. *Mars communis* was a proverb, like its equivalent in Greek.

2. Gaius Trebellius had originally, as tribune, opposed the cancellation of debts, but then supported it – and was sued by his creditors.

Plancus Bursa, too, is there,[1] and others of the same type, whose single-minded aim and effort seems directed to showing that to recall them from exile would be to cause grave damage to our country. As for Lucius Decidius Saxa[2] and Cafo, they spend their time seducing the allegiance of men who have no idea what they are doing. A couple of boorish rustics, they have never seen the government of our state properly functioning, and lack the slightest desire to do so. The acts they are defending are those not of Julius Caesar but of Marcus Antonius. The unlimited possession of Campanian land has distracted them.[3] I am surprised that they do not feel ashamed when they see that they have actors and actresses of mimes as their neighbours!

To suppress these pestilential characters, we ought surely to be pleased that Marcus Brutus's army has joined our endeavours. You cannot describe him as intemperate or violent! You might, on the contrary, feel he has shown almost excessive patience. He has never in his life entertained an immoderate thought or performed an immoderate action; never erred on the side of too much or too little. Marcus Brutus, members of the Senate, devotes his entire will, all his intentions, his whole intellect to serving the authority of the Senate and the freedom of the Roman people. Those are the causes which he keeps in mind, and is eager to defend. What patience could effect, he has tried. Since it did not prove successful, he has now decided he must oppose force by force.

And so to him, senators, at this critical juncture in our national affairs, you should vote the same honours as on December the twentieth, at my instance, you voted to Decimus Brutus and Gaius Caesar, whose private enterprises and actions were approved and commended, on that occasion, by your authority. So now, that is to say, you should make a similar decision in favour of Marcus Brutus. For what he has done is to get together, speedily and unexpectedly,

1. Tribune in 52, he had been successfully prosecuted by Cicero as a leader of the riots that followed the death of Publius Clodius Pulcher. Julius Caesar had restored him from exile in 49. He was the brother of Lucius Munatius Plancus, whom Caesar had made governor of Gallia Comata (northern Transalpine Gaul).

2. Saxa (tribune in 44) was subsequently defeated and killed in a Parthian invasion (40).

3. This land, allotted to ex-soldiers, was referred to in the Fifth Philippic.

a large and powerful force of legions, cavalry and auxiliaries, for the protection of our country.

With his name should be associated that of Quintus Hortensius. For when he was governor of Macedonia, he gave his services to Marcus Brutus and became his most trusty and reliable helper, in the task of mobilizing an army. Regarding Marcus Appuleius[1] I move another and separate commendation; for Marcus Brutus, in his letter, bears witness to his having taken the first initiative in urging him to raise an army.

So let us take notice of this letter which Gaius Vibius Pansa Caetronianus, as he indicated, has received from Marcus Quintus Caepio Brutus[2] and which has been read out at this meeting. In the light of it, I put forward the following proposal:

'Whereas through the endeavours, and strenuous labours, and gallant actions, of Quintus Caepio Brutus the proconsul, at a most difficult time of national emergency, the province of Macedonia and Illyricum and the whole of Greece, and its legions, army and cavalry, are duly under the control of the consuls, the Senate and the Roman people. Quintus Caepio Brutus the proconsul has acted rightly and in the best interests of the state, and in harmony with the noble traditions of himself and of his ancestors, and in accordance with the precedents of the rightful government of our country. These deeds of his earn and will continue to earn the full approval of the Senate and Roman people, and Quintus Caepio Brutus, proconsul, is authorized to defend, protect and preserve the safety of the province of Macedonia, Illyricum and the whole of Greece. Moreover, the army which he has created and got together shall remain under his command, and he shall levy and employ, if need be, for military operations, such public funds as exist and are available for his use, and shall borrow, from any source that he deems fit, whatever funds he needs for such activities, and shall requisition supplies of food, and ensure that he himself and his forces shall remain as close as possible to Italy.

'And whereas the letter of Quintus Caepio Brutus, proconsul, has made it clear that the courageous exertions of Quintus Hortensius

1. An official (proquaestor) in Asia, who had handed over the state funds to Marcus Brutus.

2. This was the name of Marcus Junius Brutus after his adoption by his uncle Quintus Servilius Caepio, the husband of Hortensius's daughter, in or before 59.

have likewise been of great value to the state, and that his aims have coincided, at all times, with those of Quintus Caepio Brutus, proconsul, and whereas that, too, has been of the utmost service to the state, it is decreed that Quintus Hortensius, proconsul, has acted correctly and properly, and in conformity with the national interests; and that it is the Senate's pleasure that, with the assistance of a quaestor or proquaestor and his own deputy, he should continue to be the governor of the province of Macedonia until his successor be appointed by senatorial decree.'

THE LAST PHILIPPICS AND WHAT FOLLOWED

Cicero's opposition, in the Tenth Philippic, to the proposal that Marcus Brutus should be deprived of his Macedonian command duly convinced the Senate. But soon afterwards he was less successful in his Eleventh Philippic, in which he moved that the governorship of Syria should be conferred on Marcus Brutus's principal associate in the murder of Caesar, Gaius Cassius Longinus (though Cassius took matters into his own hands, and forced his Caesarian rival Publius Cornelius Dolabella to commit suicide).[1]

In the Twelfth Philippic Cicero objected to a proposal that a second deputation should be sent to Marcus Antonius, in which he himself was to be included; and the proposal was abandoned.[2] *At the end of the month Pansa joined Hirtius before Mutina (Modena). Cicero's Thirteenth Philippic of 20th March again declared that peace with Marcus Antonius was out of the question, and urged Lepidus, etc., not to compromise. Then, in April 43, followed the first of two battles of Mutina between the senatorial forces and Antonius, in which Pansa was mortally wounded. Cicero's Fourteenth and last Philippic (21 April) eulogized him and the other Republican commanders, and delivered a funeral tribute to their soldiers who had lost their lives. On 27 April came the second battle of Mutina, in which Antonius was defeated. This might have seemed a good result of*

1. Cicero claimed in a letter to Cassius (*To His Friends*, XII, 7, 1) that his proposal would easily have been carried had it not been for opposition from the consul Gaius Vibius Pansa Caetronianus – whom he had praised so warmly, e.g. at the beginning of *X Philippic*.

2. Cicero had, in fact, been ambivalent on the subject, and on his own inclusion in the deputation (*XII Philippic*, 2–3, 6).

Cicero's Philippics, *and so were the Senate's decisions that, at long last, Antonius should be outlawed, that Marcus Brutus's and Gaius Cassius Longinus's control of their provinces should be confirmed,*[1] *and that Decimus Brutus should be awarded a triumph. But Hirtius had been killed in the battle, so that the field was left wide open for Gaius Caesar (Octavian), under whose command Julius Caesar's ex-soldiers – about whom Cicero talked so much – had now placed themselves, so that Octavian was now the military master of Italy.*

Then came the ultimate disaster, as far as Cicero was concerned, for Marcus Antonius, Marcus Aemilius Lepidus the governor of Narbonese (southern Transalpine) Gaul and Nearer Spain (whom the orator had mistakenly praised, and whom Antonius, after his defeat at Mutina, had escaped to join), and Octavian (whom he had likewise praised, in ludicrously misguided terms) joined forces to form the Second Triumvirate. This meant the end, first of Cicero himself, who had screwed up his courage to oppose Antonius, and then of the Republican form of government for the restoration of which he had yearned, and for which now, it proved, he had given his life.

Cicero was hunted down and killed on 7 December 43 BC, *and the Republic died when Caesar's assassins Marcus Brutus and Gaius Cassius Longinus met their deaths in the following year, after the battle of Philippi, won by the troops of the Triumvirate. Eleven years later Antonius (with Queen Cleopatra VII of Egypt) was defeated by Octavian at the battle of Actium, and the imperial epoch, or 'principate', was about to begin. Octavian, soon to be called Augustus, named it 'the restored Republic', but this autocracy, however tactful, was the very antithesis to the Republic to which Cicero had devoted his life – because the system installed by Augustus left no freedom of speech or action for people with his own Republican tastes.*

1. They were also granted superiority (*imperium maius*) over all eastern governors.

APPENDIX I

SOME OF THE ARGUMENTS USED IN *For Balbus*

The translation of *For Balbus* presented here concentrated on two points, the attitude of the Romans towards the enfranchisement of foreigners and Cicero's justifications for his own change of policy, in that he was now, in the interests of stable government, supporting a cause dear to the members of the autocratic First Triumvirate, which, in fact, he hated.

But the case also involved a number of rather intricate technicalities, which were omitted from the translation offered above but may be briefly mentioned at this point.

Cnaeus Pompeius Magnus (Pompey the Great) gave Roman citizenship to Balbus under the *Lex Gellia Cornelia* of the consuls Lucius Gellius Poplicola and Cnaeus Cornelius Lentulus Clodianus in 72 BC. The law empowered Pompeius to confer citizenship on individuals. Balbus's enemies based their objection to his enfranchisement on the *Lex Papia* of the tribune Gaius Papius (65), which was designed to stop the illegal exercise of citizen rights by expelling from Rome all foreigners who resided outside Italy (the political purpose of the law was to weaken Julius Caesar and his friends by driving from Rome their numerous foreign supporters).

These opponents of Balbus argued that, just as the people of Gades (Balbus's city) as a whole could not become Roman citizens unless a Roman law offering them this citizenship had been formally accepted by themselves, so, also, an express acceptance of the *Lex Gellia Cornelia* by the community of Gades (which had evidently not been received) was necessary to confirm the grant of citizenship to Balbus. That amounted to saying that the city to which a non-Roman belonged had a right to veto his acceptance of Roman citizenship. Cicero pointed out (a) that this was theoretically untenable and based on no precedent, since no member of an allied state (*civitas foederata*, which is what Gades was) had ever been prosecuted for his assumption of Roman citizenship, on the ground that his own state 'had not given its own consent', (b) that the people of Gades were, in fact, on Balbus's side, supporting the principle that it was legitimate for any individual among them to gain the citizenship of Rome.

Gades, as has been mentioned, was an 'allied' community, bound to Rome by a treaty.[1] The prosecutor took care to argue that these 'federated' states were excepted from the operation of the *Lex Gellia Cornelia* unless they had formally adopted it themselves. Cicero elaborately and in detail, and on the whole correctly although not without some moments of unfairness, rebuts such arguments. The prosecutor also sought to contend that, because some treaties incorporated stipulations forbidding Rome to receive members of the other contracting party as citizens, the same restriction should be assumed to apply to the treaty with Gades, although it was not explicitly stated in the treaty. Cicero, in reply, stressed this non-inclusion – and added that even if the treaty had been officially sanctioned by the Roman people, as, in fact, it never had been, it would not have included such a clause. He also maintains that even if such a clause had existed in the treaty, it would have been overridden by the *Lex Gellia Cornelia*.[2]

In the passages I have selected for translation, I have omitted certain conferments of citizenship which Cicero included. These are the following. Publius Caesius, knight of Ravenna, by Cnaeus Pompeius Strabo (father of Pompey, consul 89); Alexas of Heraclea in Lucania, by Publius Licinius Crassus (consul 97); Aristo of Massilia, and nine slaves of Gades, by Lucius Cornelius Sulla (dictator 81); Quintus Fabius of Saguntum, by Quintus Caecilius Metellus Pius (consul 80); Hasdrubal of Gades, and the Ovii (Mamertini) of Messana, and Fabii of Utica, and Saguntines, by Cnaeus Pompeius Magnus (Pompey).

1. The various classes of communities in the Roman provinces included citizen colonies (only a few until Caesar's time), Latin colonies (of which the officials were Roman citizens), 'free' states (*liberae*), and free and treaty-bound states (*foederatae*). All were, in fact, subject to Rome, although legal rights were more or less scrupulously respected.

2. Here Cicero is on more dangerous ground than elsewhere, since his argument involves the assumption that the Roman law overrides, or ought to override, treaty obligations. Yet the *Lex Gellia Cornelia* contained a clause providing that none of its enactments should prevail against other 'sacrosanct' arrangements. The prosecution pointed out that a treaty was 'sacrosanct' (though Cicero argued that this did not apply to the Gaditan treaty, since it had not been formally ratified at Rome).

APPENDIX 2

Minor Orators Mentioned in the *Brutus*

Cicero, in the interests of thoroughness, mentions the following additional orators, whose names have not been included in the translation.

Sections 77–81. Older contemporaries of Marcus Porcius Cato the elder: Gaius Flaminius (consul 223, 217), Gaius Terentius Varro (consul 216), Quintus Fabius Maximus Verrucosus Cunctator (consul 233, etc.), Quintus Caecilius Metellus (consul 206), Publius Cornelius Lentulus Caudinus (praetor 203), Publius Licinius Crassus Dives (consul 205). Younger contemporaries: Gaius Sulpicius Galus (consul 166), Tiberius Sempronius Gracchus (consul 177, 163; richer style), Publius Cornelius Scipio Nasica Corculum (consul 162, 155), Lucius Cornelius Lentulus Lupus (consul 156), Quintus Fulvius Nobilior (consul 153), Titus Annius Luscus (consul 153), Lucius Aemilius Paullus Macedonicus (consul 182). Other contemporaries of Cato the elder: Aulus Postumius Albinus (consul 151), Servius Fulvius Flaccus (consul 135), Servius Fabius Pictor, Quintus Fabius Labeo (consul 183).

Sections 94f. Reckoned as orators of moderate ability: Lucius Mummius Achaicus (consul 146; simple and archaic), Spurius Mummius (his brother), Gaius and Lucius Aurelius Orestes, Publius Popillius Laenas (consul 132), Gaius Popillius Laenas (his son).

Sections 96f. Quintus Pompeius (consul 141; the first of his family to attain the consulship), Lucius Cassius Longinus (consul 127; not eloquent but influential; his ballot law was opposed, at first, by Marcus Antius Briso), Cnaeus Servilius Caepio (consul 169), Quintus Servilius Caepio (consul 140).

Sections 108f. Publius Cornelius Lentulus (consul 162; leader of the Senate), Lucius Furius Philus (consul 136; scholarly, and good Latin), Publius Mucius Scaevola (consul 133; knew law and politics well, and argued acutely), Manius Manilius (consul 149), Appius Claudius Pulcher (consul 143), Marcus Fulvius Flaccus (consul 125), Gaius Porcius Cato (consul 114), Publius Decius (tribune 121; turbulent in life and speech), Titus Quinctius Flamininus (consul 123; painstaking).

Section 135. Quintus Caecilius Metellus Numidicus (consul 109; dignified), Marcus Junius Silanus (ditto), Marcus Aurelius Scaurus (consul 108; pure diction), Aulus Postumius Albinus (consul 99; ditto), Postumius Albinus (priest; his brother), Quintus Servilius Caepio (consul 106; ruined by popular odium), Gaius Memmius (tribune 111; mediocre orator but fierce prosecutor), Lucius Memmius (his brother), Spurius Thorius (tribune *c.* 118, modified the *Lex Sempronia agraria* of Tiberius Sempronius Gracchus), Marcus Claudius Marcellus (fought the Teutones 102), Publius Cornelius Lentulus Marcellinus (his son).

Sections 169f. 'Allied' and Latin orators: Quintus Vettius Vettianus, Marsian (known personally to Cicero), Quintus and Decimus Valerius of Sora (literary), Gaius Rusticelius of Bononia, Titus Betutius Barrus of Asculum (the most eloquent; e.g. speech against Quintus Servilius Caepio, quaestor *c.* 100, grandfather of Marcus Brutus). Earlier: Lucius Papirius of Fregellae was considered the best.

Sections 175f. Decimus Junius Brutus (consul 77), Lucius Cornelius Scipio Asiaticus (consul 83), Cnaeus Pompeius Strabo (consul 89; father of Pompey), Sextus Pompeius (his learned brother), Marcus Junius Brutus (lawyer), Gaius Billienus (self-made, very distinguished), Cnaeus Octavius (consul 87).

Sections 178ff. Quintus Lucretius Vespillo (good at private suits in Sullan period), Quintus Lucretius Ofella (better at public speeches), Titus Annius (of Velina tribe), Titus Juventius (slow and cold but clever), Publius Orbius (praetor in Asia 63), Titus Aufidius (ditto 70), Marcus Vergilius (tribune 87; his brother), Publius Magius (his colleague; more voluble).

Section 182. Somewhat younger than Gaius Julius Caesar Strabo Vopiscus: Gaius Aurelius Cotta and Publius Sulpicius and Gaius Scribonius Curio (all discussed later), Quintus Varius Hybrida (tribune 91), Cnaeus Pomponius (tribune 90), Lucius Fufius, Marcus Livius Drusus (tribune 91; Marcus Brutus's great-uncle), Publius Antistius (discussed later).

Sections 222f. Inferior to the best: Lucius Fufius (see foregoing: good prosecution of Manius Aquilius, consul 101), Marcus Livius Drusus (see foregoing), Lucius Licinius Lucullus (see *For Murena*), Marcus Junius Brutus (tribune 83; Marcus Brutus's father), Marcus Licinius Lucullus, Marcus Octavius (who arranged the abolition of Gaius Gracchus's corn-law; not the man of the same name who opposed Tiberius Gracchus),

Cnaeus Octavius (consul 76; not the consul of 87), Marcus Porcius Cato (father of Cato the younger), Quintus Lutatius Catulus the younger (consul 78), Quintus Servilius Caepio (grandfather of Marcus Brutus, who left the Senate to become a knight), Cnaeus Papirius Carbo (consul 85, 84), Marcus Marius Gratidianus (praetor 85), Lucius Quinctius (tribune 74), Marcus Lollius Palicanus (tribune 71).

Section 230. Contemporaries of Quintus Hortensius Hortalus: Marcus Pupius Piso Frugi Calpurnianus (consul 61), Marcus Licinius Crassus Dives (the triumvir), Cnaeus Cornelius Lentulus Clodianus (consul 72), Publius Cornelius Lentulus Sura (consul 71).

Sections 240f. Decimus Junius Silanus (consul 62; Marcus Brutus's stepfather, idle but able), Quintus Pompeius Bithynicus, Lucius Octavius of Reate, Gaius and Lucius Caepasius (quaestors), Gaius Cosconius Calidianus (voluble).

Section 305. Gaius Scribonius Curio (consul 76; noted here because he no longer spoke after his entire audience left during one of his speeches), Quintus Caecilius Metellus Celer (tribune 90), Quintus Varius Hybrida (tribune 91; author of the Varian Law), Gaius Papirius Carbo Arvina (tribune 90), Cnaeus Pomponius (tribune 90), Gaius Julius Caesar Strabo Vopiscus (aedile 90). Most of these are also mentioned elsewhere in the *Brutus*.

Section 308. Publius Antistius, Marcus Pupius Piso Frugi Calpurnianus (again), Cnaeus Pomponius and Gaius Papirius Carbo Arvina (again), Lucius Marcius Philippus (consul 91; discussed elsewhere).

MAPS

ATLANTIC
OCEAN
GALLIA COMATA
GALLIA
NARBONENSIS
GALLIA
CISALPINA
NEARER
SPAIN
FURTHER
SPAIN
Rome
ITALY
SARDINIA
MEDITERRA
SICILY
NUMIDIA
AFRICA
Boundaries of the Empire
Boundaries of Provinces
0
500
1000 km
0
500 miles

THE ROMAN EMPIRE IN 51 BC
N
SCYTHIANS
Cimmerian Bosphorus
EUXINE SEA
(BLACK SEA)
R. Danubius
LLYRICUM
PONTUS
BITHYNIA
MACEDONIA
ASIA
CILICIA
ACHAEA
SYRIA
CYPRUS
NEAN
SEA
CYRENE
EGYPT

ITALY
CISALPINE GAUL
Insubres
Mediolanum
Placentia
R. Padus
Parma
LIGURIA
Regium Lepidi
Mutina
Bononia
Pistoria
Faesulae
Pisaurum
Ager Gallicus
R. Metaurus
Sena Gallica
Arretium
UMBRIA
L. Trasimenus
Iguvium
ETRURIA
Camerinum
PICENUM
Asculum
Spoletium
Reate
R. Tiberis
Sabini
Rome
Marsi
Ostia
Hernici
LATIUM
Volsci
Arpinum
see inset
Suessa Aurunca
APULIA
Ager Falernus
Beneventum
Cannae
SARDINIA
Cumae
CAMPANIA
Nola
Neapolis
Compsa
Brundisium
LUCANIA
Tarentum
Velia
Heraclea
Tempsa
Croton
Vibo Valentia
Bruttii
Sila Forest
Locri Epizephyrii
Rhegium
SICILY
N
Tibur
R. Anio
R. Tiberis
Rome
Marsi
Tusculum
Hernici
Ostia
Alba Longa
Sora
Lanuvium
Arpinum
LATIUM
Volsci
Pontine Marshes
Suessa Aurunca
0
100
200 km
0
50
100 miles

SICILY
Tyrrhenian Sea
C. Peloris
Sicilian Strait
Messana
Tyndaris
Apollonia
Soluntum
Panormus
Eryx
Segesta
Thermae
Himera
Halicyae
Tauromenium
Mt Aetna
Lilybaeum
Agyrium
Centuripa
Henna
Catana
Sicilian Sea
Heraclea Minoa
Acragas (Agrigentum)
Leontini
Megara Hyblaea
Syracuse
Netum
Helorus
Pachynus
Odyssea
N
0
50 km
0
30 miles
Libyan Sea

SOUTH-EASTERN EUROPE
THRACIA
ILLYRICUM
MACEDONIA
EPIRUS
Byzantium
Propontis
Dyrrhachium
Apollonia
Abdera
Thasos
Pydna
N
Larissa
THESSALIA
Pharsalus
Cynoscephalae
Aegean Sea
Mytilene
Lesbos
0 100 200km
0 50 100 miles
Actium
Thermopylae
AETOLIA
Orchomenus
Mt Parnassus
Chaeronea
Delphi
Mt Helicon
Thebes
BOEOTIA
Rhamnus
Athens
Piraeus
ATTICA
Phalerum
Chios
Samos
Sicyon
Corinth
Ceos
PELOPONNESE
ARGOLIS
Argos
Sparta
LACONIA
Rhodes
Cimmerian Bosphorus
Euxine Sea
Crete
Gortyna

THE EAST
Euxine Sea
(Black Sea)
Thracian Bosphorus
Heraclea Pontica
Sinope
Byzantium
Calchedon
Propontis
Nicaea
BITHYNIA
R. Halys
PONTUS
Cyzicus
Nicopolis
Troy
MYSIA
GALATIA
ARMENIA
Aegean Sea
ASIA
Magnesia
LYDIA
PHRYGIA
CAPPADOCIA
Ephesus
Miletus
CARIA
Caunus
Perga
Cnidus
CILICIA
Carrhae
R. Tigris
MESOPOTAMIA
R. Euphrates
ASSYRIA
SYRIA
Tyre
PHOENICIA
ITURAEA
Mediterranean Sea
Babylon
BABYLONIA
Ascalon
CHALDAEA
PERSIA
PARTHIA
N
Lampsacus
Cyzicus
Dardanus
Troy
TROAD
Tenedos
Mt Ida
Adramyttium
MYSIA
Stratonicea
Pergamum
Cyme
Temnus
ASIA
Magnesia
Smyrna
IONIA
LYDIA
Ephesus
Alabanda
Miletus
CARIA
Mylasa
0
300 km
0
200 miles

N
ATLANTIC
OCEAN
GALLIA
COMATA
R. Rhenus
Helvetii
Tigurini
R. Rhodanus
GALLIA NARBONENSIS
(NARBONESE GAUL)
Avennio
Massilia
Narbo Martius
GALLAECI
R. Iberus
Numantia
NEARER
SPAIN
FURTHER
SPAIN
Saguntum
Dianium
Mediterranean Sea
Munda
Gades
NUMIDIA
AFRICA
0
500 km
0
300 miles
WESTERN EUROPE
and NORTH AFRICA

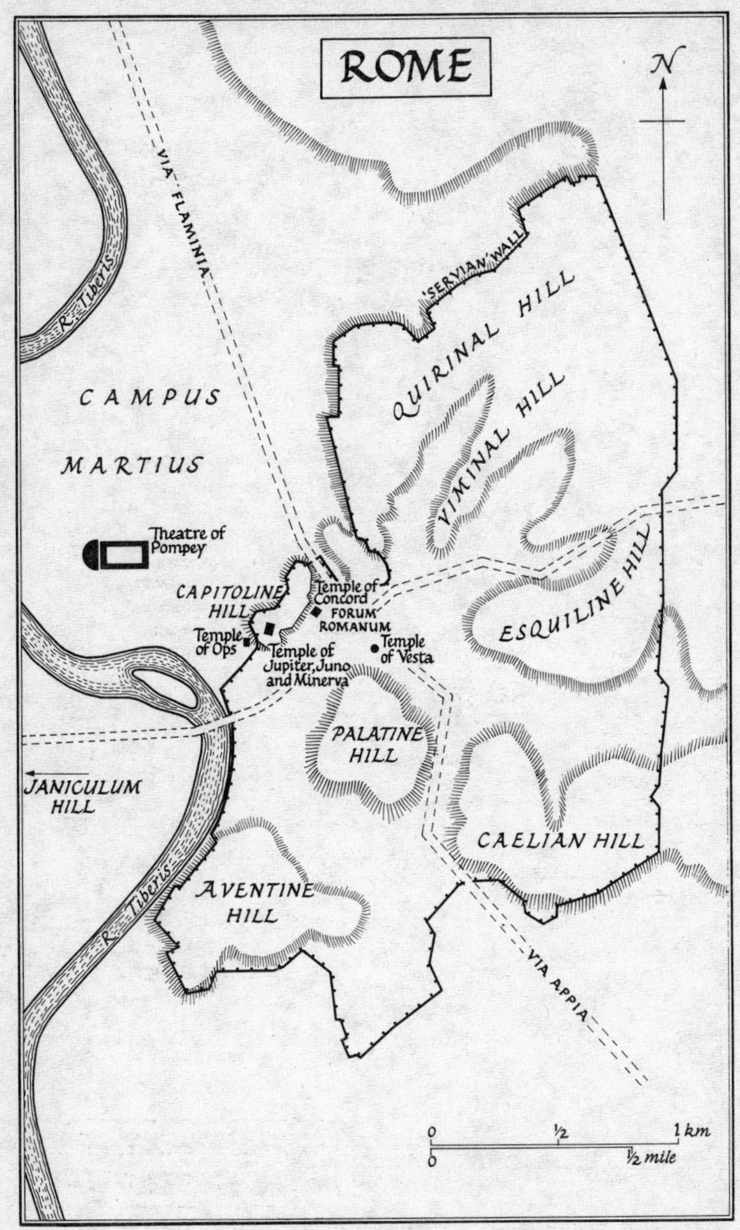
ROME
N
VIA FLAMINIA
R. Tiberis
'SERVIAN' WALL
QUIRINAL HILL
VIMINAL HILL
CAMPUS
MARTIUS
ESQUILINE HILL
Theatre of Pompey
CAPITOLINE HILL
Temple of Concord
FORUM ROMANUM
Temple of Ops
Temple of Jupiter, Juno and Minerva
Temple of Vesta
PALATINE HILL
JANICULUM HILL
CAELIAN HILL
AVENTINE HILL
R. Tiberis
VIA APPIA
0
½
1 km
0
½ mile

FURTHER READING

F. E. Adcock, *Roman Political Ideas and Practice*, University of Michigan Press, 1959.

M. Beard and M. Crawford, *Rome in the Late Republic: Problems and Interpretations*, Cornell University Press, 1985.

Cicero, *Letters to Atticus* (ed. D.R. Shackleton Bailey), Cambridge University Press, 1965–70.

Cicero, *Letters to Friends* (ed. D.R. Shackleton Bailey), Cambridge University Press, 1977.

Cicero, *Letters to His Brother Quintus and Brutus* (ed. D.R. Shackleton Bailey), Cambridge University Press, 1991.

Cicero, *Murder Trials* (ed. M. Grant), Penguin Books, 1975.

Cicero, *On the Good Life* (ed. M. Grant), Penguin Books, 1971.

Cicero, *Selected Political Speeches* (ed. M. Grant), Penguin Books, 1969.

Cicero, *Selected Works* (ed. M. Grant), Penguin Books, 1960.

F. R. Cowell, *Cicero and the Roman Republic*, Penguin Books, 1948.

T. A. Dorey (ed.), *Cicero*, Routledge & Kegan Paul, 1965.

A. E. Douglas, *Cicero*, Classical Association, 1968.

D. Earl, *The Moral and Political Tradition of Rome*, Thames & Hudson, 1967.

H. Frisch, *Cicero's Fight for the Republic*, Copenhagen, 1946.

M. Fuhrmann, *Cicero and the Roman Republic*, Blackwell, 1992.

M. Gelzer, *The Roman Nobility*, Blackwell, 1969.

C. Habicht, *Cicero the Politician*, Johns Hopkins University Press, 1990.

G. Kennedy, *The Art of Rhetoric in the Roman World 300* BC–AD *300*, Princeton University Press, 1972.

W. K. Lacey, *Cicero and the End of the Roman Republic*, Hodder & Stoughton, 1978.

A. W. Lintott, *Violence in Republican Rome*, Oxford University Press, 1968.

J. M. May, *Trials of Character: The Eloquence of Ciceronian Ethos*, University of North Carolina Press, 1988.

T. N. Mitchell, *Cicero: The Senior Statesman*, Yale University Press, 1991.

L. Perelli, *Il pensiero politico di Cicerone*, 1990.

E. Rawson, *Cicero: A Portrait*, Allen Lane, 1975.
R. Seager (ed.), *The Crisis of the Roman Republic*, 1969.
D. R. Shackleton Bailey, *Cicero*, Routledge & Kegan Paul, 1971.
R. E. Smith, *Cicero the Statesman*, Cambridge University Press, 1966.
D. Stockton, *Cicero: A Political Biography*, Oxford University Press, 1971.
R. Syme, *The Roman Revolution*, Oxford University Press, 1939.
L. R. Taylor, *Party Politics in the Age of Caesar*, Cambridge University Press, 1949.
L. R. Taylor, *Roman Voting Assemblies: From the Hannibalic War to the Dictatorship of Caesar*, 1966.
B. Vickers, *In Defence of Rhetoric*, Clarendon Press, 1988.
T. E. J. Wiedemann, *Cicero and the End of the Roman Republic*, 1991.
N. Wood, *Cicero's Social and Political Thought*, University of California Press, 1988, 1991.

INDEX

[illegible]

In [illegible]: Please write to [illegible]

[illegible]

READ MORE IN PENGUIN

In every corner of the world, on every subject under the sun, Penguin represents quality and variety – the very best in publishing today.

For complete information about books available from Penguin – including Puffins, Penguin Classics and Arkana – and how to order them, write to us at the appropriate address below. Please note that for copyright reasons the selection of books varies from country to country.

In the United Kingdom: Please write to *Dept. JC, Penguin Books Ltd, FREEPOST, West Drayton, Middlesex UB7 OBR*

If you have any difficulty in obtaining a title, please send your order with the correct money, plus ten per cent for postage and packaging, to *PO Box No. 11, West Drayton, Middlesex UB7 OBR*

In the United States: Please write to *Penguin USA Inc., 375 Hudson Street, New York, NY 10014*

In Canada: Please write to *Penguin Books Canada Ltd, 10 Alcorn Avenue, Suite 300, Toronto, Ontario M4V 3B2*

In Australia: Please write to *Penguin Books Australia Ltd, 487 Maroondah Highway, Ringwood, Victoria 3134*

In New Zealand: Please write to *Penguin Books (NZ) Ltd,182–190 Wairau Road, Private Bag, Takapuna, Auckland 9*

In India: Please write to *Penguin Books India Pvt Ltd, 706 Eros Apartments, 56 Nehru Place, New Delhi 110 019*

In the Netherlands: Please write to *Penguin Books Netherlands B.V., Keizersgracht 231 NL–1016 DV Amsterdam*

In Germany: Please write to *Penguin Books Deutschland GmbH, Friedrichstrasse 10–12, W–6000 Frankfurt/Main 1*

In Spain: Please write to *Penguin Books S. A., C. San Bernardo 117–6° E–28015 Madrid*

In Italy: Please write to *Penguin Italia s.r.l., Via Felice Casati 20, I–20124 Milano*

In France: Please write to *Penguin France S. A., 17 rue Lejeune, F–31000 Toulouse*

In Japan: Please write to *Penguin Books Japan, Ishikiribashi Building, 2–5–4, Suido, Tokyo 112*

In Greece: Please write to *Penguin Hellas Ltd, Dimocritou 3, GR–106 71 Athens*

In South Africa: Please write to *Longman Penguin Southern Africa (Pty) Ltd, Private Bag X08, Bertsham 2013*

READ MORE IN PENGUIN

A CHOICE OF CLASSICS

Aeschylus	**The Oresteian Trilogy**
	Prometheus Bound/The Suppliants/Seven Against Thebes/The Persians
Aesop	**Fables**
Ammianus Marcellinus	**The Later Roman Empire (AD 354–378)**
Apollonius of Rhodes	**The Voyage of Argo**
Apuleius	**The Golden Ass**
Aristophanes	**The Knights/Peace/The Birds/The Assemblywomen/Wealth**
	Lysistrata/The Acharnians/The Clouds
	The Wasps/The Poet and the Women/The Frogs
Aristotle	**The Art of Rhetoric**
	The Athenian Constitution
	Ethics
	The Politics
	De Anima
Arrian	**The Campaigns of Alexander**
St Augustine	**City of God**
	Confessions
Boethius	**The Consolation of Philosophy**
Caesar	**The Civil War**
	The Conquest of Gaul
Catullus	**Poems**
Cicero	**The Murder Trials**
	The Nature of the Gods
	On the Good Life
	Selected Letters
	Selected Political Speeches
	Selected Works
Euripides	**Alcestis/Iphigenia in Tauris/Hippolytus**
	The Bacchae/Ion/The Women of Troy/Helen
	Medea/Hecabe/Electra/Heracles
	Orestes/The Children of Heracles/Andromache/The Suppliant Women/The PhoenicianWomen/Iphigenia in Aulis

READ MORE IN PENGUIN

A CHOICE OF CLASSICS

Plautus	**The Pot of Gold/The Prisoners/The Brothers Menaechmus/The Swaggering Soldier/Pseudolus**
	The Rope/Amphitryo/The Ghost/A Three-Dollar Day
Pliny	**The Letters of the Younger Pliny**
Pliny the Elder	**Natural History**
Plotinus	**The Enneads**
Plutarch	**The Age of Alexander** (Nine Greek Lives)
	The Fall of the Roman Republic (Six Lives)
	The Makers of Rome (Nine Lives)
	The Rise and Fall of Athens (Nine Greek Lives)
	Plutarch on Sparta
Polybius	**The Rise of the Roman Empire**
Procopius	**The Secret History**
Propertius	**The Poems**
Quintus Curtius Rufus	**The History of Alexander**
Sallust	**The Jugurthine War** and **The Conspiracy of Cataline**
Seneca	**Four Tragedies** and **Octavia**
	Letters from a Stoic
Sophocles	**Electra/Women of Trachis/Philoctetes/Ajax**
	The Theban Plays
Suetonius	**The Twelve Caesars**
Tacitus	**The Agricola** and **The Germania**
	The Annals of Imperial Rome
	The Histories
Terence	**The Comedies (The Girl from Andros/The Self-Tormentor/TheEunuch/Phormio/ The Mother-in-Law/The Brothers)**
Thucydides	**The History of the Peloponnesian War**
Virgil	**The Aeneid**
	The Eclogues
	The Georgics
Xenophon	**Conversations of Socrates**
	A History of My Times
	The Persian Expedition